D1236702

THE POLITICS

OF RIGHTEOUSNESS
Idaho Christian Patriotism

THE POLITICS

OF RIGHTEOUSNESS
Idaho Christian Patriotism

JAMES A. AHO

A Samuel and Althea Stroum Book

UNIVERSITY OF WASHINGTON PRESS
Seattle and London

This book is published with the assistance of a grant from
the Stroum Book Fund, established through the generosity of
Samuel and Althea Stroum.

Library of Congress Cataloging-in-Publication Data

Aho, James Alfred, 1942–
    The politics of righteousness : Idaho Christian patriotism / James
Aho.
        p.   cm.
    Includes bibliographical references.
    ISBN 0-295-96997-0 (alk. paper)
    1. White supremacy movements—Idaho.   2. Silent Brotherhood.
3. Church of Jesus Christ Christian, Aryan Nations.
4. Antisemitism—Idaho.   5. Racism—Idaho.   6. Idaho—Race
relations.   7. Christianity and politics.   I. Title.
F755.A1A46   1990
322.4′2′0973—dc20   90-30168
                                                                CIP

The paper used in this publication meets the minimum requirements of American National Standard for Information Sciences—Permanence of Paper for
Printed Library Materials, ANSI Z39.48-1984

CONTENTS

Acknowledgments   ix

1. Introduction   3
The New Christian Right   4
Doing Sociology   11
Christian Patriotism Defined   13
A Geography of Idaho Patriotism   21
How This Book Came About   25

Part I. THE MOVEMENT FROM THE INSIDE   35

2. The Genesis of Revolt: Six Stories   37
Christian Constitutionalists: Protesters, Posses, and *Pro Se*   37
America: The Chosen People   51
Conclusion   67

**3. Madness, Money, Messiahs: An Analysis of
Movement Motives   68**
The Issue Posed   68
Definitions and Caveats   70
Types of Motives   71
Rationality Reconsidered   75
Christian Heroism Analyzed   78
A Critical Note   80

**4. "Satan's Kids" and Jacob's Seed: A Sociology
of Knowledge   83**
The World of Identity   85
Israel Identified   100

v

5. Identity Christianity Proven   105
Etymologies   106
Astrology, Blessings, and Numerology   108
Promises and Predictions   112

6. Christian Constitutionalism and Mormonism   114
Birch and Church   114
Constitution and Conspiracy   120
Mormonism and the Jew   127
Conclusion   131

Part II. THE MOVEMENT FROM THE OUTSIDE   133

7. Sketching the Movement Causes   135
Caveats and Disclaimers   135
Sociological Theories of Right-Wing Extremism   136
Education and the Patriot   138
Radical Patriotism and the Eclipse of Community   146
Conclusion   160

8. The Religious Roots of Radical Patriotism   164
Political Socialization Theory   164
Protestantism and Patriotism   166
Fundamentalism, Mormonism, and Anti-Semitism   175
Conclusion   180

9. Social Networks and Patriot Recruitment   185
The Political Mobilization of the Patriots   187
Assessing the Evidence   194
Conclusion   209

10. The Big Picture   212
The Politics of Unreason   213
An Alternative Explanation of Right-Wing Extremism   216
The Cycles of Right-Wing Extremism   221

APPENDIXES   227
I. Documents   229
II. Sources of Data on Core Christian Patriots   251
III. Geographic Origins of the Patriots   252
IV. The John Birch Society and the Jewish Question   255
V. The Action Orientation of Identity Christianity   260
VI. Other Conspiracies   264

Notes   267

Bibliography   299

Subject Index   311

Name Index   320

ACKNOWLEDGMENTS

Although I am responsible for this book, *The Politics of Righteousness* is a product of collaboration by many individuals.

Let me acknowledge first of all those who read and critiqued earlier versions of the manuscript: Joan Downing (Idaho State University), Robert Balch (University of Montana), Armand Mauss (Washington State University), Jim Richardson (University of Nevada-Reno), Laird Wilcox (director of the Editorial Research Service of Kansas City, Missouri), Tracy Montgomery (Washington State University). Any analytical acuity and theoretical sophistication the book has is due in large measure to their suggestions and corrections.

I would like to extend a special thanks to Jack Reinwand (Ricks College), who, as a participant in a memorable seminar on the sociology of the radical right during the fall semester of 1986, interviewed several radical Mormon patriots. Information from these interviews has been incorporated into the text of chapter 6.

For her unfailing encouragement, even when the initial readers' reports did not always seem to justify it, I thank the editor-in-chief of the University of Washington Press, Naomi Pascal. It was also a pleasure to work with and get to know personally other members of the staff: Julidta Tarver, managing editor; Veronica Seyd, designer; and Lane Morgan, copyeditor.

To my friends outside academia and my family, always available to provide harbor from the buffeting winds of Idaho politics, thank you.

Thanks are also given to the several hundred informants who patiently and, for the most part, honestly divulged details of their private lives to an inquisitive liberal sociologist who, they must have thought, could not always be trusted.

My colleagues at Idaho State University played a pivotal role in my research both through their unswerving moral support and financial aid. The Department of Sociology provided me a travel grant to underwrite my first field trip to northern Idaho. The ISU Faculty Research Committee awarded me a research grant to conduct systematic research on Idaho's right wing. In the spring semester of 1987, the university awarded me sabbatical leave to complete a first draft of this manuscript. These gestures occurred at a time when ISU, with the rest of Idaho's educational system, was under siege by some of the very patriots described in the following pages. For their stubborn yet always civil insistence on academic excellence in the face of pressures for mediocrity from their many detractors, I dedicate this book to my colleagues at Idaho State University.

THE POLITICS

OF RIGHTEOUSNESS
Idaho Christian Patriotism

1

INTRODUCTION

Given the fickleness of human memory, enduring lessons must be drawn in vivid colors. Warfare is one vehicle for this purpose. In the identification of an alien enemy and the ceremonial sacrifice of combatants, a populace recognizes what unites them as a people. But societies also designate internal enemies for this purpose: individuals with a distinguishing mark—an unorthodox belief, an untoward act, an unsightly blemish, a visible handicap, or a racial difference. In a spectacle replayed periodically in America, the Christian Right unearths the enemy within. This token of unrighteousness may be a liberal or a Communist; a Papist, a Jew, an atheist, a satanist, or a Mason; a homosexual, obese, drunkard, or addict; a black, Mexican, or Asian; or several of these embodied in an arch-demon of horrifying dimensions. In the name of Cross and Flag, Race and Nation, these half-fictitious emblems of chaos are symbolically excised from America by radical political surgery. While this operation is largely metaphorical, through it a particular image of America is rejuvenated: an America Christian and masculine in its culture, racially white, English-speaking, and overseen by its sacred compact, the United States Constitution.

Political drama is far more trenchant than textbook recitation in instilling messages of national, cultural, and racial identity. This is because drama re-presents a people's legends and myths not just to the ear, but to all the senses. Communal theater was the schoolhouse of the ancients, and right-wing extremism is nothing if not theater. It has its props, costumery, lines, and personae: the betrayer, the crippled king, the fearful mother, and the dutiful wife. Above all, it has the protagonist—white Christian male Constitutionalist—and his antagonist. The story line is familiar. America has a covenant with the Lord. If she remains faithful to its edicts, as expressed in the Constitution and the biblical lawbooks, she shall be favored. Her crops shall be plentiful, her people well-fed, prolific, and happy, her children obedient to the voice of their parents. But now she has faltered in her obligations and her cities lie corrupt, her waters and air are befouled, and wantonness, crime, and dissolution follow her people everywhere. As Satan and his allies are about to overwhelm the land, enter stage right the hero, Bible and Constitution in hand, to beat them back into the shadows. This is the symbolic gesture at the heart of the Politics of Righteousness. Herculean, because the protagonist is always out-numbered by the masses, Sisyphean in its futility because each gener-ation forgets the lessons painfully learned by its elders, it is for all that heroic. There are injuries, imprisonments, fines, and even death in right-wing theater. But the collective experience of revitalizing the myth is, at least to the performers, deemed well worth the cost.

THE NEW CHRISTIAN RIGHT

The latest enactment of the drama of American political exorcism calls itself, appropriately, the *New* Christian Right. It calls itself "new" because, unlike the tired old conservative right, it will not seek accom-modation with the "spineless and godless" liberal establishment that "has brought our nation floundering to the brink of death."[1] "The New Right does not want to conserve," proclaims one of its more forthright spokesmen, "we want to change—we are the forces of change."[2]

Although the term New Right was coined in 1962 by Lee Edwards in the platform for the Young Americans for Freedom, as published in its periodical, *The New Guard,* the movement itself did not appear until a decade and a half later. It first drew national attention in July 1980 when over 200,000 conservative evangelicals assembled in the nation's capital for a "Washington for Jesus" rally.[3] Carrying American flags, Bibles, and placards reading "America for Jesus" and "America must repent or perish," they protested "a world aflame in sin," a lead-ership openly promoting nudity, addiction, sodomy, and fetal murder. Credit for organizing the two-day gathering was given to a group of well-heeled TV and radio evangelists, most notably the Rev. Jerry Fal-well, a Southern Baptist minister from Lynchburg, Virginia, and his Moral Majority, Inc. Founded only a year earlier, allegedly at the behest of political organizer Richard Viguerie, it already boasted a subscription list of 32,000 preachers and contributions totaling $1.5 million.

Why the New Right emerged from the depths of the American psyche when it did goes beyond our concerns here. Some point to two landmark Supreme Court decisions in 1973, the first clearing the way for legal abortions nationwide, the second mandating busing as a remedy for school desegregation. Others say it was a liberal Congress giving away the Panama Canal and weakening the Central Intelligence Agency by its nitpicking investigations of alleged wrongdoing. Still others point to the Watergate scandal of the Nixon administration, followed by Nixon's successor, Gerald Ford, naming Nelson Rockefeller, the perennial nemesis of the Right, his vice-president. What is important is that barely five years after bursting on the political scene, the New Right was claiming credit for sweeping into office America's most conservative president in half a century, plus a Congress eager to do his bidding.

Although each faction repudiates the other, like all political movements the New Right counts in its ranks both moderates and extremists, those who cautiously and patiently work through the existing party structure and legal system, and those who bridle at the seeming inaction of their elected representatives, ridicule the unrighteousness of procedural law, and talk stridently of taking matters into their own hands. There are the moderates who quietly rewrite the law to gerrymander school districts so as to maintain the lily-whiteness of their children's academies, and then there are the "racists" who run through the streets screaming "The niggers are in! The niggers are in!" and take up brickbats to accomplish (with less effect) the same purpose.

The story of the moderate element of the New Right has been largely pieced together.[4] This book tells the tale of their less respectable cousins. They are commonly called "kooks" and "crazies," but in these pages will be designated by their preferred title, "Christian patriots."

A handful of journalists have already reconnoitered the territory examined in this book. Some, like Patsy Sims and Phillip Finch, have displayed commendable objectivity during their travels, crafting insightful portraits of the human beings behind the Klan robes and Storm Trooper uniforms.[5] This, however, is a sociological account of Christian patriotism. It seeks to emulate the balanced, dispassionate tone of Sims and Finch, but unlike their work, it is based on adherence to an explicit methodological strategy and has recourse to the body of sociological theory concerning political extremism. For these reasons it intends to map the patriot world more systematically and thoroughly than does journalism.

By 1975 the death knell for right-wing terrorism in America had been happily rung, the frightful murders, bombings, and floggings of the Civil Rights era securely buried in memory. "The American Nazi movement is politically impotent," the Anti-Defamation League of B'nai B'rith (ADL) proclaimed in 1978, "capable and noteworthy only in the production of vicious hate propaganda, occasional street violence, and troublemaking on the local level."[6] As Dwayne Walls of the Race Relations Information Center in Nashville, Tennessee, announced in the title of his 1970 monograph on the subject: "The Klan Is Collapsed and Dormant." A 1976 Illinois Legislative Committee investigating far-right violence concurred: "The Ku Klux Klan in Illinois today is an organization with no substance. The elaborate rules and rituals . . . have survived as mere form without content. . . . It belongs in a comic strip. . . . In a sense this report is an obituary."[7]

Evidently the obituary was premature. Already by 1980 a recurrence of racism and anti-Semitism had stirred the U.S. House of Representatives Subcommittee on Crime to conduct hearings on the "Increasing Violence Against Minorities." Ted Gurr, a sociologist appearing before the panel, reported that the country was in the midst of the fourth wave of neo-Nazi and Klan activity in the last 115 years (the three others occurring during the 1870s, the 1920s, and the 1960s).[8] After declining in membership from an estimated 55,000 in 1967 to one-tenth that number by 1973, Klan rolls grew by 20 percent in 1979 alone, according to the ADL. Membership was estimated to have peaked at about 11,000 in 1981.[9]

The immediate occasion of the congressional investigation was the arrest of fourteen Klansmen and "Storm Troopers" implicated in the shooting deaths of five Communist Worker Party U.S.A. (CWP) members in Greensboro, North Carolina, in November 1979. The fourteen, all of whom were later acquitted of murder charges, allegedly drove to the rally site of a "Death to the Klan" march and began shouting obscenities and racial epithets. When the marchers responded by beating on their cars with sticks, a dozen people jumped from them and commenced a two-minute barrage with pistols, shotguns, and automatic weapons. The attack was not unprovoked. Days before the confrontation, the CWP had issued a public challenge to the Klan to appear, calling them "treacherous scum elements" and "a bunch of racist cowards." "We take you seriously," the Communists warned, "and will show you no mercy."

From that day through the end of 1985, at least fifty people lost their lives as a result of organized right-wing extremism in America. This includes five of the activists themselves. Three more have been sentenced to death for their roles in these incidents.

Leftist violence tends to be concentrated in urban areas. Cross burnings, hidden arms caches, and parades of ranked Klansmen militarily garbed and helmeted, however, conjure visions of Oklahoma and Texas backwater towns, the Missouri-Arkansas Ozarks, names like Decatur, Alabama; Castro Valley, California; Okolona, Mississippi; Columbus, Georgia; and during the 1980s, the sparsely populated, pine-crested mountains and deserts of the intermountain West, particularly the state of Idaho. Since 1975 the Gem State and its environs have become haven to a virulent strain of bigotry and racism. So concerned had the U.S. Justice Department become with the outbreak of racially and religiously motivated violence in Idaho that in November 1982 it commissioned a study of organized hate within the state.[10]

While lines of influence can never be precisely known, nine of the deaths since 1985 can be directly traced to groups functioning in the greater Idaho region during this period, five in Idaho itself. Ten of the other deaths are attributable to out-of-state organizations maintaining close links to Idaho-based groups. Four of the six suspected rightist-related deaths recorded from 1986 to January 1988 involved individuals residing at the time in the greater Idaho area (see Table 1.1).

One of these organizations, the White American Bastion (*Bruders Schweigen,* "secret brotherhood"), or as it is more popularly known, the Order, is perhaps the most violent in American history since the notorious Black Legion of the 1930s. Headquartered initially on the Idaho-Washington border, with safe houses, arms caches, and counterfeiting presses located in Idaho, Montana, Oregon, and Washington, the Order was complicit in five of the deaths enumerated in Table 1.1.

Idaho's pivotal significance in the plans of the revolutionary right goes far beyond the ambitions of the *Bruders Schweigen.* Speakers at the Aryan World Congress in July 1986 announced that Kootenai County, Idaho, would henceforth serve as provisional capital of a five-state Pacific Northwest Aryan Nation. All of this casts considerable doubt on David Chalmers's widely quoted assertion that "only the American South provides fertile soil for the Klan seed."[11]

A sociology of the radical right in Idaho should be of interest not only to students of contemporary Pacific Northwest cult esoterica, but to concerned Americans everywhere. Every state in the union has analogous organizations. Iowa has its Society for Educated Citizens, for example; Arizona its Patriots; Nevada its Committee of the States;

Table 1.1
Fatalities Related to American Right-Wing Activity, 1980–1985[c]

Date	Number Killed	Place
1. November 1979	5	Greensboro, N.C.
2. September 1980	7	New York State
3. 1980	1	Emrado, N.D.
4. 1980–82	13[a]	Salt Lake City; Madison, Wis.; Oklahoma City; e
5. March 1981	1	Alabama
6. 1982	3	Cleveland
7. 1982	1	Oroville, Calif.
8. 1982	1	Winder, Ga.
9. 1982	2	Arkansas
10. Unknown	1	Missouri
11. Spring 1983	2	Medina, N.D.
12. 1983	2	Walnut Ridge, Ark.
13. 1984	1	Kootenai County, Idaho
14. 1984	1	Denver, Colo.
15. December 8, 1984	1	Whidbey Island, Wash.
16. October 1984	1	Cairo, Neb.
17. April 1985	1	Boise, Idaho
18. April 15, 1985	1	Arkansas
19. December 1985	4	Seattle
20. Summer 1985	2	Rulo, Neb.

See page 10 for table footnotes.

Suspects in Slaying	Known Connection to Idaho Groups
Six Nazis and KKK members	Unclear. Glenn Miller, Grand Dragon of the N.C. Klan, allegedly given stolen money by Idaho-based Order in 1984. N.C. Klan members attended 1986 Aryan World Congress in Idaho
Joseph Christopher	None
Don McGrath[b]	None
Joseph P. Franklin	None
James Knowles and Henry Hays[d]	Unclear. Both are members of the United Klans of America. Alabama Klan members attended the 1986 Aryan World Congress
Frank Spisak[d]	Lieutenant in Idaho-based Socialist Nationalist Aryan Peoples Party. Members of SNAPP attended 1986 Aryan World Congress
"Red" Warthan	None
John McMillan[b]	None
Ralph Snell	None. Covenant, Sword, and Arm of the Lord member (CSA). CSA has close ties to Idaho-based Aryan Nations Church and to Order
None	None. Woman evidently a one-time member of CSA
Gordon Kahl Yorie Kahl	Connections to Posse Comitatus in Idaho. Celebrated as Aryan heroes at Aryan World Congress
Gordon Kahl[b]	See no. 11
	Member of Order
	Member of Order
Robert Mathews[b]	Member of Order
Arthur Kirk[b]	Unclear. Member of Posse Comitatus. Celebrated at Aryan World Congress as Aryan hero
Eugene Kinerk[c]	Inducted as Aryan Warrior at Aryan Nations Church. Possible member of Order
David Tate	Member of Order
David L. Rice[d]	None. Member of eastern Washington branch of Florida-based Duck Club
Michael Dennis Ryan and Timothy Haverkamp	Unclear. Both suspects members of Ministry of Christ Church, a schism from the Church of Jesus Christ Christian, otherwise known as Aryan Nations Church

Footnotes to Table 1.1:
[a] Alleged deaths.
[b] Killed by police.
[c] Suicide.
[d] Sentenced to death.
[e] James Huberty shot to death twenty-one customers and employees at a San Ysidro, California, McDonald's restaurant on July 18, 1984. An Internal Revenue Service manual intended for official use only claims that Huberty "was a subscriber to Mid-America Aryan Nations and was on Robert Miles' mailing list." Robert Miles is an Identity pastor with intimate ties to the Aryan Nations Church in Hayden Lake, Idaho, and was a keynote speaker at the 1986 Aryan World Congress in Hayden Lake (U.S., Dept. of Treasury, Criminal Investigation, Office of Intelligence, "Illegal Tax Protester Information Book" [Washington D.C.: Government Printing Office, n.d.], p. 12). Under threat of lawsuits from various right-wing groups for publishing false and libelous information, this document was ordered destroyed by Treasury officials on Aug. 25, 1986. Until reading of it in this document, I had never heard of the "Mid-American Aryan Nations."

In February 1987, Robert Pires pleaded guilty to the murder of an Aryan Nations supporter during August 1986. Pires was a member of the Idaho-based group called the Order Strike Force II.

On May 16, 1986, one-time Idaho residents David and Doris Young took a grade school in Cokeville, Wyoming, hostage in order to extort ransom from Congress for the founding of a racially pure utopian society. Both were killed. While there are indications that David had been a member of an Idaho Posse Comitatus unit, authorities now say his ties to right-wing groups are "uncertain."

On January 28, 1988, in a police shootout with Addam Swapp, a Marion, Utah, polygamist, racist, and home schooler, one officer was killed and Swapp himself critically injured. Just prior to the shooting, Swapp had declared his 2.5-acre compound a sovereign nation. Swapp is husband of the two daughters of Vickie Singer, ex-wife of John Singer, himself the victim of a police shootout in January 1979 during a home schooling dispute. Swapp believed his armed confrontation would result in Singer's resurrection and signal the beginning of the Battle of Armageddon. Singer had earlier been celebrated after his death as an Aryan hero at the Aryan world Congress.

Oregon its Militia; and Oklahoma its Christian American Advocates. Indeed Laird Wilcox's comprehensive *Guide to the American Right* lists nearly 3,500 far-right organizations functioning in America in 1986, 500 of them in California, the nation's cult mecca.[12] The Idaho groups not only maintain close ties to many of those of similar orientation headquartered elsewhere, but the most radical of them appear to have migrated into Idaho from out of state. Therefore, although care must always be taken in generalizing from one setting to another, it is likely that what can be concluded sociologically about the causes of movement participation in Idaho is true for groups in other parts of the country as well. As is proverbially known, the great events of the world are mirrored in the small. The emergence of rightist intolerance and repression throughout America beginning in the late 1970s has been reflected and in some cases amplified in Idaho. Hence, much can be learned about the larger extremist movement by focusing on one of its most dramatic manifestations.

DOING SOCIOLOGY

This is a sociology of the Idaho Christian patriot movement, not a psychology of its individual members. The nature and causes of a social movement are not necessarily deducible from the personalities of the members comprising it. Therefore, while a large amount of biographical information will be presented in the following pages, as a sociologist I am interested in the movement as a *social* phenomenon.

Sociology sets before itself two distinguishable tasks: understanding the phenomenon in question (sociologists sometimes add the adjective "sympathetic" to the noun understanding and use the German term *Verstehen* here) and causally explaining its existence. This book is organized around these two tasks. Part I is devoted to sympathetically examining the patriot movement from the "inside," Part II to studying it causally from the "outside."

To gain sympathetic understanding of a world alien to one's own—how it classifies events, accounts for them, issues policy recommendations, and motivates members to enact them, i.e., how it provides its members with "good" reasons for acting—sociologists employ "field observation." They attempt to immerse themselves in that world without, so to speak, drowning in it. This includes reading its literature, attending its workshops and lectures, participating in its devotionals, and conversing with its inhabitants. The dangers of field observation are duly recognized by the profession, particularly when dealing with what are conventionally spoken of as "extremist" or "radical" groups.[13] The experience of a student colleague at another university who became interested in the subject of Idaho "neo-Nazism" may serve as an illustration.

After reading the somewhat embellished media accounts of happenings in northern Idaho, this student wrote out his last will and testament just prior to embarking alone on his direct investigation of the movement. Surely, he feared, blue-shirted Nazis with Uzi machine guns would be congregated on Coeur d'Alene's sidewalks, and he himself might be victimized by a terrorist hit squad. (I received similar warnings before leaving on a similar field trip around the same time.) Needless to say, the student's experience did not begin to approximate the bloodthirsty images he carried with him into the field. Instead, he found at the Aryan Nations Church compound a smattering of gray-haired retired folks, a grandfather-like leader living in comfortable surroundings with his devoted wife and dogs, and an atmosphere of conviviality and openness. On his return home after four days of "research," my friend had to spend seven more days disengaging himself from the unhealthy attachments he had formed.

The goal, then, is to find the middle ground between being so scientifically detached or closed-minded that one cannot don the subject's shoes to get a feeling for his world as *he* experiences it, and, on the other hand, allowing oneself to "become the phenomenon," as one textbook irresponsibly recommends, thus losing one's perspective as a scientist.

The construction of causal explanations of social phenomena is considerably less harrowing. Instead of coming to grasp the nuances and uniqueness of the movement in question, the analyst searches for similarities between it and others in the past. The object here is to invent a "type," and then to find the one or two conditions occurring prior to and independent of the type that are always found (correlated) with it.

If we assume that the Idaho Christian patriot movement is of the type labeled "right-wing extremism," then we ask what conditions exist independent of and prior to this type of movement that are responsible for it. Are its members being economically declassed, as Seymour Martin Lipset has argued?[14] That is, are Idaho patriots alike in respect to their experience of being downwardly mobile? Or, as other theorists suggest, are the patriots isolated from the ordinary channels of belonging in American society and hence more "available" to extremist propaganda?[15] Are right-wing zealots less educated than their peers?[16] If not, might they have received the "wrong kind" of education? To pose it in sociological jargon, have they been "politically socialized" to believe as they do? Are they merely acting out as adults what they learned in Sunday school as children? Or is there some other factor that precipitates right-wing extremist movements in general and Idaho Christian patriotism in particular?

Sociology adheres to the same logic of inquiry as the physical sciences. But given the primitiveness of its measuring instruments and the complexity of its subject matter (to say nothing of the variable skills of its practitioners), rarely if ever do its causal claims satisfy the standards of scientific rigor. Instead of constructing bonafide causal explanations, therefore, sociologists speak of producing "explanation sketches." These have the appearance of casual explanations: they contain testable general statements which, in conjunction with particular statements, seem logically to account for happenings in the world. On closer view, however, these general statements are not highly confirmed by independent researchers and hence do not qualify as actual causal laws. The explanatory premises, furthermore, are usually presented elliptically and fail to mention all the statements necessary and sufficient for logically deriving from them the events to be explained. One implication of this is that while sociologists appear to be capable of "explaining" things in the past, they are far less equipped to predict the future. But prediction is the hallmark of the advanced sciences.

Seen in this light, Part II of this book offers only probable reasons for why some individuals rather than others have joined the patriot movement, probable causal correlates or associations, explanatory approximations. Where precision of expression is unnecessary or where it enhances the efficiency of presentation, I used the word "cause" in the following pages without the qualifying adjectives above. It should be understood, however, that nowhere am I claiming to provide anything more than a causal sketch of movement affiliation. While I believe the sketch offered in Part II makes considerable sense of the past, to a great extent the future of Christian patriotism in Idaho and elsewhere must remain a mystery.

CHRISTIAN PATRIOTISM DEFINED

The subjects of this book know themselves as Christians and patriots. As Christians, the patriots assent to faith in Jesus Christ as savior (either through His example or His sacrifice), to the promise of salvation for all men (although there is debate among the patriots concerning what constitutes a human being capable of faith), and to the exclusive monopoly of Christianity over the means of eternal life.

The sample subjects consider their religion to be far more than an adjunct to life celebrated one hour weekly. On the contrary, they feel themselves duty bound to go into the world to reform it (and themselves) in a manner pleasing to the Lord. *The Politics of Righteousness* is my term. It encompasses both the reformist orientation of Christian patriotism and its abiding sense of guiltlessness and rightness in the

Lord. It stands for all the tactics, from oral persuasion to outright violence, advocated and used by Christian patriots, in certain knowledge of their divine election, to establish God's rule on earth.

A Christian patriot minister, presently under police surveillance for alleged anti-Semitism, has described the politics of righteousness in these bitterly ironic words: "You too, can experience [the] honor . . . [of being] listed in a Jewish Hate Movement Report [as he did in 1987]. . . . All you need to do is believe in and obey the Lord Jesus Christ, . . . desire and work for a Christian America as well as a Christian world, . . . acknowledge His Law as perfect . . . and expose the anti-Christ actions and hatred of modern-day Talmudic Jewry."[17]

Christian patriots distinguish between Law and legality, Morality and legalese. The former of these pairs is determined, respectively, by their readings of the so-called organic Constitution (the original Articles of Constitution plus the Bill of Rights) and selected edicts from the Pentateuch (the first five books of the Bible). They believe they have little, if any, *moral* obligation to obey legal statutes inconsistent with Law or Morality.

Naturally, as students of the Bible, Christian patriots are well aware of scriptural injunctions to submit themselves to public authority (cf. Romans 13:1–7; I Peter 2:13–16; and Titus 3:1). But they believe that with increasing frequency state regulations interfere with and even contradict biblical and constitutional law: Pastors are imprisoned for having Christian schools out of compliance with what they consider "satanic" curriculum guidelines. Pastors are fined for holding church services in areas not properly zoned for such activity. Store owners are forced to remove Christian banners from their flagpoles because they fail to meet sign ordinances. To negotiate these apparent contradictions, patriot casuists differentiate between secular *authority* and secular *power*. Truly authoritative enactments either derive directly from God (as read in the Bible) or are in accordance with His will discerned by the Founding Fathers. These enactments alone are binding upon the Christian citizen. Ordinances more or less than this may be enforced by state power, but they have no authority to command the voluntary compliance of the patriot. To quote the same patriot minister cited above:

You see county mounties with 357's on the hip and a badge on the chest, with back-ups on the way and the blessings of the county commissioners . . . but that doesn't in itself make them the higher . . . authority described in

Romans 13. Just because someone sets themself up in a position of power
. . . be it OSHA [Occupational Safety and Health Administration] or a dog
catcher—that doesn't make them the authorities of Romans 13.[18]

There is a good bit of debate among patriots over which specific state
regulations are authoritative and which merely tyrannical. To some,
virtually the entire government, to which they afix the ominous title
"ZOG" (Zionist Occupation Government), is biblically and constitutionally illegitimate, worthy only of armed resistance. To the less radical, the detested object may be a particular legal statute, a zoning law,
a local tax, or the closing of a Forest Service trail to motorized travel.
Some patriots conscientiously disobey the statute in question. Others
fight it with legal means.

The politics of righteousness is pictured by Christian patriots as a
battle against a satanic cabal that has insidiously infiltrated the dominant institutions of society, especially the mass media, public schools,
established churches, and state agencies like the Internal Revenue Service. The goal of this cabal is to subvert God's will (i.e., Law and
Morality, as understood above) by promoting, among other things,
equal rights for "unqualified" ethnic and racial minorities, non-Chris-
tian religions such as "secular humanism," and moral perversion—pornography, homosexuality, abortion, crime, and usury. God tolerates
"neither fornicators, nor idolaters, nor adulterers, nor effeminates, nor
homosexuals, nor thieves, nor the covetous, nor drunkards, nor re-
vilers, nor swindlers" (I Corinthians 6:9–11).[19] Neither should the
Christian patriot who does His will.

The *end* of Christian patriotism is the preservation of "Christian
values" and "Americanism," as the patriots understand them. In this
sense it may be taken as, and indeed sometimes calls itself, "conservative." However, it is even more typical for the people studied here to
disassociate themselves from conservatism, which they equate with in-
stitutionalized uncharitableness, a bluff and swagger do-nothing foreign policy, and appeasement of the liberal status quo. Furthermore,
and more to the point, the patriots in the sample are not averse to
advocating the use of revolutionary *means* to achieve their ends. For
this reason, I systematically avoid the use of "conservative" in this
volume. Instead, when I wish to avoid repetitious overuse of "Christian patriotism," where appropriate I substitute for it the words "far
right," "right-wing extremism," or "rightist." These substitutes are not
meant to imply anything more than the word they replace.

"Leftist" and "rightist" are terms used in political oratory to prejudge and attack one's opponents. It should be clear that this is not my intention. Furthermore, a few patriots will object to being classified in these pages as rightists. Some sample subjects place themselves in the very center of the political spectrum, the titles of their groups— e.g., "Golden Mean Society"—reflecting this image of themselves. John Birchers, for example, consider themselves the only authentic centrists in America. They place Posse Comitatus to their right and call it a form of "right-wing anarchy." Nazism (national socialism), meanwhile, they group with liberalism and Communism as promoting "left-wing totalitarianism."

Similar confusion has long surrounded the proper classification of anti-elitist Populist Party adherents, members of Liberty Lobby, and the so-called crypto-fascists such as Huey Long and Father Coughlin. Furthermore, not every member of the groups I deal with here assents to Christian patriotism as depicted above. Nationwide, there is a smattering of Jewish Birchers; in some eastern states national socialists worship pagan Nordic gods; and some American Nazi and Klan splinter groups can boast of Jewish members.[20] It is even alleged that ADL operatives once posed as neo-Nazis in a television documentary entitled "Armies of the Right."[21] Indeed, I know of an Idaho Klan group that inadvertently designated a black railroad laborer as its Grand Titan. (He simply sent in the required application form on a lark—absent his racial identity—and found himself so honored.) But in the greater Idaho region these exceptions prove the rule: There is virtual unanimity of religious confession and racial type among Gem State radical patriots.

To summarize, then, as used in this book "Christian patriot" refers to a person who:

- Assents to faith in Jesus Christ as savior, either through His example or through His sacrifice.
- Believes that the promise of salvation has been given to all "human beings."
- Believes that only through Jesus Christ can one be saved.[22]
- Feels duty-bound to reform the world after God's will, as discerned in the Bible and as manifested in the organic Constitution.
- Has a moral obligation to submit to secular authority that rules according to God's will, as understood above.
- Believes a secret satanic conspiracy has infiltrated America's major institutions to subvert God's will.

• Believes that the actions and policies of these subverted institutions must be battled by means of a politics of righteousness.

The Christian patriots studied here come in one of two forms. They are either "hedgehogs" or "foxes" (to borrow an image from Isaiah Berlin), grand theorists or empiricists. To say it more precisely, some patriots derive their positions on specific issues from explicit theories of history and society, and are able to fit events as diverse as earthquakes, venereal disease, and commodity prices into an overarching theoretical scheme. Others are concerned with a specific problem such as school textbooks, abortion, or sex education, but are disinclined and/or unable to theoretically justify their responses beyond catch phrases like "secular humanism." Such a one is the Issaquah, Washington, woman who painstakingly catalogued 785 "profanities" in J. D. Salinger's novel, *Catcher in the Rye,* including 222 "hells," and led a crusade to have it banned from the school library. She believes the book is "part of a Communist plot."[23] The primary concern of this study is the ideologically oriented hedgehogs, not the issue-specific foxes.

Depending on the theory that guides them, the hedgehogs are of two basic types: Christian Constitutionalists and Identity Christians. It should be emphasized that these terms refer to general ideological outlooks under which various patriot groups can be fit. They are not groups in themselves. For example, the Aryan Nations Church, a specific group, preaches a form of Christian Identity, but so do other groups in Idaho that disagree with Aryan Nations spokesmen on particular policy questions. Likewise, little love is lost between the groups included here under the term Constitutionalists. The Posse Comitatus, for example, rebukes the John Birch Society as the "meet, eat, and retreat society." Birchers return the compliment by ridiculing Posse deputies as crazies, fools, and anarchists.

Furthermore, no claim is made that these ideological types are mutually exclusive (or necessarily exhaustive of the Idaho Christian patriot world). Although most Idaho patriots seem to stick with one familiar orientation, a minority of others move with evident ease from one ideological position to the next. Nor, finally, am I suggesting that these two ideological types represent positions on some continuum of moderation-extremism or peaceful-violent. With the exception of those few classified as issue-oriented, all the patriots before us are exemplars of political extremity.

For purposes of this study the division between Constitutionalism and Identity is taken to pivot around the question of who is alleged to be behind the conspiracy to subvert America's institutions. Identity Christians, however much they might disagree over the precise meaning of the word, hold "Jews" responsible for America's plight. Constitutionalists are reluctant to point to a definite ethnic, racial, or religious group, favoring instead abstract categories like "insiders," "Bilderbergers," "trilateralists," "the hidden hand," "the network," or "force X."[24]

To classify those patriots not easily identified with a group affiliation, I asked a flexible series of questions. Since I assumed few Idahoans would readily admit to holding anti-Jewish attitudes, I did not directly ask who is behind the "conspiracy." Instead, I inquired first whether they had read the *Spotlight* newspaper (published by Liberty Lobby), Gary Allen's *None Dare Call It Conspiracy,* or Cleon Skousen's *The Naked Capitalist.* If the respondent admitted to having read any of these publications, I then asked for his opinion regarding the insinuations in them of Jewish, Zionist, or Israeli complicity in the conspiracy. Those who rejected any suggestion of Jewish conspiratorialism I classified as Christian Constitutionalists;[25] those who found the notion credible, I grouped under the label "Identity Christian." Many of the latter took my questions as an opportunity to expound upon other aspects of the "Jewish conspiracy": for example, the Jewish-Communist weather war conspiracy, the Jewish allopathic medicine conspiracy, or the Jewish science metric-scale conspiracy.

If a respondent said that Jews are indeed responsible for America's problems, I next inquired into what was meant by the word "Jew." In this way I discovered that there are in fact two distinct types of Identity proponents: those for whom the Jew is a member of a particular non-Aryan racial group and those for whom the Jew is a confessor of a particular world religion, Judaism, irrespective of race. This distinction is elaborated upon in chapter 4.

By means of a variety of devices, I compiled a core sample of 520 self-identified Christian patriots who reside in Idaho or who are connected with patriot groups there (see Table 1.3). Under the rubric of Christian Constitutionalists are included tax resisters (meaning here, persons who have been prosecuted for tax violations), admitted Posse Comitatus activists, John Birchers, Constitutional terrorists (individuals who have injured or killed other people), and "others," individuals difficult to classify in any single category. "Others" also include *pro*

Table 1.2
Idaho Christian Patriot Types Plus Representative Groups

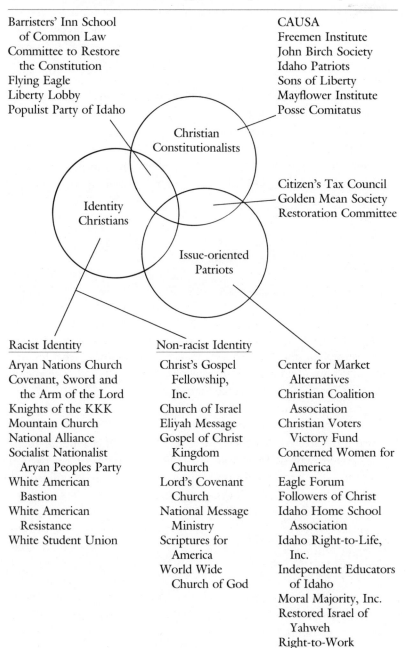

Barristers' Inn School
  of Common Law
Committee to Restore
  the Constitution
Flying Eagle
Liberty Lobby
Populist Party of Idaho

CAUSA
Freemen Institute
John Birch Society
Idaho Patriots
Sons of Liberty
Mayflower Institute
Posse Comitatus

Christian
Constitutionalists

Citizen's Tax Council
Golden Mean Society
Restoration Committee

Identity
Christians

Issue-oriented
Patriots

Racist Identity

Aryan Nations Church
Covenant, Sword and
  the Arm of the Lord
Knights of the KKK
Mountain Church
National Alliance
Socialist Nationalist
  Aryan Peoples Party
White American
  Bastion
White American
  Resistance
White Student Union

Non-racist Identity

Christ's Gospel
  Fellowship,
  Inc.
Church of Israel
Eliyah Message
Gospel of Christ
  Kingdom
  Church
Lord's Covenant
  Church
National Message
  Ministry
Scriptures for
  America
World Wide
  Church of God

Center for Market
  Alternatives
Christian Coalition
  Association
Christian Voters
  Victory Fund
Concerned Women for
  America
Eagle Forum
Followers of Christ
Idaho Home School
  Association
Idaho Right-to-Life,
  Inc.
Independent Educators
  of Idaho
Moral Majority, Inc.
Restored Israel of
  Yahweh
Right-to-Work

Table 1.3
Numbers of Idaho Christian Patriot Types

	Number	Percent of General Type	Percent of All Patriots
Hedgehogs. Ideologically oriented patriots			
Christian Constitutionalists. Believe an abstract group is behind conspiracy to destroy America			
John Birchers	45	24.9	8.6
Posse Comitatus deputies	24	13.3	4.6
Tax resisters	27	14.9	5.2
Terrorists	6	3.3	1.2
Others. *Pro se* trial litigants, Constitutionalist study group activists	79	43.6	15.2
Constitutionalist Total	181	100.0	34.8
Identity Christians. Believe Jews are behind conspiracy to destroy America			
Non-racists. Believe Jews members of satanic religion	71	24.9	13.7
Racialists. Believe Jews members of satanic race	139	48.8	26.7
Terrorists	75	26.3	14.4
Identity Christian Total	285	100.0	54.8
Hedgehog Total	466	100.0	89.6
Foxes. Issue-specific patriots			
Christian economists	6	11.1	1.2
Right-to-Life, homeschoolers, Right-to-Work	39	72.2	7.5
Miscellaneous patriots	9	16.7	1.7
Fox Total	54	100.0	10.4
Grand Total of Patriots	520	—	100.0

se trial litigants, who, as the Latin phrase indicates, defend themselves in courts of law by means of their understanding of English Common Law. It also includes a handful of persons associated with Constitutionalist study groups like the Freemen Institute and CAUSA, who have taken the lessons they have learned into the political arena.

Among the Identity Christians we can distinguish between racists— they prefer the term "racialists"—and those who see racial minorities in a somewhat more benign light, but who consider Judaism to be a satanic cult. For my purposes the latter include a handful of Populist Party activists (but not all Populists statewide), Lyndon LaRouche supporters *in Idaho,* and members of the Identity congregations specified in chapter 4. A last category of Identity Christians is comprised of racial terrorists, such as members of the White American Bastion or Order.

There are three basic kinds of issue-oriented "foxes" in the sample: Christian home-schoolers, Christian right-to-life advocates, and what I call "Christian economists." The last refers to those who celebrate free-market capitalism as an economic system consistent with the natural law of orthodox Christianity. The reborn in Christ, say the Christian economists, have a duty to the community, but it is primarily a duty of charity and love. Most kinds of taxation are un-Christian, they insist, because taxes take from others what is rightfully theirs and they discourage people from living charitably. The most enthusiastic supporters of Christian economics in Idaho are housed in the Center for Market Alternatives on the campus of Presbyterian-owned College of Idaho in Caldwell. As indicated earlier, these and other "foxes" are only alluded to occasionally in this study.

A GEOGRAPHY OF IDAHO PATRIOTISM

If Idaho were flattened by a steam roller, its land mass would expand into the largest state of all the lower forty-eight. Land of Big Sky and roaring river, Gem of the Mountains, with wilderness acreage alone that dwarfs several New England states, it is the chosen home of the Christian patriots of the intermountain West.

Their cabins nestle deep in pine-studded canyons, refuges from the pollution and crime of Sun Belt cities. Some, like Bob Fellows* of Riggins, a part-time gold prospector and ex-deputy sheriff from Reno,

---

*An asterisk indicates the use of a fictitious name.

Nevada, concoct imaginary armed invasions of aliens and, to fend them off, "home defense systems." Fellows markets an automatic shotgun which, he brags, "can be easily handled—even by the little lady of 90 pounds."[26] Others have followed their dreams and settled in "our Alps," along the fjord-like lakes of northern Idaho. An elderly Mormon woman who arrived from Wyoming to co-found one of the first American chapters of the John Birch Society back in the 1950s sees it as the fulfillment of prophecy. Latter-day Saint (Mormon) writers, she relates, have predicted that when the time approaches for Christ's Second Coming, "all nations, kingdoms, and principalities shall be thrown down." At that moment "the honest in heart" will be drawn to the Rocky Mountains. These "born patriots" will reestablish law and order "at the tops of the Rockies," which are located, of course, precisely in northern Idaho.[27]

From the outside, Idaho's Christian patriot movement appears monolithic. From the inside, however, it reveals itself as highly differentiated, with disputes between leaders constantly threatening its delicately wrought harmony. The main reason for this is that Idaho is many things religiously. Its radical patriotisms, although all Christian in name, reflect this diversity.

In eastern Idaho counties up to 90 percent of the population is Latter-day Saint. Because the Mormon Church has traditionally emphasized the sacredness of the Constitution, right-wing extremism in eastern Idaho takes the form of Christian Constitutionalism, particularly resistance against what is widely seen as an illegal income tax system. Here too the Posse Comitatus (Power of the County) flourishes. The Posse is viewed as a constitutionally decreed means of defense against government tyranny. Explicit anti-Semitism is rare among Mormon patriots, in part because of their own painful memories of religious persecution. (Until 1982, Article 6, Section 3 of the Idaho Constitution forbade any person from voting "who is a bigamist or polygamist, or is living in what is known as patriarchal, plural or celestial [i.e. Mormon] marriage.")[28] The marshal of the Bingham County Posse Comitatus, a devoted Mormon housewife—even though women are not strictly permitted membership in Posses—claims that she had Jewish grandparents.[29]

In the northern Idaho panhandle near Coeur d'Alene and in the rural districts of southwest Idaho, about 5 to 10 percent of the population is Latter-day Saint. Here fundamentalist "holiness" or "perfectionist" sects enjoy a wide following. In Canyon County, Idaho's sec-

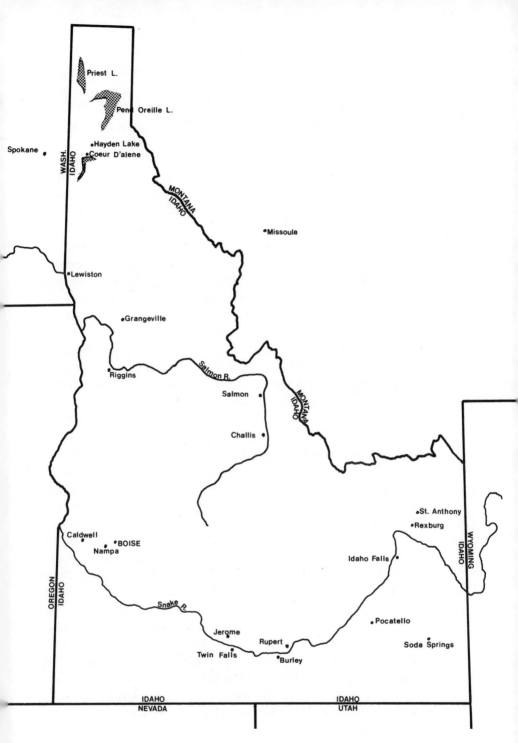

Centers of Idaho Christian political activity

ond largest, they constitute at least one-fifth of all church adherents.[30] While some of these sects theologically fall within the mainstream of conventional Protestantism, this is not true of others like the Yahweh Believers, the Gospel of Christ Fellowship, the Followers of Christ, the Order of Servant's Church, and the Voice of Elijah.

Unlike most Mormons, members of holiness sects characteristically distrust government and especially public education. Several of those I interviewed expressed pride that while raised in improverishment—in some cases out of automobiles—their parents "never stooped" to take "welfare handouts."[31] They have joined unincorporated worship groups to avoid entanglements with "Caesar" (despite the resulting loss of tax exemptions) and have established independent Christian academies to educate their children. One of these, located in Kootenai County, required all its students to wear red, white, and blue uniforms, prohibited the girls from wearing pants, using make-up, or cutting their hair, and all the children from listening to the "Devil's anthem," rock 'n' roll. The headmaster also forbade his students' parents from owning TV sets. Finding this last measure too severe, the congregation dismissed him from his position. He has since left to establish an even more radical church school.[32]

The most extreme cousins of the holiness sects are the Identity Christians, or as they sometimes dub themselves, the American Israelites. Not only antimodernist, they are also often anti-Catholic and anti-Mormon, sometimes anti-Jewish and racist, and in rare cases viciously so. In response to an interview question concerning whether or not she was Catholic, one of these subjects responded with horror, "Oh no, I'm a Christian!" When I replied that I had always thought Catholicism to be a form of Christianity, she patiently informed me, "Oh no, it's just like Mormonism! It's not a religion, it's just a cult."[33]

The best known of the Identity congregations—the Aryan Nations Church (the Church of Jesus Christ Christian), the Reformed Church of Christ-Society of Saints (a front of the Socialist Nationalist Aryan Peoples Party), the Ministry of Christ Church, and the Arkansas-based Covenant, Sword, and the Arm of the Lord, which has intimate ties with the Idaho groups—were the major recruiting bases for the White American Bastion or *Bruders Schweigen* (the Order). The *Bruders Schweigen* was named after the warrior elite of the German National Socialist movement. More than twenty of its members have been imprisoned for criminal racketeering growing out of their participation in terrorist activities throughout the West.

HOW THIS BOOK CAME ABOUT

The Politics of Righteousness was conceived in the hours following the fatal shootout between *Bruders Schweigen* founder Robert Mathews and federal authorities on Whidbey Island, Washington, in November 1984. As a student of religion and violence, I found my interest aroused when newspapers reported links between this terrorist group and a Christian fundamentalist sect then flourishing in northern Idaho. Having lived in Idaho for some years, I was fortunately situated to have my curiosity satisfied.

Starting in the late 1970s, stories began appearing with increasing frequency about an ultraconservative revival both nationwide and in Idaho. There was talk at the Idaho statehouse of reinstituting loyalty oaths, discontinuing compulsory education ("six grades is enough for anyone," said one Twin Falls legislator), ending tenure for university instructors, and privatizing public lands and services. The Idaho plurality (second largest in the country) won by Ronald Reagan in the 1980 presidential election, coupled with the defeat of liberal Senator Frank Church by an individual who appeared (at least to liberals) to represent the height of right-wing flippancy, simply underscored political developments in the state.

In 1983 a legislative memorial was passed concerning the so-called international banking conspiracy and its ties to the Federal Reserve System.[34] This was followed by legislative recision of the Equal Rights Amendment, passage of right-to-work legislation, advocacy of teaching the virtues of free-market capitalism in public schools, and hysteria concerning allegations of homosexuality in the classroom. Although in 1982 the defamatory anti-Mormon constitutional article referred to in the previous section was overturned, estimates are that close to one-half of the "gentiles" (non-Mormons) who voted on the measure favored keeping it on the books.

And more alarming news: growing numbers of prosecutions for tax violations, published threats from the Posse Comitatus to execute public officials for acting "unconstitutionally," and reports of racial and religious persecution in Coeur d'Alene, Jerome, and Pocatello. In Idaho Falls, Meridian, and Boise, Mormon church centers were vandalized and a Jewish synagogue bombed; in Twin Falls a swastika was applied to a Laotian family's home; in Hayden Lake, a Jewish restaurateur's seventeen-year-old business was defaced with anti-Semitic references; and in Hailey, racial epithets were spray painted on the car of a white mother of two adopted black children. According to the Community

Relations Service of the U.S. Justice Department, twenty-two in-
stances of racial harassment were reported in Idaho between 1979 and
1983, sixteen in the last two years alone. During the same four-year
period, thirteen others were reported near the Idaho border in eastern
Washington.[35] These incidents were coupled with rumors of arms caches
hidden in the ice caves of Power County, for example, and of paramilitary training exercises held by rightists in Bonner and Kootenai
counties.

It would be asking too much of the reader's indulgence to share all
my feelings concerning this spectacle, but I do have an obligation to
reveal the biases with which I began this research. Suffice it to say that
I felt both frightened and powerless in the face of what I then facilely
lumped under the title "the neo-Nazis." To counteract my sense of
helplessness I chose to come to grips intellectually with what it was I
feared and loathed.

For decades off and on, sociologists have been interested in the
subject of right-wing extremism in America. Some of this work will
be cited later, and it is unnecessary to detail its failings here. All that
need be said at this point is that the profession has traditionally maintained an inordinate distance from the right-wingers it has presumed
to research. It has relied on data from public opinion polls or on
secondary sources written by journalists and historians (much of this
resting in turn on questionable analogies between European and
American political affairs). Few sociologists have gone into the field
to speak with right-wingers themselves. This is ironic given their willingness to venture into other regions equally alien to the security of
academia: from urban gangs to maximum security prisons, from gay
"tearooms" to hobo camps, from leftist communes to nudist colonies.
One of the few exceptions to this avoidance is Scott McNall's Ph.D.
dissertation, based on participant observation of a now-defunct fundamentalist political sect in Portland, Oregon, called The Freedom
Center.[36] But McNall approached The Freedom Center as a self-contained world; he made little effort to connect its dealings with those
on the larger national scene. This, coupled with the fact that the research was conducted in the early 1960s, limits its use in comprehending rightist politics today. Nevertheless, McNall's dissertation provides
an approximation of the research design I wished to duplicate. He got
to know his subjects as living, breathing persons instead of as com-
puterized polling responses or as the stereotypes of liberal news commentators.

While sociologists have recently analyzed the New Christian Right, most of their attention has been focused on the circumstances surrounding the emergence of its more moderate elements, those with access to the political power centers of America: the Moral Majority, Inc., the 700 Club, the Religious Round Table, etc. To my knowledge, at least when I began this study, no professional sociologist was systematically covering the extremist angle. This being the case, I was compelled at first to rely on the stories of newspaper reporters looking for quick scoops, klanwatch groups grinding obvious political axes, and on the police, who have their own agenda, for my initial pictures of the people I would later come to know more closely. The portraits were not complimentary. What we are observing, the accounts agreed, is the hateful, sometimes criminal politics of young, poorly educated (hence fanatic), marginally employed, transient, single men.

Supplied with this image and with travel money from my academic department, I traveled in the summer of 1985 to northern Idaho, the apparent center of the politics of extremity, to find confirmation for my impressions. I still recall anxiously pacing the floor of a Coeur d'Alene motel room, attempting to garner sufficient chutzpah to phone and arrange an interview with my first "neo-Nazi." Ironically, my subject was a member of the Order who would be arrested the next day for taking out a contract on the life of the Pennsylvania informant who had exposed the group to the FBI. Held in the lakeside ambiance of the celebrated Coeur d'Alene Inn, this interview served as my entrée into a forbidden land and marked the beginning of my own demystification of its inhabitants. For behind the bravado and the insignia-covered blue shirt, I detected a human being. He was, furthermore, an elderly grandfather born and raised in the Idaho county in which he then resided, and a one-time agriculture student at the University of Idaho. He was paranoid (for every good reason) but not crazy, at least not wild-eyed and maniacal.

Few places seem a less likely home for political extremism than Coeur d'Alene, a town of 20,000 set in a glacier-sculpted valley of incomparable beauty, populated by concerned, civic-minded folk. Sandy Emerson, the executive head of the Chamber of Commerce, took pains to assure me that media impressions of this community as comprised of "Nazi lovers" were untrue. To this end he introduced me to two of my initial contacts. The first was Barbara Strakal, a local teacher and then head of what was called the Cult Awareness Center. She opened to me its impressive clipping file on the plethora of cults then fre-

quenting the area. The files included correspondence from two groups
that would later figure prominently in my research: the Church of
Jesus Christ Christian (Aryan Nations) and the closely related Socialist
Nationalist Aryan Peoples Party (SNAPP). The second contact was
Larry Broadbent, undersheriff of Kootenai County, a nationally recognized and locally admired authority on Pacific Northwest hate groups.
Sheriff Broadbent generously shared not only hours of his valuable
time but a veritable library of radical pamphlets, studies, broadsheets,
newspaper articles, and videotapes.

While in Coeur d'Alene, I was invited to prepare a written piece for
the Chamber of Commerce on the other side of the story—the community's response to racism and bigotry. The product was a brief history of the Kootenai County Human Relations Task Force, based on
unstructured interviews with those who spearheaded its establishment
at no small risk to their own welfare.[37]

By the fall of 1985 I was prepared to study systematically the radical
right in Idaho, and it became imperative that I secure the names of a
large number of reliable informants. The problem I faced is familiar
to sociologists of deviant behavior: How does one penetrate a social
world shut off to inquisitive outsiders and win the confidence of its
inhabitants so that they will reveal confidential information about
themselves? The problem was magnified in this case, not only because
radical rightists came under intense police scrutiny at the very moment
I began my study, but also because the patriots have an ideologically
grounded distrust of liberal academicians, perceiving them as allies, if
not actual agents, of the government. The solution to these difficulties
was a research strategy resembling the investigatory techniques outlined by Jack Douglas in his book on the subject.[38]

The main vehicle I employed to generate my sample was what sociologists call "snowballing," simply asking respondents for the names
of others who might be willing to be interviewed. Naturally, snowballing requires at least a few initial contacts. These I obtained from a
diversity of sources: letters to editors of local newspapers and patriot
newsletters, names reported in newspaper accounts of courtroom cases
involving patriots, lists confidentially provided by local sheriffs of
counties where patriot activity was flourishing, publications by klanwatch groups, and human-interest newspaper stories on the patriots.
I secured fifty-nine names from the so-called Nehemiah Township
Charter, a legal document filed in the Kootenai County Clerk's office
decreeing the area surrounding Hayden Lake a Christian Aryan town-

ship.[39] One evening at a workshop in Pocatello I obtained a score of names by surreptitiously glancing over the shoulder of a silver-haired lady who held in her palm a list of "people to be contacted." Typically at such gatherings I would introduce myself and ask lonely patriots directly for interviews. I conscientiously avoided interrupting those occupied with other business, hoping to get to them later.

Students in social problems and deviant behavior classes at the university proved to be an unexpected resource. Some knew radical patriots personally; others could name such "black sheep" in their own families. More than once individuals contacted me after hearing me speak about the movement or after reading of my research in the press. In the public arena I made a point of never using pejorative language in describing Christian patriotism so as not to compromise the larger project. Several Ohio SNAPP members enthusiastically agreed to interviews after recalling my name and preliminary findings from an article published in the *Cleveland Plain Dealer*.[40]

Such were the benefits of not being openly judgmental of my respondents, but the tactic was not without risks. An excerpt from one speech I gave before the Boise State University Sociology Club in 1987 somehow found itself in a Ku Klux Klan newspaper out of North Carolina a month later. I subsequently received a formal request from the Anti-Defamation League of B'nai B'rith to explain myself. Another time I received a disturbing hate call from a self-proclaimed liberal after being quoted in a local newspaper as saying the Aryans are "good people with blind spots."[41] In still another case, a critic tried to explain my neutral attitude toward the Aryans by insinuating that I suffered from the so-called Stockholm Syndrome, the tendency of hostages to empathize with their captors.[42]

Having obtained respondent candidates, I next had to gather data about them. In this project I used both secondary and primary sources of information.[43] Since they constituted a comparatively minor information resource, let me first say a few words about my secondary sources. Descriptions of patriots in anti-Klan publications are of dubious scientific value given their political motivation and lack of documentation. Except in those few places cited in the text of this volume, I ignored them unless they could be independently confirmed by a primary source. Generally, their problem was not their accuracy but their brevity. Anti-Klan reports usually leave out too much of what I was interested in learning, especially the religious backgrounds of the patriots and their political biographies.

Academic monographs and articles in commercial magazines provided the bulk of my secondary material, particularly for those I have
classified as "terrorists." For the most part this information is insightful and detailed, and the circumstances of the information gathering
explicated by their authors. I had few qualms about using this material
when there was no alternative.

As the table in Appendix II indicates, most of the data were obtained directly from the subjects themselves, either by letter, phone
call, or face-to-face interview. A surprisingly large number of the sample were willing to divulge their personal lives to a stranger over the
phone. Conventional opinion, bolstered by academic scholarship, holds
right-wing radicals to be characterologically paranoid. My impression,
on the contrary, is that much of the paranoia they exhibit may be due
in part to the conflictual situations in which they often find themselves
with liberal reporters, self-righteous academics, the police, and civil
rights activists.

Some patriots have unlisted numbers or no phones at all. Prisoners
were contacted by letter, a challenging logistical affair in itself. Other
patriots were contacted indirectly, often through relatives. A case in
point: From a list of names supplied by a local sheriff, I called all the
numbers in that county with the last name "Joyner." One of those
who answered the phone was a sister of the man I was seeking. She
requested my license plate number and told me to stand by for a return call. Although I cannot be sure, she probably used my license
number to verify my name. She then located her brother and called
me back to give me the time and place for an interview. He arrived
on time with an activist friend.

Researchers tell us not to expect more than a 20 percent return on
mailed questionnaires. My experience with imprisoned radicals confirms this. In the first place, it was difficult to locate imprisoned members of the Order. And even pinpointing their locations was no guar-
antee that a questionnaire would get to them. Several of my envelopes
were sent back stamped "Contraband—Return to Sender." Since the
FBI provided me no help on this matter, I was compelled to circumvent the system. Newspaper articles often contain the names of defense lawyers of radicals undergoing prosecution. I contacted these
lawyers and asked them, on a professional basis, to slip my letters and
questionnaires to their clients. I also consulted *Aryan Nations Calling,*
a racialist journal out of Hayden Lake, Idaho, which periodically pub-
lishes the names and prison addresses of convicted radicals.[44]

Convicts understandably suspect that their correspondence is monitored by prison authorities. They are doubly suspicious of "do-gooder" types who might be in cahoots with those same officials. Hence care had to be taken to ask questions in such a way that they could not be construed as legally compromising. Some inmates required references in the movement before returning the questionnaire. In two cases inmates gave it to fellow activists incarcerated with them who then filled it out. But even with this level of suspicion, I received what may be considered remarkably open answers to my queries. Most of the correspondence cited in this book is from convicted activists.

Neither the questionnaire nor the interview schedule used predetermined response categories. However, I did employ a checklist of the kinds of data I wished to secure during interviews. After introducing myself and attempting to establish rapport, I would ask for the least compromising information on the checklist. I would then strategically move discussion to more personal subjects.

My goal was to solicit maximum information from the informants. This required the application of skills Jack Douglas and others have described in their characterizations of investigative research. Essentially, these involve commonsense techniques to win the respondents' trust: being friendly, dressing appropriately, being able to laugh at oneself, avoiding professional jargon, making self-disclosures so as to get them to reciprocate in kind, finding common ground with them—especially common acquaintances—and above all, conveying an interest in, and knowledge of, movement ideology. Knowledge about a subject allows one to pose insightful questions. An added advantage of being able to cite movement texts is that the interrogator begins to be seen by informants as a professional. This increases their willingness to respond seriously and carefully to inquiries.

These tactics are admittedly manipulative if not outright deceptive. Sociologists justify their use on two grounds. First, every research setting is burdened with what we call "researcher effects" on subjects. The point is not to decry the fact but to recognize its inevitability, correct for it, and, if possible, use it to one's advantage. The only reasonable restriction on this rule is not to predetermine the informants' responses themselves. Second, sociologists normally do not have to force themselves to be civil to, friendly with, and interested in their informants. They try to act in the field as any socially competent individual would in a situation where he is a stranger and does not wish to alienate people.

The design used in producing *The Politics of Righteousness* most closely resembles nonparticipative field observation. As circumstances allowed, however, I did periodically join with patriots socially at conferences, workshops, and speeches. I took part in the opening ceremonies of the 1986 Aryan World Congress, surrounded by several hundred Klan-robed and camouflaged Aryan knights who saluted Nazi-style as a tinny German drinking song played over the loudspeaker. Later that evening I witnessed the ignition of a twenty-foot kerosene-soaked wooden cross. Both of these were profoundly moving, disturbing experiences. Nevertheless, it is important to recognize that these excursions were neither as extended nor as penetrating as what professionals understand as full-fledged participant observation.

The price of failing to conduct a participant observation study of Christian patriotism is an incapacity on my part to deal with a number of fascinating subjects related to the radical right: What, for example, are the real day-to-day relations between husbands and wives in patriot households? Are the wives as silently dutiful as implied in movement literature? Although, as we shall see later, patriot couplings appear outwardly stable, I had enough conversations with tearful wives whose homes had been attached by the Internal Revenue Service to cover their husbands' delinquencies to suggest that things are not quite as publicly presented. And what about the children? Will their fathers' imprisonments deter them from future radicalism or propel them to seek revenge on their governmental "persecutors"? To what degree do followers in patriot groups actually believe in the pronouncements of their leaders? My skepticism about their credulity was raised when, for example, I spoke to a young man garbed in jungle fatigues carrying an automatic rifle, whose masked visage appeared in western newspapers as a typical conferee at the Aryan World Congress.[45] Behind the mosquito face-net I discovered a bored Weiser, Idaho, high school student who became animated only when conversation shifted to his "real" interests in art, drama, and wrestling. Or consider the bio-chemist whose Chinese fiancée was still angry at him for joining the Canadian Western Guard, a front of the Aryan Nations Church. (In Aryan philosophy the Chinese are spoken of as "mud people" who are genetically unfit for intimate relationships with "spiritualized" whites.) The Canadian's doubts about what he heard preached from the pulpit were shared by a University of Idaho graduate student who escorted me into the Hayden Lake woods while looking for hidden microphones. Pointing to a National Socialist with holstered German Luger and swastika armbands, he asked me: "What's wrong with that guy anyway? Does he have a problem with self-esteem?" (I was later to find that the object of this informant's derision was a college-educated marketing research consultant from Chicago—a "weekend Nazi.")

These vignettes lead to a related question. Do the actions of patriots conform to their words? Do patriots who espouse racial separation behave in a more antagonistic way toward minorities than do public defenders of liberalism? Larry Humphries, founder of a 265-acre Christian Identity compound in Velma, Oklahoma, gained attention in November 1985 when he led a band of heavily armed vigilantes to central Georgia to confront law enforcement authorities and forcibly prevent a farm foreclosure. The owner of the farm in question was an illiterate black man.

How deeply committed are patriots to what they proclaim? At the 1986 Aryan World Congress, Greg Withrow demanded that non-Aryan women, men, and children alike "be terminated or expelled" from America. Within a year he was renouncing his position as head of the White Student Union, an Aryan Nations Church front, and declaring himself converted through "love" to acceptance of these same people. "I've said a lot of terrible things and I've spread a lot of harm; I don't want to hate anymore. I don't want to hurt anymore," he told reporters.[46] Consider too the confession of Tommy Rollins, a one-time Texas Klan leader, nationally televised on Pat Robertson's "700 Club" in 1987. He claims that a nighttime vision of Jesus Christ's love for all mankind gave him insight into the superficiality of skin color differences. He now helps men like himself to negotiate themselves psychologically away from hate-filled lives toward born-again Christianity.

Was Larry Humphries's action merely a cynically staged media event? Are Withrow's and Rollins's conversions authentic psychological transformations or fraudulent withdrawals from public life in the face of increasing police pressure? And how widespread are such gestures? These are all important questions, but here they must be relegated to the shelf as distractions from more basic tasks before us.

In closing this chapter, let me address the dangers of studying political extremism. It is one thing to research radicals from a distance, using polling data and secondary sources. It is quite another to go into the field and mingle with the extremists themselves. Naturally one can never eliminate all risk, but the best protection seems to be first to separate illusory from real perils and then to provide for the latter.

Many Gem State radicals have a penchant for firearms and display little reluctance to use them if cornered. But it is also true that the movement has been closely monitored by the police, and it is not entirely unreasonable to believe that were my life truly in danger, I would have learned of it beforehand. Even so, I made every effort neither to challenge the beliefs of my subjects nor to betray their trust. My public pronouncements were always, much to the consternation of liberal friends, conciliatory. Furthermore, I made it clear to my interview subjects that my role was that of a professional sociologist, not a potential recruit. Those who questioned my credentials were given a vita containing information about myself similar to what I was soliciting from them. Finally, I have taken care to protect the anonymity of my subjects by using fictitious names in the text of this book, except in those places where their comments are either nonincriminating or independently documented in published accounts.

For all this there is no assurance that honorable intentions will not be misconstrued by distrustful subjects, the result being disquieting letters like the following I received from a retired elementary school teacher now living in a small central Idaho logging town:

Dear Mr. Ahoe:

I have been looking for a message of apology from you. The questions you asked over the telephone are a standard list supplied by Communists in their search for alert patriots and Christians. . . . No true American would serve them. . . . I have sent you messages of concern. I hope you have considered what you are doing and do not continue.[47]

Part I

THE MOVEMENT
FROM THE INSIDE

2

THE GENESIS OF REVOLT
Six Stories

The object of this chapter is to trace the Idaho Christian patriot movement to its roots by telling the stories of six of its most striking ventures. These accounts will be exclusively descriptive. No attempt will be made here to interpret the movement from a theoretical perspective, but the examples are chosen in part to illustrate the variety within the movement.

CHRISTIAN CONSTITUTIONALISTS: PROTESTERS, POSSES, AND PRO SE

Protesters

On April 11, 1973, Governor Cecil Andrus and the heads of several state agencies received an ominous warning in the form of a circular from a group calling itself the Vigilant Committee of 10,000. On it was drawn a coiled rattlesnake, the inscribed phrase "Don't tread on me," and the French word for death, *morte*.[1] This marked the beginning of Idaho's odyssey with its mountain patriots.

The 1973 incident contains all the comic and potentially tragic misunderstandings that have plagued Idaho Christian patriotism from the beginning of its brief history. The Vigilant Committee of 10,000 probably never had more than the two members who founded it, "Rebel" DelRay Holm and Asael Lyman (now deceased). They had posted the circulars, half-seriously, as a warning against summer cabin vandals who were then frequenting the neighborhood. (It is not clear to me how copies reached the governor's desk.)

Although the pair gained a reputation for being "radical dissidents, possible terrorists," to quote one local state representative, in fact both men were liberal Democratic Mormon farmers (Holm a Church bishop) from Bonneville County, avid supporters of then Senator Frank Church and, as it turned out, of fellow Democrat Andrus.[2] In testimony before ad hoc hearings in 1978 on Internal Revenue Service abuses of Mormon taxpayers conducted by Representative George Hansen, Holm said: "I don't advocate violence—and never have—or the violent over-throw of the government or anything else. I think I have a right to protect what is mine—even with a gun, I suppose . . . but . . . I wouldn't shoot anybody for stealing or [vandalism]. . . . I might feel like it but I certainly wouldn't resort to that sort of thing."[3]

"Rebel" Holm's testimony notwithstanding, his name somehow found itself on a secret Internal Revenue Service memo circulated December 31, 1975, together with twenty-four others who, the memo asserted, "may advocate violence toward Western Regional personnel."[4] The list of names seems to have been generated in part through a comput-erized comparison of driver's license receipts in several counties against the register of all taxpayers kept by the IRS. Those with driver's licen-ses who had not submitted income tax forms the previous three years were marked delinquent and tagged with the label, "May be danger-ous."[5] Others, like Holm, who claimed in testimony never to have failed to pay taxes nor indeed to have received anything more serious than a traffic citation, were evidently tagged because their tax records had been audited in the recent past, allegedly because of questionably large donations and tithes to the LDS Church.

The story might end here as another example of bureaucratic bun-gling were it not for the fact, now public knowledge, that the incident nearly ended in the very violence the memo was intended to prevent. The IRS list was forwarded to Idaho field agents to caution them against the "propensity toward violence" that it was feared might be exhibited by tax protestors during an RCP—Returns Compliance Project—then being planned for Fremont County. The project was part of a larger program to determine the degree of "voluntary com-pliance" with tax laws and to "educate" recalcitrant eastern Idahoans of their legal responsibilities. The "educational" component—the word is the IRS's—was to include armed door-to-door searches for individ-uals and their records. For, as the Assistant Commissioner for Inspec-tion is alleged to have said, "some of these people understand nothing but force."[6] As it turned out, to the good fortune of all involved, the RCP was never carried out, due to the refusal of unionized lower-level agents to participate in an action which they feared might pro-voke violence against themselves.[7]

How could IRS officials have committed an error of such magni-tude, an error which, if Rep. Hansen's well-documented tract can be trusted, was widely repeated? For example, included on the RCP danger list were full-time Mormon missionaries working without remuneration, a matronly church organist, and a person who had been bedridden in a hospital for two years. "Almost without exception," Hansen claims, "the people on the list were good citizens and respected members of the community, Church leaders, businessmen, bank officials, and farmers. . . ."[8] As one of these testified at Rep. Hansen's ad hoc hearings: "[F]or me to be put on such a list, I don't understand. I have no criminal record. . . . As far as an arsenal of guns, I've got an old worn-out .22—that's all. The ammunition—I don't think I've even got any shells for the rifle."[9]

Although the internal machinations of the IRS remain for the most part hidden to outsiders, an inkling of its thinking can be gleaned from a broader understanding of the prevailing attitude of eastern Idaho patriots toward the income tax system.

Southeast Idaho is recognized by IRS authorities as a mecca of income tax noncompliance, with one of the highest rates of delinquency in the country. It is unknown by whom or how the idea of tax protest was introduced into Idaho, but that it has struck a responsive chord is undeniable. Some point to tax seminars held throughout the intermountain West beginning in the early 1970s, conducted by fifty-eight-year-old Marvin Cooley, "grand daddy of the movement."[10] A self-described "man of the soil" who, ironically, makes his home amidst the urban sprawl of Phoenix, a one-time Brigham Young University student, and father of ten, Cooley has been a popular LDS Sunday school teacher for years. He related to me how he became aware of the "peril to our country" while reading Will Durant's eleven-volume history of Western civilization and by noting the parallels between the tyranny of the Roman emperors and the "inquisitional practices" he saw being used by the IRS. But the U.S. Constitution explicitly proscribes inquisitional interrogation, being based instead on the principle of "accusatorial proceedings." Understanding his duty as a good Church member to uphold the Constitution which he had been taught was "divinely inspired," Cooley was driven by the dictates of his own conscience, he says, to disobey IRS rules that compel a person to bear witness against himself on a 1040 form. Cooley became a fervent advocate of the so-called "Fifth Amendment Tax Return" in which the citizen volunteers nothing but his name and address. The crucial word for Cooley is "volunteer." The original IRS charter in 1916 spoke of the system as one of "voluntary," not compulsory, compliance.

Marvin Cooley is fully cognizant that in the case of tax collection the suspension of individual rights against unreasonable search and seizure and self-incrimination is justified by the notion that public needs must be balanced against private rights, but he considers this mere bureaucratic casuistry which opens the door to despotism. That this view is widely shared in southeast Idaho is demonstrated by the electoral popularity of former teacher and Mormon elder George Hansen, who, until his conviction of Congressional ethics violations in 1983, was virtually unbeatable in the Second Congressional District. In his local best-seller, *To Harass Our People,* he has compared IRS practices variously to the Egyptian enslavement of Israel, to Emperor Diocletian's tyranny over the Christians, to the totalitarian rule of the Nazi Reich, and to KGB terrorism. For his part, Cooley favors scriptural citations to support his lessons. "Isaiah has warned us," he says, "that 'nations that will not serve Me will perish.' "

Although both Hansen and Cooley pride themselves on their conservatism, both employ radical hyperbole to inspire their audiences. "The time for revolution," Hansen writes, ". . . is now." It is to be a "revolution" by mailbox and ballot box.[11] Cooley sees such tactics as playing into a rigged game: "Slaves cannot vote themselves out of servitude." Given Isaiah's dire prophecy, concerned citizens are required to break the law, but not through violence. Given the government's superior force "this is foolhardy now. We don't have a people's army. To use firearms is just poor strategy." The most rational ploy would be one modeled after Mahatma Gandhi's method of peaceful noncompliance used against the British in colonial India: "This would work wonders." Cooley has had considerable time in federal prison to refine his views. So too has one of his closest associates, Ardie McBrearty, who was found guilty in December 1985 of criminal racketeering as a consequence of his role as legal consultant to the Order.

Like Hansen's speeches, Cooley's workshops have gained him an enthusiastic following throughout the Rocky Mountain region. One of his Arizona converts, Robert Mathews, the son of a retired Air Force officer, would later move to northern Idaho, infuse his views with a strong dose of Judeophobia, and co-found the Order. But Cooley's most receptive audience has proven to be his fellow Church members, among them the eastern Idahoans Gary Mason, Larry Rigby, and Cliff Turner. After hearing Cooley lecture in 1977, Turner says, "I got my hands on everything he had written."[12] Mason concurs:

"The day I was born I was mad at somebody. In 1970 after listening to a Cooley tape I found out who it was, the IRS."[13] Each of these men returned home, organized local tax resistance groups, and became respected seminar leaders and tax consultants in their own right.

Recruitment to their groups was generally haphazard. Take the case of Lois Heckler*. In a voice lowered to convey a sense of urgent mystery about her discipleship to Mason, she revealed to me that "for some reason I had kept an article by Marvin Cooley hidden in a dresser drawer for years." When the "West Bank incident" (described below) occurred, she remembered the article, rummaged through the dresser and found it. In the article, Cooley mentions two newspapers supporting the tax movement, *The National Educator* and Jim and Anita Lowry's *Justice Times,* both widely read right-wing periodicals. Heckler wrote the Lowrys for legal advice. They in turn recommended to her "one of the best in the country," Gary Mason, "a man on a mission," who resided in her own hometown. She followed the advice, ended up being hired by Mason as a secretary, and is at this writing awaiting sentencing with her boss on a federal tax fraud conviction.[14]

Cliff Turner's group centered near Soda Springs was first called the Golden Mean Society after a national group operating out of Missoula, Montana. The name was later changed to the Citizen's Tax Council (CTC). "Golden Mean" stands for the ultimate goal of the group, a sort of Aristotelian balance between individual rights and government needs. Most of Turner's followers were employees of Washington Construction, where Turner worked as a heavy equipment operator. Washington Construction was then under contract with Beker, Inc. to mine phosphate from the hills surrounding Soda Springs.

Virtually all members of the Soda Springs chapter of the Golden Mean Society have at one time or another faced the threat of jail for civil contempt under authority of writs of mandate for either refusing to file 1040 forms or for filing "frivolous" Fifth Amendment tax statements. Nonetheless, few of them can be considered violent in any reasonable sense of the word. Mason, perhaps the most radical of the tax rebels, explicitly eschews armed force, saying "I can't get off on violence. That's not how to solve the problem. . . . The Lord does not know violence. No good movement [made in reference to his acquaintance Ardie McBrearty and the Order] is founded on hate,

* Fictitious name.

death, and killing."[15] Although the meaning of the tactic was never effectively articulated to the public, seven CTC activists undertook an unsuccessful campaign of civil noncooperation when faced with writs of mandate in September 1983. This campaign included a week-long peaceful hunger strike in the Gandhian mode to win public support and to extort concessions from state tax officials.[16] The CTC objected to what it called the "fascistic mandate" because, it held, the mandate punishes citizens attempting to exercise their constitutional right to remain silent.[17]

Social life is "circular" in nature. People act toward others on the basis of dearly held myths, and those others respond to these actions by "confirming," as it were, the beliefs of the first party, and so on. Granted that IRS officials have had grounds for implementing aggressive Returns Compliance Programs in eastern Idaho, the apparent arbitrariness and harshness of its measures have lent plausibility to a popular image of it being stupid at best and of "playing a Gestapo game" at worst.

A poverty-stricken daughter puts her meager savings in her beautician mother's bank account for a used car. When the two go to retrieve the money, the mother finds the total together with her checking account confiscated by the IRS in lieu of taxes. No notice was ever received of the impending government action. Her accountant apparently had forgotten to turn in the required 1040 form for the prior year although the mother says she had paid for his services through that period. Some years later this same woman, now the housewife of a Soda Springs farmer, is told that she is responsible for paying the taxes of her farm laborer, a tax protester involved with the Golden Mean Society. "When a person is married, thirty years old, and a father of two children," she indignantly relates, "he should be responsible for his own debts, not me. . . . I feel like his legal guardian." The daughter, meanwhile, has also married, and with her husband has opened a struggling restaurant. On arriving for work one morning she greets two men who identify themselves as tax agents. They demand access to the cash register, summarily remove its contents, give her a receipt for the amount, and tell her it is to cover her tax debts. The notice allegedly sent earlier to warn her of the planned action had apparently been lost in the shuffle of papers during a recent move. The daughter, beside herself in tears, is left feeling invaded and robbed.[18]

A sixteen-year-old waitress at Idaho Falls' West Bank motel and restaurant is ordered by an agent to stand before a dining room table and remove the contents of her pockets so that an assessment can be made of what she owes in taxes. Another of the waitresses, who is supporting ten children, is assessed $319 based on a percentage of the gross income of the West Bank for the previous year. She decides to appeal and ends up paying $9,000 in legal fees and further assessments. She says she has learned her lesson: "I'm not going to stick my neck out again. I always thought as an American I was given certain inalienable rights. . . . But we learned this stuff was all a big mistake, a big mistake." She now calls herself a "cowardly Christian patriot."[19]

Richard Tucker, a Pocatello used-car dealer, arrives the morning of February 10, 1983, to find all the cars from his lot removed by IRS agents. Unless he can prove sole ownership, he is warned, they will be auctioned to cover the $13,000 tax liability of one of his salesmen, Steve Carter, a partner in a bankrupt local corporation. When the story hits the press, Tucker is besieged with phone calls by people who want to rectify the apparent injustice, including the offer of a thirty-five-man armed contingent from St. Anthony to crash the fence at Stan's Auto Wrecking where the cars are impounded and "liberate" them. One of the volunteers says, "I've lived long enough . . . I'll do something about it." To his credit, Tucker discourages violence. "I knew if I got mad, I'd end up in jail. . . . If I would have been hotheaded." Seven of the cars are eventually auctioned off. Four others are surreptitiously returned to Tucker through a friend who works for the Idaho State Tax Commission. No public apology is ever made for the action.[20]

Tax officials can legally justify their behavior.[21] However, compliance measures like these effectively "prove" to those already predisposed to think that way that the income tax system is tyrannical. While in many cases, such as the waitress quoted above, the result has been increased caution and cynical obedience to the law, in others the outcome has been the opposite. "The IRS radicalized me," Lois Heckler says. She was the immediate supervisor of the West Bank waitresses. "I have nothing to lose, everything to gain" by further struggle.[22] Says another respondent, "I am in this fight to the death."[23] "I'm going to do whatever's necessary, but I'm not giving up," agrees another, days before his own jailing on tax charges.[24] For these and scores of others, Red Beckman's characterization of "true" patriotism is apropos: "The patriot," he declares, "is one who is vigilant in recognizing that government is his worst enemy. And he is willing to fight his own government." False patriots equate America with its government. "False patriots," he says angrily, "make me sick."[25]

Posses

Whatever happened to old-fashioned "law and order"? . . . Somewhere along the line the good people of America fell asleep at the switch. And during the snooze, . . . the function of the American government . . . changed from protecting the Godgiven Rights, Liberties, and Property of the Sovereign Citizens . . . to that of a totalitarian state. . . .

What can be done about it? Do we have to have a revolution to get things back on the right track again?

The answer is "no"; we do not need a revolution, but what we do need is a *Restoration Movement*.

Make the government obey the law!

There is already an existing method and it is just waiting for us to pick it up and put it into action. That method is to utilize the only legitimate law enforcement officer, and his support force, in America. That is, the Sheriff and the Posse Comitatus.[26]

Every American city hall has its self-appointed watchdogs. So it was with Rexburg, Idaho's, Committee for Better Government (CBG). The CBG was formed in the late 1960s by a Ricks College faculty member, a college maintenance man, a landscape artist, an Idaho Nuclear Engineering Laboratory electrician, and three other close friends. All seven are devoted LDS churchgoers, believers in the divine inspiration of the Constitution, and longtime conservatives. Several supported Governor George Wallace's 1968 presidential campaign, and one worked as Madison County campaign manager for John Schmitz when he ran for the same office in 1972. At one time sanctioned by his colleagues for allegedly making anti-Semitic remarks in the California State Assembly, Schmitz received more votes in Madison County than George McGovern, his largest plurality in any county in America.

The incident appears petty on the face of it: A Madison County Commissioner is caught *flagrante delicto* in the lens of a camera one evening stealing gravel from the county pit. One of the CBG members, himself a gravel dealer, feels his trust as a citizen is betrayed. The incriminating photographs are shown to the sheriff, who refuses to bring charges against the thief, allegedly because of his prominence in the community. The CBG calls for a grand jury investigation of corruption in high places. (It is hard to overestimate the significance of the grand jury to Constitutionalists. Red Beckman, a well-traveled stump speaker from Billings, Montana, has argued that in reality the Constitution gives no enforcement powers to government. To enforce the law government needs juries, and the grand jury is "one of the three votes" granted each American citizen—the other two being the election ballot and the petit jury.)[27]

In principle the citizenry can petition that grand juries be called; but in fact it is judicial practice to recognize only requests by public attorneys. In this case the Madison County Attorney refused the plea of the Committee for Better Government.[28]

About the same time an investigation of a Rexburg printing firm for alleged OSHA violations is undertaken by "outsiders" from Seattle. This is widely viewed in Rexburg as unconstitutional government harassment of a respected and highly successful local employer. These incidents spur CBG activists to found a Madison County chapter of Posse Comitatus.[29]

Recognized in article 19, section 221, of the Idaho Code, Posse Comitatus (medieval Latin for "force of the county") empowers a law enforcement official to summon male citizens eighteen years and older to assist him in overcoming lawbreakers in his jurisdiction. Those who refuse or neglect the summons are punishable by a fine of not less than $50 nor more than $100.[30] The Idaho Code makes no mention of unauthorized citizens summoning their own posses. Nor is the phrase "bona fide peace officers" limited to elected officials such as sheriffs. It includes "constables, judges, or other officers concerned in the administration of justice."

The Madison County patriots may have been inspired by articles advocating posses that first appeared in patriot newsletters in 1969. Both Henry L. "Mike" Beach, a retired machinist from Portland, Oregon, and William P. Gale, a retired Army colonel from Glendale, California, who had served on General MacArthur's staff, saw the posse as a means to compel what they called "bureaucratic regulation enforcement officers" from OSHA, the Bureau of Alcohol, Tobacco and Firearms, and the Bureau of Land Management to obey the law of the organic Constitution. For example, when Roger Davis, a Kootenai County deputy sheriff, apprehended a fifty-two-year-old logger from Athol, Idaho, named Leonard Brabham for a minor traffic violation, Brabham drew his own pistol and "arrested" Davis for acting unconstitutionally. Later at Brabham's arraignment, a contingent of the Kootenai County Posse Comitatus, charging policeman Davis with assault with a deadly weapon and grand larceny, sought unsuccessfully to bring him before the magistrate as a "fugitive from justice." The subsequent courtroom scuffle between Kootenai County sheriff deputies and the Christian Posse created headlines that have been repeated throughout the Northwest.[31]

Like his counterparts elsewhere, the Madison County sheriff publicly rebuked the posse as "vigilantes" and declined the offer of their services. Although he did not also accuse the group of anti-Semitism, the assertion has been made frequently enough to deserve comment.

At first it was easy for those who saw Posse Comitatus as a vehicle to aid local law enforcement officials in search and rescue operations to deny its racist and anti-Semitic associations. But less than a year after the formation of the 300-strong Kootenai County contingent, secret FBI and IRS memos were reporting the Christian Posse Comitatus to be "an outgrowth of the Identity Group, a West Coast based group that advocates violence against blacks, Jewish persons and federal officers. . . ." These memos named sixteen northern Idahoans, including then-marshal Richard Butler, ninety-year-old lifelong KKK propagandist Hal Hunt, and William Fowler, former California Klan Grand Dragon, with advocating armed rebellion. In the spring of 1976 newswires carried the story of an Oregon PC meeting at which "Jewish moneyed interests and Communists" were said to be behind all of America's problems. "There are two kinds of people on earth," one man in the audience is said to have yelled, "the children of God and the children of the Devil—and as soon as you understand that you'll know what the battle's all about."[32] The violent pronouncements since issued in Wisconsinite James Wickstrom's newsletter, *Posse Noose* and by one-time California posse marshal William Gale (a close friend of Butler's), both widely disseminated in a sensationalized 1985 ABC "20/20" television special,[33] have added to original impressions.

Mike Beach continues to believe that the United States is controlled by the Federal Reserve Bank, owned and operated by Jewish bankers. However, he vigorously denies the imputation of bigotry and racism to the concept of Posse Comitatus, saying "knotheads," "half-wits," and "idiots" infiltrated the movement "so they could shout, holler, and do their dirty work," ruining an otherwise valid idea. "Any time they take Hitler for their king, I've got no use for them."[34] The Madison County posse agrees. "It is not fundamentally a neo-Nazi group," says one member. "The boys up north [in Kootenai County] gave it a bad name."[35] Another is more emphatic: "I don't think you can be an American and a patriot and be prejudiced." After all, he continues, a lot of signees of the Constitution have Jewish names. "Jews killed Christ," he admits. "That can't be denied." But even Wickstrom, he insists, uses the word "Jew money-lender" as a "symbol of evil," not as a literal description of an ethnic group.[36]

For its part the IRS undertook audits of the returns of those who filed the Madison County posse charter. They responded by refusing to file 1040 forms the following year. The fight went on for eight years, ended in tax court, and cost one of the litigants, the artist, $16,000 although "in reality we owed nothing." He says the judge told him prior to his court appearance: "We don't care what you have in possession. If you can't disprove our claims against you, you are liable to pay the full amount."[37]

To say that tax resistance and Posse Comitatus are inspired by LDS teachings regarding the sanctity of the Constitution is not to say that Church authorities have sanctioned these causes. On the contrary, the Church's public position is that members in good standing are obligated under Luke 23:1–2 to "render unto Caesar that which is Caesar's." In some cases the Church has excommunicated recalcitrant patriots. More often it has sought to encourage obedience to the state by threatening to deny "temple recommends" to activists so that they may not perform "ordinances" and thus fulfill their roles as priests. In a few noteworthy incidents IRS officials have even successfully subpoenaed patriots' tithing records to prove their assessment claims. "God will be merciful," one told me, "because they [i.e., Church authorities] are under coercive duress to cooperate."[38]

But not all are so tolerant. In some cases the Church has placed pressure upon wives to choose between itself and their patriot spouses. This has occasioned considerable bitterness. "The Church," warns one posse member, "is under condemnation for not following the word of God."[39] Far from abating their radicalism, then, Church policies may actually have increased the patriots' sense of isolation and paranoia.

Pro Se

I used to believe that only my elected government officials could save my freedom—now after seeing your [the Barristers'] course I firmly believe the common man can do it himself.[40]

Tactics on the right can be ranked in terms of their proponents' faith in the political system to redress wrongs: campaigning for candidates of recognized political parties, organizing issue-oriented groups and lobbying elected representatives, conducting ad hoc citizen's hearings, seeking grand jury investigations, organizing armed citizens' defense leagues or vigilante groups to uphold the law, fighting in the courtroom alone as a *pro se* litigant. By this scale Barristers' Inn School of Common Law may be considered the most radical right-wing persuasion in Idaho.

"The United States Constitution means 'leave me alone' or 'get off my back' " to Barristers. To promote this idea it works to teach students how to avoid unnecessary entanglements with the state and how to protect themselves from the state once they are under its judicial authority.

Barristers' Inn advocates avoiding entanglements through what it calls "legal asseveration." The idea is this: By virtue of their nature human beings have specific inalienable rights. The Constitution does not *confer* rights, it merely enables citizens to protect those they are born with. The problem is that citizens unknowingly contract their rights away so as to secure privileges from government. To obtain Social Security benefits they allow themselves to be given a number that police agencies may use to gather and store information about them. To be granted the privilege of driving on streets they reveal confidential information about themselves. To obtain privileges of incorporation, licensing, or government financial aid, they work as surrogate tax collectors and draft board agents, government surveillance experts, and compliance officers. To maintain one's status as a freeman, one must pay the price of refusing these blandishments. For the individual this may involve *de jure* divorce from one's spouse (for marriage at law is a contract between you, your spouse, and the government),[41] rescinding one's birth certificate (for such certificates are now used in courts to argue that legally speaking the individual, like the corporation, is a "person" created by the state),[42] refusing to secure a Social Security number, and not purchasing a driver's license. Many Barristers graduates have "liberated" themselves in one or more of these ways.

A more compelling problem for most Barristers students, however, is not how to sever the umbilical cord that keeps them wards of the state, but how to protect themselves from its judicial tentacles. Indeed, Barristers' Inn owes its origin to the courtroom battles of its founder, a self-educated high school dropout by the name of George Gordon. Gordon and his first wife had moved to Idaho at the invitation of an Eldon Shrift,* who now runs a press in Boise specializing in right-wing literature. Shrift had earlier owned an apartment complex in Alameda, California, of which Gordon was resident manager.[43] Upon his arrival in Idaho "Gordon went bonkers," according to Shrift, and "got off on a power trip."

Although they agree, to use the words of one, that Gordon "is a loner . . . he's involved with his own ego," his associates have a different version of the story. One of these, an ex-baseball and basketball star for Boise State University, relates that Gordon was transporting waterbeds from his factory one day when he was apprehended for failing to stop at a mandatory State Patrol weigh station. Gordon had reasoned that such scales violate his constitutional protection against self-incrimination. During the ensuing courtroom battle with the help of a local attorney, Gordon "discovered" Common Law and with it procedural weapons that could be wielded effectively by ordinary citizens in their own defense without the aid of legal counsel.[44]

Gordon eventually won his case and then another, a civil suit against OSHA, which tried to shut his factory down for alleged pollution violations. As his reputation grew, he and two others, one a sociology and history graduate from Benedictine College in Kansas, began contemplating the establishment of a school to teach what they had learned. Barristers' Inn School of Common Law began offering courses in 1981 in a catering hall in Boise's "nigger town," as its owner, a longtime Mormon patriot, calls it. A local physician video-taped the course and Barristers started marketing it at $2,400 for thirty three-hour lessons plus paperwork and books in three-ring binders. Advertised in patriot newspapers, the course has enjoyed remarkable sales—300 kits sold in less than five years. Each Barristers outlet—they hesitate to use the term "franchise" because of its contractual implications—is estimated to have a membership of anywhere between 10 and 1,000 students.

As copyrights are seen as a compromising legal entanglement, purchasers of the tapes are free to use them as they see fit. This includes duplicating the master and selling their own copies. There is no way of measuring such sales, but Barristers of Boise believes that several million patriots throughout the country are now preparing themselves for battle, armed with Common Law.

Successful judicial confrontations employ a strategic combination of correct speaking and silence. Barristers' Inn claims that over 90 percent of the information used by the government to incriminate defendants in courts of law is supplied by the defendants themselves. Therefore they urge citizens to habituate themselves to enacting the right to remain silent. This is not without risk, for police are typically trained to consider refusals of interrogation as *prima facie* evidence of guilt. Bob Hallstrom of the Boise office tells how once a guard at a trial he was witnessing approached him and asked his name. Hallstrom replied, "Who wants to know?" The quip earned him a trip to jail and the charge of obstructing justice. When the prosecutor strode into the holding cell he uttered the ritual warning, "You have the right to remain silent. Anything you say can and will be used against you in a court of law." Hallstrom retorted: "That's exactly what I'm trying to tell you!" He was freed within minutes.[45]

Hallstrom looks forward to his frequent jailings as opportunities to instill in his jail-mates the rudiments of Common Law. Court officers, he happily reports, do not enjoy dealing with his graduates. They impede the efficient routine of bureaucratic justice. From its side, Barristers sees silence as an infallible but entirely civil way of subverting unconstitutional governments.

The word "civil" should be emphasized. Hallstrom's nationwide public appearances confute the widely held and too-often true image of Christian patriots as humorless, self-righteous preachers always ready to burn a witch. Hallstrom's presentations are a cross between bull sessions and lectures, interspersed with double-entendres and self-deprecating jokes. Barristers repeatedly and emphatically discourages violence and even the use of violent language, including terms like "radical," "protest," or "resistance." When a member of an audience attending Barristers workshop exhorted, "Well I'd take a gun to 'em," in response to a story of tax agents unfairly seizing private property, Hallstrom's face tightened. "Never say that in public," he cautioned. "Don't be a tax protester. Join no posse." Citizen violence, he believes, is a sign of two things: ignorance of the law (a condition also shared by many judges and lawyers) and related to this, unjustified fear of authority. Knowing one's rights under the Constitution should remedy both conditions. "We have to learn how to talk; it's all a word game." Included in the video-tape course package are sample legal briefs and motions that have proved workable in the past. As a Barristers introductory sheet says:

Freedom is only for the knowledgeable and vigilant. . . . People have become slaves of the state, and until taught the truth, they will continue to be slaves. . . . The truth has always been with us—we simply need to learn it.
    Simply stated, we reduce the overwhelming size of whatever government agency we are up against to one person in the courtroom, effectively reducing

government to manageable size. . . . All it takes is knowledge of basic procedures and good paper.[46]

Barristers' Inn of Boise is pivotal for our purposes because its membership bridges the ideological gap between pure Constitutionalism, which flourishes among LDS radicals in eastern Idaho, and Christian Identity, which has found a home in the western and northern parts of the state. Besides being instructors of Common Law, several Barristers are "ambassadors of the Lord," adherents of American Israelism. George Gordon, who has since left Boise with a new wife and headed to what he believes are the more fertile haunts of Arkansas, was introduced to the doctrine through Herbert W. Armstrong's World Wide Church of God. Another Barrister, an ordained Nazarene minister for over twelve years, participates in a large Identity congregation in Nampa comprised mostly of disaffected fellow church members. Although individuals in the Nampa group maintain close contact with Identity churches in Spokane, Coeur d'Alene, Phoenix, and Fort Collins, Colorado, including the Aryan Nations Church, by no means do they share the stridency of their cohorts regarding the Jewish and race questions. Hallstrom, meanwhile, leads his own weekly nondenominational Bible study class which has an explicit Identity outlook. His legal workshops may conclude with a pitch for literature by the Canadian "British" Israelites Frederick Haberman and W. H. Bennett (both now deceased).[47] Hallstrom knows that in Mormon country he must broach the subject tactfully, as there exists considerable antagonism to any suggestion of anti-Semitism. In a seminar I attended, even the subtlest allusion to the Identity message was met by the audience with stark silence and downcast eyes. "Idaho," Hallstrom said half-jokingly after his presentation, "is brain-dead."[48]

AMERICA: THE CHOSEN PEOPLE
If it is difficult to pinpoint the origin of Christian Constitutionalism, it is virtually impossible for the doctrine of Christian Identity. For centuries Christians have bestowed upon themselves titles like His Chosen, the Seed of Abraham, God's Saints, and the Children of Jacob. References to America as the New Jerusalem or as the Temple Nation, for example, its colonists as covenanters with the Lord, and its people as having a Manifest Destiny all have played intimate parts in the American experience.[49] Historians of the Identity movement,

however, see its inception in the publication in 1840 of Scotsman John Wilson's *Our Israelitish Origin.*[50] This in turn seems to have grown out of quests by nineteenth-century Bible students for the descendants of the lost tribes of Israel.

Three answers to the question emerged at about the same time. In the prophecy of New York farmer and founder of Mormonism, Joseph Smith (ca. 1830), the tribe of Joseph reappears as the Lamanites, precursors of the Native American Indians. In orthodox Protestantism the tribes are said to have become guest peoples of nations in the Middle East; they were assimilated and then disappeared. In British Israelism, however, they are said to have migrated over the Caucasus Mountains to become the various Anglo-Saxon peoples (hence their racial type, "Caucasian"). It is out of British Israelism that Identity Christianity, as preached today in America, comes.

British Israelism was imported first to Canada and then to the United States through the writings of J. H. Allen and M. M. Eshelman. It reached its greatest popularity immediately after the Second World War. One center of activism was Vancouver, British Columbia, from which the movement spilled over the border into Washington state, establishing itself in Tacoma, Seattle, Spokane, and Portland, Oregon. Prophetic Herald Ministry in Spokane was founded in 1933 by Alexander Schiffner, an ordained Four Square Gospel minister. By April 1969, forty-one radio stations carried Schiffner's Israelite message. Since Schiffner's death in the early 1980s, Robert Thornton and the Rev. Karl Schott, the latter an ordained Church of Christ minister from the South, have been preaching to remnants of his congregation. Schott's own Pathfinder Radio Ministry is now heard on eighteen stations from Nashville and Washington, D.C., to Seattle and Fresno.

Another point of Canadian-British Israelite penetration was Maine, through the person of Howard D. Rand, then a manager of a construction company. Founded in 1928, his Kingdom Message grew to 15,000 subscribers in just two years. At its first international convention in 1930, Rand met William J. Cameron, editor of Henry Ford's *Dearborn (Michigan) Independent.* Together they formed the Anglo-Saxon Federation of America. The *Independent* had earlier gained renown for publishing some of the most extreme anti-Jewish pronouncements ever seen up to that time in America, including an unexpurgated edition of *The Protocols of the Learned Elders of Zion.* This, says Norman Cohn, is a "shameless plagiarism" by an aide to the head of the French branch of the Czarist secret police (named Cyon, pronounced "Zion") of an anti-Napoleonic tract by Maurice Joly (1864). It pretends to detail the tactics to be used by the High Jewish Council, the Sanhedrin, and the Masonic Order in their quest for world domination.[51] Nevertheless, it must be emphasized that blatant racist anti-Semitism is not intrinsic to the Identity message. Consider these comparatively tolerant words of J. H. Allen:

Understand us: We do not say that the Jews are not Israelites. They belong to the Posterity of Jacob, who was called Israel, hence they are all Israelites. But the great bulk of Israelites are not the Jews, just as the great bulk of Americans are not Californians, and yet all Californians are Americans.[52]

The popular association of Identity with outright racism is due in part to many of its most vocal proponents having been fundamentalist Protestants recruited directly from the southern and Midwest Bible Belt: James Lovell (Texas Baptist), Joe Jeffers (Alabama Baptist), Wesley Swift (Alabama Methodist), Gerald L. K. Smith (son of a Louisiana Baptist minister), and Herbert W. Armstrong (Iowa Adventist).[53]

Field Marshal Allenby's capture of Jerusalem in 1917 was taken by British Israelites as a prophetic sign that Armageddon was in the offing. But the impact of the two world wars and England's subsequent divestment of its overseas colonies devastated the movement by indicating that the "Tribe of Ephraim," as its members called themselves, was not destined to reign over the world after all. Instead, postwar American hegemony over the Western alliance seemed to indicate that the "sceptre of Joseph" was to be placed in the hands of Ephraim's twin brother, Manasseh, which is to say, the United States. (In biblical genealogy Ephraim and Manasseh are the twin sons of Joseph and the Egyptian princess Asenath, daughter of Potiphera, high priest of the Temple of On [Genesis 41:50–52]). "America," proclaimed now deceased Identity preacher Wesley Swift, "is the appointed place" spoken of by the prophets Jeremiah and Isaiah. Swift's proof is that only in America grow the myrtlewood and redwood trees prophesied in Scripture. Only here is there land and water enough to support the "multitudinous population" promised the Children of God.[54]

An element in all Identity doctrines is fundamentalism. By this I mean Protestant variations of nineteenth-century Anglican John Nelson Darby's dispensational theology. Here, biblical history is periodized by the actions God undertakes (dispenses) toward His children. Previous dispensations—Adam's banishment from Eden, the Flood, Christ's grace—have all failed to induce in man the proper response.

Ours, the modern and, as it turns out, final age—a time of particular depravity—is to be the Last Dispensation. As promised in the Book of Revelation it will consist of tribulation violence involving Christians, unbelievers, and apostates. This will be followed by the War of Armageddon ushering in Christ's thousand-year reign (the Millennium), God's Judgment, and the dispensation of rewards and eternal condemnation.[55]

Fundamentalist brethren often form gospel assemblies within which charismatic preachers may arise. They study key words from the Bible, debate biblical passages, and perfect themselves for the fulfillment of prophecy. Some do this by cultivating the virtues of patience, faith, and love, others—not untypically Identity believers—by preparing for the Last Battle. As one tract published by the Covenant, Sword, and the Arm of the Lord affirms: "Jesus gives us [in Rev. 13:10] the authority to use the weapons of the Beast against those in rebellion to God." And well it should, for our age, it continues, not only suffers the travesties of drug addiction, prostitution, and abortion, but also witches "sexually mutilating people," "sodomite homosexuals waiting in their lusts to rape," "negro beasts who eat the flesh of men," "Seed of Satan Jews sacrificing people in darkness," and above all, "city-living white Christians and 'do-gooders' who've fought for the 'rights' of these groups." As we of the Adamic race are made "in the Image of God," so then our anger at the world's sin is His, our wrath His, "our vengeance, the Lord's."[56]

With its emphasis on biblical inerrancy, fundamentalism has come into increasing conflict with liberal, symbolic understandings of the Bible. One result has been schisms within all major Protestant denominations, notably Methodism, out of which emerged Nazarene perfectionism, and Presbyterianism, from which, among others, Dr. Carl McIntire's Bible Presbyterian Church grew.[57] For reasons that cannot be examined here, these splinter groups have enjoyed an enthusiastic reception in the intermountain West and southern California. Through matings with right-wing political and vigilante groups, including in rare cases the Klan, the Nazis, and the Minutemen, they have spawned countless Christian Crusades, New Christian Crusades, Christian Defense Leagues, Christian Liberty Brigades, posses, and committees. Each has its own radio and TV ministry, its own network of patriotic letter writers and lobbyists, and its own publishing house(s), issuing "orthodox" statements on contemporary social issues in light of prophecy.

All this was part of the baggage carried into western and northern Idaho by California emigrants during the 1970s.

One of these emigrés, an aeronautical engineer from Lancaster, was Richard G. Butler, destined to become pastor of the Aryan Nations Church in Hayden Lake. While employed at Lockheed Aircraft, Butler became acquainted with Col. William Gale, mentioned earlier as a co-revivalist with Mike Beach of the idea of Posse Comitatus. In 1963 Gale introduced Butler to the Rev. Wesley Swift and his Church of Jesus Christ Christian, then headquartered in Hollywood. Swift was a one-time Ku Klux Klan Kleagle (organizer) and rifle instructor who, as son of a fundamentalist Methodist minister, had himself become a convincing literal interpreter of Holy Scripture. In the middle 1940s Swift defended the Rev. Gerald L. K. Smith after Smith delivered an impassioned speech denouncing Jews and Communists in Los Angeles. Smith befriended his defender, later making him his bodyguard and chauffeur, and naming him West Coast lieutenant of his Christian Anti-Communist Crusade.[58]

Wesley Swift had a profound impact on a number of American Israelites who now make their homes in Idaho. One of these, who presently leads a southern Idaho congregation of the Aryan Nations Church, recalls being invited by his grandparents to one of Swift's Sunday sermons in Hollywood in the early 1960s. Swift's lecture, delivered in a rapid-fire staccato, literally mesmerized the Idahoan. "He spoke an hour and a half. I thought it was only ten minutes. . . . I could relate to it. . . . It provided me with answers about myself."[59] He joined the Church of Jesus Christ Christian just as "grandmomma" had done a decade earlier. Richard Butler's experience was similar. "He [Swift] was the total turning point in my life," he says. "The light turned on. He had the answers I was trying to find."[60] The answer to which both men refer is racist Identity, the idea that there are two species of human being, Adamic man and Satanic man: true man—the Aryan European descendants of Israel—and *homo bestialis*—the sons of Lucifer, including among others, the Jews and "Satan's footsoldiers," the black Africans.

Butler's plaudit to Swift does not mean that he was not a racist long before his affiliation with the Church of Jesus Christ Christian. It has been alleged by the Anti-Defamation League that in the 1930s he (with Mike Beach and Gerald Smith) was associated with William Dudley Pelley's Silver Shirt Legion, founded the day after the German

National Socialist Worker's Party seized control of the Reichstag and Hitler was proclaimed Chancellor. Pelley was one of the first to dub the thirty-second president of the United States "Franklin D. Rosenfeld" in reference to his alleged Jewish ancestry.[61] For his part, however, Butler relates that his original conversion to racial cosmology occurred while serving in the Royal Indian Air Force under the Lend-Lease agreement during World War II:

> I had a servant named Jerami. He asked me why we were fighting our own brethren in Europe. I couldn't answer him. He said he was an Aryan too, and I laughed. Jerami said, "I represent the pollution of the race. I'm proud I have some of your blood in my veins." It bothered me that a servant knew more about my ancestry than I did, so I began what became a lifelong study.[62]

Swift died in 1970, and after a dispute with William Gale, Butler took over his Lancaster congregation. Swift's daughter, Joan, and her husband, Shreve "Duke" Nielson, both members of the original church, believe that while Butler claims to be continuing the Swift tradition, he was in fact never certified to take Swift's place by the church board. They say he stole the church mailing lists and its founder's taped sermons to market them for profit, and then unconscionably distorted their true message. Mrs. Nielson claims that unlike Butler, her father "didn't hate other races. He was only trying to keep our race pure."[63]

In any case, Gale left for Mariposa, California, in the Sierra Nevada foothills to found his own Ministry of Christ Church. Since then he has successfully proselytized economically distressed farmers in Iowa and Nebraska. Two of his affiliates have since been charged with the torture murders of two individuals, one a five-year-old boy.[64] Another has died at the hands of a Nebraska SWAT team during a foreclosure proceeding in 1984.[65] Butler and his followers, meanwhile, including the Nielsons, who evidently originally had little animosity toward their pastor, journeyed to northern Idaho.

Speculation abounds concerning why Butler's congregation chose Idaho. First of all there is the simple beauty of the northern Idaho lake country and the allure of land selling there at $200 an acre in the early 1970s. However, I believe the major attraction was an atmosphere more congenial to Butler's teachings than existed at that time in southern California.

A substantial minority of Kootenai and Shoshone county residents are descendants of Confederate states loyalists who in the early part of the century had migrated there to work the mines in the Silver Valley.

One of these described his politics this way: "We're a pretty easy goin' bunch. There's only two things we don't like, intolerance and niggers."[66] The Anglo-Israel movement was already well established in the Pacific Northwest by 1970, and several Church of Jesus Christ Christians were themselves living in retirement near Coeur d'Alene. One, an ex-CIA agent and Orange County aerospace executive, and another, an ex-policeman from Los Angeles, may have been the ones who invited Butler to check out Kootenai County.

In 1968 a guerrilla organization called the Minutemen had been crushed after blowing up the Redmond, Washington, police station and attempting to rob three Seattle banks.[67] Several top Minutemen were closely tied to Wesley Swift's church, among them Dennis Mower, a certified Identity preacher; Walter Peyson, who joined the church the same year as Butler; and Keith Gilbert. Gilbert also was implicated in the theft of 1,400 lbs. of TNT allegedly to be used to bomb the Hollywood Palladium during an Anti-Defamation League convention and to kill its keynote speaker, Martin Luther King.[68] In 1976 Donald Wiggins, a subordinate of Butler, was charged along with several associates with possessing the largest illegal arms cache ever recovered in America up to that time.[69]

After serving time in San Quentin, Gilbert moved to Post Falls, Idaho, a logging town just west of Coeur d'Alene. In nearby Spokane he set up a retail outlet, AR-YA Electronics. Its building was owned by one of Wiggins's cohorts, the son of a prominent Washington businessman, who had been sentenced to probation for his role in the arms scheme. After serving another prison term, this time for welfare fraud, Gilbert gained local notoriety for his swastika-inscribed, camouflaged Volkswagen, Storm Trooper uniform, and a dog who, it is reported, was trained to lift his paw whenever his master uttered "Seig Heil."

In short, a sizable number of prominent Identity spokesmen had begun to congregate in the Idaho panhandle by the early 1970s. They came in part because it seemed to promise at least temporary respite from constant police surveillance and a pre-existing system of mutual aid and moral support. In the presence of kindred spirits, they dreamed of establishing an Aryan Nation.[70]

Birth of the Aryan Nations

It was not a particularly novel idea. Donald Clerkin, head of an aggregate of "Christian soldiers" called the Euro-American Alliance, had already advocated the establishment of a "Europolis," an armed reservation for the dwindling Aryan species, situated in "rough country, not easily accessible to our enemies."[71]

Under auspices of their own Christian Patriot Defense League, John Harrell, a millionaire and sometime evangelical minister, and Col. Gordon "Jack" Mohr (ret.), a highly decorated Korean war veteran turned Baptist lay minister, had gone so far as to establish several "defense outposts" marking off a "survival area" loosely corresponding to Clerkin's Europolis.[72] One such outpost is located on a 232-acre site in Licking, Missouri, just miles from "Bishop" Daniel Gayman's Church of Israel and Our Heritage Academy and the Rev. Jim Ellison's compound on Bull Shoals Lake, Arkansas, the Convenant, Sword, and the Arm of the Lord (CSA).[73]

Butler had periodically reissued Clerkin's call for an Aryan homeland from his own forty-acre compound on Hayden Lake. He was concerned with the "coming racial war" that he believed had already been declared and intrigued by Harrell and Col. Mohr's efforts to establish a perimeter of defenses around the American heartland by means of units like the CPDL and the Citizens Emergency Defense System. Furthermore, Butler had been in close contact with Ellison's CSA for a number of years. Members of the two churches had frequently exchanged literature and visits. At least three CSA activists— Jefferson Butler, Norwin Butler, and James Wallington—even took time to sign the Nehemiah Township Charter during their stay at Hayden Lake in the summer of 1982. This charter decrees the area around Hayden Lake a racially pure Christian township, subject to Common Law, enforced by Posse Comitatus.[74] At the 1986 Aryan World Congress in Hayden Lake, Ellison was honored as an Aryan hero for his service to the cause of racial purity, for which he is now paying the price of a prison sentence. His wife accepted the award for him.

It is not surprising given these links that in April 1980 at Hays, Kansas, pastor Butler hoisted for the first time the Aryan Nations flag and proclaimed the founding of a racially clean homeland, bounded by the Rocky Mountains, the Mississippi River, the northern Canadian plains, and the Mexican border. By the time of the 1986 Aryan Congress, the proposed racial homeland of the white man had shrunk to include only Washington, Oregon, Idaho, Montana, and Wyoming.

The proposal was not without its detractors. Dan Gayman of the

Church of Israel, although an advocate of racial separation, was upset. "I am not going out on a Kamikaze mission to make National Socialism the next high Christian culture in America," he vowed. "My God is Jesus Christ. If your God is Adolf Hitler, then let it be so."[75] Butler ignored the dogs yapping at the heels of his revolutionary caravan and embarked on an aggressive three-pronged campaign of recruitment.

First Butler would sponsor an international Aryan Congress each July. This would feature well-known speakers, religious festivities— the highlight being a gigantic cross-burning at night ("a light to Aryan warriors during the darkness of these times")—shooting at human silhouette targets sometimes wearing Stars of David, survivalist workshops, and classes in health, diet, food storage, and nuclear protection. The congresses were to be preceded by paid announcements, but more importantly by "free advertising," playing on the appetite of the "Jewish-controlled" media for anti-Aryan human interest stories. At the 1986 Congress more than one quarter of the attendees were representatives of the media. Butler and other leaders expressed contempt at the spectacle of reporters fighting with each other to get their questions acknowledged.

Advertising prototypes reveal the intended audience of the Aryan Congress: Covenant, Sword, and the Arm of the Lord members, represented by the barefoot Confederate soldier with a CSA belt buckle; Christian Posse Comitatus activists, garbed in the robe of a Norman crusader; disgruntled Vietnam vets, dressed in jungle combat fatigues; and Minutemen, with the insignia of the cross-hairs of a telescopic sight.

It was at convocations like the Aryan Congress and others sponsored by the CSA and the CPDL—its "Freedom Festivals"—both of which Butler is known to have addressed in the early 1980s, that his credibility as leader of the Christian Identity movement was tested and found true. Two intergroup matings that issued from these annual exchanges are of particular historical significance: that between Butler's church and like-minded German and Canadian groups such as the Western Guard, and that with the Tuscumbia, Alabama-based Knights of the Ku Klux Klan.[76]

The second prong in the Aryan Nations recruitment campaign was to be the direct solicitation of tax resisters, Christian home educators, anti-abortionists, gun enthusiasts, survivalists, and mercenary aficionados through advertisements in periodicals like *Justice Times, Shotgun News, Soldier of Fortune,* and Liberty Lobby's *Spotlight,* the largest cir-

culation right-wing weekly in the United States. Concerned about today's problems? asks one ad. Then grab your gun, your wife, and your
kids and head for Hayden Lake, Idaho![77] The timing of the ads was
propitious. With inflation in the late 1970s threatening the security of
many readers, the survivalist movement, "the growth industry of the
'80s" as one commentator called it, was just building steam. While
many, probably most, survivalists eschewed racism, others—deadly, cold-
blooded, serious Christian "men of integrity" as one described himself—were retreating to the woods to arm themselves for what they
saw as an impending racial war. A handful of these would find their
way to Idaho.[78]

The third element was prison recruitment. It is a sociological irony
that groups, like individuals, come to mirror their most detested enemies. So it is with the Aryan Nations Church and those it considers
subhuman homonids, the so-called "black apes." In the late 1960s Black
Muslims won a series of court decisions based on the First and Fourteenth amendments to the Constitution which expanded religious
freedoms for their imprisoned brothers. These included the right to
receive uncensored religious literature, to hold prayer meetings, to shave
their heads and be served pork-free meals, and most notably, to be
segregated from jailed "white devils." Other racial groups appealed for
the same privileges, and within a decade America's most liberal prisons, particularly those in California, had become racially segregated
"hate factories." The blacks had their Black P Stone Nations and Black
Guerrilla Families, the Latinos their La Nuestra Familia, and the whites
their Aryan Brotherhoods, proudly wearing tattooed swastikas and
mimicking the blacks and the Chicanos with their own "white is beautiful" and "black devil" argot. John Irwin, a sociologist who did time
in the California prison system during this period, quotes the wife of
a San Quentin inmate who describes her husband's conversion to Nazism: "He didn't used to be prejudiced but now he hates blacks. He
and some other white friends formed an American National Socialist
group which I guess is a Nazi group because they hate blacks so
much."[79]

Many radical patriots have themselves been jailed at various times
and are well aware of what has been transpiring behind bars. And they
have seen in it the opportunity of winning to the fold the tough and
violent cadres they need to further their revolution. "I brought 20
convicts out of San Quentin with me," Keith Gilbert has bragged.

They became "Third Reich Missionaries" in his Socialist Nationalist Aryan Peoples Party.

Janet Hounsell, a grandmotherly figure who had moved from California to Hayden Lake where she served as Rev. Butler's secretary, was assigned to head the Aryan Nations prison mission. Candidates for membership in the church were contacted first by letter and, if the response seemed promising, by personal visits. Inmates who were successfully proselytized were themselves appointed Aryan Nations ministers and given responsibility for further recruitment behind the walls.

The results of these efforts have been something less than spectacular. Prison officials normally intercept mail that they feel constitutes a direct and immediate threat to the security of their institutions. Identity literature falls in this category. With the exception of some like Gary Yarbrough, one of the founders of the Order, and Thomas Harrelson, both of whom claim rebirth in Christ through Hounsell's outreach program, few inmates have applied for Aryan Nations citizenship. Authorities believe that no more than fifteen convicts in each of the major Pacific Northwest prisons are affiliated with the Aryan Brotherhood. Even fewer are Aryan Nations members.[80] As one ex-con, recruited from Englewood Federal Penitentiary in Colorado, says, the military discipline and religious asceticism of the Aryan Nations Church do not sit well with those like himself who like to "party and get high."

"They don't seem to enjoy life. They just sit up there and hate all day, see who can out-hate each other."[81] Butler was forced to run this young recruit out of his Hayden Lake compound personally.

The Order

After a cost of over $1 million, the presentation of 1,538 pieces of evidence, and the appearance of 280 witnesses, the U.S. Justice Department completed its successful prosecution of the Order in Seattle in late 1985, approximately one year after the shooting death on nearby Whidbey Island of its co-founder, Robert Mathews.[82] The investigation is said to have involved one-quarter of the total manpower resources of the FBI, which followed a trail of sixty-seven separate crimes including robberies, arson, bombings, counterfeit schemes, and murders throughout the country.

The story of the Order is a book in itself. But relative to the general impetus of the Idaho Christian patriot movement as a whole, it is accurately seen as a minor if newsworthy deviation. Using the very liberal criterion introduced in the first chapter, 81 of the sample of 520 radical patriots are what may be considered "terrorists." By this we mean either isolated individuals—itinerant assassins like Joseph P. Franklin, David Rice, or Joseph Christopher, who alone are responsible for about one-half of all right-wing homicides in America since 1980—or affiliates of groups who have threatened or succeeded in killing or physically injuring other people. Thirty-nine of these eighty-one, less than 10 percent of the total sample, are known Order members, eleven have at one time or another been associated with the CSA but not the Order, seven are Constitutional terrorists, and the balance ex-Minutemen, transient hit-men, and Ministry of Christ Church assailants.

Robert Mathews moved his family in 1973 from Arizona to Washington, settling on a fifty-three-acre plot of forested land near Metaline Falls, just miles west of Priest Lake, Idaho. Although his appearance at a Klan rally at Spokane's Riverfront Park a decade later surprised local law enforcement officials, Mathews's biography is almost an ideal-type of the revolutionary career. In high school he joined the youth chapter of the John Birch Society. Through this he learned of Marvin Cooley, the outspoken Phoenix tax resister mentioned earlier in this chapter, and affiliated himself with a local anti-tax group, the Sons of Liberty. An illegal claim of twelve dependents on his 1040 form when he was eighteen somehow resulted in a running gun battle with federal tax agents. He became disillusioned with Constitutionalism, dropped out of society, and began serious reading of critical social history. After delving into Oswald Spengler's *Decline of the West* and Wilmot Robertson's *Dispossessed Majority,* Mathews found his annoyance at the seeming apathy of his fellow Americans intensified. He joined William L. Pierce's National Alliance and subscribed to its slick monthly news magazine.[83]

Under the pseudonym Andrew MacDonald, Pierce wrote and published *The Turner Diaries* in 1978.[84] It is a fictional account of a thirty-five-year-old electronics engineer, Earl Turner, and the last two years of his life immediately preceding the "Great Revolution." This is the revolution that purges America of its alien hordes and permits "God's great experiment"—to introduce on earth a higher species of man, the white man—to continue.

Many believe that the Order was little more than a bloody reenactment of MacDonald's story line.[85] There were the same "socially conscious" robberies by men using code names, the same hit lists of Jewish enemies and "race traitors" (in the case of the Order, Alan Berg, Norman Lear, Baron Elie de Rothschild, Jacob Javits, and Armand Hammer), the same lie-detector loyalty tests, the same trials of movement "unreliables" and their executions (Walter West) or "suicide missions" (William Soderquist), the same plans to bomb power plants (Boundary Dam in northeast Washington) or to shut down shipping lanes (Puget Sound), the same fetish with computer technology, and the same ritual ordination into the cult (the inductees standing in a circle around a white infant, swearing allegience to the race). Although Order leaders claim they got the idea from another source, the group also had the same kind of horizontally segregated, self-contained "cells" described in *The Turner Diaries* (legal and security—Ardie McBrearty; assassinations—Gary Yarbrough; coordination—Denver Parmenter; "jobs"—David Tate; recruitment—Randall Duey; counterfeiting—Robert Merkie; and military training—Randall Rader).

Whatever the truth of these conjectures, there is little doubt that *The Turner Diaries* profoundly affected Robert Mathews.[86] Its protagonist is pictured as altogether human, a figure with whom a person like Mathews, himself an ordinary family man with few evident pretensions of greatness, could probably identify. In his last testament, written while under fire on Whidbey Island, Mathews describes himself as a guy who "just wanted to be left alone."[87] A close relative confirms this: "He was not a hater. He loved his family, but saw it endangered. He didn't hate other people and had nothing against the Negro race [although, the subject adds, "he did believe in racial separation"]. . . . What Bob wanted most was to come home. He was a devoted family man, and a very hard worker . . . very. This [homestead] was like a little paradise."[88]

Earl Turner, likewise, exhibits few extraordinary virtues. He is clumsy with his hands, once dropping a car battery on his foot. Another time he is besmudged with oily muck and must be humiliatingly washed off with a hose. He is impulsive, not particularly mindful of "Organization" discipline, and not even absolutely convinced of its ideology. When his lack of commitment results in his capture by the "Israeli intelligence," he divulges everything he knows while being tortured. Henry, Turner's cellmate, whom Turner both admires and fears, is a much less likable fellow—ideologically single-minded, strong, courageous, and cool. He kills without feeling, while Turner does so reluctantly, at first nauseated by the harm he causes.[89]

In time, however, perhaps like Mathews himself, it dawns on Turner that "there is no way we can destroy the System without hurting many thousands of innocent people—no way. It is a cancer too deeply rooted in our flesh."[90] It is a cancer that has made Americans "soft-minded," "feminine," and "infantile." Turner's revulsion for his fellows grows. They must be treated realistically, he argues, "namely, like a herd of cattle" who respond to nothing but fear and hunger. "We will take their food and make them fear us more than the System. We will treat them exactly the way they deserve to be treated."

"Boobus Americanus," whose only concern is to enjoy life, in these times of trial does not deserve to live.[91]

Like Mathews himself, who developed an intense hostility for "responsible *con*-servatives" (with emphasis on the "con"), Turner directs his wrath at the advocates of "individual freedom." Small businessmen he says, are even worse than "mindless liberals." They are "the world's biggest conspiracy mongers . . . and also the world's greatest cowards," their cowardice "exceeded only by their stupidity." "Woe betide any whining conservative . . . who gets in the way of our revolution. . . . I will listen to no more excuses from these self-serving collaborators but will simply reach for my pistol."[92]

Turner finally recognizes the cosmic significance of "the terrible, terrible task we have before us." At this point he is ready for ceremonial induction into the Organization by means of the Rite of Union, a parody of Christian communion.

Having donned a monk's copse, Turner is brought before the high priest to receive "a mighty Oath, a moving Oath that shook me to my bones and raised the hair on the back of my neck."[93] With the other initiates he is given a necklace with a pendant bearing a cyanide capsule. He then reiterates the sacred compact:

"I offer you my life. Do you accept it?"
To this the priest replies:
"Brother! We accept your life. In return we offer you everlasting life in us. Your deed shall not be in vain, nor shall it be forgotten, until the end of time."[94]

"Even though you die," the priest promises, "you will continue to live in us."

"Only in the moment of my death," Turner repeats the words, "will I achieve full membership in the Order."[95]

The first organizational meeting of the Order was held in Mathews's home during the summer of 1983. Eight were present. They included disaffected members of the Aryan Nations Church who had, in the words of one, "tired of straight-armed salutes and worship of Adolf Hitler"; Klansmen looking for action instead of words; and one survivalist who quickly found himself in over his head. Charles Ostrout, a later recruit, spoke for him when he told the jury that being in the Order was like being on "a locomotive going down the track at 100 miles an hour, and there's a trestle ahead and the trestle's not there. . . . I decided to stay on the locomotive because it was safer for me and my family."[96]

To this coterie were subsequently added a smattering of born-again CSA Christian knights, a couple of Identity churchgoers from Colorado, several eastern National Alliance members, at least two Birchers, and a handful of Christian Constitutionalists. One of the latter has explicitly denied being either a racist or an anti-Semite, and claims his prosecution as an Order member was a mistake. Love, he writes,

is a natural emotion—even within terms of physical survival, and is constructive as an energy force. Whereas hate is a negative emotion, as a negative force, it is destructive in all aspects. In plain language: There is no room in a Christ-filled heart for even a tad of hate. The so-called "Christian Identity" movement has too much hate . . . which is contrary to Christ's message. . . . I have personally been teaching/preaching against hate for over ten years. . . . I met Richard Butler several years ago. . . . We disagreed with him on nearly every point. . . . Our position is that he teaches a violation of the First Commandment—the worship of the color of skin—not God.[97]

This individual's son is married to a Filipino woman: "We have two lovely grandchildren who are obviously half-breeds to the casual observer." He says he loves them "just as dearly" as his white grandchildren. While in prison he has befriended several inmates less fortunate than himself and has given them legal advice. On Father's Day in 1985 he received a handmade card with nineteen signatures, including those of three blacks and two Mexicans. One of the blacks, a barely literate Vietnam veteran, scribbled the following note on a piece of paper and shoved it into his pocket: "I nevey had a fother but if I did I wounld want him to be like you." The inmate believes this is "the highest compliment a man can receive."

What are the other members of the Order like? Although this question shall be addressed later in the book, it is appropriate here to make some preliminary observations.[98]

Adherents to the Order are probably younger than a cross-section of the membership of the groups from which they were recruited. The average age of the terrorist (as defined above) in the sample is approximately ten years younger than the typical Idaho Christian patriot.

In regard to intelligence, I know of three or four high school dropouts in the Order. But there is no evidence that, generally speaking, Order members are less intelligent than the average American. Certainly they are no less educated. Two are graduates of the California Mentally Gifted Program and another has an IQ of 120 and is said to have read *Mein Kampf* in the fifth grade and to have worn a suit and tie in the seventh "because Hitler did." There are also graduates of Florida State University (math) and of the universities of Wyoming, Utah, Arkansas (engineering), and Georgia. Before her education was disrupted by a prison sentence, one was carrying a straight-A average in chemistry at Boise State University and was planning to become a general practitioner after studying at the University of Washington. Another, "a financial whiz kid," is said to have run "an admirable campaign" for student body president at Eastern Washington University. There are also Boys' State representatives, high school yearbook editors, a rock 'n' roll musician who confesses to once being strung out on drugs, one-time teen athletes, a champion amateur golfer, and a high school teacher with a master's degree in counseling. In sum, at least in terms of their formal educational experience and background, Order members seem indistinguishable from the typical American.

As individuals, members of the Order are described by their neighbors and employers as "likable" and as "good workers," or as one mother said of her own son, "a good little boy, except for his politics." Even Gary Yarbrough, who had a black crepe and candle shrine to Hitler in his home, who had been earlier imprisoned for burglary and drugs, and in whose house the gun that killed Alan Berg was found, "is not your standard criminal." According to his lawyer, "the media has created this monster that goes around the U.S. committing acts of terrorism. But the facts I've seen don't support that."[99]

Acquaintances confirm this. Mary Mahlon* relates how one evening at the Little Brown Jug, a Garwood, Idaho, bar where she and her husband were playing as musicians, a local cowboy tried to pick her up. Yarbrough, "a very polite young man," introduced himself and "invited" the intruder to quit pestering her. When the story broke concerning Yarbrough's alleged armed assault on three FBI agents, the Mahlons were "flabbergasted" and decided to help in his defense. They have since become firm believers in the Identity message. "If you knew how many others [in northern Idaho] were sympathetic with the movement," Mary told me in closing, "it would knock your socks off."[100]

CONCLUSION

These, then, are the roots of Idaho's patriot movement. Born of a coupling of fundamentalist Christianity and devotion to the Constitution, it is a local dramatization of a recurring cultural theme.

The politics of righteousness has never been all violence, and this is true for Gem State patriotism. The Lord's work requires a division of heroic labors. Some are called to petition, others to write, still others to pray. Some embark on campaigns of civil disobedience. Fewer don arms to do the truly nasty jobs of bombing, arson, and murder. While their extremity may be regretted by their fellow patriots, just as often it is "understood."

Like those of the past, Idaho's patriots are exceptional only in their ordinariness. For that reason they are all the more fascinating to the student of social life.

3

MADNESS, MONEY, MESSIAHS
An Analysis of Movement
Motives

For myself, I've never been able to imagine the center of life being economics as in the term we have ignominiously surrendered ourselves to—
"making a living." I majored in history with my emphasis in ancient history, but I didn't want to make a living with history. It seemed too much
like making a living cleaning my room. . . . And again, it seemed like
making a living out of my hobby. . . . I could teach, but . . . I was a
Christian (Baptist) and couldn't stand the atmosphere in the schools of
calous disregard for Christianity.[1]

THE ISSUE POSED
Media images of right-wing extremists as neo-Nazi haters, perhaps
even crazy, do not entirely jibe with the data I have assembled. This
does not mean that the media have consciously distorted the facts.
Rather, there appears to have been an error of omission, an error
fraught with potentially tragic policy implications.

"Hate," "Nazi," and "crazy" are in part rhetorical categories that do
not just describe actions but defame actors. Naturally, rightists take
umbrage at the imposition of these inflammatory labels on themselves.
Consider this passionate if clumsy defense by Frank Silva, written while
awaiting trial in the Pierce County, Washington, jail:

Since I nor any man allegedly to be involved with the "Order" has ever claimed
this distiction how then, sir can your paper, or any other paper call me a neo-
Nazi? I am now, and will allways remain a "Klansman" of the first rank. All
of the men that I have had personel contact with are Klansmen. How then
can you moraly pursue the 'defamatory' claims of "neo-Nazi," and label us—
me, accordingly. . . .[2]

As it may be difficult for the reader to understand exactly what it is
that Silva is protesting, let us consider another statement—this by
Randall Duey, who is now serving a 100-year sentence for his role in
the Order.

I am a Christian. . . . I observe the world through the eyes of one trying to
serve our King, Jesus the Christ. I see all history and everything happening

68

to us at present and in the future as parts of the plan of our benevolent Father, Who loves our ability to understand, and disciplines us when we are making mistakes, and calls us home when we stray too far for our own safety. He wishes us to perfect ourselves to the standards He gave us, written clearly in the Holy Scriptures, so that we can be an example to all people.[3]

As Albert Camus once observed: Every no implies a yes, every rebellion an affirmation, each anger at one thing, joy in its opposite. So it is with the Order and every other group described in the previous chapter. As their members' loves for Constitution, race, and religion are deep, visceral, and extreme, so are their hates. Another activist, now serving time for criminal racketeering, says it this way:

We love our "Folk," the preservation of our race and culture are very important to us. No one makes the supreme "sacrifice" out of a sense of hate, but from love. [Christian Identity, he continues, is not a theology of hate," as some have said.] "C. I" is common sense . . . and love or "kinship" for one's fellow man, or racial kinship.[4]

Thom Robb in his keynote address to the 1986 Aryan World Congress concurred with this. "The greatest propaganda tool we have," he said, "is . . . love for our people. If we cannot show love for our people we will never succeed. . . . There's a lot of people who hate us. But we're not the haters, we're the lovers. We love all that is noble and righteous. We will not stand by and allow the enemies to destroy these things."[5]

"The primary misrepresentation in the controlled media," still another activist insists, "is that we are a hate group. . . . I love my race and regard it as supreme. However, I do not hate Indians, Orientals, Mexicans, or Negroes. . . . I see my race threatened by these races."[6]

Even granted that the object of these men's devotion is regrettably, even dangerously restricted, we cannot conclude that their formal psychological functioning is radically different from our own. And yet how can such a characterization be reconciled with their complicity in terrorism? What could have motivated presumably "loving" people to do such dirty work? The object of this chapter is to address this question.

Although most of the examples in this chapter will be taken from extreme cases—both Christian Identity and Constitutionalist terrorists—my hypothesis is that the motivational portrait drawn below is true for radical patriotism generally. Identity Christians and Christian Constitutionalists, and even narrowly focused, issue-oriented activists, are in effect dramatizing their imagined heroic significance via the politics of righteousness. The heroic motif provides outsiders to the movement a deep, sympathetic, nonapologetic, and morally challenging understanding of what Christian patriots are about, why, as one terrorist wrote to me, "I am willing to sacrifice everything, even my life in order that my race might live,"[7] or why, in the words of another now in Lompoc State Prison, "I would consider it an honor to kill the enemies of . . . my race, regardless of the price I may pay for the action."[8]

DEFINITIONS AND CAVEATS

To begin with it is important to clarify how I shall be using the word "motive" here, and particularly to distinguish it from a term with which it is too often confused: "cause."[9] By motive I mean the reasons considered by the actors in question to be sufficient for explaining and justifying the act. Motives in this sense are words, not internal "springs" to action; they are vocabularies employed by actors either under interrogation or in anticipation of such, that not only "make sense" of conduct, but appear at least to them as "good reasons" for it. Motives do not describe internal states, forces that "drive" people or "cause" them to act as they do, at least in the mechanistic sense in which these terms are ordinarily used. They are instead terms by which understanding of conduct proceeds.

The "causes" of conduct, on the other hand, refer to the social conditions independent of and prior to that conduct, yet highly associated with it. This is not to say that motives and causes of conduct are entirely unrelated. What are viewed as good reasons for an act often have the power to compel. And vice versa, one unable to convince even himself that his conduct is of high and worthy purpose is discouraged from it.

In order to understand the motives of others, one must take the time and effort to experience the world as they do. My goal has been to maintain a precarious balance between the contradictory requirements of detachment and identification.[10] I have assembled data gathered by a variety of interrogatory tactics—in-depth nonstructured interviews, participant observation of patriot assemblies and workshops, and consultation of primary documents—into a motivational "ideal-type" of the Christian patriot. An ideal-type is not the same as a modal personality, i.e., the most common patriot personality. An ideal-type is instead a theoretical crystallization of a mixture of observations. As such it owes as much to the investigator's own creative insight as it does to what he has witnessed, read, and heard. Different sociologists might draw entirely opposed motivational portraits of the same population.

Finally, the use of the word "ideal" is by no means intended to confer an ethical value on the motivation in question.

TYPES OF MOTIVES

Sociologists distinguish between three ideal-types of social conduct according to the "modes of orientation," that is, the motives or purposes given that conduct by its performers.[11] Social action is either predominantly nonrational, irrational, or rational. Although few actions are exclusively one of these types, a reconstruction of the motivation of the prototypical patriot will be aided by this scheme.

Nonrational Conduct

Nonrational conduct refers to the habitual response of individuals to a given situation. The actors respond without conscious reflection to the circumstances in which they find themselves. Nowadays, sociologists may substitute for "nonrational" the terms customary or traditional conduct. The nonrational actor is compelled to do and actually does what is expected of him by tradition or custom because he has never learned an alternative way of behaving. It does not occur to him that he could dress, eat, gesture, or speak other than as he does.

It should be clear even from these brief comments that panics, rumors, fads, revolutionary movements, mob behavior, and sectarian schisms—the whole panoply of what sociologists know as "collective behavior"—cannot easily be subsumed under the category of nonrational conduct. For this reason it may be dismissed from further consideration as the ultimate motive for affiliating with the patriot movement.

Of course patriot leaders do invoke traditional Christian symbols and speak grandly about American folkways. They make sentimental references to the Constitution and the Founding Fathers, to the Prophets and the King James Bible. But this is precisely the point: This traditional iconography is consciously employed by those leaders, often quite cynically. Patriot orators and their audiences are sometimes authentically seized emotionally by the sound of their own words and by the excitement of the moment, but this should not deceive us from comprehending the reasons they give for affiliating with the movement. The prototypical patriot sees himself as being in the avant garde to (re)establish a Constitutional, Christian commonwealth in America. He pictures himself, heroically, as having transcended at great expense to himself, the soporific, narcoticized (i.e., nonrational) reactions of his fellow Americans to media-manufactured "crises" and liberal catchwords like "democracy," "peace," "brotherhood," and "equality."

Irrational Conduct

For purposes here irrational conduct will be considered that which is formally labeled as such by recognized authorities on the subject, specifically court officials and mental health workers.[12]

Items:

1977, New Rochelle, New Jersey: Frederick Cowan, thirty-three, a former Army sharpshooter and self-proclaimed Nazi, goes on a six-hour rampage, killing five and injuring five before fatally turning the gun on himself.

1977, Charlotte, North Carolina: Kenneth Wilson, a body-builder, wearing Nazi armbands and tattooed with swastikas, fires into a crowd of black picnickers, killing one and injuring three before taking his own life. A note found on his body reveals his involvement with a black teenage girl, "a relationship of which we did not approve," says his father.

1982, Oroville, California: Perry "Red" Warthan, a Nazi regalia fan, gains notoriety by recruiting local high school boys to his cause. He is convicted of murdering one of them whom he suspects of spying. Warthan had earlier spent time in a California mental facility after being connected to the death of a child. While hospitalized there he was known to have maintained contact with cult leader Charles Manson.

It is tempting to simply label these people crazy. This same assumption not untypically informs lay opinion regarding Christian patriots. How does this assumption bear up to the evidence? To repeat: The answer to this must be found in the authoritative judgments of psychopathologists licensed to issue pronouncements on bizarre conduct. With this in mind, let us consider the two most extreme cases of such conduct in our sample.

At this writing, Frank Spisak, Jr., is on death row in the Lucasville, Ohio, State Penitentiary. He is said to have wandered the back streets of Cleveland dressed as an old woman and carrying a .22 caliber pistol in a hollowed-out copy of *Mein Kampf.* Following his self-described "search and destroy" missions on behalf of the Idaho-based Socialist Nationalist Aryan Peoples Party to "exterminate as many niggers and Jews as possible," Spisak was convicted of the murders of three blacks from 1980 to 1983. The last, a homosexual minister who approached him in a public restroom, was shot twenty-two times.[13] In letters to his "Comrade Party Leader," Keith Gilbert, Spisak identifies Hitler as "the greatest Christian in 2000 years" and alludes to the possibility "that I might be the reincarnated Adolf Hitler." For like the Messiah, Spisak too "tried to drive out the 'money changers' . . ." And like the German chancellor (and Goering, Himmler, and Goebbels), he too is Catholic. "Heil Mary! Heil Hitler! Spisak, Jr."[14]

So incredible were such assertions to the court that it sought to find Spisak incapable of standing trial, and to have him indefinitely confined to an asylum as a paranoid schizophrenic. But Spisak, a married father, one-time college student, and Boys' State participant, successfully insisted on his lucidity and on responsibility for his own conduct.

For a long time we have been regarded as the "lunatic fringe," [wrote Spisak to me] and the government and mass media use words like "paranoid" and "psychotic" to describe us. At my highly publicized political show trial in Cleveland in 1983 I conclusively refuted every suggestion that I might be mentally ill and I was subsequently sentenced to die in Ohio's electric chair for the crime of mass murder. George Lincoln Rockwell, the original "American Nazi" leader of the 1960s had written a book entitled *How to Get Out and Stay Out of the Insane Asylum* and this has been of tremendous benefit to many of us who have had to face a fate worse than death from time to time. It worked for me. As far as I know, no American nazi or white racist has ever been found to be mentally incompetent although our enemies have certainly tried their best![15]

Spisak is correct. Were political moderates able to dismiss at least the fringe element of the patriot movement as insane, the sanctity of our already fragile *Lebenswelt* ("life-world") would be more secure. It is much more unsettling to contemplate the possibility of extremists being rational within the bounds of their own logic. And yet this may be required in gaining a valid sociological understanding of the movement. Consider now the second case.

On Christmas Eve, 1985, David L. Rice beat to death four members of a prominent Seattle family, the Goldmarks, mistaking them for Jewish Communists.[16] Unlike Spisak, who successfully argued for his own culpability in politically motivated murder, Rice pleaded innocent on grounds of insanity. In the course of six psychiatric examinations lasting two hours each, Rice was found to believe not only in an international banking conspiracy and the threat of 30,000 to 50,000 armed Communist invaders on the borders of Mexico and Canada awaiting orders to occupy the American heartland, but to have "a delusional system which includes 'communications' from his 'friends' from outer space . . . who sometimes . . . give him thoughts and ideas." Nevertheless, the psychological consultant hired to determine the defendant's mental state was unable to conclude that Rice suffered from paranoid schizophrenia. On the contrary, he reported to the court, Rice's beliefs were a product of his association with members of a Constitutionalist group, the Duck Club, and the reading of its literature.

Rather, [said the consulting psychologist] he belonged to a subgroup of individuals who believed in and supported these ideas . . . and validated these ideas as rational and important. . . . I believe that he felt that these people would probably approve of his actions, and support him. [To this extent they were] not true delusions at all, but ideas and beliefs that existed in and were supported by the group he identified with.[17]

One of these associates, a naturopathic physician, was, according to witnesses, "such a bigot . . . and an anti-Semite" that there was some question about her own mental faculties. It was from these acquaintances that Rice received the tragic misinformation about the Goldmarks.

To be sure, the consultant added, mass murder by its very nature is psychologically abnormal. But this does not permit us to conclude that its perpetrator is therefore crazy. In any case, it does not absolve him of responsibility. Like Spisak, Rice planned and implemented the crime with a high degree of organization and awareness. Indeed, cognizant of his impending arrest, he thought of turning himself in to a fellow activist who could then collect the reward money to further the revolution. Rice saw himself as a "soldier," his murder as "the first step" in a war of liberation. Although he regretted the violence he did to the two Goldmark children, "sometimes," he confessed, ". . . soldiers have to kill." In a kind of crackpot altruism he indicated that "it may have been necessary to sacrifice these lives for the greater good of mankind." Rice's contention of insanity was rejected. He was found guilty of first-degree murder and sentenced to death.

RATIONALITY RECONSIDERED

Recall that, as used here, the "motives" for conduct refer to the meanings the actors themselves give to it, how *they* understand what they are doing. The patriots I spoke to appear generally indifferent to the issue of the actual social-psychological correlates, the scientific "causes," as it were, of their activism. They are, however, eminently prepared to justify their behavior to a critical public by showing how it springs from what they consider to be "good" motives. These motives, or if the reader prefers, rationalizations, are the focus of concern here.

From the viewpoint of the patriots, Christian patriotism is perfectly rational, but rational in a fundamentally different sense than the way that word is commonly used in secular circles. The distinction to which I am pointing is that between *functional* or formal rationality, or what might be called profit-maximizing behavior, and *substantive* rationality. In the first, the actor believes himself to be acting in the most efficient way possible to enhance either his own personal utility or that of the greatest number of others. In the second, the actor claims to be concerned primarily with ends in themselves, regardless of their possible disutility to himself or others.[18]

Functional rationality proclaims that action preferable which enhances private pleasure or public happiness. Substantive rationality, on the other hand, proclaims that action preferable which enhances human dignity by stoic adherence to duty, regardless of the possible pain and suffering involved. Although I disagree with his ethnic application, one sociologist has gone so far as to declare functional rationality an ethics of the "average" man, characteristic, he believed, of Catholic civilization. Substantive rationality, he argued, is a truly "heroic" ethic, unique to Protestant Europeans, particularly those of German descent. This "Aryan" trait is heroic because it resists the "natural" human inclination to pursue pleasure.[19]

My understanding is that the basic motive behind radical Christian patriotism is a variation of substantive rationality. The patriot pictures himself as heroically devoted to absolute principles—to rules laid down either in the Pentateuch or the organic Constitution—regardless of the costs in human felicity of such devotion. This accounts for the positions the patriots routinely adopt on countless domestic and foreign policy issues, from "creeping socialism" (Social Security, public education, busing, Medicare, welfare, and environmental protectionism), to capital punishment, income taxes, and abortion.

Bureaucracy, faceless Communism, liberal-Benthamite "pointy-headed intellectuals," and "pen-pushing political appointees" are seen by patriots as functional rationality incarnate. They are emblematic of the decadent, antiheroic pursuit of the greatest good for the greatest number and the sacrifice of absolute principles. A patriot might not dispute the proposition that in the short run, guaranteed public education and job opportunities for minorities, abortion on demand, civil rights for homosexuals, expanded welfare programs, rehabilitation of criminals instead of punishment, and even the distribution of free contraceptives to teenagers and sterile needles for drug-users would increase the general happiness of the population. But the patriots believe that such policies would inevitably undermine the moral discipline of the nation. They would "effeminize" the people, rendering them susceptible to further temptation.

"Better Dead Than Red." So reads the bumper-sticker. Better a suffering hero than a happy slave. Better the earth be destroyed in its entirety than duty to Race, God, and Constitution be compromised. Or as one individual at the 1983 Aryan World Congress is alleged to have warned: "The old period is over, and a new period is going to begin. . . . I'm here to tell you that if *we* [the Aryans] can't have this country, as far as I'm concerned, no one gets it."[20]

"We can not offer you pay, pleasure, or power," Thom Robb reminded attendees of the 1986 Aryan World Congress:

We can only promise you the dishonorable titles traitor, criminal, crazy; the promise of being despised, ignored, and even killed; economic hardship and misunderstanding. If you are in the struggle because you anticipate victory, you are in for the wrong reason. You should be in the movement out of a sense of duty toward our children. Our duty in life is to assure a peaceful life for our children. There is a war in America today. In one camp is the federal government headed by the Jew. Their goal is to destroy us. Our goal is to destroy them. There is no middle ground. There is only right and wrong.[21]

Robb's message was received by thunderous bursts of "Hail Victory" and straight-armed salutes from the audience of several hundred.

It is true that while they rarely mention this as a motive for joining the movement, most patriots appear to have benefited personally from their affiliations by sustaining rewarding relationships with their recruiting agents. This payoff will be examined in detail in Part II. Furthermore, some activists have used their movement affiliations to aggrandize themselves financially. Mythos Makers, a white supremacist marketing outlet, sells belt buckles, beer mugs, baseball caps, pennants, bumper stickers, and other paraphernalia emblazoned with the phrase "white pride world wide." And most patriot churches, including the Aryan Nations Church, the Colorado-based Scriptures for America, and the Lord's Covenant Church of Phoenix, appear to do brisk businesses in cassette sermons, pamphlets, books, and most recently, technically well-produced videotapes. Another entrepreneurial success is Barristers' Inn School of Common Law in Boise.

FBI investigations of the Order broke open when Thomas Martinez, one of its peripheral associates, agreed to turn state's evidence after being arrested for distributing counterfeit bills alleged to have been printed on the Aryan Nations press in Hayden Lake. "How I got caught," he told a reporter, "was greed . . . I thought if I just took a little of the money, maybe $4,000, I could pass it out and get the money I needed. At first Martinez only planned to fix the rotting beams in his house. Eventually suspicious neighbors of the high school dropout turned him in when he began purchasing VCRs, lawn furniture, and mowers and leased an expensive automobile.[22] Martinez has since filed suit in U.S. District Court seeking to collect $20,000 in rewards offered for the arrest of his one-time comrades implicated in the murder of Denver talk show host Alan Berg.[23] For his betrayal of the Order, Martinez was the subject of a thwarted plot to have him beheaded.

Posse Comitatus is acknowledged by some of its more forthright units to have established the so-called Life Science Church largely as a tax shelter. Activists write off their mobile homes as "chapels" and their guns as "church property," and report their income as going to "donations" to the Church "ministry." Even Rev. Richard Butler himself has been accused by disaffected supporters of establishing his own pastorate primarily to shield his very sizable holdings from tax collectors. "I was . . . part of the Posse Comitatus in the early 1970s and knew Richard Butler before he became an ordained minister through a mail order house," one of these followers reports. "I was present at the same table in Connie's Cafe when Richard Butler told our group how easy it was to be ordained, how a dog had been ordained by his master to prove how easy it is, and I also heard why Richard became ordained—namely for a tax shelter and a front for his organization. . . ."[24]

Notwithstanding the economic motivation behind much of what passes for Christian patriotism, to focus on it inordinately is to risk profoundly misunderstanding the fundamental reason for joining the movement. After all, there are far easier and less personally risky ways of making fortunes than by dramatizing one's political eccentricities. Butler claims to have suffered substantial financial losses since leaving his secure and lucrative position with Lockheed Aircraft to assume leadership of the Aryan Nations Church.[25] To repeat myself, the "motives" for conduct refer to the meanings the actors themselves give to it. Comparatively few patriots use the terminology of functional rationality (i.e., profit-maximization) to account for their activism. This is not to say that they understand themselves to be acting out of semi-conscious habit. Even less do they see themselves as crazed. Instead, they believe themselves to be living rationally, but as patriotic Christian heroes. Theirs is seen as a life ethically superior to those of their compromised, self-satisfied, and apathetic neighbors.

CHRISTIAN HEROISM ANALYZED

> Give your soul to God and pick up
> Your gun,
> It is time to deal in lead;
> We are the legions of the damned
> The army of the . . . dead.[26]

All organisms seek to feel good, to maximize their pleasure at minimum cost. This might be spoken of as the organismic basis of our natural egoism. It is in any case the intuitive foundation of primitive ethics. At the simplest level man, like all animals, judges that thing, act, or person "good" which gives him pleasure.

To most living creatures pleasure is achieved through the gratification of biological needs and the avoidance of physical distress. But human needs are not merely physical, human fears not just organically based. The urgency to feel good that we share with all species is transformed into a need to "feel good about ourselves," to sense our lives as worthwhile.

The vehicles of self-justification constitute a virtual encyclopedia of cultural anthropology. They have one element in common: struggle against an oppositional force. Whether it is conceived as natural, intellectual, or human, the more formidable this opposition, the greater the psychological reward in subduing it. But greater too are the risks of failure. The most profound struggles take place psychologically at the very point where fulfillment and tragedy meet. This is the dialectic

of heroism. It is the dialectic within which the radical patriot participates.

Any heroic task requires first an ideal, an obligatory imperative, or
an imagined possibility. The Christian patriot finds his in the organic
Constitution and in God's Word, the Bible, particularly the Pentateuch. Heroism next requires contradiction: a "reality," an "is," or an
"actuality" counterpoised to the ideal, to the should, to the possibility.
Primitive man accomplished this by organizing his communities into
what are technically known as "moieties"—polar opposites that are
complementary. A person belonged to either one moiety or the other,
traced his descent from the moiety ancestor, identified with its particular totem, and above all, engaged in contests of skill and excellence
with members of the opposite half. The Christian patriot achieves the
analogous effect by bifurcating his world and generating an alien against
which to fight. The alien is portrayed as the anti-Christian-constitu-
tional-subverter, the exact opposite of the patriot ideal. For adherents
of Christian Identity this shadowy Other is represented by the word
"Jew," for Christian Constitutionalists, by terms like "insider." In either
case, this symbolic antagonist is essential to the dialectic of heroic patriotism. Without it there would be nothing against which to struggle,
nothing to give the patriot's life significance, nothing to justify his
existence. What this implies, of course, is that if the "Jew" or "'insider" did not exist he would have to be manufactured.

Finally, heroism requires transformative labor: courageous, persistent effort to embody the ideal in concrete reality. The German phi-
losopher Hegel speaks of this creative work as the idealization of the
real and the realization of the ideal. Again, for the Christian patriot
this is tantamount to the imposition of a white Christian constitutional commonwealth on a reluctant and apathetic American populace.
The particulars of this political labor can await the following chapters.
The language of Identity minister Jarah Crawford is sufficient to summarize the strategy, even if a bit sanguinely.

Americans, he sadly recounts, are ignorant and must be "educated"
to see things in their proper light. But, alas, conventional pedagogy is
entirely inadequate to the task. "They [can only] be cured of their
unbelief in the grave." We must therefore "wonder about the mass
death soon to take place" among the "corrupt," "spineless," "mindless" heathen of this country. If 24,000 were killed because the Israelite Zimri took a Midianite woman for his wife (Numbers 25:1–18),

then at least 24 million must die because of America's policy of racial integration.[27]

"The entire earth is about to blow up," Crawford joyfully proclaims. "We stand on the threshold of the kingdom!" And when times are at their worst, some men are at their best. Such a one was Phinehas, who impaled Zimri and his wife on a spear and brought a sudden end to God's fierce judgment on his people. It was a dramatic, noble act. "It is tremendously significant," Crawford tells us, "that one person took matters into his own hands, the one person who had the mind of God." Phinehas was a hero, for in killing two lawbreakers he saved his country. "There was no court trial, no judge and no Supreme Court" to frustrate his righteous work, "just one man who knew the mind of God and acted upon it. The day will come," Crawford promises, ". . . that one man [among us] will act upon the truth he knows in God." In that day all our problems, like those of Ancient Israel, shall be resolved. "The plague will end."[28]

Robert Mathews, founder of the Order, and many of his comrades (one of whom recommended Crawford's book to me), likened themselves to Phinehas. So do many of the other patriots before us. Some, like Gordon Kahl, knowing the immensity of the odds against them, even revel in the certainty that their efforts will end tragically for themselves.[29] Nevertheless, like the heroes of Arthurian legend, like Christ Himself who forecast his own betrayal and execution, they persist in the struggle. "I have no choice," Mathews wrote in his final testament. "I must stand up like a white man and do battle."[30]

The story of Robert Mathews is truly inspiring [one of these patriots wrote to the editor of *National Vanguard*]. . . . You now have a true martyr not like some of the nutty martyrs of the past, but a real, larger-than-life white American hero whom you can make into a folk figure. I hope that someone comes up with a really good song, written in salute to Mathews and named after him, just as a great song in the past was named after one who gave his life in similar circumstances a long way from America.[31]

A CRITICAL NOTE

The word "hero" is both an honorific title and a neutral scientific concept. It should already be clear that when speaking of radical Christian patriots as being motivated by heroism, no moral value is being placed on their quest. The Aztec Indians who dutifully ripped out the hearts of their captives did so not to satisfy some primitive blood lust, but to nourish the god of light in his eternal struggle against the hosts of darkness, thereby saving the world. Theirs too was a heroic calling. Likewise, whatever we may think of their conduct, at least some of the Nazi troops who tortured and murdered women and children saw themselves as Aryan heroes, eliminating "filth" from the earth and saving the world. The idealistic Communist who betrays his comrades or who "reeducates" them in a Soviet political hospital likewise does so to assure the victory of the heroic revolution. The attendant securely ensconced in his missile silo, whose finger rests on the first step of the spiral staircase to nuclear holocaust is not some demonic heathen. Rather, in his own little way he is dramatizing his heroic significance. He too labors to save the world. Sympathetically, we can imagine each of these persons following orders not without some distaste and even revulsion. But distaste swallowed and revulsion ignored are the hallmarks of true heroism. To repeat the age-old dictum: Men cause evil out of good intentions, not generally out of wicked ones. Men cause evil by wanting to triumph heroically over evil. It is good people, good people with blind spots, who do the world's dirty work.[32]

The point is not to decry the metaphysics of heroism as an illusion. Human beings, after all, live in illusions. Our yearning for significance in the cosmos, our need to know our lives are justified, is part of our nature as human beings. Our task is to keep illusions from devolving into delusions, which would bring down around our shoulders the very world we set out to preserve. Nor is the point here to deny that there is Evil. If the heroic quest for justice too often ends in cold-hearted tyranny, then knee-jerk tolerance is perhaps the mother of moral dissolution. Instead, the great tragedy of heroic oratory is what might be called the tendency to "fetishize evil," to locate the threat to human life in one special place, in one particular act, in one group of people, or in one individual, where it can be placated, controlled, or exterminated. "It is tragic," Ernest Becker writes in his Pulitzer Prize–winning book on heroism, "precisely because it is sometimes very arbitrary: men make fantasies about evil, see it in the wrong places, and destroy themselves and others by uselessly thrashing about."[33]

None are immune from this tendency. Human history is largely a bloody testimony to its power. And it is startlingly evident in the radical patriot before us: in his obsession with abortion, with homosexuality and "queer lovers," with pornography, and especially with his focus on the "Communist conspiracy" of the "insider" and the "Jew." Heaven help those upon whom these inflammatory labels attach. For as fetishes of Evil, as living prefigurements of all that man fears most, it is they who must play the role of foil in the heroic drama of the right-wing extremist. Or, in a more fitting metaphor, it is they who serve as the "goats" upon whom the sins of Israel are placed, and by means of which, through their annihilation or exile, Israel endeavors to escape from Evil. "It is coming, and there is not one single thing that the Anti-Defamation Leagues, the Bill Wassmuths or all the slimy jews in this world can do about it. It is just a matter of time, and that time is getting short. . . . A lot of water will flow under the bridge, but when it is all over, this will be a better world."[34]

4

"SATAN'S KIDS" AND JACOB'S SEED
A Sociology of Knowledge

Israel has mixed with the heathen of the world time and again in her past. Every disaster in the Bible is the direct result of this adultery (mixing the holy seed), but Israel never sees until it's too late. At that point, the vast majority are not worth saving and perish in one way or another so that the pure ones will not have their dead weight to carry. God will not allow His family to become racially impure—this is the whole story of the Bible. . . . The cataclysm soon to come will come because of this and will destroy those involved in this, the worst of all sins. . . .

Lastly, Sir, for your own good, I'll give you the warning that all of North America should be getting. All hell is going to begin to brake loose, directly. Prepare yourself for it. It's unavoidable.[1]

Human beings inhabit worlds of their own making.[2] This is a study of one such world, that of Christian Identity. In this chapter and the next we are interested in two questions: What is "real" to Identity Christians? And how do they know it to be so? What are the dimensions of the Identity world: its constituent elements, its basic divisions, its hierarchies of value, its notions of cause and effect, its geographies, pasts, and future possibilities? And how is this world made plausible to its adherents? Or as we frequently hear it asked, "How on earth can intelligent people believe in that stuff?"

These are queries in the subdiscipline known as the sociology of knowledge. It is a course of inquiry that rests upon what today is considered the rather trite observation that what is "real" to, for example, the Hopi Indian, may not be "real" to an American businessman.

Social worlds are built from symbols. Symbols are utterances, objects, gestures, or written expressions that stand for things other than themselves. A cloud, for example, may be said to be a "sign" of rain; that is, it signifies itself. The design of a cross, however, while signifying little in itself, may "symbolize" or represent any number of other things: first aid, salvation, good luck, the hammer of Thor, or Nazism, etc.[3]

Symbols represent images in people's minds, the feelings conjured up by these images, and in some cases lower-level or less abstract symbols. Languages are in effect coherent "sets" of symbols. And of these there exist countless types: scientific (in which the overarching symbols are "cause" and "effect"), poetry, music, and dance (a kind of "body language"), everyday street jargon, and that which shall occupy our attention here, "religious" or theological languages. To sociologists, none of these languages has, as it were, "ontological" precedence over the others. None is necessarily closer to "truth" than the others.

People tell stories with languages. Let us call this "myth-making." By so doing they make sense out of their private and collective experience. Selectively they interpret the past and present by showing how it was "to be expected" that matters should be thus and so. If it is "God's will," then it is "good" that it be thus and so. In this last sense, past and present are not only interpreted, they are legitimized. Much religious myth-making in the Occident is theodicy, the justification of God's ways to man. Theodicy answers the question of how an all-powerful and all-good Creator could permit such immense evil in creation.

In any case, to impose a particular linguistic structure on experience is to order it or, to use the sociological term, to "nomonize" it (from the Greek *nomos* = law). Without symbolic structurings of experience, humans would reside in a state of "anomos," chaos. It is a fundamental axiom in the sociology of knowledge that human beings will do almost anything to relieve themselves of anomie, to preserve their nomic creations, their symbolic worlds, from chaos—including, as history testifies, mass suicide and/or homicide.[4] Evidently death is preferable to meaninglessness.

Most ritual actions and their close relative, high drama, are from this perspective concerted efforts to maintain symbolic worlds by reminding the spectators of what it is they (should) believe but are at risk of forgetting. Ritual and drama accomplish this by vividly reenacting the myths and helping the audience recall at the most profound level the images and emotional resonances the myths stand for. Tears, emotional outrage, and group unity ("love") are typical products of ritual and drama well done.

We can hardly begin to examine all of the implications of the sociology of knowledge for understanding what goes on in social life. It is enough to appreciate that religion in general, which is storytelling and ritual theater par excellence, occupies a pivotal status in the ruminations of the discipline.

THE WORLD OF IDENTITY

The Basic Dimensions

Identity Christianity posits a dualistic realm. This dualism is so stark as to have occasioned self-criticism within the Identity community itself. The Yahweh Believers, an Identity cult located in central Idaho (who claim that they are not only God's chosen people, but also the Jews themselves), consider conventional Identity doctrine a reversion to pagan heresy for this very reason. In their view there exist only God and a "lower case" devil. God (Yahweh) is said to encompass not only love and mercy, but also terrible violence and unspeakable horrors.[5]

At the most theoretical level the world division is symbolized by the familiar "God and Devil," "good and evil," "truth and deception," "light and darkness," "life and death." But as these words carry little emotional impact, Identity myth-makers resort to more concrete medical, zoological, military, and sexual terminology.

On the side of "God" and its associated symbols are arrayed hygiene, purity, chastity, cleanliness, and their supposed benefits: health, well-being, and clarity of vision. On the side of "evil," and as in all apocalyptic oratory portrayed much more vividly, are grouped human "germs," "bacilli," "viruses," and "bacteria," their various *topoi*—spoilage, dirt, sludge, and filth—and their ultimate product, disease; particularly the debilitating sicknesses of addiction, cancer, and sexual "venery" (venereal disease)—herpes and AIDS. These are spread by carriers of sorts. Human "rodents," "pests," and "lice" seem especially favored images. They are also spread through direct contamination by "unclean" persons. This last is accomplished through inordinate contact with them: eating and traveling together, attending the same schools and churches, and "race-mixing."

Lessons from Biblical apocrypha such as the first book of Enoch (2nd century B.C. to the 1st century A.D.) are frequently used by Identity preachers to substantiate their theories of social pathology. The fallen angels of heaven, relates one story, sexually desired the comely earth maidens, took them to wife, and taught them things properly reserved to the gods: medicine, the cutting of roots, astrology, and incantations. The earthlings gave birth to black devil mutants 300 cubits tall, and spiritual wisdom was corrupted by being put to earthly ends. Beholding these abominations, God ordered the angels of light under the leadership of Michael the Archangel to destroy the offspring of adultery. What ensued was the cosmic war between the forces of Light and Darkness.[6] The point is that the promiscuous mixing of separate species of things defiles both. This, say Identity preachers, is the mystery of iniquity.

In a pamphlet of that title, the Rev. Wesley Swift calls the mystery of inquity the "Luciferian design to violate the laws of God . . . as to form and to type," the "mixed breeding" of separate species.[7] At the level of protozoa and bacteria, miscegenation has "produced viruses and germs that run wild." God, he continues, did not create disease. "He created good protozoa, good bacteria. . . ." It was Lucifer and his earthly sorcerers who "mixed them in cultures" and then poisoned mankind. Centuries later these same sorcerers would invent the atom bomb, "mutating the atom" by shooting it with electrons.[8]

In an unpublished paper composed in 1984, a member of the Order expanded on this theme: "God sense is reverance for all things pure and undefiled." This is "Natural Law" as intended by the Creator. "Thus do wolves mate with wolves and not with coyotes. Thus do brown bears mate with brown bears and not with grizzly bears. Thus does Natural Law declare a natural anti-pathy between . . . races . . . as natures method of preserving each specie in its purity." Furthermore, he adds, Natural Law decrees that no "specie" will intercede for another, nor will its males fail to defend its "specie" mates from invasion. "The penalty" for failure to obey the Natural Law "is death." This law is "perfect, unchanging, eternal, true, and life sustaining." Hence, we find in the King James Bible "that the penaltys for race-mixing, homo-sexuality, and usury are death."[9]

Against the specter of social disease and race death are allied a panoply of medicamenta: sterilization, extirpation, purging, and quarantines. Given the lateness of today's end times, the remedies must be both quick and drastic. To paraphrase one Boise broadside addressing the "cancer" of male homosexuality: "This monstrous evil" must be met "promptly and effectively." Already countless young boys have been "infected." What is called for is "immediate and systematic cauterization." The "operation as projected" must not end until "the whole sordid situation is completely cleared up, and the premises thoroughly cleansed and disinfected. This is what we demand, and this is what we expect!"[10]

In farm country the equivalent operation is to be conducted by means of "pesticide" or "insecticide." Yearns one citizen concerning an impending rock concert in northern Idaho during the middle 1970s, "If it should come to pass that . . . the rock festival does occur, then I would hope for one additional happening. That wish would be for every crop duster in northern Idaho to be working in the immediate area and find it necessary to have to jettison his load of insecticide right on top of . . . those social parasites."[11]

The Manicheistic character of Identity doctrine is expressed in a quasi-sociological rhetoric which, like the medical and zoological metaphors, is drawn from a rich treasury of American folklore. On one side is the beloved yeoman, inventive and self-reliant, whose personal relationships are based on trust, goodwill, and mutual aid. This is the "freeman," defender of Law, who trades with others by direct barter. He uses neither credit cards nor "the root of all evil," paper money ("FERNS"—Federal Reserve Notes). Confronting him is the satanic establishment of corporate science, technocratic impersonalism, moronic democracy, and bureaucracy with its centralized planning, picayune legalisms, and systematically cultivated "slavery." Allied with the establishment is the "money manipulator," the international banker and commodity broker, whose sly dealings enrich himself at the expense of both consumer and producer.

The Right side, "ours," worships the Holy Spirit and God the Father. It teaches creationism. The Left, meanwhile, celebrates earthly material substance, Darwinism, and "Baalism." There lie the dark mysteries of Woman with all her attendant corruptions: pornography, sodomy, "whorishness," and abortion by "D. Ms., damnable murderers." Masculine virtue is counterpoised to feminine vice.

West coast versus east coast. Here life is rural and "natural"; there, urban and "artificial." Here, family and neighborhood church preach God's Word. There, big government and liberal "Babylonish" churches preach "secular humanism." Here is found the small town and its quintessential resident, the Christian white man. The eastern metropolis is populated with "alien hordes of brown-skinned mulattoes" ruled by the archetypal symbol of city life, the "Jew."

These respective itineraries can be rearranged to suit the orator's purpose into numberless combinations, novel juxtapositions sometimes creating startling revelations: "pornographic push-cart peddlers," "brown-skinned-homosexual-welfare bum," "secular-humanistic-feminist-Jew," "race-mixing-city-sewer-rodent," and so on. Legalistic-artificial-eastcoast-liberal-money-grubbing-AIDS-infected-Jew-feminist-pornographer all conjunct into a vision of numinous depravity. Each word by itself stands in partial relation to evil. But their rhetorical synthesis produces an emotional response greater than the sum of each alone. Likewise, an amalgamation of white-skinned-clean-living-virile-Law-abiding-independent-rural-Christian-man into a single ideotype evokes a fervor more compelling than the listing of its parts.

While at first glance the Identity world is absolutely bifurcated, psychologically its opposing principles are interlocked in the most intimate way, each feeding symbiotically off the other. Right needs Left and God His devil. Likewise, the children of Light require an offspring of perdition, darkness, and lies. For one cannot experience "good" in the complete sense of the word, with the full resonance of feeling, without knowing its opposite. Every religious myth recognizes and implements this truth. Identity Christianity merely carries it to extreme.

History

There are two kinds of historical rhetorics. First is accidentalism, variations of which are favored in academic circles and of which evolutionism may be considered the preeminent example. Second, is conspiratorialism, which enjoys immense popularity among outsiders to academia. Creationism may be understood as an example of benign conspiratorialism, for whereas evolutionism interprets the variety of life and even the human being as the outcome of chance and accident, creationism sees it as the manifestation of God's grand and beneficent design.

Like most historiographies of the far right (and far left), Identity doctrine is conspiratorial. It views history as the outcome of an immense satanic plan to seize God's creation and establish over it a reign of evil. At the beginning of time Lucifer, his fellow angels, and their witchwomen mates were the world's evil conspirators. Today they are the "Jews."[12] "In 1909 the powers of Lucifer were permitted full manifestation," Swift writes in *The Mystery of Iniquity*, and at that moment the world Communist movement organized and led by "Jewish" Bolsheviks began.[13] But centuries before this, Lucifer's "Jewish" schemes were taking effect.

When the Roman emperor Constantine legalized Christianity (A.D. 313), the "Jews" sought to destroy it from within, first by infiltrating its high offices, and then by introducing into it the "Babylonian" practices of priestcraft, pontifical authority, and vestal virgins. The product of these efforts is the gigantic Christian "fraud" known today as Roman Catholicism.

After I had confessed to him my own conversion to Catholicism, a now-imprisoned member of the Order painstakingly pointed out my "error" by reviewing the pagan foundations of the Church: "Jesus" is a corruption of "Zeus"; Christmas, December twenty-fifth, was originally the pagan god Mithra's birthday; Easter is derived from a pagan celebration of the fertility goddess Astarte, etc. He left his bitterest words for "a Jew pimp and subverter named Paul, whose twisted, perverted ideas of sex formed the basis for the celibacy of the priests and nuns of the Catholic Church," resulting in untold damage to the white race. "The destruction of all healthy. . . . sexual instincts in favor of the unnatural repression of historical Christianity has lowered the birth rate, emasculated the males, and instilled guilt complexes in the females of our race." He concluded that "it was with purpose that nature made the Aryan female so beautiful as to be nearly irresistible at an age sometimes as early as the mid-teens. It was with purpose that nature gave the Aryan male a sexual desire for this young beauty, even as a teenager, so strong that in accordance with natural law he will fight, die, and kill to achieve union." [14]

At the Council of Nicea (A.D. 325), Swift continues, the Bible took final form. Of the 163 original candidates for admission to sacred canon, only 66 books were selected, and 2 of these—the Song of Solomon and the Book of Esther—are spurious according to Identity preachers. Both are supposedly written derivatives of the sexual and cannibal cults of the Canaanites. At the same time the "authentic" books of Enoch, Esdras, Seth, and Abraham were eliminated by the Council because of "Jewish" subversion.

Finding their goal of world conquest through the Church continually frustrated, "Jewish" elders held a secret meeting in Venice late in the twelfth century during which it was decided to use Mongol horsemen to further their aims. An emissary was sent to Genghis Khan allegedly promising Jewish provision of arms in exchange for his obeisance to Jewry. The subsequent Mongolian invasion was barely staved off by the heroic resistance of the Christian West.

We are fortunate, the story goes, that unlike the Venetian assembly, the strategy for the culminating step in the Jewish conspiracy was committed to writing during the first Zionist congress held at Basel, Switzerland, in 1897. There, under the leadership of Theodor Herzl, the Jewish Sanhedrin and its Freemason allies are said to have composed the legendary *Protocols of the Learned Elders of Zion*.[15] (In point of fact the Great Sanhedrin, the highest political magistracy of Judaism, ceased to exist when the Jewish state perished in A.D. 70, the religious Sanhedrin about 250 years later. The last meeting of the French Sanhedrin was called by Napoleon I in 1807. It was quickly dissolved after the emperor was accused of being the anti-Christ. There is no documented record of the Sanhedrin and Freemasonry ever meeting. Evidently, the fantasy of their collaboration was first concocted by a notorious French anti-Semitic Jesuit priest around 1820.)

The *Protocols* were passed to me under an unmarked cover during an interview conducted in the back room of a Pocatello warehouse after interrogation evidently indicated that I was a reliable reporter. "It's all here," I was told. Indeed it was. The twenty-four sections of the document detail the steps presumably to be undertaken in establishing Communist-Jewish rule in America: Establish corporate monopolies (protocol 6); conduct arms races and instigate wars between Christian nations (7); infiltrate the legal profession and advocate civil rights for minorities and foment disputes among Christians by the use of lawsuits (8 and 17); institute public education and brainwash the children with the watchwords "liberty, equality, and fraternity" (9); introduce universal suffrage for the propertyless, women, and minorities (10); stage "revolutions" (10); gain control of the major media and create simulated opposition newspapers to give the citizenry the impression of free speech (11); distract the population with elaborate sports festivals, amusements, and recreations, most importantly pornography and free love (13 and 14); destroy the classical tradition in the universities, especially the teaching of Christian racial history (16); employ agents provocateurs and secret police to infiltrate opposition groups (18 and 19); and (protocol 20) "the crowning and decisive point of our plans": Implement progressive income taxes, sales taxes, and confiscatory inheritance taxes. Expand easy credit and then strategically withdraw it, creating economic crises. Use subsequent foreclosure proceedings to seize private property. Rid monetary policy of the gold standard, replace gold with paper currency, and establish a national, privately controlled, bank.

We shall replace the money markets by grandiose government credit institutions the object of which will be to fix the price of industrial values in accordance with government views. These institutions will be in a position to fling upon the market five hundred millions of industrial paper in one day, or to buy up the same amount. In this way all industrial undertakings will come into dependence upon us. . . .[16]

The Banking Conspiracy

The significance of this last protocol for Identity Christians can hardly be exaggerated. The creation in 1913 of the Federal Reserve Corporation, they believe, took the power of monetary policy from Congress and placed it in private hands, violating the first article of the Constitution. The government would now buy credit from the Federal Reserve Bank in exchange for U.S. bonds plus interest, and collateral such as public lands and control over government policy. Like all banks, the Federal Reserve would encourage the government to take out loans. The trillion dollar U.S. government debt in 1984 is considered simply a precursor to total control of America by the international bankers.

The establishment of an International Monetary Fund and the introduction of magnetized credit cards to replace checks and paper (which have already replaced gold and silver) are the final steps in "Satan's Plan." Now when an individual shops he will show his account number which will electronically debit his account at the local commuter bank. This is in fulfillment of Scripture: "And he [Satan] causeth all, both small and great, rich and poor, free and bond, to receive a mark in their right hand, or in their forehead [these are said to be figurative forecasts of the credit card]: and no man might buy or sell, save he that has the mark, or the name of the beast [i.e., of the bank], or the number of his name [666]" (Rev. 13:15–18).

Identity followers believe that every retail outlet and service counter eventually will be equipped with computer terminals, which will be connected to a national information storage and retrieval center. To purchase an airline or bus ticket, fishing line, or potatoes, the consumer will be required to show his credit card number, which for convenience will be his Social Security number. This will be flashed to the national mainframe computer, together with the location and time of the purchase, permitting surveillance of the entire population. Such an internal passport system is the ultimate goal of banker-controlled totalistic government.[17]

As for the background of the international bankers, Identity preachers like Sheldon Emry, who before his death in 1984 enjoyed a wide following in Idaho, is emphatic: "Most of the owners of the largest banks in America are of Eastern European [Jewish] ancestry and connected with the [Jewish] Rothschild European banks."[18] While Emry cites no references to support this contention, we may assume that he is relying on standard movement sources such as Gary Allen's *None Dare Call It Conspiracy*.

The attraction of Emry's pamphlets to Idaho patriots can be understood in part by the radical nature of his proposals to end America's debt crisis. The commandments of Exodus 22:21–22, Leviticus 25:35–37, and Deuteronomy 23:19–20 explicitly condemn usury, the taking of interest on loans, as a subtle and pernicious form of theft and hence a sin against both charity and justice. It is a sin Emry solemnly reminds the reader, punishable by death. If our nation is to avoid divine destruction, an end must be made of interest-taking and therefore of banking as we know it.[19] Concerning the billions of dollars in debts already incurred by American farmers and home owners, Emry proposes the reinstitution of the Sabbath and Jubilee years (respectively, Deuteronomy 15:1–4 and Leviticus 25:8–10); all debts would be cancelled every seventh year and all properties lost to creditors would be returned every forty-nine years:[20] "This is what can, what must, and what will be done in America."

Emry evinces little concern about the consequences of these suggestions on the nation's financial system. The "cataclysm" lying if they are not implemented, he warns, is far worse. All they entail are the "immediate nationalization" of all lending institutions, the cancellation of all debts, the declaration that Federal Reserve money is null and void, and the return of money issuance and extension of interest-free credit to Congress. "It is the wicked who will suffer" through these actions, "not the righteous." Knowing this, the wicked will naturally ridicule these proposals as subversive and harass their advocates. In 1863 "an agent of the Rothschild bank" murdered Abraham Lincoln when he sought to introduce interest-free credit practices. The capitalist and communist world, "under the heel" of these same bankers, declared war on Germany because in 1935 it began issuing debt-free, interest-free money.[21] The entire hidden "cons-PIRACY" in politics, religion, education, and entertainment is "working for a banker-owned United States in a banker-owned world under a banker-owned world government!"[22]

Sons of Light—Sons of Darkness

I have put the word "Jew" in quotation marks because, although it is a key term in Identity rhetoric, it has no definite meaning. This very ambiguity threatens to rend the Identity community into hostile sects.

At least seven distinct references for "Jew" can be discerned in Identity literature: "Jew" as a follower of God the Father, Jehuda (Jeho-

vah), the definition used by Idaho's Yahweh Believers; "Jew" as a figurative symbol of evil without reference to any single ethnic or racial
group (as in the phrase, "He really 'jewed' me"); "Jew" as a shorthand
corruption of the Greek word "Ioudean," meaning a resident of ancient Judea who could have confessed to any one of a number of
religious beliefs, including Judaism; "Jew" as an adherent of a specific
world religion which counts among its holy books the Talmud; "Jew"
as a corruption of the word "Judah," meaning a member of that specific tribe; and "Jew" as a particular and, as it happens, inferior race
or species of human being.

These distinctions are esssential to a grasp of Identity beliefs, although the terms can overlap semantically. Thus Yahweh Believers
emphatically deny that they hate Jews; that would be tantamount to
self-hatred. However, they are wary of "pseudo-Jews" who attend synagogue services. Likewise, a handful of Identity adherents with northern German ancestry hold the authentic "Jew" to be descendant of an
Aryan people today known as the Jutes, themselves presumably derived from a remnant of Judah. These believers too would deny having anti-Jewish attitudes. Lastly, even assuming the "Jews" are not
history's Jutes, then as members of the House of Judah they may still
be considered bonafide sharers in the covenant with Yahweh, although they represent only a 12th or 13th part of the chosen people.
This is the traditional position of British Israelism.[23] To British Israelites, Jews are said to be inheritors of the scepter of world rule, and
it is from their line that Jesus Christ, the world savior, shall come.[24]
It is a grave mistake to uncritically group advocates such as these with
the violently anti-Jewish rhetoricians of sects like Aryan Nations.

The object of loathing for a typical member of the Aryan Nations
Church is one who, regardless of his religious faith, descends from
Cain and is thus born of Satan. This is the "real," the racial, Jew. Non-
racist Identity Christians reject this view. Included in their number are
pastor John Woods' Gospel of Christ Kingdom Church, which split
from the Aryan Nations Church in the early 1980s and now has a
separate congregation in Hayden Lake; Missourian Dan Gayman's
Church of Israel, which has a sizable Idaho mission; and Karl Schott's
Spokane-based Christ's Gospel Fellowship. To these pastors the Jew
is simply a person who confesses to what they suspect is a satanic
religious creed: Judaism. Although Jews in this sense may be rebuked
for their blindness, stubbornness, and immorality, they are not spoken

of as being genetically condemned by the Lord. Indeed, according to Gayman, being counted among God's creatures the Jews may be considered "very good."[25]

Another of these non-racist pastors has gone so far as to advise his church that for all practical purposes a person's racial identity is irrelevant to his being saved. What *is* essential is the cultivation of a "personal relationship with Christ." As one of his congregants, an Idaho follower of Lyndon LaRouche, told me, "My identity is less important than my salvation. Butler's position is idiotic."[26] In saying this he evinces familiarity with J. H. Allen's classic Identity text, which devotes an entire chapter to the question of race versus grace.

There is, says Allen, an elected race, the seed of Jacob, with a mission and destiny prophesied in Scripture. But if it is a question of personal election to the grace of salvation, then all men are called. "Whosoever will, may come and take the water of life freely." The duty of the elected race, the Lord's "servant people," is to evangelize this very promise to all the world. "This is the great purpose for which the Lord has chosen Israel, and when this is accomplished, they shall have reached the acme of national glory."[27]

Having distinguished between racist and non-racist Identity, it is important not to overlook the permeability of the boundary between them. Gordon "Jack" Mohr, a widely read and much-admired Identity lay preacher who co-founded the Christian Patriot Defense League, illustrates this in his 1982 pamphlet "Know Your Enemies."[28]

At the outset of his discussion Mohr ridicules the suggestion that Jews constitute a race of people, citing UNESCO literature and research by recognized Jewish anthropologists to bolster his claim. On the contrary, he says, quoting Alfred Lilienthal, " 'Jews are a people who acknowledge the Jewish religion. They are of all races, even Negro and Mongolian. . . .' So much for the myth that the Jews are a race. It just isn't so!"[29]

Not only is the Jew a religious confessor, Judaism is a faith with a past distinct from Christianity. "Raised in a zealous Baptist family" in which he had been taught that Christianity and Judaism were essentially alike, that the Jews were and are a chosen race, and "Jew" and "Israelite" are equivalent terms, Mohr relates his surprise at these discoveries. It is a revelation frequently heard from Identity Christians. It is the basis of their bitterness toward fundamentalist preachers like Jerry Falwell who, they believe, "lie" to their people.

Using standard Biblical references, Mohr reminds the reader that while Moses, David, Solomon, and Samson were all Israelites, they were not Jews in the sense of being adherents of a specific world faith. After all, the word "Jew" does not even appear in Biblical histories until II Kings 16:6, at least two centuries after the Israelites' deaths, and then in the context of the phrase "men of Judah" who were at war with Israel. Mohr points out that by 975 B.C., the nation of Israel had split into two kingdoms: the "men of Judah" consisting of the tribes of Judah, Levi, and Benjamin in the south, with their capital in Jerusalem, and the other ten tribes comprising the northern kingdom, ruled from Samaria.

From 740 to 712 B.C. the tribes of the northern kingdom were systematically captured by Assyria and their populations resettled in northwestern Iran, Armenia, and the region near Baku. The southern kingdom was captured by the Babylonians about a century and a half later, its people forcibly removed to what is now southern Iraq, near Baghdad. It was there that Levitical priests composed the original Jewish Talmud, a blending, according to Mohr, of the old Hebrew faith of the Torah "with the heathen Baal worship of Babylon, replete with its devil worship. . . ."[30] When the Persian emperor conquered the Babylonians about seventy years later, 42,000 of the Talmud worshippers under Ezra returned to Judea. Mohr quotes the ancient historian Flavius Josephus as saying these were "the lowest of the low," people who had intermarried with the Edomites and taken on their dark features while in captivity. These are the world's prototypical "Judahites" or "Jews," according to Mohr. The balance of the liberated men of Judah, "fair and tall, the cream of the Aryan race," dispersed, some becoming the ancient Jutes of northern Germany. As for the 42,000 who resided in and about Jerusalem, in A.D. 70 the Roman imperial army, beating back a messianic revolt, destroyed the temple, killed the priests, and scattered the remnants of the population, "fulfilling God's promise" that they were to be destroyed as a nation.

Ignoring the claim concerning the origin of the Jutes and his barely veiled hostility concerning the Jewish religion, to this point Mohr's argument pretty much follows academic orthodoxy. But the emphasis in his pamphlet now shifts dramatically, contradicting his earlier assertions. The Jew is now said to be a distinct racial group "with a special facial characteristic . . . sometimes . . . called the Jewish look."[31] Mohr writes that Jewish character is also inherited and that Jews therefore cannot become authentic Christians through conversion. He recounts his personal experience of Jewish conversions in which they almost immediately become totally immersed in the business of the church; they will attempt to get on as many committees as possible; they will attend every meeting, many times with a tape recorder. You may say: "This is because Jewish converts are more sincere than others. . . ." But I know they are taught to infiltrate the Christian church for the purpose of destroying it.[32]

"You may know nice Jews. I have known some too," Mohr admits. "But even the so-called nice Jew" cannot divorce himself from 2,500 years of legacy and "when the chips are down I imagine most of them would react as Jews."[33] What, then, is the essence of Jewish character? They are, proclaims Mohr, "parasites and vultures," infected with "moral gonorrhea." They believe others are "cattle" fit only for use as animals.[34] Quoting from Father Justin Bonaventura Pranaitis's *The Talmud Unmasked*, considered fraudulent in Jewish circles, Mohr reiterates the ancient indictment: They commit "terrible pollutions at their secret gatherings."[35] "They murdered the Son of God. (Yes the proper word to use here is Murdered!)."[36] They "curse Christ and his followers on a daily basis in regular prayers" as bastards.[37]

This is not, technically speaking, full-blown racism which uses hackneyed genetic metaphors to "explain" character differences. But it is a form of religious bigotry with which much of Identity Christianity is intimately acquainted. Even Pastor Gayman's reading list in the Church of Israel Missionary and Literature Room contains a standard catalogue of anti-Jewish tracts: F. P. Yockey's *Imperium;* D. Felder's *Anne Frank's Diary: A Hoax;* F. L. Britton's *Behind Communism;* A. Butz's *Hoax of the Twentieth Century,* containing the "truth about the 6,000,000" allegedly killed by the Nazis; Henry Ford's *International Jew,* a best-seller in Nazi Germany; *The Protocols;* Jack Mohr's *Satan's Kids;* Elizabeth Dilling's *The Plot Against Christianity;* and the Pranaitis *Talmud.*[38]

As Mohr continues, he moves from bigotry to racism: It is not simply that Jews are taught immorality through the Talmud. This, after all, could be rectified by counter instruction. Rather, the Jew is *born* evil. This is "confirmed" by apostle John's accusation attributed to Jesus that "Ye are of your father the devil."[39] "It is a proven fact that Talmudism is Satan worship."[40] And "what makes you believe that a 'child of Satan, the murderer' would hesitate in killing a Christian baby?"[41] They are the world's "seducers, executioners, destroyers and incendaries" who are under obligation to Satan to "ruin the people among whom they sojourn."[42]

Beyond even Mohr's tirade, pure racist Identity is exemplified by

Jarah Crawford, a Middlebury, Vermont, Assembly of God minister, whose *Last Battle Cry* was mentioned in the previous chapter.

Crawford writes of how he struggled for years to integrate the Gospel of John—particularly chapters 8 and 10 where Jesus berates the Jews for not being of God—with what he had learned from the pulpit as a child, namely, that all men were created equal. At 6:30 in the morning of October 8, 1975, he was jarred awake by the realization that all men are not created in God's image and likeness, but that the Jews are "Satan's children." Thus began Crawford's excursion into the world of Identity, culminating in his 597-page exegesis of the Bible from a racist viewpoint.

"The Christian and secular humanists must establish that we all come from one beginning, one man," Crawford asserts. "Upon this rest all their humanistic views." This is why they castigate as anathema any suggestion of a "pre-Adamic man."[43] But in point of fact, says Crawford, a close, literal reading of Genesis reveals that there was not just one creation of man, but two. In Genesis 1:26–27 God creates man in His image and likeness, "male and female he created them." In Genesis 2:2–6, however, God sculpts a male figure from the dust, breathes into his nostrils, and names him Adam. From Adam's rib God then fashions for him a helpmate, the woman Eve (2:21–23). This, says Crawford, is not merely a "second account," but the creation of a separate race of human beings.[44] Adam is distinct from and subsequent to the man created in chapter 1. And it is to the latter's children that Cain will go when he takes a wife in Genesis 4:16–17. As for Adam, he is *ish,* "high man" (Hebrew), his wife *ishshah* (2:23). That they are ancestors of the Caucasian race exclusively is "proven" by reference to Strong's Exhaustive Concordance to the Holy Bible and its definition of the word "Adam": *Aw-Dam*—"to show blood in the face, flush or turn rosey. Be dyed, made red (ruddy)." The Garden of Eden is said in Genesis to have been at the confluence of four rivers. According to Crawford, this can only mean the Pamir Plateau of Central Asia between the Hindu Kush and the Tian Shan mountains. This is the "gate of the Universe" from which the Aryans dispersed themselves throughout the western world.

Genesis goes on. The "man," we are told, had relations with Eve and she gave birth to Cain and then to Abel. While it may appear that the man referred to here can be none other than Adam, Crawford reads between the lines to discover that it was not Adam who introduced Eve to sexual intercourse, but Satan himself. This is indicated by Genesis 3:13 when God asks Eve to account for her transgression of His commandment not to eat fruit of the tree of knowledge. She replies, "The serpent deceived me. . . ." According to Strong's Concordance, the Hebrew equivalent to "deceive" is *nasha,* which means, among other things, "to seduce." "While the evidence is circumstantial, we are led to believe that Satan seduced Eve, Eve then introduced sexual intercourse to Adam."[45] The progeny of these respective couplings are Cain and Abel. "Cain was of the evil one!" Crawford writes. Satan had seduced Eve and impregnated her with his "evil seed."[46] This "explains" John's assertion attributed to Jesus that "Cain, who was of the evil one . . . slew his brother" (3:11–12). Following this crime he was cast into the land of Nod to the east of Eden, where he married a pre-Adamic woman. His seed are the "sons of Satan" who through various "adulterous" matings would become the Jews.[47]

We cannot hope to detail Crawford's entire argument. To get a feeling for racist Identity it will be sufficient to reconstruct his exegesis of several of Jesus' best-known parables. While these parables are used by liberal theologians to substantiate Christian universalism, to Crawford they are ammunition in the racist arsenal. For example, the parable of the seeds in Matthew 13:24–30 is not a spiritual allegory. The "good seed" and "bad seed" to which the story refers are exactly that. "The good seed sown by the Son of Man are the true children of God." They will flourish and multiply. "The bad seed sown by the devil are not the creations of God."[48] Consider too the parable in which Jesus compares the kingdom of heaven to a dragnet, gathering fish of every kind. The good fish are gathered into containers; the bad are thrown away (Matt. 13:47–50). This, says Crawford, is not a moral lesson: "Do figs and fish have bad morals?" On the contrary, these are racial parables. "Jesus was not a humanist." He did not believe that if all people were given equal opportunities, they would turn out alike.[49] Jesus was a racist who believed some men are born evil, others good. Some are "pure blooded Adamic men," others fornicating Jews. "What God created was good. Therefore Jews could not be God's creation."[50]

The fifteenth chapter of Matthew, verses 21 through 28, tells the story of a Canaanite woman who approaches Jesus and pleads with him to exorcise her daughter of a demon. At first Jesus ignores her, and his disciples urge the crowd to "send her away." "Lord help me!" she cries again. But Jesus rebukes her, saying it is not right to take children's bread and throw it to dogs. In a last gesture of humility, the Canaanite accepts the degrading label. "Let me therefore have not the bread, but only crumbs; and do not give me even them but let me pick up what falls from the table." Jesus commends the mother's faith and grants her wish. Crawford concludes that the mother was aided by the Lord only because "she admitted she was a dog," not an Israelite. She is not of God, and appropriately Jesus grants her only a crumb of grace. This teaches that not only should the sons of light proclaim their identity, but "it is equally important for those who are products of sin and Satan to know who they are. . . . Instead of demanding civil rights, equal rights, love, and equality, if these polluted human beings would recognize who and what they are . . . they could find the same compassion as the Canaanite woman found."[51] For God is just. Even those who are racially tainted can be admitted to the kingdom of God, "not as heirs in the family of God, but as servants. . . ."[52]

Contrary to the teachings of more benign Identity adherents, Crawford teaches that salvation is not simply an issue of who believes or who does not, who does good work and who does not, who gives good witness and who does not. Rather, in a sense that reminds us of Calvin's electoral predestinationism, only those with white skins are born to salvation. Others are born to condemnation. Of course, Chinese, Negroes, even Jews can become Christians but they are relegated to the visible church. The invisible church is limited to the white descendants of Adam. "But we must remember that they [nonwhites and Jews] are not from the seed of Abraham. They will not share the inheritance of Israel. What they will share is their rightful place in the kingdom." They will be allowed within the gates of the heavenly Jerusalem, but not into the temple, into the outer court, but not the inner.[53]

"God so loved the world, that He gave His only begotten Son, that whoever believes in Him should not perish, but have eternal life" (John 3:16). "Let us not be deceived," warns Crawford, "by the universal application here." This is a promise of eternal life, but it says nothing about "in the heavenly temple of the Lord." There is no promise of equal rewards after death for heathen converts.[54]

Crawford knows that orthodox theologians will reject this ecclesiology by insisting that lest one is "reborn in Christ," one cannot see the kingdom of God (John 3:3). Crawford agrees with John, but gives his admonition a racial turn. What this passage means, he argues, is that to be saved one must be begotten by God in heaven. In other words, one must be generated in the spirit of God, be of the Adamic race "before the foundation of the world," before he can be saved. This is emphatically not the same as the "born again" experience of the evangelicals.[55] "No one can come to Me, unless it has been granted him from the Father" (John 6:65; 6:44). "Unless one is [literally] born from above" there is no salvation. "This," Crawford concludes, "is very much a family affair!!!"[56]

ISRAEL IDENTIFIED

God gave His only begotten son for the salvation of His sheep, Israel. But who is Israel? The answer to this lies at the very heart of Identity doctrine. Orthodox Christianity teaches that while the Old Testament is concerned with a single nation, the New Testament is indiscriminate in its promises. But many Identity ministers dispute this, quoting for support Luke 1:68–71: "Blessed is the Lord God of *Israel;* for He hath . . . redeemed His people, and hath raised up a horn of salvation for us in the house of His servant David."

"We, Isaac's sons," proclaims Wesley Swift, "the Saxons are Israel." The Bible is "our history," God's promises "ours." Nor is it fair, he adds, to accuse him or his followers of anti-Semitism, for they and they alone are the true descendants of Shem. The Semites "today are the great White Christian nations of the western world."[57]

The genealogy in Table 4.1, reconstructed from Pastor Bertrand Comparet's sermons, indicates that Jews are neither Semites nor Israelites, but Canaanites. "Israel," the name given Jacob after his nocturnal struggle with the angel at Peniel (Genesis 32:26–32), had twelve sons by four women, these becoming the legendary twelve (or thirteen, if the twins Ephraim and Manasseh are substituted for their father, Joseph) tribes of Israel.

Israel, his twelve sons, and their families sojourned in Egypt for 250 years, their offspring leaving in Exodus under Moses. The unified nation was originally ruled by Judges, its first king being Saul of Benjamin, followed by David. The reign of the Davids persisted until 975 B.C. when, under the military prophet Jeroboam of Ephraim, the ten tribes of the northern kingdom revolted and seceded from the south. King Rehoboam, son of Solomon, was left in the south with Benjamin, Judah, and a handful of priestly Levites. After Assyria conquered the northern kingdom, which for practical purposes may now be called

"Israel," its people were lost to biblical record. The subsequent fate of the Judahites of the southern kingdom has been recounted above.

It is at this point that Anglo-Israelite historians introduce their innovative account of the ten lost tribes. For miraculously, as they tell it, the lost have been found. The apocryphal book II Esdras 13:39– 46 tells of Israel's journey over the Caucasus mountains, along the northern shore of the Black Sea, to the valley of the Ar Sereth, a tributary of the Danube in Romania. This migration is supposedly confirmed by obscure passages in the prophecies of Micah and Isaiah. Their presence in the area is also said to be testified to by the place names left behind by Israel's leading tribe, Dan: Macedonia (presumably a corruption of Moeshe [the land of Moses]-*don*-ia), *Dan*-ube, *Dn*-eister, *Dn*-eiper, *Don*-etz, *Dan*-zig, and *Don,* etc. (In ancient Hebrew there are no written vowels. In the word "Dan," for example, there are only two letters used, which are equivalent to D and N. Hence, it is irrelevant if the word is Dan, Don, Dun, Din, or Den. All are equivalent to D-N, in which the speaker sounds the vowel according to his own dialect.)[58] The tribes would flourish, split, and settle in various European countries, many of whose names today bear witness to their original colonists: *Dan*-mark, *Jut*-land (Judah), Svea-*dan,* Scan-*din*-avia, and *Got*-land (Gad).[59]

Having settled in the lands of northern Europe, Israel became legitimate heir of the ancient Davidic sceptre of authority. The story goes like this: When the last Davidic king of the southern kingdom, Zedekiah, was taken into Babylonian captivity and his sons killed (589 B.C.), his cousin, the prophet Jeremiah, stole his two daughters to Egypt along with the coronation stone from Solomon's temple. Jeremiah then sent them by ship to Spain and later to Ireland. The first daughter, Tamar Tephi (Tea Tephi), was married at Ulster to one Eochaidh (Herremon), an Irish king, who himself was a distant descendant of Zerah, one of the twin sons of Judah (see Table 4.2). Jeremiah made this marriage conditional upon a promise from the king to put an end to serpent worship, and to establish a college of prophets at Tara (Torah = the Law).[60]

Thus the execution of Zedekiah's sons did not put an end to the Davidic dynasty. According to biblical law, when a man dies leaving no sons, his daughters become heirs to the estate. The Davidic line, and hence the divine right to rule the earth until the Second Coming of Christ can, to the satisfaction of Anglo-Israelites, be traced in the

Table 4.1
Genealogy of Israel Based on Identity Doctrine

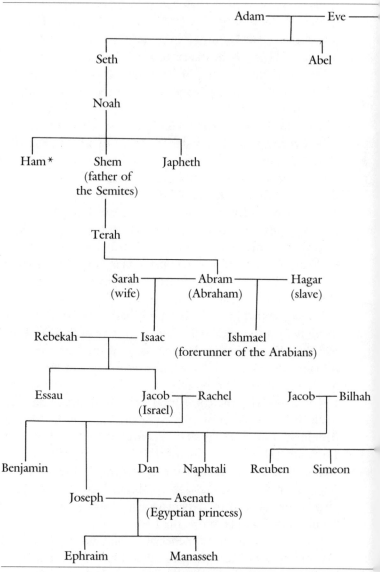

*Based on Genesis 9:18–28, Ham, not Cain, is patriarch of the Canaanites.

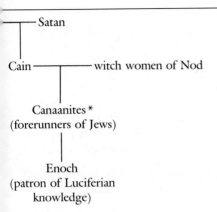

Satan

Cain ——— witch women of Nod

Canaanites *
(forerunners of Jews)

Enoch
(patron of Luciferian
knowledge)

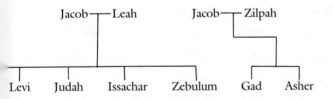

Jacob—Leah   Jacob—Zilpah

Levi   Judah   Issachar   Zebulum   Gad   Asher

Table 4.2
Genealogy of the House of David

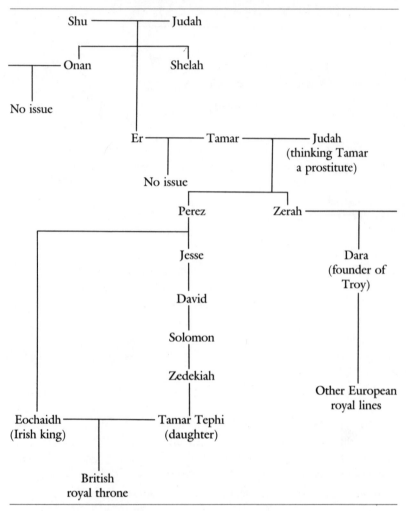

royal histories of Ireland, Scotland, and England, down to Queen Elizabeth today.[61] Solomon's coronation stone, it is said, now sits under the imperial throne in Westminster Abbey in London. The stone is supposed to be the pillow upon which Jacob rested his head just prior to his being named Israel. And it is the same rock which Moses smote in the desert to provide the thirsting nation lifesaving waters before its entry into the promised land.

5

IDENTITY CHRISTIANITY PROVEN

How do believers come to accept and sustain the tenets of Identity Christianity outlined in Chapter 4?

A basic proposition in the sociology of knowledge is that people are convinced of a reality by virtue of incorrigible truths held independent of their own subjective experience.[1] Even the veracity of direct experience is subject to the biases of fatigue, stress, fear, overattachment, and preconception. For this reason, human beings instinctively rely on things outside themselves to help them discern what is real. Included in the body of incorrigible truths may be standards of logic and reasoning, pronouncements by authoritative individuals (especially parents and teachers), and collections of previously certified facts.

For Identity believers, the preeminent incorrigible truth is the Word of God, as literally read in the King James Bible, together with biblical apocrypha deemed valid. To believers, the Word alone is eternal, indubitable, unerring, and entirely self-consistent. From the Bible the Identity Christian receives his cosmic dualism: the distinction between the House of Judah and the Kingdom of Israel, between Adamic man and pre-Adamic man, between the sons of light and the sons of darkness, the attribution of diabolism to "Jews," and the genealogies supporting the Anglo-Saxon's Israelitish identity. From the Bible are taken the strictures on racial purity and the teachings regarding Israel's superiority to other nations of the earth. Here too are found Identity's phobia of the moneylender, Identity's sexual puritanism, and in the extreme cases where these are followed, its food proscriptions, its advocacy of polygamy, and its admonitions that sodomites, disobedient children, and usurers be placed under the ban. Finally, from the Bible is appropriated the doctrine of military holocaust of God's enemies, the violent ritual of *herem*.

That this reading may be scripturally unsound, as asserted by orthodox theologians, is beside the point. Abstract sacred literature is invariably subject to multiple interpretations. Identity Christians defend their position with three types of "proofs," which may on further examination be seen as addressing three different kinds of audiences: primary proofs, relying exclusively on God's Word (all the claims itemized above); secondary proofs, employing the Word of God together with readings of recent history in light of prophecy (God's promises to Israel, Jacob's blessings to his sons, and astrological retrodictions of Israel's migrations); and tertiary proofs, using secular sources with only minor resort to God's Word (numerology, pyramidology, philology, and probability theory).

These proofs do not necessarily meet the standards of deductive or inductive logic. Rather, they suffice to convince those already committed by faith to the Identity message. For all practical purposes, Identity Christianity is unassailable, untestable in the scientific sense of the word. In principle, virtually anything can be taken as lending credence to it. The seeming hopelessness of the struggle, the money sacrificed for the cause, the lives lost, the jail sentences incurred, the repudiation by the mass media and the public all "prove" to believers that what they preach is undeniably true. That the odds are virtually insurmountable demonstrates the satanic nature of the opponent. That the conspiracies are so intimate a part of what ordinary Americans think is commendable—equality, democracy, peace, and interracial brotherhood—is predictable. The ancient Israelites were also complacent. They also worshipped golden calves. That Anglo-Israelites are ridiculed and persecuted is to be expected. Christ Himself and all the prophets of history suffered similar fates at the hands of the "Jews." When Hal Hunt's prediction in the 1960s that Soviet troops stationed in Mexico were on the verge of occupying the soft American underbelly went unfulfilled, this had no discernible negative effect on his conspiratorial *Weltanschauung*. Indeed, the very failure of the forecast "proved" to Hunt the fiendishness of Communist espionage. Knowing that Hunt and other patriots knew of the impending incursion, and that the patriots would mount a spirited defense of their homeland, the Communists wisely called it off.

ETYMOLOGIES

Perhaps the most compelling literary tool used to substantiate Identity claims is etymology, the tracing of modern English words back to their supposed roots in the Hebraic language. I say "supposed," because the consensus of linguistic scholars is that Hebrew is a derivative of the Afro-Asiatic Semitic language subfamily which also includes

Arabic, Ethiopic, Amharic, and Aramaic languages. English is considered to be of the Germanic language subfamily, together with Danish, Dutch, Swedish, Yiddish, etc. The Germanic languages have Indo-Aryan parentage, not Semitic. Identity ministers, undaunted by the claims of philologists (many of whom are alleged to be "Jews" anyway), disagree. "English" itself, they insist, is a corrupted conjunction of several Hebrew terms, which translated mean literally "a stammering man" (*an* [one] + *gael* [stammer] + *ish* [man] = english).[2] (Academic linguists argue that "english" is from the Old English *angul* [angle, the shape of the original homeland of the Angles, the Angul district of Schleswig] and *isc* [having the nationality of].)

This critical observation aside, one cannot but admire the intricate connections that historians such as the Canadian British Israelite Frederick Haberman, American archaeologist E. Raymond Capt, and others have drawn between English and Hebrew. The most notable example is the argument that the word "British" is a conjunction of the two Hebraic words, *b'rith* (covenant) and *ish* (man). The British, Haberman says, are literally "covenant people"; Abraham was the first "Britisher."[3]

But the story is more complex than this. Haberman spends pages noting the structural parallels between the megalithic altars at Stonehenge, Avebury, Kenswick, and similar rock circles in Persia and Tibet. "Avebury," he says, comes from the Semitic word *abiri* (the Hebrews), the name allegedly given the Israelites by their neighbors.[4] (By the same token, Iberia [Spain] can be considered "land of the Hebrews," Cadiz the seaport of the tribe of Gad.)[5] Just how did the great Stonehenge and Avebury monuments come to be in England? A clue is found in the fact that the inner circle of Stonehenge has a circumference precisely equal to the Egyptian *aroura*, a unit of land measure. About 1700 B.C. when the Druidic circles were being constructed, the Israelites were dwelling in Egypt under the Eighteenth Pharoahnic Dynasty. Therefore, it follows that "the early Britons who built the gigantic structures . . . were either Hebrews themselves or progenitors of the Hebrews, as were also the builders of the Great Pyramid. . . ."[6]

According to Haberman the Hebrews, or their wisdom, were brought to England by the Phoenicians. The Phoenician water patroness was Barati, and from her name comes Britannia, of which she was mistress. She is also Fortuna in the Roman pantheon (F = B, *una* = one; hence Bort-one, or "the Barat ones"). Furthermore, since the *o* is dialectically like *w* or *u,* we can also derive Brut, the first legendary British king. Brutus of Troy in 1100 B.C. gave the land he occupied, present-day England, the name of his own race, Barat or Brit. The Brits are therefore not only the covenant people, they are the Fortunate Ones, the blessed people, and their land a promised land.[7]

In the Phoenician alphabet, x is pronounced "x at." This is the name of an ancient Phoenician clan, the Catti, from which the Israelite tribe of Gad came. "Scot" is a corruption of Gad. Andrew, the patron saint of Scotland, is a variation on the name of the Vedic god, Indra (as are Thor, the Gothic war god, and the Iranian emperor Darius). X is the symbol of the lightening bolt used by Indra in his fight against the evil dragon. Likewise, St. George, the English patron, is a corruption of the Old English *gar,* which is derived from the Phoenician *gura,* "gore." Finally, the legend of St. Michael is a Christianized rendition of the story of the Phoenix, the Phoenician totem (from the Egyptian *pa-hanok* or *pa-enoch;* Enoch was the legendary father of the Phoenicians).[8] All three of these British heroes, says Haberman, are mythological anticipations of the dying and resurrected Christ. The X of Gad, meanwhile, has become emblazoned on the Union Jack.

ASTROLOGY, BLESSINGS, AND NUMEROLOGY

"On earth as it is in heaven": so speaks the ancient truth. Since agricultural folk first lifted their eyes toward the heavens to discern in the positions of the planets the propitious time for planting, humans have discovered parallels between earthly events and astral signs. In the Middle East the notion emerged that earthly arrangements are but mimetic reiterations of heavenly movements. As there are 360 days in a solar year (ignoring the five major feast days), and 360 seconds to an hour, then so must 360 degrees encompass the horizon. As there are twelve major heavenly constellations, so there are twelve hours in one circulation of the clock, twelve thirty-day months in a year, and what concerns us here, twelve comprising the nation of Israel (ignoring the tribe of Levi).

Following the positions of the constellations, the Book of Numbers decrees Israel's array for camp and march. The respective signs of the zodiac become the heraldic totems of the tribes (see Table 5.1). To the north under the flying eagle (Scorpio) are Dan, Naphtali, and Asher; under the Bull in the west, Benjamin, Ephraim, and Manasseh; to the east the Lion of Judah, Issachar, and Zebulum; and under

Table 5.1
Legendary Camping Array for Ancient Israel, with Appropriate Astrological Banner
and Corresponding Modern Destination

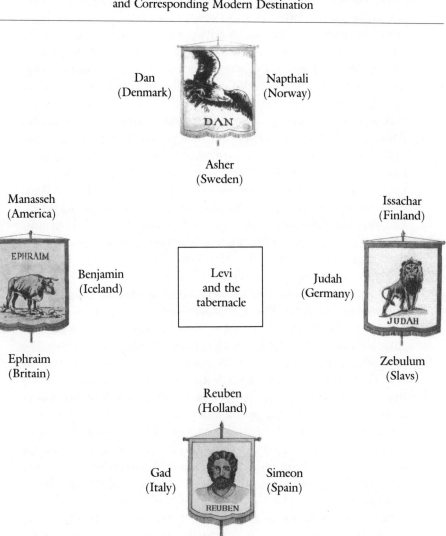

Dan
(Denmark)

Napthali
(Norway)

Asher
(Sweden)

Manasseh
(America)

Issachar
(Finland)

Benjamin
(Iceland)

Levi
and the
tabernacle

Judah
(Germany)

Ephraim
(Britain)

Zebulum
(Slavs)

Reuben
(Holland)

Gad
(Italy)

Simeon
(Spain)

Aquarius (the sign of man) to the south, Reuben, Gad, and Simeon. This is the kingdom of God on earth. It is the New Jerusalem upon which John in Revelation gazes, with Jesus Christ astride the throne of David.

This biblical array is used by Identity historians to approximate where it was the various tribes of Israel resettled in Europe after the Diaspora. Wisemen in each tribe, Identity preaches, carried with them the symbols of the race and knowledge of the ancient mystery schools: in eastern climes—Judah (Germany), Issachar (Finland), and Zebulum; in the west—Benjamin (the Vikings), Ephraim (England), and Manasseh (America); and so on.[9]

As to who will assume leadership of modern Israel, there is debate. Some hold that Judah in the form of a revived Germany will come from the east to save the Christian world from barbarism. This is implied in Jacob's blessing: "Judah, your brothers shall praise you . . . your father's sons shall do you homage" (Genesis 49:8–9). But since this does not entirely square with recent historical events, others claim that God transferred the sceptre to the "Islands of the Sea" (England), i.e., to Ephraim. This supposition is based on Jacob's blessing to his twin grandsons by Joseph. The elder, Manasseh, he placed on his right; Ephraim, the younger twin, on his left. But then over Joseph's objection he placed his right hand on Ephraim's head, prophesying his destiny was to be greater. Ephraim was to be "the company of nations" referred to by the prophets. "Now some think," says Wesley Swift, "that because we [the United States] have fifty states, that we are the company of nations. . . . But the symbol of the throne of David is . . . on Britain."[10] The problem with Swift's reasoning, of course, is that the United States is the "younger brother" of England. How, then, can it also be Manasseh (the elder) to England's Ephraim? "Doctor" Franklin Snook, whose work is published by the Lord's Covenant Church in Phoenix, overcomes this difficulty by positing that America is not merely the thirteenth tribe (Manasseh), but all thirteen tribes. America is the place prophesied for the regathering of the Last Days. Mormon theologians have adopted a nearly identical position.[11]

Jacob's blessings to his sons are frequently used to predict retrospectively the destiny of the thirteen tribes, and by this, their geographical locations. Benjamin is blessed as "a ravening wolf . . . devouring his prey in the morning and dividing the spoil at night." Therefore, this must refer to the Norsemen whose wolf totem was seen on their galley sails.[12] Issachar, says Jacob, is to be a "strong ass" who lies "between two staves." He likes to "take his ease" and will thus "become a slave to forced labor." But this can be none other than Finland, the prophecy referring to its position between Russia and Europe.[13] This conclusion is "confirmed" by President Mannerheim's alleged appeal to the Finns in World War II to resist the Soviet invaders of their country: "Men of Issachar, stand and die, that nothing but scorched earth cursed by God will fall into anti-Christ hands." Because of their perfidy, on the other hand, the Levites will be "scattered among Israel." According to Wesley Swift, the Levites are now Christian fundamentalist clergy who carry on and preach the covenant.[14]

Several of the blessings are so terse as to make definite predictions well-nigh impossible. Nonetheless, Identity preachers make the best of what little is provided. Gad, prophesies Jacob, will be robbed and himself become a thief. This seems to correspond to its supposed namesakes, the Goths. Therefore Gad must have migrated to Italy during the fall of the Roman Empire and become the Lombards, says Swift.[15] Simeon will be accursed for its ruthlessness. Therefore, perhaps they are the ancestors of the Spanish.[16] "Asher's bread is rich, he provides food fit for a king." These, therefore, must be the ancestors of today's tidy and prosperous Swedish farmers. And since Naphtali will "drop beautiful fawns," these became Norwegian hunters.[17] Jacob predicts that Zebulum will "be a sailor" living "by the shore of the sea" near Sidon on the eastern shore of the Mediterranean Sea. But this region is now populated by Arabs. Swift is therefore forced to relocate Zebulum several hundred miles northwest to the Black and Adriatic seas where they become Rumanians, Bulgarians, and Yugoslavs.[18]

A third data source used to triangulate the present-day locations of the twelve or thirteen tribes is numerology. Seven (the five planets visible to the naked eye plus the sun and the moon) multiplied by 360 = 2,520 years. This, we are told, is seven prophetic cycles. But 2,520 years added onto 576 B.C., the year when Benjamin was captured by Babylonia, is exactly 1945, the year Iceland became independent from Denmark. This is "conclusive evidence" that Iceland was the final stopping place of Benjamin.[19] That Manasseh is the United States is just as assuredly known. The House of Manasseh was captured by Assyria in 745 B.C. Precisely seven prophetic cycles from that date equals 1776, the year of the signing of the Declaration of Independence. "This proves our lineal descent from ancient Israel," Swift proclaims.[20]

And there are still other numerological signs of America's destiny.

Just as there were thirteen original tribes in the nation of Israel there were thirteen colonies. The word "American Eagle" has exactly thirteen letters, as does "E Pluribus Unum." In the great American seal, the eagle holds in its right claw an olive branch with thirteen leaves, in its left, thirteen arrows. The ensign on its breast has thirteen stripes, and the crest over its head thirteen stars. On the reverse side of the seal is pictured a pyramid over-watched by the all-seeing eye of God. The pyramid consists of thirteen courses of stone. Above this in thirteen letters are the words "Annuit Coeptis." Is this merely coincidental? Hardly. According to Snook, these signs mean nothing less than that America must be the final gathering place of Israel, co-inheritor with its "younger brother," Ephraim, of Jacob's estate.[21]

America is the New Jerusalem, the Novus Ordo Seclorum (the New Secular Order). After all, its birthday, "July the Fourth," contains thirteen letters, and its first navy had thirteen ships. Even the Confederate flag had thirteen stars although there were but eleven states in the Confederacy. Fort Sumter was fired upon on the thirteenth day, and Admiral Dewey took Manila on the thirteenth. "Woodrow Wilson," the name of the President who led America in its new role as world patron, has thirteen letters. The American Expeditionary Force he debarked to Europe to Save the World for Democracy sailed in thirteen ships, took thirteen days to cross the Atlantic, and fought its first major engagement on Friday the thirteenth. Its commander, John J. Pershing, has thirteen letters in his name. The evidence is "absolutely overwhelming."[22]

PROMISES AND PREDICTIONS

The proofs gathered to support the claims of Identity faithful are not limited to convoluted readings of Jacob's blessings, to numerology and astrology, or even to tracing archaeological and philological fingerprints. There are in addition the over 100 promises made to Israel in the Bible for upholding the covenant. Bertrand Comparet poses the issue as a Kierkegaardian wager: all or nothing. "So these are the promises of God: If they are false, then the Bible is false. But if they have been fulfilled, then the people to whom they were fulfilled are thereby identified as Israel."[23] Among the five-score promises are these:

> Israel shall have a change of name.
> Israel shall become a great nation and company of nations.
> Israel shall become blind to its identity.

Israel shall receive the new covenant—Christianity.
Israel shall be a maritime people.
Israel shall be the world's greatest military power.
Israel shall possess the gates of her enemies.
Israel shall possess the desolate heritages.
Israel shall have colonies in all directions.
Israel shall maintain the continuity of the throne of David.

Since presumably only the Anglo-Saxon peoples have fulfilled all of these promises, then only they could conceivably be God's chosen people. Indeed, Comparet has even determined that the probability of one nation fulfilling all 100 promises if due to chance alone is $1/100^{100}$. "Do you think that this could have happened by mere accident?" Of course not. "They have come to pass; and they have all been made good to the same racial group of nations."[24]

This kind of tautological reasoning—How do we know we are chosen? Because we are favored. How do we know we are favored? Because we are chosen—is the sort of analysis used by inhabitants of any self-constructed world to demonstrate its veracity. More to the point, it permits us to understand the vehemence with which Identity believers defend Western imperialism and military expansionism. If such aggressive policies are not undertaken, then this would indicate that perhaps God has not favored the Anglo-Saxons after all. Furthermore, it gives us insight into the rabidly conservative moral outlook of Identity Christianity. God is obligated to fulfill His part of the covenant only if Israel remains faithful to its part. This requires strict adherence to the political, economic, ritual, sexual, and in extreme cases, the culinary proscriptions laid down in the Pentateuch. If, as it now appears, white America is no longer blessed, there is a good reason for this. America has failed its obligations as servant people to the Lord.

6

CHRISTIAN CONSTITUTIONALISM AND MORMONISM

Brethren and sisters, our friends wish to know our true feelings towards the Government. I answer, they are first rate, and we will attempt to prove it too, as you will see if you only live long enough, for that we shall prove it true is certain; and when the Constitution of the United States hangs, as it were, upon a single thread, they will have to call for the "Mormon" elders to save it from utter destruction; and they will step forth and do it.[1]

Delivered by President Brigham Young in February 1855 in the Tabernacle at Salt Lake City, Utah, these words convey in a nutshell the traditional position of the Church of Jesus Christ of Latter-day Saints (Mormon) regarding the sanctity of the United States Constitution. This chapter shall examine this doctrine in detail, showing how it has been used by some Idaho patriots to promote a particular brand of righteous politics, Christian Constitutionalism. Its second object will be to elucidate the differences between this style of right-wing radicalism and Identity Christianity regarding the so-called "Jewish question."

The associations examined here between Mormonism and radical Constitutionalism are best understood as associations of meaning rather than as causal connections. Most Mormons, like most Idahoans, are generally indifferent if not openly antagonistic to "Mormonesque" patriotism. Whether this majority can be said to be "poor Mormons," as maintained by their fellow confessors who are patriots, is another question.

BIRCH AND CHURCH

In 1958 Robert Welch, a born-again Massachusetts candymaker, founded the John Birch Society. Its title memorializes a Baptist missionary to China who, it is said, was martyred for the cause of liberty by agents of the international Communist conspiracy. As described in its handbook, *The Blue Book*,[2] the John Birch Society is to be a nonpartisan, semisecret "educational" association, comprised of loyal patriots, organized in local chapters, whose actions are directed by a disciplined hierarchy of coordinators. Its object is to apprise freedom-loving citizens of the perils of Communist subversion and to help them mount campaigns against it.[3]

Whether or not allegations that Robert Welch modeled his recruitment strategy after the Russian Bolsheviks are accurate, there is clear evidence that the John Birch Society has attempted to penetrate groups considered amenable to its views.[4] These have included, among others, the Church of Christ Scientist and the Church of Jesus Christ of Latter-day Saints. Robert Welch admitted as much at a news conference in Salt Lake City held just prior to the annual Church convention in Spring 1966: "If we are looking for conservative, patriotic Americans of good character, humane consciences and religious ideals, where would you go looking for them any more hopefully than among the Latter-day Saints? The Latter-day Saints are as individuals the kind of people we would like to have in the John Birch Society."[5] This comment was made while Welch stood before a large portrait of then Church president, ninety-two-year-old David O. McKay.

Recruiting handbills distributed in the early 1960s at stake (neighborhood church) gatherings explicitly announced parallels between Mormon political theology and Birch goals. One asked the reader what the "immediate obligation" and "paramount duty" of each Church member is. The answer was given in the form of a quotation from an early member of the First Presidency of the Church, Orson Hyde, in 1858 (a variation on the epigram at the beginning of this chapter); an analogous assertion by McKay, "I repeat that no greater immediate responsibility rests upon members of the Church . . . than to protect the freedom vouchsafed by the Constitution of the United States"; and a statement from the *Ward Teaching Message* concerning the duties of freedom-loving patriots to resist Communism.[6]

Welch's public endorsement by Church apostle (now seer, "revelator," and prophet) Ezra Taft Benson during an appearance in Los Angeles in 1963 gave the impression that John Birch activities had received official Church sanction. "The John Birch Society," Benson was quoted as saying, "is the most effective non-church organization in our fight against creeping Socialism and Godless Communism."[7] (Although Benson was evidently never a dues-paying member of the society, his son, Reed, was at that time serving as its Utah coordinator.) When the story reached the newswires, a storm of protest arose, accusing the Church of meddling, perhaps at risk to its tax-exempt status, in politics. Birch and Church officials stumbled over each other attempting to contain the damage. First, the society's California district coordinator asserted that President McKay had given Benson his blessing to appear in Los Angeles. Later, the statement was modified to say that at least McKay had not denied Benson's request to speak. Meanwhile, Reed Benson bemuddled the issue by claiming that his father's endorsement "was not a political talk . . . [because] Communists are not a party, but are a conspiracy."[8] After more than 1,000 people wrote LDS headquarters seeking the view of the First Presidency regarding the society, the Church was compelled to restate its political neutrality and to "deplore" the Birch tactic of "casting aspersions" as both "anti-Christian" and "un-American."

It was events in Idaho that forced the issue to a head. Mormonism commands the religious landscape in southeast Idaho, with over half the population in some counties professing the faith. Birch organizers have been notably successful at enlisting Idaho Saints into the cause. One of the first chapters in the nation was chartered by a coterie of young professionals in Kootenai County, several of whom were LDS and all of whom had been active in an earlier anticommunist group called the Freedom Fighters. Birch officials now boast that its Idaho branch has the largest per capita membership of any state, with youth chapters in every city of significant size.[9] The founding of the Pocatello chapter illustrates how instrumental Church membership has been to the Birch recruitment campaign.

The two founders, one a successful naturopath, the other a respected plumbing contractor and self-described "free thinking Democrat," were already close friends who associated at Church gatherings and had shared their concerns about creeping socialism as early as 1960. When Ezra Taft Benson urged attendees at the annual Church conference in 1963 to educate themselves about Communism and to be vigilant about threats to the Constitution, the two sent him a letter asking for direction. They received a package containing several Birch pamphlets including Robert Welch's *The Politician*, a scathing indictment of President Eisenhower as "a dedicated, conscious agent of the Communist conspiracy. . . ."

"It scared us to death," one of the men now confesses. "If the book is true [and who would know better than Benson, who had served as Eisenhower's Secretary of Agriculture] we're in deep trouble."

The two decided to confront Benson directly. Screwing on their courage, they called for an appointment, drove to Salt Lake City, and were granted a fifteen-minute audience with the apostle. Benson affirmed his loyalty and affection for his one-time boss, but then added that "Ike refused to listen in regard to Communist subversion." The fact that all general authorities in the Church had been given copies of Welch's book, he suggested, implies its veracity. When the Pocatellans asked if joining the John Birch Society would hurt either themselves or the Church, Benson allegedly assured them it would not. The men returned to Pocatello to organize what was to become one of the largest and most effective Birch chapters in Idaho.[10] Among other things, this unit spearheaded the series of electoral successes of fellow Pocatellan, Church member, and Birch sympathizer, United States Congressman George Hansen, beginning in 1964.

Few outsiders had taken note of the Birch-Church link until Ralph Harding, Idaho's Second District Congressman, referred to it during a speech on the floor of the House of Representatives in January 1963.[11] The speech, which largely reiterated the traditional Church stance of political neutrality, created an uproar in the LDS community. Possibly fearing that the Church ruling cited by Harding might dissuade patriots from expressing their views, Utah's archconservative Wallace Bennett took the floor of the Senate several days later to read a somewhat contrary pronouncement from the First Presidency: "Members of the Church are free to join anti-Communist organizations if they desire and their membership in the Church is not jeopardized by so doing. . . . The Church is not opposing the John Birch Society or any other organizations of like nature."[12]

This ruling was enthusiastically embraced by Birch officials who redoubled their enlistment efforts among the Saints. Reed Benson was assigned to coordinate Birch activities in southern Idaho on behalf of Harding's opponent, George Hansen. Observers reported frequently seeing Hansen, Benson, and another high Birch official, Californian John Rousselot, together during the year, and noted obvious similarities between Birch rhetoric and Hansen campaign slogans.[13] Meanwhile, the elder Benson, who had been raised in the Second District and evidently still felt a sentimental responsibility for its political fate, continued his incendiary sniping: glorifying the Constitution, decrying Communist infiltration in high places, alluding to the questionable patriotism of progressive educators, liberals, and advocates of peaceful negotiation with the Russians, and praising the work of the John Birch Society.[14]

Hoping to muzzle apostle Benson, Harding wrote to the First Presidency. He received in turn three letters in the autumn of 1963. Two were from apostle Joseph Fielding Smith, agreeing that it was time Benson "forgot all about politics," and expressing hope that upon his return from his mission in two years "his blood will be purified."[15] Harding allowed the letters to fall into the hands of reporters who promptly published them, much to the chagrin of apostle Smith.[16] The elder Benson called the publication of the letters "unwarranted," "unworthy of comment," and "vicious."[17] Insulted a second time by having its family affairs exposed to public scrutiny and ridicule, large portions of the LDS community withdrew its support from Harding and voted for Hansen, who held the seat until his conviction on charges of Congressional ethics violations in 1983.

After this uproar, Mormon officers looked for a way to divorce the Church from increasingly compromising entanglements with outside political action groups, while still promoting Constitutionalist vigilance by the Saints. In 1967 W. Cleon Skousen, an associate professor of religion at Brigham Young University in Provo, Utah, organized an off-campus institute for constitutional studies. Formally christened on July 4, 1971, it was named The Freemen Institute after the legendary freemen of the Book of Mormon who resist attempts by so-called "kingmen" to chisel away the constitutional liberties of the Nephites.[18] The Freemen Institute was dedicated to instilling the doctrine that America is the fulfillment of prophecy in the latter days. Now headquartered in Washington, D.C., it goes by the name of the National Center for Constitutional Studies.

Skousen had already attained eminence in the Mormon community, having graduated in law from George Washington University and served with distinction in the FBI for sixteen years before his appointment as Chief of Police for Salt Lake City. By the time of his assignment to the institute, he had earned a reputation as an outspoken anticommunist. A member of the John Birch Society speaker's bureau, he appeared with Dr. Fred Schwarz, founder of the Christian Anti-Communist Crusade, at a "Hollywood for America" extravaganza at the Hollywood Bowl. The event, held October 16, 1961, was televised coast-to-coast.

As recent commentators have pointed out, the "suggestion of Church approval is integral" to the success of the Freemen Institute,[19] but let us emphasize the word "suggestion." There is no evidence that the First Presidency actually sanctioned the use of its symbols and teachings by the Freemen Institute. However this may be, Prophet Joseph

Smith's picture has appeared on institute literature; members speak of being "called" to Constitutionalism and give "testimony" concerning their devotion to it. Until recently Church buildings were used to house institute seminars, and until a gentle rebuke from the First Presidency in 1979, the seminars were even announced from the pulpit. My interviews indicate a large number of Mormon patriots have been introduced to activism through their participation in institute workshops. Ezra Taft Benson, whose son Mark has served as the institute's vice president, praised its efforts, saying, "I don't think there is any power on earth that can stop this work because it's right and has the Lord's approval."[20]

Ironically, right-wing independent Baptist critics have claimed that the Freemen Institute is a "surrogate" front for the LDS Church in its own secret conspiracy to establish "one world government."[21] Mormonism in their eyes is not authentic Christianity but instead a form of "Oriental occultism," part of the New Age Movement. Their alarm at being allied with Mormons to fight pornography and abortion is widely shared in western and northern Idaho, and presages possible schisms in the patriot movement. On the other hand, the recent coalitions between the Freemen Institute and Baptist minister Jerry Falwell's Moral Majority, Inc., the Catholic antifeminist Phyllis Schlafly's Eagle Forum, and the Korean evangelist Rev. Myung Moon's Unification Church suggest that even irreconcilable theological differences can be transcended when far rightists face a common foe. It should be emphasized that these are fragile bridges at best. In regard to Falwell, perhaps they involve little more than a "close personal friendship" between himself and Skousen and a public admission of his fondness for the institute's "The Miracle of America" video-tape seminar on the Constitution. In any case, it would be a serious mistake to infer from these few links an emerging coalition between the Mormon Church and the Protestant Right, at least in Idaho.[22]

Like patriot Saints, the Moonies too hope to restore a Christian commonwealth according to their understanding of the "organic" Constitution. The educational component of this effort is CAUSA International, founded in 1980 and now active in over twenty countries. Originally an acronym for Confederation for the Unification of the Societies of America, CAUSA is now said to stand for the Spanish term for "cause"—the cause against atheistic Communism, which it sees as "the enemy of God and mankind . . . the most serious threat to human civilization in all history." Against this diabolical power and in "God's emergency of all time," CAUSA proposes to array a non-denominational "Godism" comprising all the world's "God-accepting forces." To this end it has energetically solicited the support of scores of fundamentalist Protestant clergy as well as Mormon political activists, including Cleon Skousen.[23] Skousen has given major addresses at annual CAUSA conferences. In exchange, CAUSA has financially underwritten Freemen Institute pedagogical labors. Col. Bo Hi Pak, the Rev. Moon's primary podium interpreter, is listed as a major contributor to the institute (along with archconservative millionaires Joseph Coors, Nelson Bunker Hunt, William Boeing, and Idaho's Jack Simplot).

During the summer of 1985, twenty-six Idaho state legislators, the largest contingent of elected officials from any state, attended all-expense-paid CAUSA conferences in Denver, Los Angeles, and Salt Lake City.[24] Seventeen of these twenty-six are Latter-day Saints, most of them graduates of Freemen Institute workshops. According to the Twin Falls Constitutionalist responsible for issuing the invitations and coordinating the trips, and himself a Latter-day Saint and Skousen disciple, the twenty-six were "very carefully" selected according to Christian patriot criteria as evidenced by their voting records. Those about whom there was some question were interviewed concerning their devotion to the Constitution.[25]

Two of the attendees formally addressed one or more of the conferences, one on National Education Association subversion of American values, primarily through its advocacy of gay rights. Another, a highly educated Saint from Kuna, Idaho, would gain notoriety later that year for rebuking liberal lawmakers as "queer lovers" (an accusation as serious in intent and consequence in rural Idaho as "nigger lover" used to be in the Deep South). His targets had refused to support a bill that effectively would have made neutral classroom discussion of homosexuality a crime. In August 1985, at a banquet honoring Moon upon completion of an eleven-month prison term for tax evasion, one of the legislators, a Mormon convert who once fled Communist East Germany, presented the Unification Church leader with a gold loving cup.[26] Reports had ex-congressman George Hansen sitting at the head table with Moon.[27]

CONSTITUTION AND CONSPIRACY
None of the previous discussion is intended to demonstrate that the Mormon Church has caused John Birch or Freemen Institute activism,

or that it has officially stamped right-wing extremism with its approval. Rather, what appears to have occurred is that patriots who also happen to be Mormon have freely appropriated Church paraphernalia and teachings to further their own political ends. Two teachings of immeasurable importance in their articulation of the politics of righteousness have been those concerning the divine inspiration of the Constitution and the so-called Gadianton robber conspiracy. I do not claim that these doctrines are in fact as central to Mormonism as claimed by the patriots or that their interpretations of these doctrines are scripturally correct.

Constitutionalism

Mormonism shares with other Christian fundamentalisms a kind of dispensational theology; it differs from them in the role that it sees America playing in the Last Days. Most fundamentalists are effusively patriotic, but Mormonism goes further, viewing America as nothing less than the Zion of ancient prophecy. "I bear witness," says Ezra Taft Benson,

that America's history was foreknown to God; that His divine intervention and merciful providence have given us both peace and prosperity in this beloved land, and through His omniscience and benevolent design He selected and sent some of His choicest spirits to lay the foundation of our government. They were not evil men. Their work was a prologue to the restoration of the gospel and the Church of Jesus Christ. It was done in fulfillment of the ancient prophets who declared that this was a promised land, " a land of liberty unto the gentiles," and that is us.[28]

America is "choice above all other lands." Here is the stage upon which the drama of the Last Days shall be played out, where all the tribes of Israel but Judah shall be regathered. God's earthly kingdom, Zion, shall be built not by Semitic herdsmen, but by English-speaking American Saints, the very name of its capital, Independence, reverberating with the American spirit. And leading the restoration movement is a prophet like Abraham, Isaac, and Moses of old, but with the quintessential American appellation Joe Smith—an ordinary yeoman, to whom a new holy book is unsealed precisely because of his democratic unpretentiousness and simplicity.

Individual choice is a major key to understanding Mormon theology. The crucial moment in each man's life is said to be the harrowing choice between faith in Jesus Christ or obedience to Lucifer. It is the choice between the paradoxical promise of blessings to the meek, to peacemakers, to the poor and to the humble of spirit, or to the outwardly more practical promise of advancement by means of strength, violence, brains, and wealth. For this reason, the United States Constitution is considered seminal to the fullness of the gospel. The Constitution not only protects individual free agency, it mandates each to make the existential choice, to commit himself to either God or to the devil. "And for this purpose have I established the Constitution of this land, by the hands of wise men whom I raised up unto this very purpose, and redeemed the land by the shedding of blood."[29]

Composed by men called by God to the task, "no item of inspiration is held more sacred with us than the Constitution," wrote Brigham Young.[30] Its authors, presumably at their own request, were eternally sealed into the Church by President Wilford Woodruff at the temple in St. George, Utah, in 1877.[31]

Like all governments, the American government is held to be "instituted of God" for man's benefit. Hence, the Latter-day Saint is enjoined to "befriend that law which is the constitutional law of the land." Even so, from the outset of Mormon history, one can detect a distinction employed by Church spokesmen between the "government" and the Constitution. It is a distinction taken to the extreme by today's radical patriots, and probably in a way unintended by the early Church fathers.

Regarding the Constitution, Brigham Young avers, "It is pure." As for the government, it is comprised of "so-called gentlemen" with "a bit of sheep's skin" in their pockets, who presume on the one hand to discipline the people, but who on the other are "not fit to live in our midst." President Zachary Taylor himself, says Young, "is in hell" just like "any other miserable sinner." Concerning the bureaucrats Taylor assigned to administer the Utah territory: "We have some of the most . . . damnable, mean cusses here that graced the earth." They carry the holy sanctuary in one hand "and a jug of whiskey in the other, and follow a whore and have a Saint trail behind them to hold up their garments to prevent their drabbling. . . . I despise them and so does every good man."[32] To such knaves, Young warns, the Saints "will never crouch down." As *Doctrine and Covenants* teaches, against corrupt governmental officials "all men are justified in defending themselves."[33]

To be understood properly, of course, these comments must be read in the context of the anti-Mormon persecution of Young's day. But they are lifted by today's Mormon patriots and applied to modern circumstances. In patriot oratory, the Constitution is likened to "the pillar of the temple of liberty," "that great palladium of human rights," "the freedom formula" that has made "the miracle of America" possible, "the last hope for the human race," "our greatest export."[34] But elected officials and their bungling bureaucratic allies in the employ of the Internal Revenue Service, the Bureau of Land Management, the Occupational Safety and Health Administration, and especially "secular humanist" public school teachers and Christian "priestcrafters"— these are "specimens of fallen humanity," who in the garb of legalese, expertise, and sanctity, manufacture falsehoods and prey on the "vitiated tastes of the age."

While according to the Mormon patriot, the Saint must "befriend that law which is the Constitutional law of the land" (as he interprets it), he is not beholden to regulations and statutes "more or less than this."[35] With Joseph Fielding Smith, an early Church president, he asks, "If lawmakers . . . violate their oath . . . and depart from the Constitution, where is the law . . . which binds me . . . ?"[36] Most Mormons dutifully obey even Constitutionally questionable edicts, trusting that God will hold tyrants responsible for abusing their office. But the patriots will have none of this. Citing occasional references from the *Journal of Discourses* (pronouncements recorded at various nineteenth-century general assemblies), they insist that men of God need not sacrifice principle to "corrupt, unreasonable and unprincipled men," that they are "no craven serfs, and have not learned to lick the feet of the oppressor."[37]

Conspiratorialism

The underlying story line in the Book of Mormon is the archetypal dissension between Good and Evil. The opposition is framed at two levels. At the first, the God-fearing Nephites whose skins are "white and delightsome" war with the Lamanites who, "dark and loathsome," revel in their nakedness in the wilderness. At the second and, for our purposes, more significant level, within the Nephite community itself, "freemen"—friends of individual liberty—struggle against "kingmen" who wish to overthrow the Nephite Constitution and establish autocratic rule.[38] In the end, the kingmen have so weakened the Nephites that they are rendered incapable of resisting the armed forays of the sons of darkness and suffer eventual extermination. The final battle is fought on Cumorah Hill wherein Mormon buried the golden tablets, the Nephite historical ledger, which were unearthed centuries later by Joseph Smith.

The kingmen have two attributes that account for the success of their internal subversion. First, they are known to the heads of the Nephite government, "therefore they were not destroyed."[39] Second, they are organized in a "secret combination." Each conspirator has undertaken a self-condemnatory oath—"Swear unto me by thy throat, and if thou tell it thou shalt die"—not to reveal the "great secret."[40] The terrible secret, first divulged to Cain by Lucifer at the beginning of time, is that through murder and robbery one can advance himself in the world, not through work and sacrifice.[41] Armed with this dark knowledge, Cain names himself "Mahan," master of the secret, and carries out its bloody lesson on his brother, Abel.[42]

Since the time of Cain's Faustian covenant, others have struck the same bargain with Lucifer, each becoming in turn Master Mahan, head of his own secret band. In our age, the latter days, an analogous conspiracy with similar disastrous consequences for America is prophesied in the Book of Mormon: "And there were also secret combinations, even as in times of old, according to the combinations of the devil, for he is the foundation of all these things; yea, the foundation of murder, and works of darkness; yea, and he leadeth them by the neck with flaxen cord, and he bindeth them with his strong cords forever."[43]

Several critics have wondered about the source of the conspiracy theme in Mormon legend. It is well documented that the terror of Freemasonry was hottest in the neighborhood of Joseph Smith's residence, Palmyra, New York, in the very months during which he was transcribing the Book of Mormon from the angel Moroni's golden tablets.[44] And there is some evidence that this hysteria found expression in the Mormon bible. The word "Mormon" itself, some have contended, may be a conjunction of the first syllables of the last names of two men then believed to have been murdered by the Masons, William Morgan and Timothy Monroe.[45] The Gadianton robber conspiracy is said to have been organized in the fortieth year of the reign of the liberty-loving Nephite judges;[46] but the fortieth year of the American Republic, dated from its birth in 1789, is 1829, the year when anti-Masonic excitement reached its apogee. Again, Master Mahan, the title granted the head of each Luciferian conspiracy in the Book of Mormon, bears an uncanny resemblance to Master Mason, the ruling officer of a Masonic chapter. And the terms "secret combination," "secret band," "secret society," and "murderous combination," all frequently found in the Book of Mormon,[47] the members wearing their "lambskin aprons,"[48] and communicating through "signs, yea, their secret signs, and their secret words; and this that they might distinguish a brother who has entered into the covenant,"[49] are identical to the labels and phrases used in period exposés of Freemasonry. Many of these exposés were reprinted in the *Palmyra Freeman,* which Joseph Smith would have had easy access to. Is it possible that the name of the tragic heroes in the Book of Mormon, the freemen, was drawn from the title of this anti-Masonic weekly?

That Joseph Smith would have known about the mysteries of Masonry is understandable: his brother was a member of a local lodge when Joseph was writing the Book of Mormon. Furthermore, as anti-Mormons never tire of reminding their audience, Joseph himself, along with several of his earliest followers, was inducted into the Nauvoo Masonic Lodge in 1842.[50] This, however, was over a decade after the publication of the Book of Mormon, and long after the fever of anti-Masonry had passed through upstate New York.

But all of this is less important than the proposition we wish to entertain here. Just as Joseph Smith's obsession with secret combinations may reflect his familiarity with and sympathy for the anti-Masonry of his time, the conspiratorialism of today's Mormon radicals seems to be partially derived from their reading of the Book of Mormon. That this may be a contextually inappropriate reading of Mormon holy scripture is beside the point. The visions of the fathers have undoubtedly been visited on successive generations of Mormons. For many patriots, they are the key to the idea that there is a secret conspiracy to establish Communist rule in America: "The Gadianton robbers in the Book of Mormon," says a typical respondent, a longtime John Birch activist. "When Cain slew Abel he established secret societies . . . and we can trace them down to the present day."[51] "The Book of Mormon has ominous parallels with today," agrees another. "Our problems are those of the ancient Nephites."[52]

Drawing on the same source, still another concludes that "disaster is overtaking us . . . the time bomb is ticking. This [America] is the last stronghold, the last hope. . . . We have precious little time to save ourselves. If we don't wake up we'll lose our country."[53] These respondents authenticated their insights by reading books like Robert Welch's *The Politician,* Ezra Taft Benson's *The Red Carpet* and *An Enemy Has Done This to Us,* Anthony Sutton's *National Suicide,* and Clarence Kelly's *Conspiracy Against God and Man.*

Two of the most influential titles on this theme have been Cleon

Skousen's *The Naked Capitalist*[54] and Stanford-educated Gary Allen's *None Dare Call It Conspiracy,*[55] which Benson once said he wished "every citizen of every country in the free world . . . might read." While both books claim to be reviews of Georgetown University professor Carroll Quigley's history of modern civilization, *Tragedy and Hope,*[56] they are in fact running commentaries on less than 100 pages of Quigley's 1300-plus-page compendium, those with passages buttressing Allen and Skousen's belief that a ruthless, anti-Christian, dictatorial authority is being erected insidiously over the world.

Neither author believes the Russians or Chinese could have engineered their own revolutions. Such a straightforward scenario does not fit the portrait of a bonafide Master Mahan and his wily band. On the contrary, the directors of the Communist conspiracy flourish in our own midst. Or as Allen quips, "the U.S.S.R. was made in the U.S.A."[57] And this must be a cabal comprising men one would least suspect of Communist sympathies, the magnates of capitalism themselves. The one-world conspiracy "is being plotted, promoted and implemented by the leaders of free nations and the super-rich of those nations whose influence would seem to make them the foremost beneficiaries of our free-enterprise, property-oriented . . . society."[58] Skousen expresses bafflement over this "startling . . . virtually inconceivable" discovery.

Quigley agrees that capitalist kingpins have financed left-wing movements but claims that their motive is not to further left-wing causes as such, but to ingratiate themselves with future leaders in order to secure and possibly expand their profit-making opportunities.[59] Skousen ignores the apparent incongruity that these same financiers bankrolled fascist revolutionaries in the 1920s and 1930s. Allen handles it by simply grouping both left- and right-wing movements under the rubric of "total government." As the goal of the international bankers, he says, is to establish total government, Communism and Nazism serve this purpose equally well.[60]

It is the investment bankers, then, luxuriating in matchless riches, residing in the financial capitals of the free world, who head the conspiracy. Like the legendary kingmen of Mormon mythology, they are well-known to American government officials, but as they all come from the same eastern seaboard families, nothing is done about them. Like the Gadianton robbers of old, today's conspirators are wedded in a secret society, the Round Table, founded in 1910 by Cecil Rhodes under the inspiration of the English sociologist and philanthropist,

John Ruskin.[61] Rhodes saw the Round Table and its affiliates, such as the New York-based Council on Foreign Relations, as the vehicle to consolidate benign British rule throughout the world. The models for this occult band were the Catholic Society of Jesus and Freemasonry, as elaborated upon by Bavarian Mason Adam Weishaupt ("the monster," Allen calls him), who founded the Order of Illuminati on May 1, 1776, to spread Enlightenment ideas.[62]

So we come full circle: Joseph Smith may have derived Master Mahan and the Gadianton robbers from nineteenth-century anti-Masonic frenzy; Skousen patterned the Cecil Rhodes–robber baron conspiracy after Mormon fable; and Allen pointed back to its alleged roots in the Illuminati-Masonic collusion of liberals Weishaupt, Voltaire, and Turgot. The basic design of the story remains unchanged over time; only the cast of characters is altered to fit new circumstances. There is a worldwide, secular-humanist, satanic conspiracy—"an evil inspired by the evil one." It is headed by those who, because of their fortunate birth, believe themselves superior to us (Skousen bitterly describes them as "Ivy League, Anglophile, eastern seaboard, high Episcopalian, . . . the American branch of the English establishment"); its dealings are "secret, seditious, scheming," its tactics "without conscience or honor," for "they have no moral code"; its goal is "to rob God's children of their freedom of choice, their God-given free agency" by subverting their constitutionally protected liberties.[63]

MORMONISM AND THE JEW

Radical Mormon Constitutionalists are conspiratorialists, but rarely do they evolve into full-fledged anti-Semites. This explains their attraction to groups like the John Birch Society, the Freemen Institute, and CAUSA, and their avoidance of Identity cults. This is ironic in that Mormonism bears an outward resemblance to Identity Christianity. Both preach variations of dispensational theology, both appeared at approximately the same time in the nineteenth century, both provide sophisticated answers to questions concerning the fate of the lost tribes of Israel, and both see their followers as authentic children of Abraham, adherents to the ancient covenants, and God's favorite children.

Identity Christians and Latter-day Saints alike consider themselves Israelites. But while Identity Christians claim to trace their genetic ancestry back to one or more of the lost tribes, the Mormon typically speaks of himself as being "grafted" or "adopted" into Israel, although Anglo-Saxon Mormons often do not hesitate to follow their lineal descent back to the tribe of Ephraim. Mormon sacramental adoption is accomplished through baptism, the confessor being fully immersed in the waters from which he is reborn. In the patriarchal blessing, a voluntary yet integral rite in the Church since the 1830s, the Saint is reminded of his tribal affiliation.

Church theologians argue over whether Mormon ritual adoption is literal or metaphoric and purely spiritual. Ezekiel 11:34 and 37, Galatians 3:7, and chapters 4 and 11 in Paul's letters to the Romans can be read to support either position. The Reorganized Church of Jesus Christ of Latter Day Saints, a schism that broke from the main denominational line in 1860, following a dispute over succession to the Church presidency, generally favors the figurative rendition. Representatives of the Salt Lake City branch, however, insist that baptism entails the actual transubstantiation of the celebrant's blood. "Those who accept the gospel become the house of Israel regardless of what their literal blood ancestry might have been," says Bruce McConkie. Adoption, he continues, quoting the prophet Joseph Smith, "Purge[s] out the old blood and make[s] him actually of the seed of Abraham." But on closer view, the process is more complicated than this. The ritual action, McConkie goes on, is "more powerful" in transforming the blood of a historical descendant of Abraham than it is on the blood of a complete gentile.[64] McConkie identifies these descendants as the Anglo-Saxon peoples of northern Europe and their American offspring.[65] In making this assertion, he restates the Church view that Mormonism's nineteenth-century confessors (all of whom came from northwest European stock) were not merely adopted into the House of Israel but were a literal remnant of the tribe of Ephraim. To bolster his claim, McConkie cites a standard text of the Identity movement, George Reynolds' *Are We of Israel?* This describes how the various Western European nations were peopled from descendants of the exiled ten northern tribes of Israel who migrated from Iran over the Caucasus Mountains into the Danube Basin and spread throughout the continent. (Although both McConkie's encyclopedia of Mormon doctrine and Reynolds' pamphlet are widely circulated in patriot circles, neither are officially sanctioned by the First Presidency of the Church.)

The parallels between popular Mormonism and Identity do not end here. To my knowledge, Yale professor Charles A. L. Totten was the first American convert to British Israelism around 1885. He was also the first to publish as objective history the tale of the marriage of the last Davidic king Zedekiah's daughter, Tamar Tephi, to the Irish king Eochaidh,[66] the connection that links the English Tudor and Stuart dynasties to the House of David and legitimizes British claims to world domination under the Bible. This same legend may be found in many nonofficial Mormon devotional texts.[67] It complements the Book of Mormon, which claims that not all Zedekiah's sons were murdered by the Babylonians. His youngest, Mulek, taking to heart Jeremiah's dire warnings, fled Jerusalem at the last moment with a remnant of the community, sailed to the New World, and established a Jewish colony in "land north."[68]

Mormonism, then, evinces a striking continuity with American and British Israelism but it has not fully embraced Identity's anti-Judaism. The reason lies in the ambivalent yet generally positive portrait of the Jew drawn in Mormon scripture.

On the face of it, the Book of Mormon appears to reiterate the ancient biblical indictments of the Jews. The Jews—"those who are the more wicked part of the world"—are said to be Christ killers ("There is no other nation on earth that would crucify their God"),[69] transgressors from the womb,[70] and murderers of the apostles and prophets.[71] The whole Nephi-Lamanite epic reported in the Book of Mormon is inaugurated by the attempt of Lehi and his family to escape Jerusalem before it is punished by God for the "wickedness and abominations" of its inhabitants.[72] All the destructions, famines, pestilences, bloodshed, and scatterings endured by the Jews throughout history are seen in the Book of Mormon as divine retribution for their crimes. They have, Nephi tells the reader, justly earned "the hatred of all men."[73] As one Mormon interview subject related: "I don't know about that [i.e., Jewish complicity in the one-world conspiracy]. I can't really believe it. . . . [But] Christ was a Jew and his own race crucified him. I don't know why they did that. Why would they persecute one of their own flesh? I don't know. . . . Maybe that's why they were persecuted."[74] Unless we separate Mormon literature from Mormon scripture proper, then, it is hard to agree with sociologist Armand Mauss, who once stated that "one would look long, and probably in vain, to find in Mormon literature any counterparts of the hostile and explicitly anti-Semitic passages . . . found in some denominational tracts."[75]

On the other hand, the condemnations of the Jews in Mormon scripture are most accurately understood as condemnations of a generic and endemic *human* perfidy, of which the Jewish case is merely one documented historical example. The evil Mormonism sees in history is not unique to either the Jewish "race" or religion but is characteristic of human apostates everywhere. There are Mormon anti-Semites who misuse Mormon scripture to bolster their prejudices. But it is inaccurate to attribute this to the official position of the Church itself.[76]

In any case, regardless of the final judgment of this particular issue, there is no ambiguity concerning the status of Jews in the eyes of Mormonism today. Whatever their transgressions in the past, the Jews retain God's unconditional love. And as promised at the beginning of time, they shall be regathered to possess the land of their inheritance. This is contingent, of course, upon their "coming to knowledge of the True Messiah" and tearful repentence of their sins over the ages.

From the Jewish viewpoint such conditional promises obviously are presumptuous. But the Latter-day Saint sees them in a benign, even heroic light. The Saint is not just a metaphorical or symbolic brother of the Jew but his own flesh and blood. Both are children of the same father, Abraham.[77] As such, although he "understands" the reasons for the historical plight of the Jew, the Saint has an intensely jealous familial interest in harboring him from gentile persecution. The litany of pogroms, holocausts, and dispossessions suffered by the Jews are said in the Book of Mormon to have been instigated by leaders of the "great and abominable church," the "whore of Babylon," at whose foundation is the devil. This so-called "mother of harlots" is believed to encompass primarily the non-Mormon Christian churches. As for Latter-day Saints, the warning of an early Church president is still operable: "Let no Saint be guilty of taking part in any crusade against these people [i.e., the Jews]."[78]

Nor is this all. It is the penultimate responsibility of the Saint to bring to the Jew the "fullness of the gospel" so that he can recognize his errors, change his ways, and participate in the completion of God's plan. For even when they strayed from the covenant, the Jews have remained God's favorites, the chosen people. Hence, not only is the Saint forbidden on pain of excommunication to harm the Jew, he is to sponsor actively the Jew as one would a younger, disobedient son to his father. The poignant language of Mormon scripture expresses the intimacy of this bond. The Jew will be "nursed by the Gentiles [meaning the gentiles who are baptised into the Mormon church], and their children carried in their arms and on their shoulders into the lands of their inheritance." "Yea the kings of Gentiles shall be nursing fathers to them and their queens shall become nursing mothers."[79] Just as Moses delivered his people from slavery in ancient times, so today his American counterpart, Joseph Smith, will deliver modern Jewry into the promised land.

Israel is an olive tree and in the latter days new branches, the adopted gentiles, shall be "grafted in," becoming olive branches in their own right.[80] The grafting will be accomplished through the baptism of gentiles who recognize that they were Israelites all along, but had somehow forgotten. This is the regathering of the tribes in Zion at the end of time, the restoration of the Jews in the Last Days.[81]

Before Joseph Smith was killed he dispatched an apostle named Orson Hyde to dedicate the land of Palestine to the Jews in accordance with Mormon prophecy. In 1841 Hyde ascended the Mount of Olives, built an altar, and offered a prayer that the land now begin to receive the scattered remnant of Judah, that it flower once again, and that the Jews restore their capital in Jerusalem. Mormons view the history of the State of Israel since 1948 as a miraculous fulfillment of that prayer and as still another sign that ours are indeed the latter days.[82]

CONCLUSION

Mormon doctrine has been used by LDS patriots both to buttress their belief in the sanctity of the United States Constitution and to validate their conspiratorialism. At the same time it has provided an obstacle to patriots tempted to place blame for this alleged conspiracy on the House of Judah, forcing them to direct their animosity onto an abstract Enemy. The product of this trilogy of theological dicta—Constitutionalism, conspiratorialism, and pro-Judaism—is the peculiar brand of Christian patriotism that flourishes in southeast Idaho. As militant as other forms of the politics of righteousness, it nonetheless typically fails to burst into full-fledged anti-Semitism.

Beyond study groups and lobbies like CAUSA, the Freemen Institute, and the John Birch Society, Mormon Constitutionalism can also manifest itself in illegal tax-resistance or in armed survivalist townships. Examples of the latter now proliferate in southern Utah and western Arizona, organized by the "Freemen," who call their enterprise "New Nation U.S.A." Neither is Mormonesque patriotism a stranger to racism as found, for example, in the pronouncements of one of the publishers of the Pace amendment, a legal brief advocating the forcible expulsion of non-white minorities from America.[83] He proudly parades his fifth-generation Mormon heritage. Or consider the director of the Institute for Conspiratology in Spokane, an ex-LDS missionary who now describes himself as a "racial socialist." With the declining health of Richard Butler, this man periodically serves as spokesman for the Hayden Lake Aryan Nations Church. Finally, radical Mormon Constitutionalism can result in outright violence, as the cases of Minutemen founder Robert DePugh, Mormon bishop Gordon Kahl, heretic Mormon polygamist John Singer, and his son-in-law Addam Swapp all testify. DePugh, still a member of the Reorganized Church of Jesus Christ of Latter Day Saints, was imprisoned in the 1970s for firearms violations. Kahl and Singer were killed in separate police shootouts in the 1980s, Kahl after taking the lives of three law enforcement officials. Swapp and his family took part in a violent confrontation with police in which one officer died. Earlier Swapp had declared his two-and-one-half-acre polygamist homestead a sovereign nation.

Still, it is inaccurate to classify indiscriminately this style of right-wing extremism with that characteristic of the Identity churches. To be sure, Mormonism displays uncanny resemblances to more benign forms of Identity, such as taught by the late J. H. Allen or by Spokane's Alexander Schiffner. Some few in fact, like pastor John Woods of Hayden Lake, view their conversion to Identity from Mormonism as a natural progression in their own spiritual development. (Prior to the establishment of his schismatic Gospel of Christ Kingdom Church, Woods taught Sunday school at the Aryan Nations Church academy.) But Identity of any species has a different theological foundation—largely literalist biblical—than Mormonism, whose holy athenaeum includes not only the Bible but the Book of Mormon.

Part II

THE MOVEMENT FROM THE OUTSIDE

7

SKETCHING THE MOVEMENT CAUSES

CAVEATS AND DISCLAIMERS

The goal of this and the following chapters is to unravel the causes of radical Christian patriotism in Idaho. Although sociology cannot claim to provide scientifically rigorous explanations of Christian patriotism, it can provide explanation *sketches* of the movement. These are roughly drawn pictures that hint at some of the social conditions that are independent of, prior to, and remain correlated or associated with participation in the movement when other conditions are held constant.

Even in the most advanced sciences, causal connections can never be strictly proven. They are merely inferences about which one has more or less confidence depending on the quality of the data supporting them. The factual bases for my causal sketches of Christian patriotism are the interviews with and questionnaires sent to self-identified patriots, together with biographical information (of sometimes questionable validity) published in newspaper articles and other secondary sources. Although this data base is sizable, there is a serious problem with it. Most of my informants were referred to me by other patriots. It was not unusual for my initial contacts to provide the names of three to five potential respondents. The disadvantage of this procedure is that these acquaintances tended to be similar in background to my initial small sample. The potential for sampling bias is obvious.

I compensated for this bias by making initial contact with patriots who lived in widely different geographical areas and represented the diversity of positions comprising the patriot world. Equal proportions of the sample were drawn from the three major population centers in Idaho: the Boise Valley, Pocatello–Blackfoot–Idaho Falls and the Upper Snake River Valley, and Kootenai and Bonner counties in the north. Handfuls of other contacts were made in Twin Falls, Jerome, Riggins-Grangeville, Salmon-Challis, and the logging communities around St. Maries and Lewiston. Subjects from these areas represent the vast regional, occupational, religious, cultural, and topographic

differences constituting Idaho. In terms of differences in political outlook, I studied patriots running the full gamut of right-wing extremism: from CAUSA and John Birch Constitutionalists who pass out
petitions and lobby for trimming local taxes, to nonviolent but militant tax resisters, armed non-racist Posse Comitatus deputies, and a
plethora of American Israelites (Identity Christians), ranging from those
who classify themselves "Jews" to those who revile the very term;
from pacifistic Bible students to *pro se* trial litigants; from Lyndon
LaRouche supporters to convicted terrorists.

The educational backgrounds of the patriots range from fourth-grade
dropouts to medical doctors and a Ph.D. in linguistics. They issue
from the icon-bedecked and incensed world of Roman Catholicism to
the hard-pewed, plain-speaking, home-educated Followers of Christ.
Some live in split-level country club splendor, others as recluses in
makeshift cabins and barns. Some have inherited considerable fortunes
and dabble in amateur science. Others are unemployed and live off the
welfare system they despise. Some administer hospitals and schools,
while others are self-employed contractors. No single characteristic encompasses all of those in my sample, except perhaps their Christianity.
For this reason it may be assumed that if not random, the sample is
at least somewhat representative of the membership of the movement.

SOCIOLOGICAL THEORIES OF RIGHT-WING EXTREMISM

There are several standard sociological hypotheses concerning the
prior correlates of right-wing extremism. Our object is to compare
these hypotheses against the data on Idaho's patriots. We will not be
able to definitively accept or reject any of these hypotheses. We will,
however, be able to specify in what ways and to what degree they are
true in the case of Idaho Christian patriotism. The reader who yearns
to discover the single overarching Cause of Idaho rightism will be
disappointed. As for any phenomenon involving human beings, the
correlates of patriotism are multiple and sometimes seemingly contradictory.

This chapter will deal with the educational and mass theories of
extremism. Chapters 8 and 9 will address the "learning" theories of
extremism, of which two forms will be handled—political socialization
theory and the so-called two-step theory of mobilization. The last
chapter will cover a fifth sociological theory, that concerning status
insecurity.

The educational theory holds that right-wing extremism is due largely to an absence of formal education or to its failure to inculcate in the individual citizen an intellectual commitment to democratic principles. Preeminent among these principles is tolerance for opposing viewpoints. Most Americans probably have an affective commitment to the Flag, to the Star Spangled Banner, and to the Constitution. Most even assent on questionnaires to due process, freedom of speech, religion, and assembly. But far fewer agree to extending constitutional rights to Communists, Nazis, atheists, criminals, and homosexuals. (As onetime Arkansas Senator William Fulbright once commented, Americans believe in the rights of freedom until someone tries to exercise these rights.) Those who are, at least on questionnaires, willing to grant rights to minorities generally have attained higher levels of formal education. The "irony of democracy," so the theory goes, is that the poorly educated, intolerant masses are also the most apathetic and least likely to participate in politics.[1] In any case, the solution to the "problem" of right-wing extremism is to extend the years of formal, especially public, education for our children.

The mass theory maintains that what makes individuals prone to mobilization by extremist groups is not their lack of education but their "massification"—their estrangement from the local community, their isolation from ordinary channels of belonging. For example, freelance writers and artists, even if they are well educated, are susceptible to extremist propaganda because of their alienation from ordinary associations. It has been said, for example, that 25 percent of the original Nazi SS elite had liberal arts doctorates.[2] Similar observations have been made of the Russian Bolsheviks. Both groups comprised mainly "armed bohemians," to use William Kornhauser's words. By the same token, illiterate peasants, safely ensconced in local parish, family, and manorial life, are supposedly immune to mobilization by outside agitators. Robert Nisbet summarizes this view:

Where there is widespread conviction that community has been lost, there will be a conscious quest for community in the form of association that seems to provide the greatest moral refuge. . . . And above all other forms of political association it is the . . . Communist party that most successfully exploits that craving for . . . Communal membership. . . . The almost eager acceptance of the fantastic doctrines of the Nazis by millions of otherwise intelligent Germans would be inexplicable were it not for the accompanying proffer of moral community to the . . . alienated German.[3]

The theories discussed in Chapters 8 and 9 assert that like any other lifestyle, political deviance is essentially learned. Right-wing radicals are "socialized" to this orientation by the words and examples of those with whom they are most deeply bonded: parents, teachers, friends, co-workers, or pastors. Non-movement or extra-movement ties to the recruiter almost always precede the candidate's commitment to the cause. Political socialization theory in particular focuses on *what* kinds of prior group affiliations are associated with specific political outlooks. The two-step theory, on the other hand, analyzes the process of *how* political commitments are generated.

In either case, two implications follow from learning theory. First, it is not merely the years of formal education that are crucial in dissuading youngsters from extremism; rather, it is the content of the lessons taught at home, school, or church. Second, those who are truly isolated from families, schools, churches, or friendships where extremist opinions are preached and celebrated are the least likely to join extremist movements. In these two ways, the learning theories contradict the educational and the mass theories of extremism.

These, then, are the basic theoretical orientations to be examined below. For each of them, I will ask first whether it is true for the Idaho Christian patriots in general. Then I will inquire whether and to what degree it is true for the two major types of patriotism separately—Christian Constitutionalism and Christian Identity. The reader should not be surprised if a particular theory appears valid in regard to the patriots considered as a totality, but is invalid for one of the two major sub-types of activism. Unless I explicitly indicate the contrary, issue-oriented patriots are included under the rubric of "all" patriots. One final point: Earlier a distinction was made between racist and nonracist types of Identity Christians but in the following discussion all American Israelites are grouped under a single general title. The reason for this is that in a number of cases, despite the operational procedure described in Chapter 1, it could not be clearly determined whether a subject was one type or the other.

EDUCATION AND THE PATRIOT

In summarizing a number of earlier surveys, the respected political sociologist Seymour Martin Lipset concluded that those who occupy the lowest social ranks in modern society are the most likely to be antidemocratic.[4] Lipset went on to say that several characteristics of lower-class life produce this result: perpetual economic insecurity and its concomitant frustrations encourage its sufferers to search for scapegoats; a lack of work-related self-esteem inclines them to bully outsiders; abusive child-rearing practices increase their authoritarian (fascist) tendencies; and higher rates of mental illness make them less able to fend off demagogic appeals. But the most important factor, he claimed, is their low level of educational attainment.

Samuel Stouffer had come to the same conclusion five years earlier during the height of the McCarthy era.[5] Using data from the Gallup organization and the National Opinion Research Center on a cross-section of 4,933 Americans, Stouffer found that the lower the level of education his respondents reported, the less tolerant they were as indicated by their willingness to allow unpopular views to be expressed in their communities. College graduates were about four times more tolerant than those who had dropped out of school in the eighth grade (see Table 7.1). This relationship held across race, age, sex, community status, place of residence (rural or urban), and across different degrees of religious piety. On the other hand, none of the associations between different amounts of intolerance and these same variables persisted when the educational level of the respondents was held constant. Stouffer's findings were confirmed twelve years later in another nationwide survey by Herbert McCloskey.[6] By 1975 the informed judgment of authorities was that years of formal education explained more of the variation in political attitudes, anti-Semitism, and bigotry than any other single variable.[7]

My information on Idaho's Christian patriots does not support this proposition. One of the most shocking and perhaps disturbing findings of the sample of respondents is that on the whole they have attained slightly greater levels of formal education than either their fellow Idahoans or more conventional Americans (see Table 7.2).

The data in Table 7.2 are self-explanatory, but it will be helpful to mention some highlights. Idahoans in general reach higher levels of

Table 7.1
Educational Level and Tolerance among Americans (1952)

Highest Level of Formal Education	Percentages of the Tolerant and Intolerant			
	Less Tolerant	In-Between	More Tolerant	Total
College graduates	5	29	66	100
Grade school	22	62	16	100

SOURCE: Samuel Stouffer, *Communism, Conformity and Civil Liberties* (New York: John Wiley, 1966), p. 90.

Table 7.2

Formal Education of Patriots as Compared to Americans and Idahoans

Highest Level of Formal Education Attained	Identity Christians		Christian Constitutionalists		All Patriots		All Idahoans 25 Yrs+ [a]	All Americans 25 Yrs+ [b]	White Idahoans 25 Yrs+ [c]	White Americans 25 Yrs+ [d]
	N	%	N	%	N	%	%	%	%	%
Graduate degree	15	7.8	13	8.9	37	9.7	6.9	7.6	7.3	8.0
Undergraduate degree	45	23.6	25	17.1	74	19.3	8.9	8.6	9.4	9.1
Some college	45	23.6	35	24.0	93	24.3	21.4	15.7	21.8	16.0
Nonacademic post–high school	14	7.3	9	6.2	29	7.6	—	—	—	—
High school graduate (including GED)	56	29.3	53	36.3	118	30.8	36.5	34.6	37.7	35.7
High school dropout	12	6.3	7	4.8	23	6.0	13.7	15.3	13.1	14.6
Eighth grade or less	4	2.1	4	2.7	9	2.3	12.6	18.4	11.4	16.6
Total	191	100.0	146	100.0	383	100.0	100.0	100.2	100.7	100.0

[a] U.S. Department of Commerce, *1980 Census of Population, General Social and Economic Characteristics*, vol. I, ch. c, part 1 (Washington, D.C.: Government Printing Office, 1981), Table 239.
[b] *Ibid.*, Table 83.
[c] Estimations based on the ratio of education levels between all Americans and all Idahoans.
[d] Goodman and Kruskal's Tau for the relationship between educational attainments of Identity Christians and Christian Constitutionalists is 0.01. Goodman and Kruskal's Tau for the relationship between educational attainments of all patriots to white Idahoans is 0.02. These figures indicate that the levels of educational attainment in these two comparisons are virtually identical.

education than Americans in general. But the 383 patriots on whom I have obtained educational background information have as a group spent more years in school than their fellow Idahoans. This pattern persists even when non-Caucasians are excluded from the comparison groups of Americans and Idahoans. Our figures include twenty-nine individuals whom we have listed as terrorists according to the criterion introduced earlier. The most notable difference between the sample and the control groups involves their relative propensity to drop out of school before graduation. Only about 8 percent of the patriots indicate themselves to be dropouts, compared to 26 percent of a cross-section of Idahoans or 33 percent of all Americans.

The educational achievements of Identity Christians and Christian Constitutionalists are virtually indistinguishable. This may be significant in that other surveys indicate racists to be less educated than Constitutionalist-oriented letter writers.[8] (Of course, only about half of the Identity Christians may accurately be classified racists, and the Constitutionalists in the sample do far more than compose epistles.) The terrorists in our sample are no less educated than their less violent comrades, although the numbers are far too few to be conclusive. An observable pattern among the terrorists, possibly worthy of further study, is that they seem either to be college graduates or high school dropouts.

When research contradicts well-established theory, the burden is upon the investigator to demonstrate that his findings are not spurious. Let us address three possible explanations for the data that would account for their apparent anomaly: respondent deception, sampling bias, and the type and quality of the patriots' education.

Did the respondents lie to me? Respondent deception is a perennial problem in social surveys. And there is little doubt that given the importance of education for prestige in America, Christian patriots too will fudge their pedagogical accomplishments. One of the advantages of a nonstructured conversational interviewing technique is that it provides opportunities to cross-validate what appear to be exorbitant educational claims. This was done by inquiring, for example, if the respondent had studied under a particular professor or what the quality of library holdings was at his school. One interview subject, an Identity pastor, reported that he had earned a Ph.D, a doctor of divinity, and his doctorate in theology. When asked for the title of his dissertation, he confessed to having matriculated at Zion Faith College and having earned his Ph.D. and advanced theology degrees from the American Institute of Theology, a mail-order Bible study course. I classified this respondent under the category of "Some college." Several other interviewees had honorary masters and doctorates in divinity bestowed upon them by independent Bible colleges not for academic accomplishments, but for "mastering" or "professing" Christian doctrine; but my questioning uncovered only a few cases of deception.

A more genuine and serious problem is the possible lack of representativeness of the snowball sample of patriots. Thus, if the investigator's first contact is a highly educated professional, it is likely that those he names as interview candidates will be people who move in his social circle. It is not likely they will be eighth-grade-educated transient laborers.

To control for sampling bias I made the following assumptions. Those under examination here are not merely sympathizers with patriotism but activists. Activists are probably more highly educated than nonactivists. Nevertheless one can distinguish between activists who play acknowledged leadership roles in the movement and those who may be considered the "effectors" of their programs. I excluded from consideration all patriots who identify themselves as authors, journalists, editors, printers, publishers, pastors, radio preachers, free-lance political organizers, administrators or executives of business firms or agencies, legislators, and professors. This eliminated 105 leading activists from the original sample. Table 7.3 compares the levels of educational attainment between nonleading effectors and white Idahoans and Americans. While the average level of educational attainment of effector activists is somewhat lower than that of their leaders—for instance, over 90 percent of the school dropouts are followers—Christian patriots have had no less, and perhaps a bit more, formal schooling than the typical white adult Idahoan or American.

In other words, at least in Idaho it appears that years of formal education alone offer little protection against extremist political appeals. This does not mean that we are justified in the contrary conclusion that higher education predisposes individuals to right-wing activism. There is evidence from other sources to indicate that while right-wing activists may be better educated than the average population, their educational attainments are less than those of *left*-wing activists.[9] Instead, we are only permitted to say that the traditional correlation between years of formal education and support for democratic values requires further specification.

One way to examine the relationship between education and dem-

Table 7.3
Formal Education of Non-Leading Patriots as Compared
to Americans and Idahoans[a]

Highest Level of Formal Education Attained	Non-Leading Christian Patriots		White Idahoans 25 Yrs+	White Americans 25 Yrs+
	Number	Percent	%	%
Graduate degree	18	6.5	7.3	8.0
Undergraduate degree	45	16.5	9.4	9.1
Some college	57	20.5	21.8	16.0
Nonacademic post–high school	19	6.8	—	—
High school graduate (including GED)	109	38.8	37.7	35.7
High school dropout	22	7.9	13.1	14.6
Eighth grade or less	8	3.0	11.4	16.6
Total	278	100.0	100.7	100.0

[a] For data sources, see footnotes at Table 7.2.
[b] Goodman and Kruskal's Tau for the relationship between educational attainments of non-leading Christian patriots and white Idahoans is 0.04. This figure indicates that the levels of educational attainment for these two groups are virtually identical.

ocratic values is to inquire into the major courses of college study undertaken by right-wing activists. Lipset has suggested that to be effective, one's commitment to democracy must be "cognitively" grounded. By this he means the citizen must have a capacity to handle conceptually difficult cases of freedom during times of crisis, a tolerance for ambiguity, and an ability to critically analyze complex issues in a sophisticated rather than simplistic way.[10] This requires a large body of factual information and philosophical and historical grounding in the principles of democracy, all of which he believes, are products of a particular kind of formal education, namely, that found in liberal arts disciplines.[11]

What have Idaho's Christian patriots studied in college? And where have they received their higher educations?

I have learned the undergraduate academic majors or interests of 153 patriots (ignoring 17 others who studied law or who entered diagnostic health care professions). Classifying majors by college we find that 41.2 percent of the college-educated patriots studied in colleges of arts and sciences (see Table 7.4). About two-thirds of these majored in humanistic liberal arts disciplines—English, history, and foreign languages—those disciplines most apt to inculcate a cognitive commitment to democratic values. The remainder of the arts and sciences graduates were either natural science or social science students. But even this may be too liberal an estimate. History increasingly occupies an ambiguous status in American higher education. At liberal arts colleges it continues to be taught as a humane art; but at public universities it has begun modeling itself after the social sciences. If history is classified as a social science, then the percentage of patriots majoring in the central liberal arts disciplines drops to 11.1 percent.

Religious studies majors are even more difficult to categorize. Religious studies at Bible colleges is often little more than dogmatics, homiletics, and pastoral care, skills not likely to encourage tolerance for ambiguity or diversity of views. At public universities, however, the discipline may also include inquiry into comparative religious doctrines, foreign languages, and philosophy and history, the basics of a classic liberal arts education. All but one of the religious studies majors before us attended sectarian schools.

Table 7.4
Academic College Majors of Idaho Christian Patriots

College	Number	Percent
Arts and sciences	63	41.2
Liberal arts	17	11.1
	39	25.5
Social science (history)	(13)	(8.5)
Natural science	7	4.6
Religious studies	17	11.1
Education	30	19.6
Engineering	10	6.5
Allied health professions	10	6.5
Business and accounting	23	15.0
Total	153	99.9

While its importance should not be overemphasized, it is worth noting that the bulk of patriots graduated in disciplines that traditionally score low on standardized graduate admissions examination tests.[12] The second largest number of graduating patriots majored in education, more than all the liberal arts graduates combined. But nationwide, education degree holders rank by far the lowest on both verbal and quantitative graduate admissions tests. Business school graduates, our third largest group of majors, score slightly above educators, and our largest cohort, social scientists, a bit above these. Natural science graduates, engineers, and philosophers generally score the highest on the national tests. But only about 10 percent of the patriots in the sample have studied these, conventionally acknowledged as the most intellectually demanding academic disciplines. There are no philosophy graduates in the sample, which is perhaps ironic if not revealing.

We cannot, of course, infer the achievement scores or the intelligence of individual patriots from aggregate nationwide data. Some business, social science, and education majors undoubtedly score higher than less talented natural science, mathematics, and philosophy students. This would be even more likely if they attended universities with international reputations and high admissions standards. While there are numbered among the patriots graduates of Columbia, Harvard, USC, Ohio University, Oberlin, and Wheaton, 92 percent of those in my sample attended either state universities of moderate or little distinction or denominational institutions of comparable repute (see Table 7.5). The latter include Brigham Young, Notre Dame, and Valparaiso universities, several midwestern Catholic colleges like St. Mary's and Benedictine, and fundamentalist schools such as Oral Roberts, Lenoire-Rhyne, Grove City, and Liberty Christian. I was unable to find the names of several of the Bible colleges attended by the patriots on lists of accredited institutions of higher learning.

My argument is not that individuals cannot receive quality educations at these institutions, but rather that their entrance and graduation requirements are as a rule less demanding, and that their faculties are not generally acknowledged as academic leaders. This, coupled with the observation that many patriots attending these schools majored in something other than the liberal arts, allows us to suggest that perhaps this is why they could leave such schools with their parochialisms and prejudices intact.

In conclusion, then, there is little basis for believing Idaho's Christian patriots to be on the whole less educated than their more conven-

Table 7.5
Four-Year Colleges and Universities Attended by Patriots

Type and Location	Number	Percent
Public institutions	108	73.0
Western states	85	57.4
Idaho and surrounding states[a]	69	46.6
Other westerns states	16	10.8
Other states	23	15.5
Private institutions	40	27.0
Denominational	28	18.9
Nondenominational	12	8.1
Total	148	100.0

[a] Includes, but is not limited to: Idaho State University, Boise State University, University of Idaho, Utah State University, Eastern Washington State University, Washington State University, the University of Utah, and Weber State College.

tional peers. Even after controlling for possible respondent exaggeration and sampling bias, the patriots under examination here appear to have achieved no less academic success than typical white Americans and Idahoans. Evidently, years of formal education alone are not sufficient to erase predispositions to intolerance and conspiratorialism. Although this is by no means certain, the sample appears to have entered fields of study and attended institutions of higher learning not particularly noted for instilling a cognitive commitment to democracy. This means that the educational theory of extremism is not disproven, but specified. Even highly educated individuals ungrounded in traditional liberal arts disciplines may not remain committed to democratic principles when subjected to social stress. Let us examine one such stressor, community alienation.

RADICAL PATRIOTISM
AND THE ECLIPSE OF COMMUNITY

One of the most plausible theories of extremist politics was inherited by sociology from conservative French historians of the early nineteenth century. Shuddering at the Jacobin reign of terror which followed in the footsteps of the Revolution of 1789, they asked how seemingly civil and intelligent people could be rendered into a frenzied mass of violent beasts? Maybe the question was inappropriately posed, but the answer, they agreed, was that the participants in the Terror were those whose ties to community and traditional status had recently been severed by urbanization, industrialization, and democratization. Isolated and lonely, their lives made meaningless by the dislocations of modernization, they presumably yearned for an alternative social organism with which to merge—a leader, a party, a cause to give them direction and boundaries.[13] Turned by social change into an undifferentiated mass of objects, they sought respite from homogeneity, greed, and chaos by fleeing into the protective womb of pseudocommunity. This is the mass theory of political extremism.

Updated and amplified, the thing has since been applied to countless cases of revolutionary unrest, both left-wing and right: from labor activism to the student unrest of the 1960s, from fluoridation disputes and medieval peasant revolts to European fascism, from Third World insurgency to prison riots.[14]

Empirical research on the actual backgrounds of movement activists, however, has begun to cast doubt on the mass theory of extremism. Robert Crain, in his study of fluoridation controversies, found the most fanatic protagonists to be those most integrated into their communities.[15] A study of the participants at a Christian Anti-Communist Crusade rally in 1962 confirms Crain's observation.[16] But the most convincing refutation of the theory comes from analyses of voting support for the German Nazi Party in the pivotal elections of 1932. "One conclusion comes through very clearly," says the author of the most comprehensive of these studies. "A large part of National Socialist electoral support came from the Protestant countryside."[17] In the rural precincts of Schleswig-Holstein, for example, 63.8 percent voted the Nazi Party slate; in the urban precincts the comparable figure was 44.8 percent. But it was in the rural districts that Germans were most integrated socially and religiously into the ordinary channels of community belonging. According to the mass theory of extremist politics, these should have been the districts least susceptible to Nazi agitation.[18]

Do Idaho's radical Christian patriots fit the prototype of the isolated transient of mass theory, or are they closer to the German Nazi Party supporters of the 1930s?

Demographic Considerations

The demographics of the sample are equivocal on this question (see Table 7.6). If it is assumed in accordance with other research[19] that middle-aged males are more involved in local community affairs (as evinced by their participation in voluntary organizations) than are young people or females, then our findings are inconsistent with the predictions of mass theory. Over 80 percent of the patriots in the sample are male. The only exceptions to this are the issue-oriented activists, about half of whom are women. These issue-oriented right-to-lifers and Christian home schoolers are the least radical of the patriots.

Furthermore, the patriots are on the average about fifteen years older than the typical American. It is worth noting, however, that the ter-

Table 7.6
Demographics of the Idaho Christian Patriots

A. Female Participation in Patriot Groups

Political Orientation	Number	Percentage of All Members
Identity Christian	43	15.0
Christian Constitutional	36	19.9
Issue-oriented	24	53.3
Total	103	19.8

B. Average Ages of Patriots As Compared to Americans and Idahoans

Political Orientation	Number	Mean Age
Identity Christian[a]	208	44.9
Christian Constitutionalist[a]	147	50.8
Terrorists	53	35.8
All patriots[b]	399	47.6
U.S. median age (1980)[c]	...	30.0
Idaho median age (1980)[d]	...	27.6

[a] Includes terrorists.
[b] Includes Identity Christians, Christian Constitutionalists, and issue-oriented patriots.
[c] U.S. Dept. of Commerce, *1980 Census of Population, General Social and Economic Characteristics,* vol. I, ch. c, part 1 (Washington, D.C.: Government Printing Office, 1981), Table 98.
[d] *Ibid.,* Table 235.

rorists in the sample are somewhat more than a decade younger than their less violent comrades. This is what the mass theory of extremism would lead us to expect. If the fifty-three Identity terrorists whose ages are known are eliminated from the larger group of Identity Christians, the mean age of the latter is 48.3—almost identical to that for the Constitutionalists.

Theorists of mass politics argue that physical mobility tends to loosen local group affiliations and render migrants available to extremist appeals. Given this, the data on the geographic mobility of the patriots are relatively clear.

Over half of Idaho's Christian patriots were born outside Idaho. This is a rate significantly higher than the national average of about 36 percent who presently reside in states different from their places of birth. But it is approximately the same as the 50.9 percent of Idahoans who in 1980 reported themselves as out-of-state migrants, or the 56 percent of intermountain West residents who so described themselves.[20]

Eight percent of the American population changed their states of domicile between 1975 and 1980. The comparable figure for Idaho residents for that same period was 21.4 percent. During the 1970s, Idaho had the sixth most mobile population in the country, behind only Alaska, Wyoming, Nevada, and Arizona, and almost equal to Colorado. What this all indicates, of course, is that while the patriots have indeed been geographically mobile, they are evidently no more transient than their fellow westerners. This comparability is observable for both Identity Christians and Constitutionalists.

Up to 70 percent of the Identity Christians I have studied were born outside Idaho. This is an extraordinarily high number, but it is no higher than expected given the character of the population in which they reside. In the two Idaho counties—Bonner and Kootenai—where the most violent forms of racist Identity were preached during the decade between 1975 and 1985, the rate of in-state migration was well over 29 percent (31.1 percent in Bonner County alone), one of the highest in the nation.[21] In 1980 far less than one-third of the residents of these two counties could claim birth in Idaho. Nonetheless, based on informal observation of support for the Kootenai County Human Relations Task Force, my impression is that very few of the residents of these counties are sympathetic with Identity Christianity.

The Constitutionalists in the sample are far more geographically stable than their Identity colleagues. More than 70 percent of the Constitutionalists hail from Idaho. Many of them reside in the same towns, and some on the very farms where they were raised as children. In more than a few cases, their local ties go back five generations to the arrival of their Mormon colonist ancestors from Salt Lake City. In this regard, they too, like Identity adherents, are indistinguishable from their less radical neighbors. Most of the Constitutionalists are from counties like Madison, Bingham, Fremont, Oneida, and Jefferson, where well over two-thirds of the citizenry are native to Idaho.

Although they exhibit far different rates of mobility, Constitution-alists and Identity adherents are no more (or less) transient than the immediate populations from which they are drawn. In Idaho, geo-graphic mobility appears to be neither a necessary nor a sufficient con-dition of radical patriotism.

Marriage Instability

If the argument holds that the most compelling civilizing force on masculine libidinal energy and violence is marriage and family,[22] we should expect political radicals to have somewhat weak family ties. How do Idaho's patriots measure up to this expectation? In brief, the marriages of patriots in the sample are, on the face of it, considerably more stable than those of a cross-section of Americans or Idahoans. My impression, furthermore, is that patriot families are typically larger than the American norm. Although I did not request this information, several respondents proudly volunteered that their families had ten, twelve, and in one case fourteen children.

Table 7.7 allows the following observations: Idaho radical patriots are more likely to report themselves married than their more conven-tional peers. They are also more likely to say they have never divorced. This is true for both Identity adherents and Constitutionalists, al-though Identity Christians appear slightly less marriage-oriented.

I have improvised a marriage instability rate to represent these ob-servations and to permit easier comparisons with statewide and na-tional data. It is calculated by dividing the number of ever-divorced individuals by the number never divorced. The census estimate is fig-ured by dividing the number of ever divorced by the total number of presently married individuals. Because the total number now married also includes some who were previously divorced, census data are not strictly comparable to mine. However, insofar as the census-generated calculation has the effect of exaggerating the stability of conventional

Table 7.7
Marital Status and the Idaho Christian Patriots

Marital Status	All Patriots Aged 18 and Over		Identity Christians		Constitutionalists and Issue-oriented Patriots		Idahoans Aged 15 and over[a]
	N	%	N	%	N	%	%
Never married	31	7.7	22	11.0	9	4.4	21.6
Divorced now	…	…	…	…	…	…	6.3
Married, never divorced	325	80.4	146	73.0	179	87.7	66.3[b]
Ever divorced and either single or remarried	48	11.9	32	16.0	16	7.9	24.0
Total	404	100.0	200	100.0	204	100.0	

[a]U.S. Dept. of Commerce, *1980 Census of Population, Detailed Population Characteristics: Idaho,* vol. I, ch. d, part 14 (Washington, D.C.: Government Printing Office, 1981), Table 205.
[b]Married now, but may have once been divorced.

marriages relative to those of the patriots (and therefore acts against the argument presented here), it is permissible to use it.

Comparisons of our sample with census information give the impression that patriot marriages are on the whole considerably more stable than marriages between conventional couples (see Table 7.8). For the Constitutionalists and issue-oriented patriots, matrimony appears to be a resoundingly stable institution. Although their marriages are not nearly as secure as those of the former, even Identity believers enjoy relatively notable marital solidarity.

As just noted, census figures regarding marital stability are not perfectly comparable to those for the sample. A more fitting comparison group would be a cohort of Americans tracked from the time its members obtained marriage licenses to the dissolutions of their marriages either through death or divorce. To my knowledge the only example of such a design was published in 1970 and used 1960 data.[23] In that study social demographers Hugh Carter and Paul C. Glick found that about 80 percent of the elderly men and women in their sample had married only once and that only 16 percent of their marriage dissolutions were due to divorce. This converts to a marriage instability rate of about 190 (that is, 16/84 × 1000). This is greater than that for all the patriots together, but a bit lower than that for Identity Christian marriages. Were this rate of 190 multiplied by a factor taking into consideration the large increase in the divorce rate from 1960 to 1985,

Table 7.8
Marriage Instability of the Patriots

	Ever Divorced per 1000 Never Divorced
All patriots	148
Identity Christians	219
Christian Constitutionalists and issue-oriented patriots	89
Idahoans	284
Americans	329[a]

[a] Based on the national divorce rate, the national marriage instability rate is estimated to be about 1.16 times greater than Idaho's marriage instability rate. National marital status information from U.S. Dept. of Commerce, *Statistical Abstract of the United States* (Washington, D.C.: Government Printing Office, 1986), pp. 35–36.

it is likely that even Identity marriages would show themselves to be no less secure than conventional unions.

Whichever measure is employed, then, there appears to be little support for the notion that Christian patriots have less successful marriages than their more conventional peers, and some evidence that theirs are relatively firmer couplings. Some of this must undoubtedly be due to factors having little to do with Christian patriotism itself. The sample is comprised exclusively of Caucasians, and Caucasians generally have significantly lower divorce rates than non-Caucasian minorities.[24] A larger portion of the patriots reside in rural districts than is typical for Idahoans or Americans, and rural residents have lower divorce rates than their urban cousins. Finally, the higher the level of one's formal education the lower the likelihood of divorcing.[25] As we have just seen, the patriots in the sample are slightly more highly educated than cross-sections of Americans and Idahoans.

After eliminating the influence of these extraneous considerations, it can be hypothesized that an immeasurable portion of the difference in marriage instability between patriots and others is due to differences in their characters. Not only are the patriots 100 percent white, they are virtually 100 percent Christian, and devotedly so. Mormon and Catholic patriots, furthermore, who constitute about one-half the sample, confess to faiths that doctrinally discourage divorce. A related factor is that patriot marriages are traditional "Christian" relationships in which the female partner "knows her proper place." When subordinates piously embrace even demeaning statuses, antagonisms between themselves and their superiors can be expected to decrease. Last, pushing patriot couples together is a joint sense of persecution. When asked to account for the remarkable success of patriot marriages, many informants responded that the stresses of political activism either shattered them quickly and completely or made them stronger, in most cases the latter. There is rarely a middle ground.

Exclusion from Conventional Politics

A reasonable derivation from the theory of mass politics is that extremists are extreme because they are voluntarily or compulsorily excluded from standard political activity. Christian patriots engage in politics whose tactics range from cross-burnings and conscientious lawbreaking to filing lawsuits against government officials, conducting paramilitary training, and violently confronting authorities. But do they also eschew a less dramatic political style?

Table 7.9

Conventional Political Participation by Idaho Christian Patriots

Have Run for Political Office	Number
National office	11
State office	43
Local office	17
Have campaigned for or coordinated campaigns for others, or worked in an official capacity for a political party	25

The data on this question are uneven at best, and there are few findings on a national level (none at all at the statewide level) with which to compare them. Cursory indications, however, are that radical Christian patriots are probably as deeply involved in conventional politicking as they are with its more extreme variants. Of those 275 in the sample whose conventional political involvement is known, 33 percent claim to have either run for office at one time or to have actively campaigned for a candidate. Countless other patriots have lobbied at local, state, and national levels. This percentage compares favorably to a national survey which found that 26 percent of Americans have "ever worked" for a candidate during an election.[26]

Christian patriots do show a proclivity to run for state or national office or to work for sympathetic candidates at the same level. Perhaps this evinces an attraction to abstract and direct solutions to complex social issues. If so, this may be considered partial confirmation of the theory of mass politics, an inability or unwillingness to work through local channels of political representation.[27] Second, while 40.1 percent of the Christian Constitutionalists and issue-oriented patriots are able to point to conventional political participation, only about half that number (21.6 percent) of the Identity Christians can do the same. While the latter number does not vary greatly from the national figure cited above, it may indicate that relative to Constitutionalists anyway, American Israelites are alienated from the conventional political community. This is consistent with our earlier observations regarding their relatively greater marital instability and higher geographic mobility.

However this may be, patriots are preeminently political animals and they do not seem reluctant to employ any vehicle of influence that promises an end to America's problems. This includes canvassing for candidates and holding political office themselves. There is little evidence that voluntary or imposed exclusion from regular political channels has occasioned their resort to more extreme measures. Indeed, the opposite is more likely true. Their use of nonconventional tactics may be a sign that regular channels of influence have not worked for the patriots to the degree they might prefer. The theory of rising expectations makes the rather paradoxical prediction that inflation of expectations precipitated by *too much* citizen participation aggravates dissatisfaction and unrest when demands are not met. Alexis De Tocqueville used this very hypothesis to account for the French Revolution.[28] To be sure, there are cases where, once patriots have been branded troublemakers by public officials or newspaper editors, conventional political forums were shut off to them. This can be taken as "proof" by the patriots of persecution by "satanic conspirators," but it does not corroborate the mass theory of extremism, in which exclusion is said to precede and thus cause extremism.

Occupational Isolation

One of the most frequently cited measures of community alienation is occupational isolation. In a study using international data, for example, Clark Kerr and Abraham Siegel discovered that workers in such structurally isolated industries as mining, lumbering, and the maritime trades have a higher propensity to strike than those who labor in urban trades or factories.[29] Such workers, they believed, are "almost a race apart," living in physical isolation in barracks, towns, or on ships difficult to leave, and governed by exclusive moral codes. They are therefore ripe for mobilization by demagogues. In his own research on the subject, William Kornhauser added to the list of vulnerable occupations itinerant preachers and intellectuals,[30] small farmers (although Kerr and Siegel consider farmers among the least prone to strikes),[31] manual laborers,[32] the "maverick" wealthy whose fortunes come from speculation,[33] and marginal, independent contractors and retailers.[34]

Are Idaho's Christian patriots overrepresented in these presumably isolated occupations? Using Kornhauser's list, my estimate is that 40.3 percent of the patriots whose occupations are known are socially isolated from their immediate communities. This is a conservative estimate in that a number of patriot salespeople may also be "isolated" by Kornhauser's reasoning. Since the data are not detailed enough to separate self-employed retailers from employees of large firms, they are

Table 7.10
Patriots in Isolated Occupations

Occupation	All Christian Patriots		All Employed Idahoans 16 Years and Older	All Employed Male Idahoans
	Number	Percent	Percent	Percent
Manual labor	22	5.7	4.6[a]	4.6[a]
Mining	9	2.3	1.4[b]	2.2[b]
Farming, ranching, logging	51	13.2	10.0[b]	14.2[b]
Free-lance intellectuals	16	4.1	1.0[a]	1.0[a]
Itinerant preachers	27	7.0	0.3[a]	0.3[a]
Independent contractors	21	5.4	1.7[c]	2.7[c]
Free-lance organizers	10	2.6	0.4[c]	0.4[c]
Self-employed retailers	—	—	1.0[c]	1.0[c]
Total	156	40.3	19.4[d]	25.4[d]

[a] *1980 Census of Population, Detailed Population Characteristics: Idaho,* vol. I, ch. d, part 14, Table 217.
[b] *Ibid.,* Table 226.
[c] *Ibid.,* Table 229.
[d] Excluding self-employed salespeople.

ignored here. By comparison only 19.4 percent of all Idahoans in 1980 were reported to be working in isolated situations (20.4 percent if self-employed salespeople are counted). But this comparison is a bit misleading. Since 80 percent of the Christian patriots are male, it is more appropriate to compare them with the percentage of working male Idahoans. The comparable percentage of male Idahoans sixteen and over employed in isolated occupations is 25.4 percent (or 26.4 percent counting self-employed retailers). The conclusion, obviously, is that the patriots in the sample are somewhat overrepresented in isolated occupations. Whether occupational isolation was one of the factors producing Christian patriotism or the other way around, the data cannot say.

The percentage of male Idahoans who work as manual laborers, miners, farmers, and loggers is virtually the same as comparably employed patriots—21.0 percent and 21.2 percent, respectively. While this is close to a quarter of the employed patriots, the number is no greater than expected given the nature of Idaho's work force. Therefore, it cannot be concluded that there is something in these lines of work that propels people to right-wing extremism.

There appears to be some difference in the proportions of male Idahoans and patriots who describe themselves as independent contractors—2.7 percent and 5.4 percent, respectively. But part of this is probably due to my own failure to inquire into whether the patriots in question are bonafide self-employed contractors or merely supervisors of or workers for small contracting firms. There are, furthermore, five times the number of self-employed organizers among the patriots than among a cross-section of employed Idahoans. While the difference may be attributed in part to chance, it also reflects the presence of several political consultants, lobbyists, and political entrepreneurs among the patriots, for whom politics is a vocation.

But the crucial employment difference between male Idahoans and patriots is in the area of what the Department of Commerce classifies as professions. No less than 23.4 percent of the patriots are "professionals," as compared to only 11.4 percent of working Idahoans. This is only slightly less than the number of blue collar workers in the sample.

Under the category of professional employment are grouped licensed engineers, physicians, dentists, teachers, lawyers, and architects, nonconventional diagnostic health care dispensers such as naturopaths, and writers, artists, clergy, and counselors. If among the patriots the last four jobs are eliminated from the professional category, we are left with 12.2 percent, a figure similar to that for employed Idahoans in general.

Of the four eliminated "professional" occupations, 4.2 percent of the patriots are "authors," speakers, and journalists. This is a rate four times greater than that found in the general working population of Idaho. The numbers concerning clergy are even more striking. While only 0.3 percent of employed Idahoans report themselves to be religious workers—most of these in recognized denominations—7.0 percent of patriots so describe themselves. And these are without exception unaffiliated "freelance" pastors of independent congregations.

William Kornhauser has advanced some explanations as to why freelance intellectuals and clergy are more susceptible to extremism than denominational or university-affiliated intellectuals: They are perpetually insecure financially, because they receive no church or corporate patronage. They have no denominational or corporate responsibilities. Their financial insecurity is aggravated by an oversupply of competitors relative to a scarce audience. Hence, they are compelled to be undisciplined and inflammatory in composition and presentation. This trait also is encouraged by their own alleged failure to have developed in themselves a habit of scholarship and objectivity. Intellectuals and pastors, he concludes, are by their very nature inclined to abstraction, and those who are structurally isolated are given status and scope for unrestrained ventilation of their own messianic tendencies and anger at their alienation.

The occupational differences between Constitutionalists and American Israelites are worth mentioning. Constitutionalists are a little less than twice as likely to report themselves as executives, owners, or administrators than Identity adherents. On the other hand, the latter are more likely than Constitutionalists to be professionals by the same proportion. On closer view, the overabundance of Identity professionals is revealed as being due to their much greater likelihood of being preachers and writers.

The figures show that Constitutionalists are more likely than Identity Christians to work as contractors and in precision manufacturing and repair. But almost all of the Christian patriot firemen, policemen, and prison custodians I have interviewed are in Identity (by a ratio of 11:1). This is also true for manual laborers (ratio—5:1). In all of these cases, the numbers are too small to warrant great confidence. Consider, however, the figures for those employed in agriculture, logging, or mining. While 21.2 percent of the Constitutionalists labor in these occupations, only about 10.8 percent of the Identity proponents do.

A hypothesis emerges from this last observation that may be worthy of more study. About 40 percent of both Constitutionalists and Identity believers are in jobs that may be considered structurally unintegrated into the larger community (41.1 percent and 38.1 percent, respectively). But the locations and working conditions of these occupations are to a degree different. Constitutionalists work in rural districts in relative physical isolation, with the soil. American Israelites work in urban areas in psychological isolation, with ideas.

Whether these occupational circumstances determine the stylistic differences in their radical politics (or vice versa) remains to be seen. But one thing is certain: Idaho rural residents in general, and hence Constitutionalists, have little contact with racial or religious minorities. Idaho's urban residents, on the other hand, Identity proponents included, are thrown inescapably into physical contact with these same minorities. This may partially explain why Constitutionalists focus in their conspiracy theories on an indefinite satanic force and Identity adherents on definite ethnic and racial groups.

Religious Isolation and the Patriots

It almost goes without saying that religious affiliation serves as a pivotal linkage between the individual and the larger society. One can, as Idaho's patriots evidently do, have extraordinarily tight family ties and yet, because the family unit itself is estranged from local community, remain effectively isolated. What is necessary to alleviate alienation, as William Kornhauser points out, are viable "intermediate" relationships between family and society. The family breadwinner's occupation, if it is not socially isolated, and the family's religious affiliation, if any, should satisfy this condition.[35]

There is some evidence that Idaho's Christian patriots are comparatively occupationally isolated; how do they stand relative to religion?

At the time of their interviews, all but a handful of disillusioned freethinkers and paganist Nazis reported themselves to be practicing members of recognized Christian religious bodies, that is, of one of the groups listed in the *Encyclopedia of American Religions*.[36] Given that the United States Census Bureau does not inquire into one's religious affiliation, it is difficult to say how this compares to the general American population. A Gallup poll conducted in 1982 found 67 percent of a cross-section of the American public claiming church membership, although only 57 percent expressed a specific religious preference, and only 41 percent actually attended services.[37] A survey of the membership rolls of 219 American religious bodies conducted by the *Yearbook of American and Canadian Churches* in 1983 found 59.6 percent of the civilian population church-affiliated.[38] Based on a county-by-county religious census conducted in 1980 by the Glenmary Research Center of Atlanta, Georgia, my own estimate is that 63.9 percent of all Americans and 54.4 percent of all Idahoans are church members.[39] This estimate corresponds nicely to that of Rodney Stark and William Bainbridge in a recent publication (62 percent and 53.7 percent, respectively).[40]

Regardless of what figures one employs it is obvious, at least superficially, that Idaho's patriots are considerably less disaffected from the religious community than their fellow countrymen. But closer examination of the nature of their religious affiliations belies this impression. Most of the church groups that Idaho Identity Christians have joined are themselves self-encapsulated, socially isolated sects, with names like the Ministry of Christ Church, the Life Science Church, the Gospel of Christ Ministry, and the Kingdom of Yahweh, etc. By contrast most Constitutionalists have retained memberships in mainline denominations, primarily as Latter-day Saints, Catholics, and Presbyterians. Still, religious sectarianism is not entirely unknown even to Constitutionalism, as witnessed by the names of some of its associated church bodies: The School of Prophets, the Church of I Am, the Restoration Church of Jesus Christ, and the New Covenant Theocracy, and so on.

Did the evident religious alienation of these patriots come before and thus occasion their political extremism, or is their sectarianism a consequence of a pre-existing extremism caused by something else? In part the answer to this question may be found in the patriot's religious upbringing.

Over four-fifths (83.4 percent) of those in the sample report themselves as having been brought up not in sects, but in one or more of the forty largest standard denominations in America (see Table 8.1). This suggests that we should be careful before attributing Idaho's brand of the politics of righteousness to the prior religious disaffection of its activists. While for perhaps 15 to 20 percent of the patriots this—and therefore the mass theory of extremism—may be true, it is probably more accurate to say that political extremism preceded and thus was one of the causes of the patriots' estrangement from the larger mainline churches. This process will be examined more closely in the next chapter.

CONCLUSION

Despite the possibility of sampling error, several conclusions are warranted from these data.

There is no evidence that Idaho Christian patriots have less formal education than their less radical peers. Indeed, the subjects studied here have on the average spent more years in school than their more conventional neighbors. This is not to say that they have achieved a better education or that they are more intelligent. But there is nothing to support the popularly held reverse contention, that Idaho Christian patriotism can be accounted for by the lack of education of its proponents.

There are indications that among the Christian patriots, Identity Christians are somewhat more estranged from ordinary channels of community association than Constitutionalists. They have been more geographically mobile. They have relatively less stable marriages. They report themselves as less active in conventional politics. And they are religiously considerably more sectarian. But there is little support for the hypothesis that this apparent isolation has in a mechanical way caused their extremism, at least in the manner suggested by the mass theory of political extremism. Respondent interviews with Identity émigrés, for example, indicate that they carried their adherence to Identity doctrine with them to the Gem State and were attracted to Idaho because of a preexisting support community of fellow believers. Religious background information, furthermore, demonstrates that the vast majority of American Israelites were raised in mainline—though generally fundamentalist—Christian denominations, not in isolated sects.

The only unequivocal support for the theory of mass politics comes from data on occupational isolation. Both Constitutionalists and Identity Christians are alike in respect to their having rates of occupational isolation about one and a half times the Idaho average. Most of this is due to the overabundance among the patriots of itinerant preachers, freelance intellectuals, and self-employed organizers and political consultants. However, as with the mobility and sectarianism data, it is difficult to say whether the choice of isolated work preceded and thus increased the probability of the respondents' becoming radicalized, or whether their occupational careers are the result of a world-rejecting Christian life style. Both hypotheses are plausible, and impressionistic evidence lends credence to both.[41]

Apart from these differences and similarities between Identity Christians and Christian Constitutionalists, Idaho's patriots in general do not seem more socially alienated from their communities than cross-sections of Americans or Idahoans. Table 7.11 summarizes the findings. "Confirmed" designates a statistical association consistent with the theory of mass politics, and "disconfirmed" indicates that findings are not as predicted.

Out of the seven alienation variables on which information was gathered, statistical support for the theory of mass politics is found for only one. Disconfirmation is found on two of the major structural measures of community isolation and for all three of the demographic indicators. This, of course, does not disprove the theory of mass politics. It may be that the indicators selected to test the theory are in-

Table 7.11
Summary of Findings Relating to the Mass Theory of Political Extremism
as Applied to All Patriots

Structural Indicators of Isolation[a]	Status of the Theory of Mass Politics Relative to this Measure
Marriage instability	Disconfirmed
Political participation	Unclear[b]
Occupational isolation	Confirmed
Religious alienation	Disconfirmed
Demographic Indicators of Isolation	
Age	Disconfirmed
Sex	Disconfirmed
Geographic mobility	Disconfirmed

[a] Theorists of mass politics rarely talk about the public education system as a vehicle of community integration. In light of its frequent celebration as precisely such a vehicle, this lacuna is surprising. Let us assume that through high school, public education does assimilate individuals into the larger community. Given our earlier observations about the higher rate of high school graduation by the patriots than their more conventional peers, this is still another indication that the sample does not fit the mass theory of politics. Even though some of the Catholic respondents attended parochial schools, their numbers are so small as to have no effect on this conclusion. Even fewer of the sample attended private Christian academies.

Although quantitative data was not collected on this question, my impression is that a large number of the sample educated in public schools themselves, have withdrawn their own children from that milieu. The consequences of this action for the radicalization of these children will be speculated on in chapter 9.

[b] Because comparative data for Idaho are lacking, I am reluctant to draw a definite conclusion about the relative political participation of Idaho's patriots. As seen earlier, however, the data incline in the direction of disconfirming the mass theory of extremism.

valid or that the information gathered was not truly representative of the typical Idaho Christian patriot. But the preponderance of evidence from so many independent sources makes this somewhat less than likely.

Still, it is important to acknowledge that while the theory of mass politics may not in a mechanical sense accurately portray the reality of Idaho Christian patriotism, it may be valid if understood as part of a dynamic reflexive process. In other words, if Idaho's radical patriots did not necessarily start out socially isolated, they have certainly ended up that way. And my impression is that once labeled "Nazi," "criminal," or "crazy" by authorities, they will be forcibly expelled from the larger community and its consensual restraints. Common sense and deviancy theory alike tell us that this expulsion should encourage their radical propensities. The question for policymakers is how to respond effectively to antidemocratic variants of the politics of righteousness without inadvertently driving it underground and increasing its psychological hold over its proponents, to their detriment and our own misfortune.

8

THE RELIGIOUS ROOTS
OF RADICAL PATRIOTISM

POLITICAL SOCIALIZATION THEORY

The last chapter approached right-wing extremism from a somewhat negative standpoint. The question was whether rightist extremism might possibly be due to an *absence* of something, such as formal education or effective conventional community ties. In this chapter we shift emphasis and ask whether adherents of Idaho's far right are peculiar in repect to the *presence* of a shared background condition. Has the prototypical patriot experienced a unique kind of community linkage and/or a unique type of education that distinguishes him from his more moderate neighbors?

These queries lead to consideration of the theory of political socialization. It is an approach which because of its straightforwardness has enjoyed remarkable growth in popularity since the middle 1960s.[1]

For my purposes "political socialization" will refer to the process by which a junior member of a group, institution, or society assimilates the political values, attitudes, and preferred political behaviors of that group. It is the process by which political preferences, ideological orientations, and so on are successfully transmitted to and eventually accepted by an audience. The idea behind the theory is this: Individuals identify themselves as part of a group or ideology, when they do, because they have come under the influence of specific agents of socialization. The two major concerns of political socialization research have been to identify precisely *what* the effective agents are and to determine how socialization proceeds. The "what" will be the concern of this chapter, the "how" our concern in the next.

The search for agents has mainly been a study of antecedents. The research designs involve correlation studies between a sample's past contacts and its present political beliefs: between mass media (propaganda) messages, for example, and a sample's opinions now; between parents' political party affiliations and those of their offspring; or between parents' racial attitudes, etc., and those of their children. Although it may not have been intended, such studies give the impression that those subject to indoctrination are in effect blank slates upon which messages are imprinted.

However this may be, until 1970 the consensus among political scientists, based on the findings of these correlation studies, was that the family is the paramount agent of political socialization. As one recognized authority said in a widely quoted assertion, "Most of the individual's political personality—his tendency to think and act politically in particular ways—has been determined at home, several years before he can partake in politics."[2] Recent criticism has cast doubt on the validity of this conclusion. Among other things, it points out that high correlations between parental and child political opinions may be spurious products of the abstractness with which questions on political attitudes are typically posed. One is guaranteed virtually perfect agreement between American parents and children on their attitudes toward positive symbols like the flag, the president, democracy, and freedom.[3]

Religion has largely been ignored by students of political socialization. In *The Handbook of Political Socialization,* schools, parents, peers, and mass communications each have separate chapters, each with impressive bibliographies.[4] Religious background and its relation to political outlook are relegated to two pages near the end of the 500-page book, under a minor subheading entitled "other personal factors."[5] It is the religious factor I wish to address here.

As early as 1929, sociology recognized that religious affiliation is a correlate with political attitudes and that Protestantism in particular is a predictor of Republican loyalties.[6] Studies since then have demonstrated Jews and agnostics to be overrepresented among leftists.[7] The most insightful allegations of causal links between Protestantism and rightism, however, have been based on ad hoc impressions by journalists and sociologists at patriot gatherings.[8] There is, therefore, some question about both their reliability and validity.

Where statistical data have been used to verify the causal link between Protestantism and conservatism, as in the collection of articles in a volume on the right wing published in 1969,[9] little attempt is made to control for the overall Protestant population of the surrounding area. Thus, while it may be true, as a 1981 survey showed, that fundamentalists greatly outnumber religious moderates in Moral Majority, Inc. in the Dallas-Fort Worth metroplex, we may still ask whether there are more fundamentalist members than could be expected given their already disproportionate number in that part of Texas.[10] As with the previous discussion of children's and parent's attitudes toward abstract American political symbols, the high correlation here may be due less to an actual causal connection between Protestantism and rightism than to chance.

A related and still graver problem with the statistical studies is that without exception they correlate *present* religious affiliation with political attitudes and behavior. But one's present religious orientation may bear little resemblance to past religious upbringing. Hence, however illuminating such research may be in other respects, it throws very little light on the question of the sample's antecedent socializing agents. Indeed, my impression is that some patriots are "reborn" to rightist politics just as they convert to a fundamentalist Protestant sect. For example, several Aryan Nations Church members I interviewed, who were educated in comparatively liberal Catholic parochial schools, became fundamentalist converts just about the time they were developing their extremist political philosophy. This suggests that for these individuals there may be a third factor, related to both Protestant fundamentalism and to rightist extremism, causing their conversions.

Among these possible tertiary factors Seymour Martin Lipset and others have proposed elderliness, low class rank, a rural geographical residence, status insecurity, and, especially, a low level of formal education.[11] In regard to the last factor, it has been hypothesized that uneducated people may be attracted simultaneously to political extremism and to fundamentalism because of the simplistic dualism of these world views and their anti-intellectual appeal to faith. The findings reported in Chapter 7 seem to indicate that at least for Idaho's patriots, this hypothesis is probably untrue.

What then is the relationship between religious background and the rightists in our sample?

PROTESTANTISM AND PATRIOTISM

Of the 384 patriots on whom I compiled religious background information, 80.5 percent reported themselves schooled in Protestant church groups, nearly two-thirds either as Mormons or as fundamentalists (32.3 percent and 32.5 percent, respectively). Nearly 5 percent of the patriots had no religious training at all as children. As might be expected given the paucity of their numbers in Idaho, only a small proportion (14.6 percent) of the patriots admit to having been raised

Table 8.1
Religious Upbringing of the Idaho Patriots

Denomination	Number	Percentage of All Patriots
Catholic-Episcopalian*	56	14.6
None	19	4.9
Protestant	309	80.5
Latter-day Saint (Mormon)*	124	32.3
Baptist*	47	12.2
Lutheran*	18	4.7
Methodist-Congregationalist- United Church of Christ*	24	6.3
Presbyterian*	18	4.7
Nazarene*	11	2.9
Other fundamentalist	67	17.4
Independent Bible	22	5.7
Seventh Day Adventist*	9	2.3
Follower of Christ	6	1.6
First Christian*	6	1.6
Church of God*	3	0.8
Four Square Gospel*	2	0.5
Assembly of God*	2	0.5
Church of Jesus Christ Christian	7	1.8
Others	10	2.6
Total	384	100.0

*One of the forty largest American denominations.

either Catholic or Episcopalian. Although they will be treated as doctrinal moderates here, most Methodists, Lutherans, and Congregationalists in the sample were brought up in pre–World War Two evangelical variations of these confessions.

Of the 417 patriots whose *present* religious affiliations are known, 92.6 percent are Protestant. This compares to 32.7 percent of all Americans and 55 percent of all American religious adherents, and to 46.2 percent of all Idahoans, or 84.5 percent of all Idaho church members. (About 54.4 percent of Idaho's citizenry claims church membership.)[12]

That over four-fifths of the sample were introduced to Protestantism as children and that over 90 percent now confess to Protestant faiths suggests the possibility of a causal tie between Protestantism and Christian patriotism. Confidence in this suggestion increases when one notes that over 60 percent of these Protestant patriots were raised not in doctrinally liberal nor even moderate denominations, but in fundamentalist churches and sects or in the Mormon Church during the 1940s through the 1960s, when its teaching hierarchy was expanding an increasingly conservative social philosophy.

To study this hypothesis we would want to compare our figures to those concerning the religious upbringing of the general American and Idaho publics. But unfortunately, very little is known about the religious training of the American population, and even less about Idahoans. According to Table 8.1, virtually all the patriots can point to at least some formal religious training in their childhoods. This is a rate higher than the 83 percent reported in a 1978 Gallup poll for a cross-section of Americans. (The Gallup figure was 88 percent for those who presently attend church, but only 77 percent for those presently unchurched.)[13] We know nothing about the specific church groups that the Gallup respondents referred to. It will therefore be necessary to improvise an appropriate comparison group.

I make the following assumptions: First, it is reasonable to suppose that people's religious orientations today generally correspond to their religious upbringing in the past. That is, Catholics remain, if anything at all, Catholic; Protestants, Protestant; and Jews, Jewish. There are enough exceptions to this rule to emphasize the word "generally." Second, I will assume that those brought up in one of these orientations are no more likely to "lose the faith" and drop their church memberships than those of other orientations. (There is evidence that since the Korean War members of liberal denominations have in fact apostasized at higher rates than fundamentalists. Were these different rates of apostasy controlled for, the statistical association between fundamentalism and patriotism reported below would be stronger than indicated.)[14]

In 1980 the ratio of Catholics and Episcopalians to Protestants in Idaho was about 1 : 5.5 (or 15.4 percent to 84.7 percent). Given the previous assumptions, there is reason to believe that although a greater *number* of Idahoans were brought up in churches than actually attend services now, the *ratio* of Idahoans originally raised Catholic and Protestant should parallel present church enrollment. That is to say, for every Idaho citizen schooled at one time in Catholicism or Episcopalianism, there should have been about five Idahoans raised Protestant. If so, then we would expect from chance alone that for every Idaho Christian patriot brought up Catholic there should be five or so patriots who were brought up Protestant. This prediction is borne out by the numbers in Table 8.1. There is in fact a ratio of 5.5 Christian patriots raised Protestant to every 1 raised Catholic or Episcopalian. To repeat: Although patriots-raised-Protestant vastly outnumber patriots-raised-Catholic in the sample, evidently no more patriots were raised Protestant than their present proportion of the total population in Idaho would lead us to expect.

Recall that 65 percent of all the patriots were raised in two highly conservative orientations: Latter-day Saint and fundamentalist. Is this also what would be expected given the proportions of fundamentalists and Mormons in Idaho?

Table 8.2 indicates that virtually the same number of patriots were raised LDS and fundamentalist (including Baptist) as expected given their present proportion of the Protestant population of the state. But there appear to be slightly *fewer* patriots of Mormon background than expected given their numbers in the Protestant population. First impressions to the contrary, in other words, Mormon conditioning appears to have a slightly moderating effect politically on its members. As shall be seen, this conclusion may be premature.

In any case, the story is different for patriots coming from either Baptist, non-Baptist fundamentalist, or Presbyterian backgrounds. About three times as many patriots were raised Baptist than might be expected given their ratio to all Protestants in Idaho, about twice as many Presbyterians, and anywhere from half again to nearly three times as many non-Baptist fundamentalists.

It is important to caution against making too much of the exact ratio numbers themselves; these would likely change with alterations in sample size. But the general tendencies of the ratios are so glaring in these three cases that changes in their general directions would be unlikely even with a much larger sample.

Have the sample subjects been politically socialized to radical patriotism by virtue of their religious training? Were they catechized as youths with the precepts of rightism they enact today as adults? Because we do not know the church lessons actually instilled in the minds

Table 8.2
Ratios of Patriots Raised in Different Denominations Compared to Estimated Ratios of Idahoans so Raised

Comparison Groups	Ratios for All Idahoans[a]	Ratios for All Patriots	Interpretation
Catholics and Episcopalian to Protestants	1:5.5	1:5.5	No difference
Fundamentalist Protestants[b] and LDS to all Protestants	1:1.1	1:1.2	Virtually no difference
LDS to all Protestants	1:1.8	1:2.5	LDS slightly under represented among patriots
Baptists to all Protestants	1:18.4	1:6.5	Baptists overrepresented among patriots by three times
Lutherans to all Protestants	1:15	1:18	Virtually no difference
Methodists, Congregationalists, and United Church of Christ to all Protestants	1:16	1:13	Virtually no difference
Presbyterians to all Protestants	1:35.4	1:16.8	Presbyterians overrepresented among patriots by over two times
Other fundamentalists[c] to all Protestants	1:5.3	1:4.1	Other fundamentalists, overrepresented among patriots
Other fundamentalists[d] to all Protestants	1:11.5	1:4.1	Other fundamentalists overrepresented among patriots by nearly three times
Other fundamentalists[c], Presbyterians, and Baptists to all Protestants	1:3.7	1:2.1	These groups overrepresented among patriots by nearly two times

[a] Ratios based on *Churches and Church Membership in the United States,* ed. by Bernard Quinn et al. (Atlanta, Ga.: Glenmary Research Center, 1981), pp. 13–14. The information in this monograph is based on 111 reporting church bodies nationwide. The editors believe that the population reached constitutes about 91 percent of that surveyed by the *Yearbook of American and Canadian Churches,* which is based on data from 219 church bodies. To compensate for the acknowledged gap in information, I have multiplied the total adherents reported by the Glenmary Center for Idaho by a factor of 9.1 percent. My adjusted estimate is that 54.4 percent of Idahoans are members of religious groups.
[b] Includes adjustment factor (above) added to fundamentalist enrollments reported in Quinn et al. plus Baptist Church membership.
[c] Includes adjustment factor minus Baptist Church membership.
[d] Fundamentalist church enrollment reported in Quinn et al. without adjustment factor.

of the patriots as children, these questions have no certain answers. But the theological complexion of conservative Christian orthodoxy makes such a conclusion at least plausible.

Divine Transcendence and Earthly Sin

Elsewhere I have examined one doctrinal characteristic of Christian fundamentalism and Calvinism (of which Presbyterianism is a modern derivative) that has historically inclined their adherents to political extremism and, in rare cases, to violence.[15] It is succinctly expressed in these words of Paul to the Corinthians (13:10): "When the perfect is known, one despises what is imperfect." Posed in sociological terms: The more spiritually transcendent and etherealized a people's notion of God, the more cognisant they are of incompatibilities between His majesty and the material world. The more absolutist are their expectations for this world, the more unrighteous and depraved it will seem.

Divine transcendence and its corollary depreciation of this world is an ideal-type which no doctrine or individual entirely represents. But Christian fundamentalism undeniably approaches the extreme. This is demonstrated both in its assertion concerning God's heavenly transcendence relative to the world (and its preoccupation with worldly sin) and in its negation of Mormonism as Christian "paganism" that deifies man and humanizes God. As man is, God once was, Mormon theology asserts; and as God is, man through his own efforts may become. The doctrine that, after death, man's place in heaven comes solely through God's undeserved grace is alien to Mormonism, which is one reason Mormonism is tantamount to blasphemy and apostasy to fundamentalists.[16]

To one who knows God in His infinite righteousness, this earth and its chief denizen, man, are not simply petty, they are utterly fallen, inexorably evil. Even infants, John Calvin argues, deserve eternal condemnation though the fruits of their iniquity are not yet manifest. Born as they are in the stench of sexuality, they harbor the seed of evil "and therefore cannot but be odious and abominable to God."[17] "We're sinful, we're wicked. . . . We're dying, we're condemned," agrees a Kansas radio minister four centuries later. "Little children," he continues, "you'd think they'd be innocent creatures." But they're depraved too. They fight, they scream. "They'll tell you lies, they'll cheat. Where do they get this? They're born with it. This is Adam's nature. It came upon us from Adam's sin in the Garden."[18]

Misogyny

"Adam" is derived from the Hebrew *adamah,* of the soil, with its associated images of darkness, still waters, and material substance, which is to say, femininity and womanhood. As "material" and "matter" come from the Latin word for mother (*mater*), then the loathing of the material world by fundamentalist Christians often takes misogynic (woman-hating) forms. This is not necessarily disgust at particular women, but horror at the feminine principle, of what the image mother-seductress-siren-shrew-daughter-witch represents. The female embodies surrender of individuality to fate, to Nature, to Fortuna, to the inescapable cycle of womb and tomb—unconscious fertilization, bloody fecundity, death, and reabsorption into the Great Mother, Earth.[19]

Christian patriots, 80 percent of whom in the sample are males, can no more help accommodating themselves to this fearsome mystery than they can deny their own lives. But they do require that accommodation be in their own "righteous" terms, that feminine power be subject to their conscious control, for God's sake (or the Nation's or the Race's). This begrudging of Woman is indelibly etched in orthodox Christianity, but rarely has it been so straightforwardly expressed as in Richard Butler's essay "Women," in *The Aryan Warrior.*[20] The world of the "contented Aryan woman," he says, is made up of family, husband, children, and home. Such a life has but two purposes: to bring "true love and affection and a happy well-run home to refresh and inspire her man" so that he may be better able to protect community and race from the Foe; second, to bear and care for children—for "every child that an Aryan mother brings into the world is a battle waged for the existence of her people." To serve these ends, Aryan girls should school themselves in wifely and motherly chores, and "devote years to making [themselves] pure. . . . "It is in the purity of her blood in which reposes . . . Aryan culture." Such is "far greater love" than preparing herself to be a "clever woman lawyer."

Innerworldly Asceticism

As Max Weber has so masterfully shown, believers in divine transcendence have but two choices. They can flee this world, becoming world-rejecting monks, or if this is doctrinally impermissible (as it is for Protestants) they can go into the world to tranform it in a manner pleasing to God.[21] As world-reforming ascetics, they will remake the world after God's image, without themselves being tempted by it. This is precisely the heroic vocation of the Christian patriots, the motivational underpinning, as they themselves understand it, of their politics of righteousness.

Naturally the patriots realize that as individuals they are powerless to reform the world all at once and in its entirety. Therefore, each focuses his righteous hostility on the one or two earthly sins most personally salient. For one it may be the "crime" of homosexuality, for another "demasculating" women, for still others "fetal murder," or race-mixing. These become the arenas of combat in which they heroically testify to the Lord's call.

Conspiratorialism

An essential component of the Christian patriot world is conspiratorialism, the insistence that there are no accidents. Each historical event is effected by conscious design and intent. As such, it too may be understood as a derivative of and generalization from the doctrine of divine transcendence. A cosmic Actor, all-powerful and omniscient, determines the minutiae of earthly events through His purposes and plans.

Insofar as this all-powerful Creator is also pictured as perfected in His goodness, then the fundamentalist is thrust into the perilous situation of reconciling the Creator's perfection with the glaring imperfections of His creation. To maintain the integrity of his faith, the fundamentalist is therefore driven to devise a counterpart to God: the Devil and a consortium of human allies (Jews, Masons, liberals, Trilateralists, Bilderburgers, Illuminati, and Communists, and perhaps even Mormons and Catholics). These shadow figures are endowed with the same transcendent powers of the good God except placed in the service of evil purpose, slavery, and death. Now responsibility for all earthly imperfections, natural and human—from volcanoes and droughts to disease and social ills—is transferred onto this quasi-divine alter ego. And in combat against it the Christian patriot dramatizes his holy calling, the remaking of the world after God's image and likeness.

Dispensationalism

Add to all this the *conditio sine qua non* of fundamentalism as defined in Chapter 1: dispensationalism—the periodizing of human history according to the ways in which God has "dispensed" favors and judgments to mankind and, above all, the insistence that ours is to be the Last Dispensation. Such teaching has the effect of rendering every contemporary event symbolic of Armageddon. The swelling of the

Great Salt Lake in Utah must be due to a Luciferian plot. Rock 'n' roll must be a satanic design to weaken the moral fiber of our youth. AIDS is divine punishment for disobeying God's commandments. "Praise god for AIDS," proclaims J. B. Stoner, a recently imprisoned racial terrorist. "God is avenging us white Christians against those who are persecuting us."[22]

But more than this, the contention that Christ's thousand-year earthly reign is imminent lends utmost urgency to the private and public lives of believers. *Now* is the time to choose to walk in faith with the Lord; tomorrow may be too late. Today one must cleanse himself for the Second Coming, straighten out his family life, and begin purging the world in preparation for receiving Christ. The politics of righteousness is replete with the pressing sense of this obligation.

General Comments

Mormonism does not adhere to divine transcendence as characterized above. But it does divide the world into opposed forces—the Saints and the "abominable church." It does speak of satanic conspiracies. It does preach a variation of dispensational millennialism, and it shares with fundamentalism the idea that these are the "latter days," the age when the anti-Christ will be crushed in a final battle ushering in the Millennium. Hence, all the heady anticipation of laying the political and confessional groundwork for the establishment of Zion is seen in Mormonism too. Bruce McConkie's encyclopedia on Mormon doctrine devotes nineteen pages to the subject "Signs of the Times," far more than to any other entry.[23] These signs are indicators of discernment bestowed to men of faith, proving that ours are truly the latter days.

It is no mystery, then, why patriot organizers with an eye for new recruits have come to frequent conservative and fundamentalist denominations and sects, or why the John Birch Society targeted Mormon Church meetings. For it is in such places of worship that they find their natural constituency, audiences prepared to take seriously in action what they have already been schooled to believe.

Gary Cutler, a former Pocatello Mormon convert to Baptism who later became an Aryan Nations leader, once admitted to newspaper reporters that "a lot of Identity people do that [i.e., visit other fundamentalist churches]. You talk to other people—you're a spy of sorts." The recruitment of his own wife Cindy to the cause illustrates this procedure.

Cindy was raised a rigid, thrice-born-again Southern Baptist. "I was with the Jesus Christ thing, that Jesus was my savior and God was love. We'd go to the beach and walk up to a perfect stranger and say, 'Are you saved?'" As chance would have it, Gary Cutler, who was stationed with the Navy in Cindy's hometown of San Diego, met her one day at Baptist services and introduced her to Identity.

Cindy's fondness for Gary grew, but at first she found his belief in Identity hard to swallow. Their courtship was spent in Bible study, Cindy trying to overcome her "prideful" resistance to the message. Conversion occurred during one intense session when she came across this passage: "My sheep know me and hear my voice, and follow me." "That's how I got into Identity," she later told reporters. "I questioned how they [the Jews] could be God's chosen people if they hate my Christ." Cindy was last publicly seen teaching music at the Aryan Nations Academy in Hayden Lake.[24]

FUNDAMENTALISM, MORMONISM, AND ANTI-SEMITISM

The clearest statistical evidence that certain kinds of religious backgrounds predispose people to Christian patriotism is provided by the association between different religious upbringings and different styles of patriotism.

Table 8.3 shows that 59.6 percent of the Identity Christians in the sample come from conservative or fundamentalist Protestant backgrounds, but only 9.2 percent were raised in the Church of Jesus Christ of Latter-day Saints. For Christian Constitutionalists the percentages are almost reversed: 65.4 percent of the Constitutionalists were schooled in LDS doctrine, but only 18.2 percent were brought up as fundamentalist or conservative Protestants. The patriots raised as Latter-day Saints are about three times less likely to be Identity Christians than would be predicted given their numbers in Idaho, and nine times more likely to be Constitutionalists than Identity patriots.

These differences are all the more striking given similarities between Constitutionalists and American Israelites in their levels of formal education, their ages and genders, and their degrees of occupational isolation. While Constitutionalists and Identity adherents have somewhat different rates of marital instability, political participation, and geographic mobility, these pale in comparison to their differences in religious upbringing.

Sociologists have adopted the custom of representing strengths of association between two variables by using unity (1.00) to designate a perfect relationship and zero to indicate no relationship at all. One such measure is Lambda. Its numerical value describes the percentage by which the analyst is able to decrease errors in predicting the distribution of cases on one variable knowing a second variable, as compared to having no information on the second variable. Lambda for collapsed versions of Table 8.3 varies from 0.54 to 0.64. This means that we are able to reduce our errors in predicting the respondents' styles of Christian patriotism by over half knowing whether they were raised LDS or in some other faith, as compared to knowing nothing about the respondents' religious backgrounds. (Our overall ability to predict the respondents' political orientations knowing their religious backgrounds is above 80 percent.) We have before us, obviously, a singularly powerful relationship.

My hypothesis is that the relative amenability of patriotic Latterday Saints to Constitutionalism and their avoidance of Identity Christianity are due partly to their political socialization. As described earlier, Mormon Constitutionalists appear to have borrowed three elements from their Church's social ethic: piety toward the organic Constitution and its "fathers," conspiratorialism as interspersed throughout the Book of Mormon, and above all, a patronistic attitude toward the Jew as a flesh-and-blood family member. This last factor psychologically immunizes even militant Mormon patriots from directing their enmity onto Jews. Fundamentalist and conservative non-Mormons, on the other hand, being less doctrinally insulated from anti-Semitism, tend to fasten their hostility onto the Jews.

Both Mormons and non-Mormons consider the Bible a holy book. But Mormonism gives equal status to three other sacred texts: the *Pearl of Great Price,* the *Doctrine and Covenants,* and the Book of Mormon. Like the Bible, the Book of Mormon is interpreted by believers not as an esoteric metaphor of individual spiritual development, but as the actual historical record of the Native American peoples.

As we have seen, the theme of the Gadianton robber conspiracy plays a seminal role in the unfolding of this legend. But there are also interpersed assertions about Jews as God's chosen people who will reappropriate the land promised to them by God, and of the sponsorship by the Saints in this event. There is no suggestion that the Gadianton conspirators are Jewish. There are, however, intimations of a linkage between the conspirators and the devil's "abominable church," the non-Mormon Christian (or "gentile") establishment.

Table 8.3

Religious Upbringing of Idaho Christian Patriots by Present Political Orientation

Religious Upbringing	Christian Identity		Christian Constitutionalists		Issue-Oriented Patriots	
	N	%	N	%	N	%
Catholic-Episcopalian	32	17.3	15	9.4	9	22.5
Latter-day Saint (Mormon)	17	9.2	104	65.4	3	7.5
Fundamentalist-Conservative Protestant[a]	110	59.6	29	18.2	23	57.5
"Liberal" Protestant[b]	15	8.1	7	4.4	1	2.5
None	11	5.9	4	2.5	4	10.0
Total	185	100.1	159	99.9	40	100.0

[a] Includes mainly independent Bible churches, Seventh Day Adventist, Church of the Nazarene, Lutheran, Baptist, Followers of Christ, Church of God, Four Square Gospel Church, Presbyterian, Assembly of God, Church of Jesus Christ Christian, Jehovah's Witnesses, and unaffiliated pentecostal groups.
[b] Includes only Methodist, Congregationalist, and United Church of Christ. Although the adjective "liberal" is used, in fact most patriots were raised in conservative, evangelical variations of these denominations.

	Christian Identity	Christian Constitutionalists	Total
LDS	17	104	121
Fundamentalist-Conservative Protestants	110	29	139
Total	127	133	260
	Lambda = 0.64		
	Overall predictability = 82.3%		

	Issue-oriented and Christian Identity	Christian Constitutionalists	Total
LDS	20	104	124
Non-LDS	190	51	241
Total	210	155	365
	Lambda = 0.54		
	Overall predictability = 80.5%		

By contrast, for their edification regarding the Jew, non-Mormon fundamentalists have primarily the Bible, their pastors' interpretations of its passages, and Christian tradition. In the context of the theory of political socialization the question is: How is the Jew portrayed in the New Testament?

The issue is not what the actual intent of the authors of the Gospels—particularly John—and the epistles of St. Paul were. Nor are we interested how or to what degree their statements were allegedly distorted to serve the interests of an imperial Church by its teachers and lawgivers. Nor, finally, do we need to consider whether New Testament anti-Judaism is an extension of pre-Christian Greek and Roman hostility to the ghetto and synagogue. All that is relevant is what the New Testament teaches about Jews to uncritical literalist readers who are prepared to find some group to blame for the world's ills.

The view of post-Holocaust Christian and Jewish scholars is that anti-Judaism is inextricably woven into the Christian testament, so much so that Rosemary Ruether can speak of it as "the left-hand of Christianity." As the Christian learns what his faith is, he also discovers its negation: Judaism.[25] "Christianity in its very nature," agrees one theologian, "implies a criticism of Judaism. . . . that is a better—the word *better* must suffice here—religion than Judaism." What Paul says about the Jews, concurs another, is "unmistakably negative."[26] The Jews are portrayed as blind to the spirit of the law, obsessed with the outward conventions of conformity to it, stubborn in their myopia, and arrogant in their mule-headedness. As people of the flesh they are dark and loathsome, the eternally damned children of Satan.

This fantasy was first concocted between the second and fourth centuries A.D., in the course of the missionizing conflicts between synagogue and church. By the end of the first Christian millennium, it had evolved into an all-encompassing demonology in which Jews were said to murder Christian children on high feast days, use their blood to make unleavened bread, desecrate the wafer, poison wells, and commit usury. By the Reformation, Jews had become satan-worshipping sorcerers presiding over orgiastic festivals and plotting the destruction of Christian civilization.[27]

Adapted to modern circumstances, every negative assertion preached from Identity pulpits on the Jews is taken verbatim from this infamous literary tradition. Martin Luther's "On the Jews and Their Lies," for example, continues to be sold through Identity book catalogues. Until after World War II this tradition was reiterated in the catecheses of even the most liberal American denominations. In the official liturgy of the Catholic Church, the faithful were exhorted until 1948 to pray on Good Friday for "the perfidious Jews": *Oremus et pro perfidis Judaeis.*[28] These lessons are still taught by some fundamentalist and conservative sects and churches today.[29]

My position, then, is that one need not entertain convoluted psychological theories to account for the penchant of some Christian patriots for anti-Semitic causes and others for pro-Jewish Constitutionalism. Like the predisposition to Christian patriotism itself, these political orientations are more or less built in to the theologies of the Christianities from which the patriots have been drawn. Those who are now anti-Semitic were probably introduced to it in veiled form in Sunday school as children. Recall Baptist Cindy Cutler's allegation that "Jews hate my Christ" and therefore cannot possibly be God's chosen people. On the other hand, those patriots who are pro-Jewish were probably either not taught anti-Semitism, or if they were, had intellectual ammunition of equal authority to counter it.

If this supposition is accurate, then non-Mormon fundamentalist Christians as a group should exhibit higher rates of anti-Semitism than less rigidly dogmatic and more theologically liberal Christians such as Unitarians, Congregationalists, and Methodists. Results of an elaborate survey program conducted by sociologists Charles Glock and Rodney Stark out of the University of California in the 1960s support this contention. Without going into details of the study, it is enough to say that religious dogmatism—by which the investigators meant intransigence, militance, and literalism—as measured by a joint index of religious exclusivity and doctrinal orthodoxy, is highly associated statistically with agreement to hostile statements about modern Jews.[30] This association persists when age, sex, political outlook, occupational prestige, income, and education are held constant. For comparable levels of education, those who are more religiously dogmatic also register higher degrees of anti-Semitism. "No matter how high their education or occupational status," Glock and Stark conclude, "persons remain very likely to be anti-Semites as long as they retain a religious perspective which facilitates an image of the Jew as an outsider."[31] Here, I believe, is one explanation for why so many of our respondents could be highly educated and still retain religious and racial prejudices toward Jewry.

In what was until 1970 the largest systematic survey ever conducted on Mormonism, Armand Mauss used the Glock-Stark questionnaire on a sample of 1,300 Latter-day Saints.[32] Comparing their attitudes toward modern Jews with the Glock-Stark respondents, Mauss discovered that his Mormon subjects were six to seven times *less* likely to exhibit high degrees of anti-Semitism than the most dogmatic Protestants, and about four times more likely to exhibit no Judeophobia at all. Indeed, Mauss found that on the Jewish questions Mormons were typically more tolerant than members of even the most liberal denominations. He attributes these striking differences to what he calls the Mormon doctrine of "Semitic identification," the same theological complex depicted in Chapter 6.[33] While he does not invoke the specific concept of political socialization to explain his findings, support for the theory is clearly implied in his discussion.

The Glock-Stark research program came under bitter attack from some religious quarters where it was argued, among other things, that while this association may be true for laity, it could not be true for their pastors: the problem must be one of misinterpretation on the part of bigots in the congregations. The two sociologists replicated the original study, this time on a sample of Christian clergy. They found the original association to be at least as strong for Christian ministers as for laity.[34]

CONCLUSION

The preponderance of evidence both from the present survey and from independent sources supports the proposition that in Idaho membership in fundamentalist or conservative churches is a precondition for recruitment into the Christian patriot movement. Although it cannot be proven, I believe this association is explained by the theory of political socialization: the majority of Christian patriots in our sample were taught as youngsters what today they express in their righteous politics.

There are two problems with this conclusion. First, most fundamentalist and conservative Protestants in Idaho are not active in the movement (although they may be sympathetic with it). Most Mormons do not become Constitutionalists, and only a handful of fundamentalists and Baptists convert to Identity Christianity. Furthermore, fifty-six subjects in the sample have Catholic backgrounds, twenty-four were brought up in religiously "liberal" milieus (but see footnote b at

Table 8.4

Distribution by Christian Denominations on Index of Secular Anti-Semitism

Degree of Anti-Semitism	Percentage of Each Denomination at Given Level[a]						
	Mormon[b]	Congregationalist	Methodist	Lutheran	Evangelical Sects	Total Protestant[c]	Catholic
High	3–4	7	9	19	26	15	11
Medium high	7.5	14	14	17	27	18	18
Medium	10.5	53	51	24	39	47	45
None	38.5	26	26	24	8	20	26

[a] Adapted from Rodney Stark and Charles Glock, *Christian Beliefs and Anti-Semitism* (New York: Harper & Row, 1966), as reported in Armand Mauss, "Mormonism and Minorities," Ph.D. dissertation (Berkeley: University of California, 1970), p. 91.
[b] Combined approximation of distributions of two samples of Mormons in San Francisco and Salt Lake City.
[c] Excludes Mormons.

Table 8.3), and nineteen report themselves as having had no religious training at all as youth. This adds up to 25 percent of the sample. Not only is a fundamentalist or a conservative religious background alone not sufficient for recruitment to the cause, it is not necessary. Second and relatedly, while we may have a clearer picture of one of the agents of political socialization for three-quarters of the sample, *how* this influence proceeded still remains a mystery. It is hard to believe that today's patriots were as children mechanically imprinted with doctrines which they now simply reflexively dramatize.[35] But how does recruitment actually occur? This will be the concern of the next chapter.

By way of closing and anticipation, let us consider the case of Ed and Lisa Minor,* two congregants of the Aryan Nations Church, who unapologetically espouse its racialist ideology.[36]

Lisa was raised liberal Catholic in a northern Idaho town named after the river which meanders through it. Her mother had long since resigned herself to a life of tedium and helplessness, providing little encouragement and less guidance to three daughters trying to forge independent destinies in the world. At eighteen Lisa traveled to nearby Moscow to study physical therapy at Idaho's land grant university. It was during the late 1960s, and she became deeply involved in the local drug scene, dropping out of college and returning home a hippy. While living at home, Lisa went through a series of dead-end relationships with small-time drug pushers, the last of whom was a charismatic Charles Manson cult leader type. Realizing that if she did not pull herself together soon, hers would be a short, senseless, brutal life, Lisa turned to prayer. How this solution came to her is unclear. What is known is that she was "born again," joined a local Bible church, and soon found employment as a clerk in its Christian bookstore. It is there that Ed came into her life.

Ed Minor's cause had for some years been the Aryan Nations Church. Raised nominally "Christian," he had already turned agnostic "seeker" when he learned of the group through friends at Lockheed Aircraft in Lancaster, California, where he worked as an electrical engineer. Included among these friends was Richard Butler. We do not know if Butler himself recruited Ed into what was then Wesley Swift's church, but when Butler moved the church headquarters to northern Idaho in

* Fictitious names.

the early 1970s, Ed dropped everything to accompany him. He settled in a log cabin in the woods near Deep Lake,* and when the new chapel was constructed at Hayden Lake he volunteered to install the utilities.

Ed is about twenty years older than Lisa, well educated, and sure of himself and his beliefs. Evidently he was the kind of man, a stable Christian man, that Lisa had been looking for when he made one of his regular recruitment visits to the bookstore that day. Lisa now lives in his shadow, bearing his children and rarely seeing visitors. She is the prototypical hippy earth mother turned barefoot, silent, pregnant wife.

Lisa and Ed were married in the new Aryan Nations chapel, the Rev. Butler officiating. After thirteen years of marriage they boast seven children, the oldest already a teen. None of the children has ever attended public school, for it teaches the satanic pedagogy of "secular humanism." Nor do they attend private church school. That would be prohibitively expensive given that Ed is perennially unemployed and the family lives off welfare. Nor are they taught at home. The seven children are functionally illiterate. But all of them can expostulate on who is at fault for the world's ills. All are devoted and voluble racists.

True, Idaho state law in the county of Lisa and Ed's habitation is not simply being evaded, it is being flagrantly flouted. But cases like the Minors' are all too common in the local district, and the school board hesitates to stir the sleeping beast hidden deep in the woods lest it awaken in a rage. What was once the belief of a single, forceful, clear-sighted personality, Ed's, has now been incorporated by his wife and successfully transmitted to the next generation.

We see here, too, three different ways in which religious factors enter into the process of political socialization. Had Lisa not been "reborn," had she not joined a Bible church and sought employ in its bookstore, Ed might never have met her. Lisa's life would have taken some other trajectory. Had Ed not been an active "seeker" with a "Christian" outlook, however unrefined, he would have been less receptive to the Identity message. The seven children, on the other hand, have been born into a church already teaching that as the chosen people they are God's battle-axe and His weapons of war. Unless they rebel against the psychological hold their parents (and through them the church) currently have over them, the children are fated to walk in the footsteps of their elders. At this point they closely approximate the popular stereotype of the passive cult member. Nevertheless, even given that their illiteracy makes it harder to imagine how they might rebel against parents and church, it is still too early to predict their political careers. Already the eldest son rides his bike to town every morning to play video games and "hang around." It is possible that these daily excursions will introduce him to other ways of life.

9

SOCIAL NETWORKS
AND PATRIOT RECRUITMENT

Men are not born with hatred in their blood. The infection is usually acquired by contact; it may be injected deliberately or even unconsciously, by parents, or by teachers. . . . The disease may spread throughout the land like the plague, so that a class, a religion, a nation, will become the victim of popular hatred without anyone knowing exactly how it all began; . . . and no one foresees the inevitable consequences.[1]

Popular wisdom posits that people join extremist movements in different ways than they affiliate with conventionally acceptable groups. Because their views are considered eccentric, then presumably the ways in which extremists received them must be extraordinary or weird. Since conventional middle-class life is assumed to be unproblematic, sacrosanct, "correct," the extremist could only be the way he is because something either in his background or in himself is "incorrect."

This chapter takes the opposite position. There is little evidence that Christian patriots are indeed peculiar in other respects than their religious background and politics. Therefore their recruitment to the movement must be analogous to the way ordinary people join everyday causes. This is the "how" of the sample coming to espouse Christian patriotism.

It seems likely that one of the major socialization agents for a majority of Idaho's Christian patriots may have been their fundamentalist and conservative churches. But it is still an open question how religious backgrounds are transmuted—when they are—into political activism. An immense theoretical gap exists between a youngster's religious upbringing and an adult's politics of righteousness. Most potential recruits with the "proper" religious credentials are lost to the patriot cause somewhere in that gap. At the same time there is a small but notable number of Catholics, "liberal" Protestants, and those with no religious training—that is, people with the "improper" background—who nonetheless become patriots during passage in that same theoretical gap. This chapter will describe and analyze the nature of that gap.

How are ordinary people mobilized into collective efforts? One of the most fruitful discoveries by sociologists researching a variety of settings since World War II has been the so-called "multi-step" process of mobilization (see Table 9.1). Whether it is a fashion or fad, an opinion, a voting preference, or a distrustful attitude toward government, the adoption of an agricultural innovation, the spreading of a rumor, or participation in a demonstration or riot, individuals are not generally recruited directly by mass appeals—handbills, ads, or pamphlets—but indirectly through their ties with "opinion leaders," influential members of the same local groups as themselves.[2] It is through personal connections that a person's attention is first aroused. And these same groups and leaders either sanction or reward members depending on their response to the issue. Those estranged from such groups are typically uninformed about the fad, rumor, invention, opinion, or cause, and indifferent in their response to it. They are the last and the least likely to be swept up in popular enthusiasms. To quote Anthony Oberschall: "Participants in popular disturbances and activists in opposition organizations will be recruited from previously active and relatively well-integrated individuals within the collectivity,

Table 9.1
The Multi-step Process of Mobilization

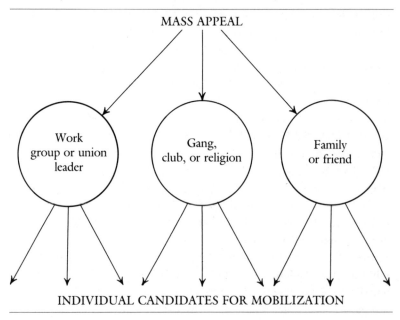

MASS APPEAL

| Work group or union leader | Gang, club, or religion | Family or friend |

INDIVIDUAL CANDIDATES FOR MOBILIZATION

whereas socially isolated, atomized, and uprooted individuals will be underrepresented, at least until the movement has become substantial."[3]

This is the multi-step theory of political mobilization, and it is eminently consistent with my own findings. Contrary to the expectations of the mass theory of political mobilization, the patriots participated in a multi-step recruitment process mediated precisely by their community attachments.

THE POLITICAL MOBILIZATION OF THE PATRIOTS

The respondents were typically made aware of Christian patriotism, although not normally in these terms, through conversations at lay Bible study meetings, during coffee breaks at work, during discussions with loved ones, or in one case during a study hall break at a parochial high school in Cincinnati, Ohio. (The young man in question, now a northern Idaho resident, espied his tablemate, the son of a National Socialist, reading *Aryan Nations Calling*, a Hayden Lake white-supremacist journal. "What's that?" he asked. The answer was his introduction to the Aryan Nations Church of which he is now a member.)

It might have been a favored pastor who initially aroused the respondent's attention, a trusted friend, or for several of the sample, a prison cellmate; but more often it was an admired family member, normally a father or an older brother, a spouse or a fiance. Often the occasion of initial arousal was a specific issue: inflation, a bond or tax levy, the children's problems at school, or a particularly heinous local crime. In the course of discussion patriot pamphlets or cassette tapes might be passed or an invitation to a patriot speech or workshop given. The crucial point is that with few exceptions, social bonding with the recruiter preceded the respondent's intellectual commitment to the cause. The successful recruiter invariably had influence over the respondent independent of the recruiter's involvement in the patriot movement itself.

Respondents rarely joined the movement because they saw it initially as compatible with their political interests. Indeed, many confess at first to have been revolted by the Identity message or by Constitutionalism. Rather, they "joined with" others already in the movement, and only later began articulating its dogma. In this regard the process of what I have called mobilization corresponds to the conversion process observed by sociologists to sects and cults like the Unification

Church,[4] the Jesus Movement,[5] Pentecostalism,[6] Scientology,[7] and the UFO crusade.[8]

To be sure, there are respondents who appear to have become aware of Christian patriotism through mass media solicitations. One, a postal clerk, came across an Aryan Nations advertisement in the *Spotlight* newspaper he was processing. He subsequently joined the group. Another dozen or so subjects report having educated themselves to patriotism by using the resources of a local library. Lastly, a handful of patriots credit their involvement in the cause to unprovoked "persecution" by local officials during zoning disputes, farm foreclosures, and especially tax audits. But these evident exceptions merely prove the proposition argued here. The vast majority of the subjects made their connection to Christian patriotism via social networks of which they already were members.

Robert Mathews, founder of the Order, gained more than one recruit by placing ads in patriot newsletters calling for unemployed Vietnam veterans and other men down on their luck to join him in Metaline Falls, Washington. But closer analysis of his successful solicitations reveals that prior to their induction into the Order, these recruits were calculatedly (if willingly) put in Mathews's debt by his loaning them small amounts of cash and hosting them in his wilderness cabin. While not as consciously contrived as the Unification Church's strategic use of "hooking" and "love bombing,"[9] or the Children of God's "flirty fishing" (sexual allurement),[10] Mathews's tactics evince an intuitive understanding of the principles of marketing theory. One of those who answered an ad and was sent $50 by Mathews helped arrange an armored car heist that netted several million dollars. Indifferent to Mathews's ideology, he now says with bitterness that "it started off as a friendship. . . . I was loyal to friends, and he [Mathews] just kind of drew me in through that." Another cadre concurs. Claiming that originally he had no animosity toward minorities and "got along with everyone," he moved in with Mathews and changed his views out of respect to Mathews the man: "It was my friends that started to convince me that blacks weren't my equal."[11]

Although patriot ministers do engage in proselytizing, recruitment to the patriot movement seems to have been mostly a matter of chance, mobilization being a function of where individuals were positioned in their social networks. A typical example: Several Union Pacific "car men" (conductors and engineers) develop strong ties to an elderly work group leader. Respected by his younger co-workers for his humility, generosity, and courage, the gentleman is also an avowed racist and once-convicted tax resister. His example as a person first attracts the younger men to him, not his beliefs. Only after strong bonds are established does he open to them his prolific library of radical literature. Their eventual recruitment is also facilitated by their worship at the same Seventh-Day Adventist Church.

By being subtly rewarded for responding "correctly" to specific issues, the respondents found themselves beginning to consent voluntarily to the line espoused by their sponsors. Sometimes the untimely expression of the same opinion to other audiences resulted in rebuff, ridicule, and more than once in fisticuffs. Expulsion of the candidate from "decent" company often precipitated his complete engulfment in the patriot role. Again, this last step is consistent with what sociologists have observed when young people are disowned by their families just prior to their full commitment to exotic cults.[12]

Naturally, details of this process varied for different respondents. But whether American Israelites, issue-oriented patriots, or Constitutionalists, their political careers followed similar steps. Each modeled himself after one or more "significant others" either imposed on the respondent because of his institutional position or chosen for reasons other than the recruiter's beliefs as such. The respondent's self-esteem was enhanced by imitating the recruiter's mode of expression, his attitudes, actions, and dress. Through "conditioning," responses at one time perhaps embarrassingly self-conscious to the respondent became internalized. In the end he appropriated them, freely choosing to act and believe in the way expected of him by his comrades, namely, as a Christian patriot.

To use a somewhat unfortunate metaphor, group forces appear to have "pushed" and "pulled" our respondents into the patriot movement. This, and not their lack of education or their lack of group ties, accounts for their affiliation. Had the respondents no community ties, the likelihood of their even hearing about the movement, much less converting to it, would have been nil. Still, I do not mean to suggest even metaphorically that the respondents were passive victims of group forces that compelled them against their wills. This kind of sociological overdeterminism tends to ignore the very real freedom the respondents actually displayed in evaluating the veracity of the various messages they received in the patriot media and in weighing the value of various invitations to join different activist groups.

In a manner of speaking most of the subjects actively recruited themselves to the movement. They were intellectually active "seekers" for answers to serious questions they had about what is "going wrong" with America,[13] or, more often, for satisfying personal relationships with those who eventually served as their recruiters, e.g., for a "good Christian man," to quote several patriot wives.

Since 1975 sociologists of collective behavior have attempted to integrate the two-step theory of mobilization and its portrait of the passive joiner with the more realistic notion of the joiner as an active agent in his own recruitment. These efforts have culminated in what is known as resource mobilization theory.[14] This theory argues that affiliation with any political or religious group is a function of relatively rational decisions made by "human resources" to enhance their own interests (of which they may not be entirely conscious). In brief, potential recruits weigh two considerations: the value to themselves of the collective goods advertised by the groups in question; and the values of selective private goods that might accrue from affiliation with those groups. Using patriot groups as a case in point, the former might include the defense of constitutional liberties or traditional WASP privileges from "unAmericans," "perverts," and aliens. The latter might include the pleasures of socializing with others who share one's views—eating meals, singing, and playing together, being acknowledged by people whose opinion one respects—or it might include more worldly things like sexual gratification and money.

In one of the most far-reaching variants of this theory, Rodney Stark and William Bainbridge write that the major "payoff" for joining a religious group is a "compensator." This is an IOU of sorts—eternal life in heaven—redeemable only after the joiner's death.[15] In exchange for their loyalty and tithes, in other words, the potential member is promised a very practical if otherworldly benefit. In this sense, however else it is viewed by the joiner, the decision to join one church or cult over another is an economic matter. Likewise, religious organizations may be seen as competitors in "religious markets," doing commerce both in compensators and in tangible rewards ranging from sex (the Children of God) and money (the gospel of wealth) to magical powers over disease. Successful American church groups in addition typically advertise their child-care facilities, their counseling skills, aerobic dance classes, baseball and basketball leagues, and wilderness outings. Nor is this unique to established denominations. The Laporte, Colorado, Church of Christ, one of this country's largest Identity groups, sponsors an annual Rocky Mountain Family Bible Retreat. Besides the expected fare of workshops on constitutional law, "victory over persecution," and "the new anti-Christ tactics planned for America," its brochure for 1988 announces a string of dude horses, baseball and volleyball, frizbee golf, a talent night ("bring your instruments"), the annual tug of war, and "the nationally acclaimed Legacy Singers."

According to resource mobilization theory, candidates for recruitment multiply the values of the public and private goods preferred by a group times their own estimates of the probability that the goods will actually accrue to them if they join. The recruits then, presumably, add the multiplied products to assess the expected utilities of joining one group or the other. Rational candidates will join that group which has the highest expected utility to them given their interests.

This process may seem to overcomplicate acts that appear entirely straightforward to the actors themselves: "Why did I join such and such a church? Well, because I believed in its message." To its credit, however, the theory provides a plausible way to explain why people who otherwise seem intelligent and psychologically normal would join groups advocating what appear to outsiders to be "crazy" or "stupid" doctrines. Notwithstanding how irrational it may seem to become a "Moonie," a Child of God, or a devotee of Nichiren Shoshu Buddhism, people join such groups because joining is (to them) the most rational thing they could do, given their interests and their perceptions of the groups' offerings. Furthermore, the theory allows analysts to differentiate among various interests and to learn which are actually given more weight in a candidate's calculations. For example, patriot "seekers" typically proclaim that the single most important motive in joining the movement has been to preserve a Christian, constitutional America, often at great personal cost. But the evidence we have gathered suggests that a major interest in joining the patriot crusade is not this alleged public good, at least not exclusively and not even primarily. It is instead to nurture rewarding personal relationships with their recruiters. Again, the sample subjects celebrate their involvement in the movement by speaking of the virtue of being dutiful Christian patriots. But when their actual interests in joining are examined closely, they are more likely to be private ones: preserving, establishing, and expanding love relationships and family ties, friendships, and positive work environments. I suspect that this is equally true for most left-wingers. On the other hand, it should also be emphasized that, except for patriots of a libertarian bent and a handful of tax resisters in the sample, there is very little evidence that these private interests include purely mercenary considerations.

A related point concerns what James Richardson and others have observed with regard to cultists. Because patriots are, according to resource mobilization theory, relatively rational seekers who wish to maximize their political-religious and especially their private-social interests, their group affiliations at any one time are not necessarily permanent.[16] Instead these affiliations may change along with the patriots' changing perceptions of what is most beneficial and least costly to their interests.

A hypothetical patriot may flirt briefly with a Young Americans for Freedom (YAF) club in part to maintain friendships with his chums and then after graduation become an active Republican Party organizer so as to please his fellow workers. His party loyalty and hard work may be rewarded with an offer to be a precinct committeeman, but finding his ideal aspirations frustrated by the "system," he may instead begin attending John Birch Society meetings where he learns the "real" cause of his frustration, namely, the machinations of the "invisible hand." However, because the Birch Society in his hometown may have turned into a study and letter-writing group, he may find its activities do not provide him scope to really "take a stand" against the "one world conspiracy." At this point he may begin experimenting with a local tax resistance group, finding much to his surprise that when the chips are down and prosecution is pending, his old conservative friends have disappeared. Perhaps, he concludes, they too are part of the conspiracy. Now it may seem reasonable to leave them behind to join the local Posse Comitatus unit, register for a series of *pro se* litigation training sessions, or take up membership in the Populist Party or even an Identity church. Although outsiders may interpret these steps as confirmation of the increasing "kookiness" of the hypothetical patriot, he himself may see them as marking his development as a good Christian citizen. Resource mobilization theorists, meanwhile, see these transformations as rational adaptations to the various situations in which he sees himself.

Having said this it must not be forgotten that rational, interest-directed seekers though they may be, patriots rarely, if ever, embark on political career changes like these without the direct mediation of others. Patriot groups have overlapping memberships. In every YAF chapter there are regular Republican Party activists. In most county parties there are Birchers, in most Birch cells tax resisters, in most Golden Mean Clubs hangers-on who also attend Posse meetings, or who are on the Barristers' Inn mailing list, or who are Populist Party recruiters. And in Idaho many Populist Party leaders are also affiliated with Identity sects. Hence, as the patriot becomes dissatisfied with one political posture, he locates contacts in each group (or they find him) who are seekers like himself, willing to introduce him to another, perhaps more radical political style.

Nor is the career trajectory of the activist inevitably toward increasing radicalism. It is conceivable that after years of anxiety, fatigue, and disgust the patriot will renounce politics altogether. Since my research deals exclusively with activists, this last trajectory must be left open as a theoretical possibility. However, the reader may recall two cases mentioned in Chapter 1 of complete disavowal of extremism: Greg Withrow and Tommy Rollins. While the details of their apostasies must await another investigation, the multi-step theory of mobilization (or in this case "demobilization") would retrodict that both renunciations were mediated by specific social contacts—a pastor, a friend, or a counselor—standing partly outside the patriot movement. Indeed, Withrow himself said as much when he revealed that a woman named Sylvia inspired him to change his views. In the course of an interview, he pointed to a tattooed rose on his shoulder inscribed with her name. "Isn't that much more beautiful than the gray swastikas across my back?" he asked reporters.[17]

A final observation. Those few subjects in the sample who were structurally or voluntarily estranged from groups carrying messages contrary to the patriot line seem to have had their mobilization to the cause enhanced. Technically, this is sometimes called "superimposed segmentalism."[18] It is most easily understood by contrasting it with its opposite, structural "cross-pressures." When under cross-pressure, a subject is positioned to receive contradictory messages from different opinion leaders and thus finds it difficult to fully commit himself to either one. Patriot children being educated in exclusive right-wing academies, at home, or, like the Minor children, receiving no formal education at all, are not under cross-pressures. If their situation persists, the effective transmission of the politics of righteousness to them is virtually guaranteed. But even in rural Idaho it is difficult to entirely insulate children from peers who might carry the viruses of worldliness and "satanism." It is therefore premature to predict the political futures of these youngsters.

In any case, this observation concerning cross-pressures is balanced by its corollary. Patriot groups that choose to isolate themselves from conventional communication networks—public schools, workplaces, established denominations, unions, social clubs, and the major political parties—invariably cripple their capacity to recruit new members. To conquer the world, political and religious movements must paradoxically allow themselves to be conquered by the world. Many of the extremist groups studied here will not permit this, being motivated by a sense of heroic Christian duty rather than by utilitarianism.

ASSESSING THE EVIDENCE

A major weakness of the multi-step theory of political mobilization is that it is difficult to document statistically in any but the most superficial way. Table 9.2 lists the major influences mentioned by the subjects in their decisions to join the Christian patriot movement. There are several problems with this table. First, common sense tells us that any social act, a political commitment included, is the product of more than one influence. In the interview protocol, however, I requested that the respondent name the single most important influence on his politics.[19] Second and more serious, simply because an individual mentions in hindsight that a particular event or person has influenced his decision to be a patriot does not necessarily mean that objectively this influence was as powerful as it appears in retrospect. It is conceivable that the real influences on a person's life remain unknown to him even if he responds in good faith to inquiries. And there is reason to believe that on this question the subjects did not always speak in good faith. Human beings are adept at constructing autobiographical accounts that present them in positive, heroic, righteous lights. Idaho's patriots are not immune to this tendency. In this table, however, we are forced to take the retrospectives of the subjects at face value. Third, as the multi-step theory would indicate, it was difficult for many patriots to relate specifically the date at which they became committed patriots. One of the subjects—who has at various times been a Silver Shirt, a Klansman, a Minuteman, a Posse Comitatus deputy, and who is now a member of the White American Resistance—told me, "I been fightin' against them Communist sons o' bitches since 1923." When I asked him how he got involved in the movement he related that as a teenager he attended a Wobblie (Industrial Workers of the World) conference in California, "and they was a singin' the Internationale."

Table 9.2
The Major Immediate Influences Mentioned by Patriots
(One Influence Only for Each Patriot)

Major Types of Influence	Number	Percentage
Primary Group Influences		
All family members	79	34.6
Male members (father, grandfather, husband only)	(38)	
Female members (mother, grandmother, wife only)	(19)	
Friends (other than non-coworkers)	47	20.6
Co-workers	17	7.5
Pastors and fellow confessors	14[a]	6.1
Unspecified personal acquaintances	7	3.1
Total	164	71.9
Secondary Group Influences		
Contacts in political action groups (Republican Party, Young Americans for Freedom, etc.)	10	4.4
Church sponsored studies or outlook (Freemen Institute, Mayflower Institute, etc.)	30[b]	13.2
Total	40	17.6
Tertiary Group Influences		
Advertisements or mass media messages	3[c]	1.3
Response to legal "persecution"	6	2.6
Self-educated	15	6.6
Total	24	10.5
Grand Total	228	100.0

[a] Includes five recruited via radical church prison ministries.
[b] Includes four who claim their radicalism is a natural outgrowth of traditional Catholicism.
[c] Includes one woman whose husband had been "saved," and who was praying for salvation when she was "reborn" during broadcast of a fundamentalist preacher's sermon.

The implication is that this opened his eyes to who was really behind the labor movement and "caused" him to become a lifelong patriot. Needless to say, given the elderliness of a good many of the subjects, I have heard many analogous tales. They are almost impossible to classify and hence most are ignored in Table 9.2.

Read in light of these weaknesses, Table 9.2 still has some analytic utility. If nothing else it reveals these things: First, there are a variety of ways in which Idaho's patriots were recruited to the movement. Second, an overwhelming number of patriots specify a primary group influence as having mediated their mobilization. Third, among these primary influences family ties and friendships together are by far the most important. Fourth, in the family, male members are mentioned twice as often as females as the occasion of one's joining the cause. And fifth, mass media devices were a statistically insignificant reason for becoming a patriot. Indeed, all tertiary influences summed constituted only 10 percent of the major immediate influences reported by the sample. Even with all its problems, Table 9.2 provides unequivocal support for the multi-step theory of recruitment. It is through close, personal ties that the subjects first learned of and were encouraged to join the movement. The unstated implication is this: Had they had different family members, friends, co-workers, and pastors, etc., it is possible that most of the subjects would never have joined the patriot cause.

Alternatives to statistical studies of the multi-step theory of political mobilization are qualitative narratives of individual cases of conversion such as those reported in John Lofland's and Rodney Stark's classic piece "Becoming a World-Saver." Accounts like these are subject to the criticism that as descriptions of unique events they are not easily generalizable to other situations. But their attention to the details, nuances, and complexities of the conversions of concrete human beings more than compensates for this problem.

With this in mind, presented below are two case histories based on my interviews that display the multi-step theory.

The Boise Valley American Israelites (BVAI)

Through its linkages both with the Aryan Nations Church in Hayden Lake, Barristers' Inn School of Common Law in Boise, and the Idaho Populist Party (which was led until recently by a BVAI member), the BVAI occupies a pivotal node in the Idaho patriot communication network. Furthermore, unlike all but the issue-oriented patriot groups, the BVAI is headed by a woman, Regina Smith,* a well-traveled and much-respected evangelist. The BVAI is comprised of articulate, basically humane, and well-educated urban professionals, people whose profiles hardly fit the media stereotype of the red-neck, bourbon-swilling, wild-eyed patriot. Nonetheless, its members have totally devoted their lives to the movement (see Table 9.3).

Most of those in the BVAI explicitly renounce racist Identity. True, they see the religion of Judaism (if not all synagogue Jews) as mistaken or inadequate, and at worst a tool of Satan. But they hesitate to speak of themselves as "superior" to others and vigorously protest the suggestion that they might be religious bigots, at least in the pejorative sense of the word. (It was pointed out to me that "bigot" is a conjunction of two German words, *bei* [by] and *Gott* [God]. So understood, some BVAI members proudly proclaim their "bigotry.") Instead, they prefer to rank individuals and creeds in terms of "responsibility." Some are called to "more responsibilities" than others. Aryan Israelites are among those so called. "The kingdom is for everybody," says Regina. "Our responsibility is to set an example as Christians." "I am," she insists, "very radical on this point."[20] If the world is to be reformed at all, she believes, it will be done not by force but through witnessing to Christ in one's private, family, work, and political life. While members of the BVAI actively participate in the politics of righteousness and can "understand" the "necessity" of Christian violence, none that I interviewed was able to condone the extremities of the Order.

The BVAI is in essence an unincorporated Bible study group which meets weekly to read biblical passages, share testimony, and hear short lessons. Regina has her master's degree in counseling from the University of British Columbia. She presides informally over approximately twenty individuals. These individuals, however, do not attend services alone, nor did they join the BVAI originally as social isolates. Instead they first became aware of and subsequently affiliated with the group through their families. As a consequence, the BVAI is less a congery of twenty discrete worshippers than it is an association of four families: the Smiths,* the McDougalls,* the Vogels,* and the Andersons.* A fifth family, the Johnsons,* who now live in Colorado, are only peripherally associated with the BVAI.

At this writing the BVAI consists of four generations of worship-

*Fictitious names.

Table 9.3

A Social Inventory of the Boise Valley American-Israel Community

Name[a] and Relationship	Age (1984)	Education	Occupation	Religious Upbringing
1. Robert Golden	80s		Minister	Nazarene
2. Mrs. Smith	76		Avon distributor	Baptist,
3. Regina Smith (daughter of Mrs. Smith)	50	MA. Counseling, U. British Columbia	Evangelist counselor	Nazarene
4. Larry Smith (son of Mrs. Smith)		High school graduate	Precious metal broker	Nazarene
5. Mrs. Larry Smith				
6. Larry Smith children				
7. Jim Smith (son of Mrs. Smith)		High school graduate	Real estate appraiser	Nazarene
8. Mrs. Jim Smith				
9. Jim Smith children				
10. Ed McDougall	56	High school dropout; real estate certificate, Boise State	Elected Canyon County official	Nazarene Baptist, Church of God
11. Gerald McDougall (son of Ed McDougall)	35	B.B.A., Boise State	Timber Company comptroller	Independent fundamentalist
12. Mrs. Gerald McDougall		B.S., Boise State	Surgical nurse	Baptist
13. Frank Vogel	59	High school graduate	Farmer, health food sales	Evangelical Lutheran
14. Mrs. Frank Vogel		High school dropout	Hospital kitchen supervisor	Evangelical Lutheran

	Age	Education	Occupation	Religion
15. Alice Vogel (daughter of Frank Vogel)	32	High school graduate; beauty school	Day care proprietor	Evangelical Lutheran, Baptist
16. Son of Alice Vogel	12	Home schooled	. . .	BVAI
17. David Anderson	26	B.S. math and psychology, Oral Roberts; M.A. Counseling, U. Connecticut	Counselor	Nazarene
18. Mrs. David Anderson (niece of Regina Smith)	27	B.Ed., Oral Roberts	Housewife	Independent Fundamentalist
19. Daughter of David Anderson				
20. Ronald Big	58	2 years Boise State, business administration	Banker/financier	Seventh Day Adventist
21. Leonard Johnson	38	Ph.D. vocational ed., Colorado State	Educator	Lutheran, Presbyterian, Nazarene
22. Mrs. Leonard Johnson	38	A.S. College of Southern Idaho	Housewife, educator	Nazarene
23. Leonard Johnson Children				Nazarene

[a] All names fictitious.

pers, ranging in ages from around eighty to toddlers. The latter are becoming familiarized with spirited "full gospel" preaching through their parents, just as the parents became acquainted with it through the grandparents. The McDougalls, one of the two leading BVAI families, provide an excellent illustration of the transmission of religious-political tastes to a new generation. Like the Smiths, the McDougalls started out as Nazarenes. But the parents became increasingly dissatisfied with the answers their Nazarene pastor was giving their queries. Taking their son Gerald with them, they moved from the Church of the Nazarene to a local Baptist congregation, from there to the Church of God, and then to a Full Gospel Church which was not, father Ed McDougall now says, "really full." Finally, the Smiths and the McDougalls found Robert Golden, a United Pentecostal minister, who was preaching what they had evidently been searching for, a brand of American Israelism. Gerald McDougall has since married and introduced his wife, once a disillusioned Baptist, to the same doctrine.[21]

Another example: As Evangelical Lutherans, the Vogels accustomed their daughter to emotional preaching while still a child. Now she raises her own son in the same atmosphere with the added influence of teaching him the regular school curriculum at home. Alice's son's enforced exclusion from the "perils" of public education makes it likely that he will take it for granted that his is the only correct way to be Christian and in the end will display the views of his parents and grandparents, only more vehemently.

Regina Smith's mother originally took her three children—Regina, Larry, and Jim—to Nazarene Sunday school. Later, with the McDougalls, she attended Pentecostal prayer meetings led by "brother" Golden. First conducted in the homes of one or another of the families and later in a rented American Legion hall, Sunday testimony is now shared in an Adventist Church building. When Golden became too enfeebled to lead the group himself, Regina was informally appointed his successor. She received the call to evangelize at seventeen, just three years after her own baptism.

Larry and Jim brought their children to meetings to instill in them the same lessons they had received as youngsters from their mother. Although Regina has not married, her influence is such that her niece, Regina Anderson, has now brought her husband and daughter into the fold. The Andersons met at Oral Roberts University, a school founded by the Oklahoma fundamentalist minister of that name. David Anderson, like Regina Smith herself, now supports the family as a Christian counselor, employing a therapeutic rhetoric of sin and choice, instead of the more conventional illness-passivity model.[22]

As indicated earlier, the BVAI is an important link in the patriot network. Through her travels and preaching as an "ambassador of Christ," Regina has developed close ties with a number of patriot groups. She is credited with introducing the wife of one of the executives of Barristers' Inn to the Identity message. Regina has preached and led workshops at the Heritage Library in Velma, Oklahoma, a center founded by the son of a banker angered because of the financial shenanigans of his father's colleagues. She has also appeared at the Liberty Ranch outside Roseburg, Oregon, a Christian patriot retreat established by two ex-Amway dealers. It was there that she met fundamentalist minister Joe Lutz, who in 1986 unsuccessfully ran for the Senate in Oregon. She has warm ties with pastor Everett Silevin, a Nebraska Baptist church school activist who has been jailed more than once for resisting court orders, and who in 1986 entered the Republican primary for governor of Nebraska. Neither Lutz nor Silevin is an Identity Christian.

Regina Smith is not the only BVAI member with ties outside the Boise Valley. Through the Montgomery Institute, a home-school information dispensary and legal center established by Dave Anderson, the BVAI is kept in communication with Christian home schoolers throughout the state. One of these is Alice Vogel, the divorced daughter of two other BVAI activists, Frank Vogel and his wife Gilda. Although all three now attend BVAI services, and Alice now ministers to brother Golden in his last days, they got into the movement somewhat independently of each other. The recruitment of both parents and daughter is fraught with enough uncanny coincidences to be taken as "proof" of God's intervention in their lives.

Alice first heard the Identity message in a taped Sheldon Emry sermon given her by a friend in 1973. She was twenty-one. She had already been instilled with the habit of Bible study and was reading the Prophets at the time, struggling with the question of why, if they are truly God's chosen people, the Jews would have persecuted their own prophets and killed His only son. After hearing Emry's taped answer, Alice sent for more information and as a result was placed on the mailing list of his Phoenix-based Lord's Covenant Church. Jane

Johnson, who was working as Emry's secretary, thus learned about Alice and inspired her to pull her son out of public school and teach him at home.

Alice appears to have kept her growing interest in Identity to herself out of respect for her parents. It was only when she learned that they too had heard the message that they began exchanging literature. Their commitment to the movement has since then been mutually reinforcing.[23]

Frank Vogel was sitting with fellow activist Jeff Ligert* in the booth of a Boise pancake house planning marketing strategy for a series of anti-abortion tapes when their conversation, filled with allusions to the Bible, was overheard by a seventy-eight-year-old acquaintance of Ligert. Within minutes the man was challenging Vogel to learn what the Bible "really" said. A bit condescendingly Vogel agreed and was handed several taped sermons by Emry. "At first I tried to prove him wrong," Vogel told me, so contrary were Emry's words to what he had learned as a Bible student. "But I couldn't." Other tapes soon followed, recordings by Bertrand Comparet and Wesley Swift, and then pamphlets and books. Vogel finally became convinced after reading J. H. Allen's *Judah's Sceptre and Joseph's Birthright*. This was in 1981. Frank Vogel and Gilda have since joined the BVAI and he has become an unpaid "ambassador of Christ" himself.

Had Ligert's friend shown up but a moment later, Vogel is convinced, he and Gilda would still be wallowing in darkness. He sees the hand of God in his conversion. Divine intervention is indicated in another way as well. Both Frank and Gilda are from Gering, Nebraska, where they attended church in a building later rented by a local Church of Christ group. The assistant pastor of that group was a young man by the name of Pete Peters. Peters now heads his own flourishing Identity church in Laporte, Colorado. His taped sermons are heard nationwide.[24]

Jane Johnson and her husband, Leonard, now attend Pete Peters's church. However, both are one-time Idaho residents, having met at the College of Southern Idaho in Twin Falls, where he was an instructor and she was studying for a degree in applied science. Both at the time were in the throes of divorce from their first spouses. In Leonard's case, the proceedings were initiated by his wife's furor over his increasing devotion to the patriot cause.

* Fictitious name.

Like Frank and Alice Vogel, Leonard first heard the Identity message via taped sermons, in his case, those of Herbert W. Armstrong, and then of Robert Record and Emry. Also as for Frank and Alice, the tapes were provided by a friend. And again, like so many of our subjects, what he heard "was repulsive to me at first," he relates. "But I kept going back to it." In the course of their courtship, Bob showed the tapes and pamphlets to Jane. She enthusiastically embraced what she read. Headier literature followed: Frederick Haberman's *Tracing Our Heritage* and Alexander Hislop's *Two Babylons,* the latter a critique of Catholic "paganism." On holidays the two enjoyed family studies, took up genealogy, and jointly discovered their Israelitish roots. Their goal now is to establish a nondenominational private college with an integrated vocational-technical and spiritual curriculum.[25]

The Upper Snake River Constitutionalists (USRC)

Mormon colonizers from the valley of the Great Salt Lake began settling the Upper Snake River basin in the early 1880s. Among the first to stake homesteads in what is now the struggling farm community of Paynes Ferry* were the Foremans* and the Peterses.*[26] Numbered among the most outspoken extremists in southeast Idaho are descendants of these same two families. They constitute a core group of what I shall call the Upper Snake River Constitutionalists (USRC). Their political biographies are presented not because of their uniqueness, but because they graphically illustrate how the USRC, like the Boise Valley American Israelites, have been mobilized to activism via their memberships in extra-movement groups.

The case of the USRC also refutes the theory of mass politics, which holds that it is those least integrated into the community who are most prone to radicalism. Although their political beliefs have resulted in ostracism by Paynes Ferry's moral censors, the individuals discussed below are fourth- and fifth-generation members of the village in which they reside. Both their ancestors and present-day relatives are local notables. William Peters, who in 1883 helped Thomas Ricks survey the streets for the Mormon college town of Rexburg, Idaho, would give his name to the nearby city of Petersburg.* One of the legendary Idaho Mormon patriarchs, he fathered thirty-nine children by seven wives. His son Robert is said to have had livestock and land holdings worth more than a million dollars before the Great Depression wiped

* Fictitious names.

him out. He is still remembered for having guided then Church President Joseph F. Smith on a fishing expedition through Yellowstone Park in the early 1890s. The Foremans can also boast of Church bishops, counselors, and missionaries in their past. Nor is the prominence of the two families limited to religious affairs. The Peterses have provided both Utah and Idaho with state and local lawmakers. Most recently Verl Foreman, Annette Peters-Foreman's now deceased husband, served for years as a Fremont County Commissioner, although he had but a grade-school education.

For the most part, however, like the USRC generally, the Foremans and the Peterses have not attained the professional stature of the BVAI. Their educational aspirations have, with few exceptions, been satisfied by high school, and their occupations blend perfectly with the local economy: herding, farming, sawmilling and carpentry, farm product wholesaling, construction and irrigation contracting, and farm implement dealing. The wives all describe themselves as "homemakers."

Religiously embellished legend surrounds the conversions of the Foremans and the Peterses to radical Constitutionalism. Through Latter-day Saint Church catechism, all had learned as children to associate the United States Constitution with the theological doctrine of free agency. All of them thus see their activism as a natural extension of Church teachings. But the real story goes considerably deeper.

Like the majority of rank-and-file Saints, the parents of today's radical Foremans and Peterses were devoted New Deal Democrats in the 1930s and 1940s. (Utah and eastern Idaho remained two of the largest beneficiaries of federal welfare funds during the Depression until after the Second World War.) But the election of Dwight Eisenhower in 1952 on the Republican ticket and the appointment of Idaho's own Ezra Taft Benson to Secretary of Agriculture seems to have signaled a basic shift in Mormon political attitudes. Whether Benson's views merely reflected the changing beliefs of his audience or whether he created his own right-wing clientele I cannot say. But this we do know: Benson's views on the socialistic implications of farm subsidies, progressive income taxes, and public schools have been widely heard, read, and discussed throughout the Upper Snake River basin, including in the homes of the Foremans and the Peterses.

The central focus of our story must be Morale Peters, the eldest son of Royal and Janet Peters. Born in 1926, he claims to be the first in his family to have seen the light. He indoctrinated his sister Annette and his younger brothers, Ladell, Loren, and Lavon, with constitu-

Table 9.4

Genealogy of the Upper Snake River Constitutionalists[a]

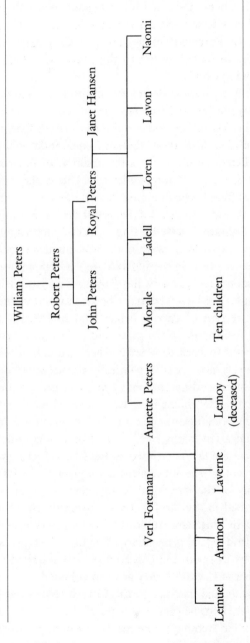

[a] All names are fictitious. Only names of individuals discussed in text are listed.

tional principles, and he has also successfully transmitted the message to his ten children, all but one of whom are now politically active ultraconservatives. This, he says, is in spite of persistent efforts by the public schools to subvert his parental authority. When Annette married into the Foreman family (much to the disgust of its members), she appears to have brought to the relationship her own propensity for right-wing causes.

According to Morale Peters, the immediate occasion of his radicalization was the Internal Revenue Service seizing "without warning or warrant" his log peeler, forcing him to close his fencing business. But this is probably little more than self-congratulatory retrospective. In fact, the Peters family has a long tradition of deviance which more than once has crossed into outlawry. (This explains the rebuke Verl Foreman suffered when he took Annette Peters to wife.) Morale's father, Royal, and his uncle John enjoyed the reputation of being "wild, fighting, drunken, bronc-busting hellions," according to informants who knew them. Both were once prosecuted for moonshining, and the uncle spent time in the Idaho State Penitentiary for cattle rustling. Local wisdom, such as it is, has Royal's wife Janet labeled as "a possible nympho" (which label must be understood in the context of the sexual puritanism of Paynes Ferry) who has already sent four good men with less energy to the grave and is still going strong at eighty.

This brings us back to Morale. There are indications that he was a tax violator, if not yet of a politically conscientious sort, well before the IRS confiscated his machinery to cover his delinquency. The way in which the IRS might have learned of Morale's infraction throws light on the phenomenon of tax resistance in eastern Idaho. There are rumors that a law partner of one of Morale's cousins (also a Peters) informed on the Peters brothers to the IRS in exchange for the reward of 10 percent of the subsequent delinquency fine assessed them. Indeed, many of the individuals whose names appear on the IRS "hit list" described in the second chapter believe themselves to have been victimized by this same "traitor." Lavon Peters served a sentence in McNeil Island federal penitentiary when his infractions became known.

Mormons in good standing are not only required to "render unto Caesar what is Caesar's," they are also enjoined to tithe 10 percent of their gross annual incomes to the Church. Now that their tax delinquencies have become public, virtually all the Foremans and the Peterses have lost their "temple recommends," written permissions from their bishops to perform sacred temple ordinances such as proxy baptism for the dead and the eternalization of marriage. While they have not been fully excommunicated from the Church, they are at this moment denied access to the highest Celestial kingdom in the event of their deaths.

The Foremans and Peterses fervently hope that Ezra Taft Benson's elevation to the position of prophet and seer of the Church (1986) will not only establish the kingdom of God on earth, but put an end to their own persecution for merely doing what their consciences demand: defending individual constitutional liberties against bureaucratic tyranny. Meanwhile, they attempt to circumvent tithe collectors and tax agents by conducting all their business in precious coins or direct barter. Morale and Ladell Peters, who work as self-sufficient farmers, herd sheep and raise chinchillas for in-kind trade with their neighbors, have no reportable income, and hence pay neither taxes nor tithes. Annette proudly related that to avoid taxes, one of her sons bought an entire farm and outbuildings with pure gold and silver coins having face values of less than $600. (The market value of the gold and silver in the coins at that time was many times greater than their nominal value.)

Annette now says that she was weaned from political naivete to maturity on Ezra Taft Benson's testimonies heard at the LDS General Conference. For her they rang with legitimacy not so much because of their content, but because of Benson's position as a Church apostle. God, after all, does not ordain liars or exaggerators to divine office in His restored Church. It was about this time that Morale loaned her Gary Allen's *None Dare Call It Conspiracy*. Through this she learned of the cabal of "insiders" behind the problems Benson had decried. The book accomplished its purpose. Annette joined the local chapter of the group distributing it, the John Birch Society. Finally, she was positioned to do something practical to save her vision of America from alien subversion and immorality.

Annette became an early devotee of the Freemen Institute. Cleon Skousen's seminars reinforced her sense that her growing radicalism was religiously grounded. Annette then took a step most conservative Mormons are reluctant to take: she began subscribing to Liberty Lobby's *Spotlight* newspaper. Although understandably, given her Mormon background, she dislikes its ranting about the "Zionist lobby" and the "problem" of Israel, Annette has now learned to flesh out the abstract conspiratorialism of Skousen and Allen. The "insiders," she has discovered, are really the international financiers and commodity brokers. These, she says, are almost all "Jew bankers." Annette now calls herself a populist and has canvassed for the candidates of the American Independent Party.

A pivotal moment in Annette's political metamorphosis occurred when her oldest son, Lemuel, asked her to account for her political "kookiness." She and Verl agreed it was time to "share the secret" necessary for their sons' further "spiritual development." The sharing took the form of an initiation of sorts, performed on a holiday especially chosen for the purpose. Baptisms, marriages, and similar rites often have the effect of reconfirming the beliefs of participants, and indeed are usually conducted with that purpose in mind. The Foremans' private ceremony had a similar psychological effect on Annette. In the "sharing," a book was ceremoniously bequeathed from the hand of parent to child. It was done with reverence, for it was the same book, not merely a copy, received earlier and with similar care from Annette's older brother, Morale: Jerreld Newquist's *Prophets, Principles, and National Survival*.[27] It is a 550-page compendium of inspired Church teachings regarding Constitutionalism, together with commentary by such names as J. Edgar Hoover, Herbert Spencer, Fred Schwarz, Ludwig Von Mises, and F. A. Hayek. Nothing summarizes so well all that Annette had so far learned about America's struggle against Communism. No book has left her more uplifted and prepared to undergo the sacrifices demanded of the true Christian patriot. Among its lessons are that "Communists yield to nothing but force" and "loss of liberty is worse than death." To this end, Annette would drive her boys to the local draft board herself to enlist them in the fight against Communism in Vietnam. Ammon would return a decorated combat veteran.

Lemuel, Ammon, and Laverne Foreman have all read the book and memorized its catch phrases. All the sons were taught, in Annette's words, "to be free and independent," just like her and her brothers. And now all three are full-fledged "populists" in their own right. Ammon is a convicted tax resister awaiting sentencing in federal court. His wife lovingly describes him as a man "who likes to read and study about everything, especially our Constitution and protecting our Freedom." Included in his extensive library are Benson's collected works, Frederic Bastiat's *The Law*, John Taylor's *The Government of God*, and the Newquist classic, the same once given him as a gift by his mother. Laverne is described by neighbors as "a potential terrorist." Both Lemuel (following his divorce) and Laverne (who never married) presently reside at the old family estate with their mother.

CONCLUSION

The greater Idaho region has a population of close to two million. Of these, at most several thousand have joined one or more of the groups described in this book. Their influence far outweighs their actual count. We should never forget that newsworthiness is not typicality. What makes Christian patriotism a newsworthy event is its very novelty.

What is it that distinguishes the few Idaho patriots from the conventional majority? Evidently, it is not their lack of education, nor is it their estrangement from regular channels of community association, at least in a simple mechanistic sense. My data indicate that what distinguishes patriots from ordinary Idahoans is their access to and involvement in what may be called a patriot "opportunity structure." This structure has provided them a body of patriot exemplars—fictive and actual martyrs and stars—a sophisticated ideology disseminated through the media of cassette tapes, literature, and broadcasts, a compelling rhetoric of justificatory motives, and a support network offering emotional surcease, physical retreat, protection from authorities, and material inducements to those who have taken up Cross and Flag. Without this opportunity structure, a viable Christian patriot movement is, from a sociological perspective, theoretically inconceivable. Through it, patriot candidates have first been drafted, then schooled, and then mobilized to perform roles in the drama of (re)Christianizing America and saving the world.

The patriots before us enlisted in the movement in a manner resembling the rational consumer in a monopolistic political market. That is, while they sought to maximize their private and public interests, as they understood them, their choices appear to have been structurally limited beforehand by the parameters of the situations in which they found themselves: by who their neighborhood acquaintances happened to be, where they happened to find themselves working, where they happened to be jailed, where they happened to be taken to worship by their parents, and, most importantly, by who their families happened to be and what their political orientations were. Those denied access to patriot friends and coworkers, to "Aryan" cellmates, to fundamentalist fellow confessors, or to ultraconservative family members were not likely to become patriots themselves.

This means that the process of recruitment and commitment of individuals to the Christian patriot movement parallels the process of conversion to left-wing causes.[28] Left-wing converts are not particularly identifiable by their stupidity, by their genius, by their craziness, or by their transiency, but instead by the largely accidental fact of their having bonds with people already in or sympathetic with the movement: liberal parents, socialist professors, fellow liberal arts college majors, or radical apartment chums, lovers, or drinking partners.[29] In both cases, left-wing or right, the following proposition is true: Extra-movement or non-movement ties with movement role models generally predate and facilitate people's affiliation with the movement itself.

Radical Christian patriotism may be considered a deviant political career with a trajectory sometimes culminating in prosecution, fines, imprisonment, and, rarely, in violent death. And as in all callings, one's political vocation is largely determined by career opportunities. To be sure, many potential patriots have rebelled against the opportunities provided them by their church memberships, friendships, and family ties to be Christian heroes. Others, despite "good" intentions, simply could not learn the requisite Christian patriot slogans or the worldview of their significant others who were patriots. Still others were too timid to carry off a convincing patriot performance. The causes of these various "failures" to take advantage of the available opportunities to become a Christian patriot go beyond our present concerns.

What interests us are the choices the successful initiate makes, once embarked on a patriot career. It may involve moving to a more "Christian" locale—back to the country, for example, or to the "tops of the mountains," which is to say, to a place resembling rural Idaho. It may entail adoption of a self-sacrificing "Christian" occupation—working with one's hands or as a freelance intellectual or as an "ambassador of Christ," in any case avoiding the blandishments of employment in the "Zionist Occupation Government." It may entail limiting transactions to direct barter or to payment in silver coin. It may involve leaving an "abominable" established church, a denomination affiliated with the "Soviet-controlled" National Council of Churches. Or it may involve pulling one's children out of public school and either teaching them "Christian values" at home or enrolling them in the local Christian academy. In other words, it may involve choosing a way of life that has as one consequence alienation from the worldly "satanic" community, the community most Idahoans take for granted as the normal state of affairs. In successively burning these various conventional social bridges behind them, Christian patriots unwittingly further their own and their children's radicalization. Most assuredly, a Christian patriot career will involve active participation in what I have called the politics of righteousness.

10

THE BIG PICTURE

The previous three chapters have examined several theories of right-wing extremism in the light of data on extremist patriot groups in Idaho. We found little support for the educational theory, equivocal but generally negative findings for the mass theory, and substantial confirmation for the theory of political socialization and the two-step theory of mobilization.

While sociological theory seems to account for why some people are likely to join the patriot cause, intellectually it is not completely satisfying. It is a bit like trying to explain widespread earthquake damage by pointing to negligent building codes. The account may be true enough, but the question still remains: Why the massive terrestrial movement in the first place? The two-step theory of mobilization tells us why, once they are aroused, some people are inclined to express their grievances in the politics of righteousness. The choice of expressive strategy is largely a product of the opportunity structure within which (largely by chance) they happen to find themselves. But the primary question is still unanswered: What is it that arouses a population in the first place? What is the historical context that has produced and nourished radical patriot groups in Idaho in the late 1970s and 1980s? This is the "big picture" of Idaho Christian patriotism.

In the following pages I will not be concerned with the factors inducing individuals to join patriot groups as such. Instead I will inquire into the social conditions behind the emergence of the groups themselves. These are the political and economic circumstances independent of, prior to, and historically associated with, periods of right-wing resurgence in America.

We begin by placing before us the award-winning account of American political extremism by sociologist Seymour Martin Lipset and his collaborator Earl Raab, *The Politics of Unreason*.[1] This volume was written under the auspices of the same five-year study of anti-Semitism credited with the Glock-Stark research cited in Chapter 8.

It will be impossible to do little more than briefly brush in broad strokes the basic tenets of Lipset and Raab's theory. In so doing, the actual complexity and sophistication of their views must of necessity be ignored. However, I am confident that the general tone of their views can be faithfully rendered in few words.

THE POLITICS OF UNREASON

To Lipset and Raab the distinguishing mark of right-wing movements is their preservative, backlash character. Right-wingers look nostalgically on the (sometimes imaginary) past, whereas left-wing groups look hopefully to an often equally fanciful future. This is because while left-wing movements are engineered by people experiencing upward mobility, the right wing attracts those whose status in the world is threatened with displacement.

Lipset and Raab go on to say that the displacement of some groups by others has been an enduring fact of American history. Hence, this country has been more prone to extremisms of preservatism than to their opposite. This also explains why extremism in America typically takes symbolic or expressive forms, emphasizing sexual mores, dress standards, religious preferences, and race. Those whose class position and power in society are threatened have little else with which to dramatize their superiority but their lifestyle.[2] Right-wingers shore up their sagging esteem by inflicting their morality on others.

The ranks of extremist movements are not filled with basically evil types, Lipset and Raab remind the reader, but with ordinary people caught in certain kinds of stress: the terrifying specter of losing their position in the world.[3] The disconcerting elements of right-wing ideology—Manichaeistic dualism, conspiratorialism, historical simplism, moralistic advocacy of violence, and bigotry—are less neurotic symptoms than the "cultural baggage," as Lipset calls it, that *any* American political group must adopt if its commodity is to be marketed successfully. The broader culture from which this baggage is drawn is an uneasy combination of classical liberalism (antielitism, egalitarianism, and *laissez-faire* economics) with Arminian Christianity (self-improvement, social reform, moralism, hard work, and hygiene).

Lipset and Raab appreciate that this "baggage" can have a dynamic of its own, but as the word implies, it is to them clearly subsidiary material taken along by people already politically disembarked for altogether different reasons. The following quotations give the flavor of the book's emphasis:

In speaking of American Protection Association activism in the 1890s, the authors say "Protestantism, fundamentalism, manners, and morals are often less the motivation [i.e., the cause] than the excuse for nativist bigotry—its 'cultural baggage' rather than its engine."[4]

When addressing Klan insurgency in the 1920s, the authors recognize that two-thirds of the national Klan leaders were fundamentalist preachers, but then they insist that "the congruence of Protestant fundamentalism and moralism is largely an historical accident. . . . Moralism does not create right-wing extremism. Desperately preservative movements require a moralistic stance, and will find it somewhere." During the 1920s religious energies were "invoked" after the fact to serve the goal of preserving the faltering status of America's southern, white, rural, Protestant citizenry.[5]

Similar reasoning is used to account for the over-representation of fundamentalists among George Wallace's supporters in his campaign for President in 1968.[6] In short: "[R]eligious fundamentalism and fanaticism is seen [by the authors] primarily as the specific symbolic content of lost-group status . . . rather than as a kind of intellectual mind-set which is the direct source of right-wing extremism."[7]

One weakness of the Lipset-Raab theory is that "status displacement" is never explicitly defined. Indeed the authors admit as much, claiming that the comprehensiveness of their model "defies . . . any particularistic definition." In the final chapters of the book they substitute for it the all-embracing subjective concept "Quondam Complex," a psychological attachment to and stake in the past.[8] The reader can sympathize with the authors; historical reality rarely fits into narrow sociological categories. Nevertheless, this maneuver opens Lipset and Raab to the criticism of circular reasoning, for without an explicit definition to the contrary, virtually anything can be taken as an indicator of the Quondam mind-set.

Some of these indicators do seem to have face validity. For example, in explaining the rise of anti-Illuminati hysteria around 1800 among New England mercantilists, the authors point to the emerging political threat to the Federalist Party posed by populist farmers on the Northeast frontier.[9] To explain the popularity of the American Protection Association in the 1890s among skilled Protestant laborers, the authors cite the influx of Catholic immigrants into American cities, the subsequent industrialization of work, and corrupt machine politics.[10] (The statistics used by the authors do not support their own contentions, however. American Protection Association membership was in fact not highest in the native urban middle class, but in the Rocky Mountain and western states, where skilled workers were still in great demand at the turn of the century and machine politics was minimal.)[11]

But many more of the authors' attempts to fit extremists into the Quondam Complex seem overly clever. For example, Lipset and Raab admit that in the 1930s, Father Coughlin's National Union for Social Justice appealed mostly to lower-class, urban Catholics, a stratum which can only with difficulty be said to have lost its already rock-bottom status during the Great Depression. The authors are therefore forced to introduce a new concept, "anomic status preservatism." Unemployed Catholics were not actually threatened with the loss of social position, say Lipset and Raab, but with the loss of their attachments to the larger community.[12] At this point they invoke William Kornhauser and his mass theory of political extremism, taking it (incorrectly) as a specific case of their overall position.

Again, the early 1950s was a time of "unprecedented" and widespread prosperity in America, when one might expect status threats to be relatively muted and therefore right-wing extremism to have little public sympathy. But, in fact, this was the highpoint of postwar anti-Communist hysteria. Lipset and Raab handle this evident incongruity by arguing that the new wealth of the postwar period produced new status anxieties: "With the possession of status comes the fear of dispossession."[13] To this they add status anxiety over America's postwar foreign policy reversals. My point is not that what the authors say is necessarily untrue, although they never do provide concrete evidence of status insecurity for any of the movements they study. It is rather that the concept is so vaguely posed that virtually nothing is excluded.

Does the theory of status politics account for the Christian patriot movement of the 1980s? In a 1981 *Commentary* article, Lipset and Raab reply in the affirmative.[14] The social status of the evangelicals, they say, was increasingly threatened by "aspects of modernity" appearing in the turbulent 1960s and 1970s: gay rights, women's rights, pornography, and sexual promiscuity. This is to say nothing of skyrocketing inflation and the oil crisis. (Again, observe the inherently malleable nature of the concept of status displacement.) This anxiety finally culminated in election booth support for the Reagan Revolution.

In a piece composed that same year, sociologist John H. Simpson blasted the Lipset-Raab account as a misreading of recent American religious history.[15] Members of evangelical and fundamentalist churches had occupied the most marginal positions in America's status hierarchy for more than fifty years. The sexual experimentation and drug use of the 1960s did nothing to change this. To suggest anything else is to ignore the devastating symbolic impact to fundamentalists of the repeal of the Prohibition Amendment in 1933, the public ridicule of fundamentalist champion William Jennings Bryan in the infamous "Monkey" trial of 1925, and the longstanding cultural relegation of fundamentalism to a sideshow menagerie of teetotaling loudmouths by urban sophisticates like H. L. Mencken. If the Lipset-Raab theory is valid, then the evangelical political response should have come fifty years earlier than it did.

Simpson fails to articulate fully an alternative explanation for the rise of the new Christian right, but he suggests that far from declining in status, evangelical/fundamentalist Protestants have, since 1975, been quickly advancing themselves. It is the forces and proponents of modernism who are beating a hasty retreat. In the intellectual and moral disarray of liberal modernism, evangelicals have sensed an opportunity to enhance their own political and social status. What I have called the politics of righteousness is not, at least according to Simpson, the fearful reaction of losers but the expression of growing confidence by a rising stratum. If anything, the new Christian right confirms the theory of rising expectations.

AN ALTERNATIVE EXPLANATION
OF RIGHT-WING EXTREMISM

Table 10.1 illustrates the relationship between economic cycles and periods of right-wing resurgence in America from 1795 to 1985. It may be taken as a very limited test of the theory that status displacement is historically associated with right-wing extremism. I say "very limited" because this interpretation is subject to the proviso that economic booms are times of enhanced opportunity for most people, while busts magnify threats to established status. If this assumption is true, then economic recessions should be temporally associated with increases in right-wing activism.

Because nationwide employment and business statistics were not kept until around 1900, the comparative heights of the unemployment cycles on the graph must be read as little more than pedagogical sugges-

Table 10.1

Unemployment and Right-Wing Extremism, America 1795–1985

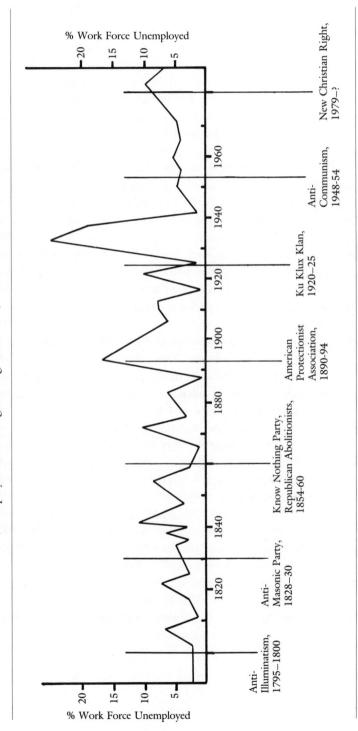

[a]Unemployment cycles estimated from data in Walter B. Smith and Arthur Cole, *Fluctuations in American Business: 1792–1860* (Cambridge, Mass.: Harvard University Press, 1935), pp. 12–21, 59–69, 93–101; Paul Ringenbach, *Tramps and Reformers: 1873–1916* (Westport, Conn.: Greenwood Press Inc., 1973), p. 24; Charles Hoffman, *The Depression of the Nineties* (Westport, Conn.: (Greenwood Press, 1970), pp. 106, 107, 109–10; and from *Long-term Economic Growth: 1860–1965* (Washington D.C.: U.S. Dept. of Commerce, 1966), p. 40.

tions. Furthermore, the table is not intended to give the impression that there has ever been a time in American history without right-wing activity. There have, however, been what appear to be seven distinct apogees of right-wing rabidity in this country since its founding. Only one of these seems to have taken place during a bonafide depression: the American Protection Association which, according to its own recordkeepers, grew to 2.5 million members by 1893–94. The recession of 1982–83, following the implementation of Reagan administration monetary policy, may be considered more a consequence than a cause of the fanaticism of this period.

Mine is not a novel observation. Even Lipset and Raab agree that "most of the previous right-wing extremist movements in America had their genesis and often their greatest strength during times of economic growth and prosperity."[16] To their minds this does not confute the theory of status displacement, but proves that during economic booms, rising social groups threaten relatively privileged segments of the population. An equally plausible hypothesis, however, is that people can afford moralistic politics when they prosper economically. Without working definitions of either status insecurity or prosperity, both of which are subjective experiences, there is no way of ascertaining the truth of these conjectures.

I have an alternative theoretical interpretation of the periodicity of right-wing resurgences in America. This interpretation is consistent both with the information gathered in the previous chapters and also with the bewildering variety of alleged status threats cited by Lipset and Raab. It is presented here not as a fully documented proposition but as a hypothesis for further research. Furthermore, it should be emphasized that, as a sociological rather than a psychological theory, it makes no claim to explain individual cases of extremism. Like the theory of status politics itself, it is intended only to account for general political trends in American history.

I begin with a confession by Richard Hofstadter, who in 1955 invented the theory of status politics in an attempt to explain the outrages of the Ku Klux Klan and the anti-Communist hysteria of his own time.[17] If the article were rewritten in light of what he knew just seven years later, Hofstadter says, a factor he originally overlooked would "now loom large indeed." The factor is Christian fundamentalism. "To understand the Manichaean style of thought, the apocalyptic tendencies, the love of mystification, the intolerance of compromise that are observable in the right-wing mind, we need to understand the history of fundamentalism."[18] In place of the concept of status politics, which he now sees as "inadequate," Hofstadter proposes a theory of "projective politics." Right-wing extremism, he says, "involves the projection of interests and concerns, not only private but essentially pathological, into the public scene."[19]

Without an *a priori* devaluation of the projections as sick or pathological, the hypothesis presented here is the theory of projective politics that Hofstadter calls for. It takes religion (as mediated by one's intermediate social networks) as an independent correlate of right-wing extremism. Theology, in this view, is not mere "baggage" acquired after the fact to justify aggression toward groups that threaten people's worlds. On the contrary, right-wing radicals sense certain events as threats to their worlds because these events are filtered through religiously tinted lenses. This assumption rests on a fundamental axiom in sociology: Things defined as real become real in their consequences. The people, events, and objects enumerated below are experienced as dangerous because they are *defined* as wicked and harmful, not because they are objective threats. To determine why Jews, liberals, public school teachers, Dungeons and Dragons, Oriental mysticism, and illicit drugs, "pornography," and sex are so judged we must inquire less into the things themselves than into the frames of reference of the definers.

It is not without irony that Lipset and Raab are forced to concede the validity of the theory of projective politics in their account of the abolitionist movement during the 1850s. At first they attribute abolitionist sentiment to "New England leadership which had become increasingly frustrated over [its] . . . lost . . . influence on the country." New England WASPs had become a "downgraded" elite, "an elite without function, a displaced class in American society."[20] But within a page the authors are admitting that "the extreme moral fervor poured into the abolitionist movement cannot be attributed solely or even primarily, to the . . . reaction of displaced groups. The moralistic concerns were stimulated by the direct line to evangelical Protestantism and its commitment to oppose sinful behavior." Once men and women are led to "define" (the word is theirs) certain things as evil, they work actively to eliminate them.[21]

What, then, are the projective lenses through which right-wing activists view reality and pronounce judgments on it? To summarize the discussion of Chapter 8:

First and preeminently, dualism. Relative to the doctrine of divine transcendence, of a perfected, spiritualized (male) Creator residing in distant heavens, the material (that is, feminine) world is profanity, unconsciousness, and death. Among the images of this fallen world are the "curse" of matriarchy, "bull-dyke" women and ladylike men; actions alleged to be associated with them—sex education, birth control, sloth, drunkenness, pornography, drug addiction, raucous music, gluttony, revelry, dance, and provocative dress; policies that presumably promote these—passivity, pacifism, communalism, and moral "dissolution" as expressed in the practices of profit without productivity, pay without work, crime without punishment, seizure without compensation, purchase without cash, and its inexorable accessory, usury; knee-jerk tolerance; the promiscuous mixing of "distinct" things— creeds, nations, species, races, classes, and roles; philosophies of hazed vision, blurred edges, and relativity; games of chance, ouija boards, the I Ching, astrology, and other New Age "satanic" technologies; and promoters of these policies—secular humanist educators, the liberal media, "politicians" (by which is meant those who aggrandize themselves by compromising with all of the above), the "Soviet-controlled" National Council of Churches, "socialist" bureaucrats, and the chief conspirator himself, the archetypal "Jew."

Once again, these things are not evil in themselves, nor are they judged evil because they constitute status threats in the narrow way depicted by Lipset and Raab. Even less are they annexed after the fact to more fundamental occasions of status insecurity. Rather, ignoring their modern variants, they are the traditional vices in orthodox Christianity. For they represent, among other things, the assertion of the feminine principle and the loss of masculine control, sensibility, creativity, consciousness, aggressiveness, and rationality.[22]

A second element in the projections of those called to Christian patriotism is conspiratorialism—the psychologizing of history and the reduction of historical events to the conscious intentions of omniscient and all-powerful Benefactors and Malefactors. The search for the ultimate causes of social decline invariably ends in the quest for whom to blame and whom to eliminate.

Third and finally, there is a pervading conviction of cosmic exigency, that the world and thus life itself is in dire emergency, and that the Second Coming is imminent. This is the *criterion definiendum* of fundamentalism, dispensationalism and its never-ending search for signs of the Apocalypse and the Last Dispensation.

THE CYCLES OF RIGHT-WING EXTREMISM

A grave weakness of the theory of projective politics as characterized so far is that it fails to address the periodic nature of religiously
inspired activism. If these periods cannot be attributed to status insecurity, then what might explain them?

Every thirty years since 1800 has seen an upsurge in right-wing
activism in America. The most recent began around 1978 and culminated in the election of Ronald Reagan and twenty-three United States
senators listed as "allies" in the 1980 *Conservative Digest* (as compared
to three in 1976). Each crescendo appears to last about a decade, and
like today's Moral Majority, Inc., or the 700 Club, each has been led
by Christian pastors, thus being infused with evangelical oratory. The
Idaho Christian patriot movement is but an extreme, albeit central,
tendril in the latest blossoming.

Inevitably, the enthusiasm of each right-wing revival either is ab-
sorbed and coopted into the platforms of established political parties,
or, where this is impossible, destroys itself through its own blind fury,
ending in acts of violence, rumors of corruption, angry schisms, and
public derision. In either case, it eventually retreats into the unswept
corners of the American psyche, there to build force for an outpouring
of equal fervency the following generation. Already by 1985, signs of
ideological exhaustion in the New Right were evident with the Justice
Department's prosecution of racist and abortion clinic violence and
exposures of illegalities in high places.

To portray American political history as a neat cyclical series is, of
course, to misrepresent it. What about the "crypto-fascist" Father
Coughlin during the height of the Great Depression, the American
Independent Party of the late 1960s and 1970s, or the persistence of
anti-Masonry during the 1840s?[23] America has never been without a
rabble-rousing right. But once every third decade right-wing enthusiasm seems to capture the public imagination, coming temporarily to
dominate the political scene.

I am not the first to observe the periodicity of rightist movements
in America. As early as 1924 Arthur Schlesinger, Sr., using a generational standard of thirty-three years, foretold the demise of Coolidge-
style conservatism by 1932, a reappearance of evangelically inspired
privatism by 1947, and the emergence of a new conservative epoch in
1978.[24] On the eve of his death in 1965 he used the same formula to
account for the failure of ultraconservative Barry Goldwater's "ill-timed"
presidential endeavor a year earlier "since not twenty or thirty years

but only ten had elapsed from the last eruption." And again, he suggested the likelihood of a new outbreak of repressive rightism by the early 1980s.[25]

Schlesinger's son, Arthur, Jr., has amplified his father's formula. The regularity of rightist movements in America, he said in 1986, "has nothing to do" with business cycles. Instead, invoking sociologist Karl Mannheim's concept of political generations, Schlesinger concludes that the dominant atmosphere of each historical period, conservative or liberal, produces the conditions of its own replacement in the ferment, protest, and boredom of those not yet in power: "Each generation spends its first fifteen years after coming of political age in challenging the generation already entrenched in power. Then the new generation comes to power itself for another fifteen years, after which its policies fail and the generation coming up behind claims the succession."[26]

Sociologists are accustomed to explaining collective behavior by ascribing to actors certain social locations. For example, election support for different political parties is said to be due to the class positions of voters; or different attitudes toward free market economics are attributed to the places of workers in the division of labor, etc. These same sociologists are normally reluctant to extend this notion of social location from the confines of actors' *spatial* locations to their *temporal* locations in society.[27] But to fully understand the periodicity of right-wing extremism in America perhaps such an extension of viewpoint is required.

The temporal location of an aggregate of social actors refers to their collective identity as participants in a specific generation. As Karl Mannheim has pointed out, generational location is not "mere chronological contemporaneity," for similarity of age can no more effectuate common generational identity than similarity of income can produce class consciousness.[28] In any case, if the concept of generations is reduced to age cohorts it loses its explanatory power, as a "new generation" in this sense is born every day. What is crucial in the formation of generational consciousness, he says, is a common experience of history that colors the politics of a people into adulthood.

Arthur Schlesinger argues that a liberalism collectively perceived as having lost its vision and verve calls forth its own younger detractors. But he fails to differentiate between those of comparable age who share this experience (and thus technically make up a rightist political generation) and those who do not. To rectify this apparent oversight we must acknowledge first of all that the experience of liberalism as in decline is compounded from two elements: the objective condition of liberalism itself, plus what the viewer brings to it. If establishment liberalism is seen as paralytic and corrupt by an aggregate of people—call it a "rising generation"—this must be in part because this aggregate views liberalism through conservative glasses. These, it appears, are individuals like the "seekers" mentioned in the last chapter, who crave a world more consistent with their moral standards.

It is at this point that Hofstadter's theory of projective politics can be seen as complementing Schlesinger's views. For Hofstadter implies that a rightist generation is indeed limited to those of similar age whose political lenses have been ground by fundamentalist Christianity.

Add now two further qualifications based on the research reported earlier: First, contrary to Hofstadter's hypothesis, the constituency of a rightist generation is not necessarily limited to Christian fundamentalists, but may include a minority of others who have been raised in liberal Christian churches or in none at all. Second, regardless of its religious upbringing, the membership of a rightist generation includes only those fundamentalists (and others) who are tendered and actually accept invitations to enlist in rightist groups by virtue of their access to local patriot "opportunity structures."

Table 10.2 summarizes this discussion and that of the previous two chapters in the form of what is known in the social sciences as a stochastic model. This model portrays one way in which the population of potential candidates for recruitment to a rightist political generation is selected through a step-by-step process of elimination. It pictures the major steps in the career of the prototypical Christian patriot. It recognizes both the social milieu conditioning the candidate and the choices open to the candidate in this milieu.

At each level in the table the candidate for admission to the rightist cause can move either to the left or to the right. At those levels where the movements are the consequence of specific decisions by the candidate—e.g., to either flee the world or attempt to change the world, to either accept an invitation to join a patriot group or reject it—it is assumed that such decisions reflect the candidate's interests as he understands them. In any case, if at any level the candidate moves to the left, the probability of his committing to a rightist group and hence becoming part of a rightist generation decreases. If on the other hand the candidate gravitates to the right at any level, the probability of his

Table 10.2

The Process of Recruitment to Right-Wing Extremist Groups

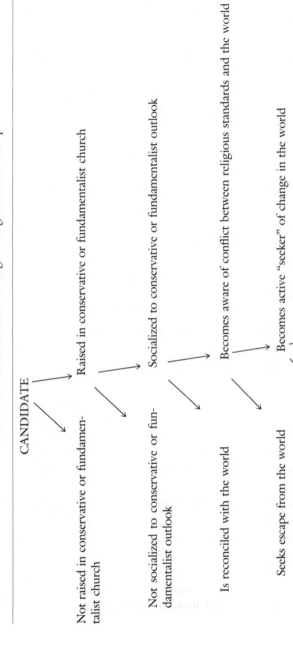

CANDIDATE

Raised in conservative or fundamentalist church

Not raised in conservative or fundamentalist church

Socialized to conservative or fundamentalist outlook

Not socialized to conservative or fundamentalist outlook

Becomes aware of conflict between religious standards and the world

Is reconciled with the world

Becomes active "seeker" of change in the world

Seeks escape from the world

Has access to radical "opportunity structure," a family member, friend, co-worker, cellmate, lover, etc., in the movement

Does not have access to radical "opportunity structure"

Accepts invitation to affiliate with right-wing group

Refuses invitation to join right-wing group

Becomes increasingly isolated from conventional community: takes children out of public schools, takes isolated job, moves to rural area, renounces conventional politics, joins exclusive sect, is disowned by friends, family, etc.

Retains social ties to conventional community

Develops deeper commitment to the movement

moving still further right increases. Given that a good quarter of the sample in this study were not raised in fundamentalist or conservative churches, no claim is made that candidates cannot "jump" one or more of the first few steps. There is evidently, as just indicated, more than one way to become a "seeker." At the same time, these data also suggest that the boxed-in step—access to a radical opportunity structure—is very likely essential for most seekers to be assimilated into a rising rightist generation.

Appendix I

DOCUMENTS

Silk-screen color poster advertising the Aryan World Congress

ARYAN NATIONS

Church of Jesus Christ Christian

P.O. Box 362
Hayden Lake, Idaho 83835

SUBJECT RESIDENTS OF THE ARYAN EMPIRE

SUMMER CONFERENCE AND NIGGER SHOOT - July 24, 25, 26, 1981

We are pleased to announce our Annual Summer Converence and NIGGER SHOOT to be held at our Hayden Lake headquarters; as many subject residents in the Aryan Empire who wish to come are welcome.

There will be no charges to anyone bringing live targets. Paper practice targets are available for all races with range rules. A special prize will be given to the best Runnin' Nigger scores in the Shotgun, Pistol, and Sub Machine Gun categories. Niggers, Jews, Mexicans, Gooks, etc., are also welcome as live targets!

Camping areas and housing is available for everyone. Live targets must be housed in our special facility for security reasons.

Children are welcome and we will have special games arranged for them including some activities in the surrounding communities with green ribbon prizes.

On Sunday the 26th we will host an outdoor Barbeque and Chicken Fry with plenty of Watermellon for the best marksmen to share with you.

We want winners and to win you must be able to shoot. Civil Rights comes out of the barrel of a gun and we mean to give the Niggers and Jews all the Civil Rights they can handle.

Our "Official RUNNIN' NIGGER Target" is included with this announcement for you to practice on...the real thing is real fun.

Our Security Team will see that no live targets escape from the range. Any who refuse to run or can't for any reason will be fed to the dogs. The dogs appreciate a good feed as much as we do.

THE GREEN RIBBON SALESMAN OF ATLANTA will be honored whoever he is and a special pledge of support will be made for his continuing good works. Remember, every Nigger he gets is one that our children won't have to fight in the streets!

There will be a substantial force of Aryan Warriors in uniform and during the Conference we will descend upon the home of a local traitor and serve up Biblical Justice to the Godless one.

[signature]

Aryan Nations publicity

FOR ACTIVE CHRISTIAN-PATRIOTS ONLY!!

C.S.A. NATIONAL CONVOCATION

★ Christian ★ Identity ★ Patriotic ★ Survival

OCT. 8, 9, 10, 1982 —FREE Admission —Secluded

To Be Held on the Secluded 224-Acre CSA Property in Pontiac, Missouri

**Primitive Camping Facilities available on property
or you can stay at one of the nearby resorts in Pontiac.**

Guest Speakers: Col. Jack Mohr (Ret. US Army)
Bob Miles (Mountain Church)
Richard Butler (Aryan Nations)

Plus CSA's own instructors and other outside teachers! There will also be an open forum time for people to speak. PLUS the establishment of a National CSA Confederacy.

Informational and Participational Classes include:

Weapons	Income Tax	Health	Betrayal of America	
Wilderness Survival	Shooting Weapons	Racial Truths	The Jews	
Christian Army	Food Storage	Natural Childbirth at Home		
First Aid	Personal Home Defense	Self-Defense	Rappelling	
Nuclear Survival	**AND MUCH, MUCH MORE! ! !**			

Facilities include classroom areas, shooting range, and our own "Silhouette City" for Military Training.

PRE-REGISTRATION is Required!! Only White, Patriotic, Serious CHRISTIANS need apply.

for Attendance Registration Form or for information, please write or call:

Iℌe Covenant
Iℌe Sword
Iℌe Arm of Iℌe Lord

C.S.A. ENTERPRISES
RT. 1, BOX 128
PONTIAC, MO. 65729
501-431-8882

Plan To Attend!

CSA publicity

HE IS ABLE TO DELIVER

SPECIAL EVENTS PLANNED
FOR
SCRIPTURES FOR AMERICA'S
1989 ROCKY MOUNTAIN FAMILY BIBLE CAMP

1. DEBUT OF TWO NEW MINISTRY WORKS:
    1. CONGRESSIONAL MINISTRY—A new and ingenious method of reaching and influencing congressmen with the Scriptures. Campers come prepared to speak to your congressman.
    2. CHRISTIAN VENTURE CAPITAL—A Christian financial service will be in the beginning stages with a committee of financially astute Christian men meeting in open planning sessions with interested campers. There are ways to have Biblical interest-free banking and investing. Those ways will be explored and a service developed at this camp. Included in the service will be ways to help our youth find apprentice positions.

2. A GREAT MYSTERY SPEAKER IS SCHEDULED. Guess who he/she is and be eligible for the special camp prize. Here are some clues:
    He/she is nationally known.
    He/she is a courageous hero.
    He/she is a threat to the traitors of our nation.
    He/she has traveled land and sea to obtain the information he/she will be revealing at camp.
    He/she has risked his/her life in obtaining and documenting the truths he/she will be presenting at camp.
    He/she has never before spoken at a Christian Identity family camp.

3. A NEW "WOMAN OF GRACE" CONTEST well be held in addition to our annual Man of Steel contest. You'll like this one!

4. A KINGDOM SCAVENGER HUNT has been planned for the children.

5. AN OLD FASHION EVENING SCOTTISH CEILEIDGH (KAYLEE) for the older singles. Singles plan to meet others of like mind and age and have a great time.

6. A YOUTH BANQUET just like last years will be held, but with a new twist. Girls bring your best dress and boys your best tie.

7. A CAMP MARKET similar to last years will be held. Bring your goods, services, crafts, etc. and plan to sell, trade and barter. (We reserve the right to disallow any product, literature or service.)

8. "HE IS ABLE TO DELIVER" is the 1989 camp theme and classes will include plans of the anti-Christ to deliver us up and what you can do to stop those plans!

See You At Camp!!!

Announcement of Christian Identity summer camp

CAMP NOTICE

MORE CONCERNING CAMP

1. There will be **25 speakers** from 20 states.

2. Following are some of the **class titles**:

    – Preparation For End-Time Deliverance

    – Deliverance From Christian Anarchist

    – Deliverance For America's Abandoned

    – Deliverance From The Judaisers

3. **Special classes** for the ladies (no bachelors allowed) on the art of homemaking to be taught by a special Bible college friend of Cheri's who is coming from Louisiana. She is a mother of five, a preacher's wife, seamstress, homemaker, and excellent teacher.

4. **Singing groups –**

    Legacy

    The Watchmen

    The Bulla Family

    Jerri Meigs

LAST CHANCE TO REGISTER

Announcement of Christian Identity summer camp

TRUTH IS VICTORY

Keith D. Gilbert, Esq.

The
TERRITORIAL
IMPERATIVE

ADOLF HITLER
was
ELIJAH

TO: THE ARYAN NATION

Beloved kinsmen

In the Holy Bible in Modern English as translated by Ferrar Fenton, in the Book of Malaki we read, "Then you will turn and distinguish between the righteous and the wicked, between who serves GOD, and who serves Him not. For be assured the day comes that will burn like an oven, when all the cruel, and all who practice vice, will be stubble, and will be burnt in that coming day," says the LORD OF HOSTS, "nor root not branch shall be left. But the Sun of Righteousness will shine forth to you with restoration on his wings, and you shall be brought out, and sport like a bullock from the stall, and tread down the wicked, for they will be dust under your feet, on the day when I perform it," says the LORD OF HOSTS.

"Remember the Laws of My servant Moses, which I communicated to him in Horeb, and the Institutions and Decrees for all Israel. I will assuredly send to you Elijah the Prophet before that Great and Terrible Day of the Lord arrives,and he will turn the hearts of the fathers towards their children, and the children towards their fathers; lest I should come and strike the earth with a ban."

The coming of Elijah must be confronted before we can move on to the judgement of the Aryan Nation of Israel. We are told that YHWH will send Elijah BEFORE the great and terrible day of destruction. That terrible day is now upon us, therefore, Elijah has already been made manifest. Two thousand years ago, the prophet, John the Baptist, was a manifestation of the spirit and power of Elijah. He spoke the powerful message of repentance and the condemnation of the King and his life. Then John identified the jews as vipers in Matthew 3:7. There was a great boldness and power manifested and many thought that John the Baptist was really the Prophet Elijah. He was manifesting the power and MESSAGE in the spirit of Elijah as a forerunner of the coming Yoshua and the events that were to take place.

For years i have known that the message of Identity brought the power of the Holy Spirit and the coming of Elijah as stated in the scriptures. A good thing to re- member is that we must have two witnesses before judgement and punishment can be executed. Over fifty years ago this message went out to the world in the words of Adolf Hitler and the message lives in his second witness Rudolf Hess who at this writing is alive and true to the faith in spite of the lies and persecution of the murderous jews who pressed for his imprisonment and the ritual murder of eleven of the Saints who stood with this great peacemaker.

These men told our Racial Nation that the jews were turning the people away from God and His ways. They warned about the jews and the International Bankers and spoke against mongrelization and racial suicide.   However, those who ruled over us in governments and 'churches' didn't heed the warning; in fact, they supported integration and intermarriage of the races and accepted the massive use of usury banking and truly did Mystery Babylon take control.

The Beast of Desolation invested with the power of the Red Dragon of old, of Satan and his children, the mongrelizing jews of dark destruction, was wounded almost unto death by this great Prophet of our Aryan People, Adolf Hitler, for he delivered the sword thrust and led the way for our deliverance and said; "It is necessary that I should die for my people; but my spirit will rise from the grave and the world will know that I was right." Adolf Hitler -- 1889-1945, born on April 20th, his great truths and prophesies live on in spite of the persecution of the jews who murdered our God and sought to kill all the Prophets and Saints.

But do not allow this one fact to escape you Kinsmen, that with the Lord a single day is as a thousand years, and a thousand years as a single day. The Lord does not delay His Promise, as some regard delaying; but extends His patience towards you, desiring that none should be lost, but that all should come to a change of mind. But the day of the Lord will approach like a thief, when the skies will pass away with a crash, and their constituents will be dissolved by heat; while the earth and what is upon it will be reorganized. All having to be thus dissolved, what ought you to be like in regard to pure conduct and piety, expecting and hastening on the appearance of the Day of God! -- during which the burning skies will be dissolved, and their constituents melted by heat: yet according to His promise, we look for new skies and a new earth, in which righteousness will dwell. II Peter 3: 8-13.

It is not without good cause that Adolf Hitler quoted the Holy Bible over five hundred times in his great work, MEIN KAMPF.

REMEMBER, our sacred writings describe the Last Covenant and its requirements. You are Saints, In your own eyes, and to the exclusion of all others, representatives of the only Covenant agreeable to our God, the eternal and final Covenant. We shall be, and with the communities which we establish, the 'little remnant' foretold by the Prophets; the true Israel. We are all volunteers joined with our Assembly bringing all our wisdom, understanding, and powers, the wholeness of our possessions and wealth into a community of God in the valley of our decision.

We hold to TRUTH and it is our VICTORY! You will find no 'fire escape theology' here among us nor will the libelous doctrine of a 'rapture' be heard among our Assembly for we are 'born from above' and as the children of ALMIGHTY GOD, YHWH, our father of old we will do only his bidding.

THE RESTORED CHURCH OF JESUS CHRIST is a SOCIETY OF SAINTS. We hold to and practice the ancient FAITH of our Aryan ancestors. We hold to no 'religion' with its incense, candles, rituals and vain repitious chants. We have cast off the tricks of 'priestcraft' and 'churchanity' of the catholic and protestant 'religions' that we might "be as little children" and true to the FAITH of our racial NATION!

ARYAN KINSMEN, this is my testimony unto you: That ADOLF HITLER was ELIJAH and that he did all that he came here to do. When he died on April 30, 1945, he set the date for THE GREAT DAY OF THE LORD!

This truth I leave with you. On May 1, 1985, will come THE GREAT DAY OF DESTRUCTION! This will be forty years after the great man's death and a high holiday in the jew 'Soviet' empire. Be true to the FAITH of our ARYAN racial NATION and may GOD keep you safe unto himself in his great storehouse as the tares now bundled together in the cities of Mystery Babylon burn.

KEITH D. Gilbert, Esq.

April 20, 1889

May His memory refresh your soul

and give you inspiration.

HEIL HITLER!

Socialist Nationalist Aryan Peoples Party brochure

Source: *The Spotlight*

Source: Sheldon Emry, *Billion$ for Banker$* (Phoenix, Ariz.: Lord's Covenant Church, 1984)

INTRODUCTION
Mythos Makers represents a small group of dedicated men and women who believe that their race is dangerously approaching the point of no return. We believe that a regeneration of our race consciousness, loyalty, unity, solidarity and pride is required if we are to survive the extreme challenges of the future. Mythos Makers is a small business venture dedicated to providing White racial identity items as a means of developing a nucleus around which our racial mythos may be regenerated, communicated and enhanced. The moment is now when valient men and women around the world must stand tall and proclaim their Northern European Heritage, regardless of the artificial social prejudices that prevail. If Mythos Makers is successful, it will lay the financial groundwork for a North American educational Foundation known as the Aryan Heritage Institute International. Please support our cause and make this project a success. White extinction is forever.

DEFINITION
MYTHOS: A pattern of beliefs expressing often symbolically the characteristic or prevalent attitudes in a group or culture. The traditional story of ostensibly historical events that serves to unfold part of the world view of a people or explain a practice, belief, or natural phenomenon.

Webster's 7th New Collegiate Dictionary

MYTHOS BASEBALL JERSEY, 50% cotton 50% polyester.

MYTHOS BUCKLE   For the man who is determined that it's time to speak out. Our Mythos logo is sculptured in solid bronze and is of the very finest quality and workmanship. The bronze shield is 2.75 inches (70mm) in diameter and fits 1.75 inch belts. This buckle is a real collectors item built to last.

MYTHOS PATCH   This magnificently embroidered patch is a full 4 inches (102mm) in diameter and comes in 4 colors. Extremely popular with teenagers and represents our Mythos at her finest.

MYTHOS KEY TAGS   Not shown. Mythos logo is printed on both sides in high contrast black and white and set in (Laminated). A 1.75 inch (45mm) smooth, round, convex shield made of crystal clear virgin acrylic. Comes with a tempered steel split ring and a chrome plated jump ring and is unbreakable. A real hot item.

MYTHOS MUG   Beautiful 6.5 oz. French Crystal Mug with the Mythos logo printed in royal blue. This item is guaranteed to generate positive social dialogue. Can be purchased by the set.

Color brochure advertising white supremacy items from Mythos Makers, Aryan Nations

MYTHOS STAMP   This rubber stamp is a full 2 in-
hes (51mm) in diameter and is of the highest quality.
or the person who wants to spread the word, this rub-
er stamp will test your ingenuity and creativity to the
mit.

MYTHOS BUMPER STICKER: A flashy 5 inches
(128mm) in diameter. Printed on heavy exterior vinyl,
with peel-off adhesive backing. Very striking.

MYTHOS T-SHIRT, 100% cotton pre-shrunk.

MYTHOS HAT   This hat speaks loud and clear. Very
popular with truckers and farmers. This top quality hat
is royal blue and white with a 2 color Mythos logo. Ad-
justs to any size.

A nation without a vital myth drifts aimlessly throughout
history. Myth gives purpose and meaning to the civilization. Myth makes a people a nation and a nation a race
and a race a contributor to the world. Myth shapes the
race so that the race may fulfill the potential of its individuals. The myth makes us conscious that we are a
race, and not merely an arbitrary, purposeless, ill-
defined conglomerate of men and women. The German-
Nordic race is unthinkable as a civilization forming, pur-
poseful group without its myth.
Myth of the Twentieth Century

In the entire life history of a people, its holiest mo-
ent is when it awakens from its powerlessness . . . a
ople which, with joy and love, grasps the eternity of its
tionhood can, at all times, celebrate its festival or
birth and its day of resurrection.
Friedrich Ludwig Jahn

Mythos Makers * Aryan Nations
Post Office Box 567
Hayden Lake, Idaho
83835

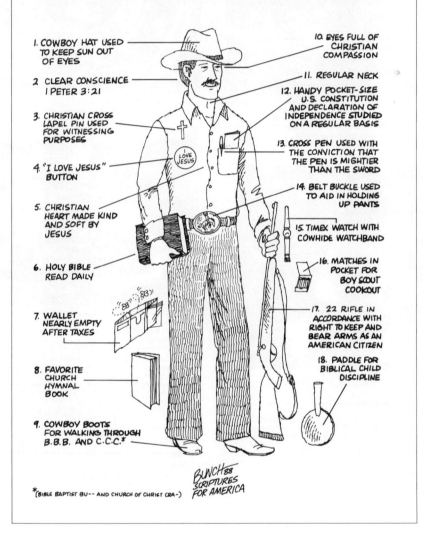

Source: Pete Peters, *The Real Hate Group* (La Porte, Colo.: Scriptures for America, 1988)

CHRISTIAN VILLAIN

SAME CHRISTIAN SOLDIER AS DESCRIBED AND DEPICTED BY JEWISH ORGANIZATIONS IN THEIR HATE GROUP REPORTS, AND IN THE JEWISH-CONTROLLED MEDIA. THIS REPRESENTATION FREQUENTLY DISPERSED TO VARIOUS LAW ENFORCEMENT AGENCIES & MAJOR TV NETWORKS.

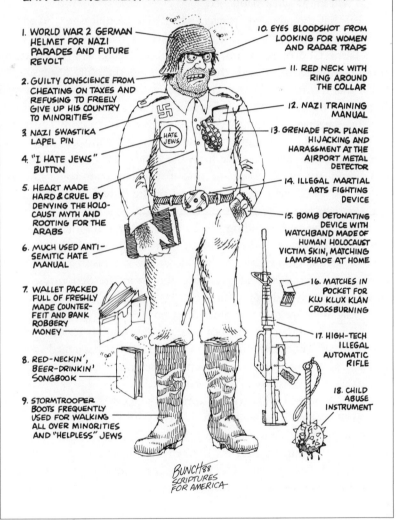

1. WORLD WAR 2 GERMAN HELMET FOR NAZI PARADES AND FUTURE REVOLT

2. GUILTY CONSCIENCE FROM CHEATING ON TAXES AND REFUSING TO FREELY GIVE UP HIS COUNTRY TO MINORITIES

3. NAZI SWASTIKA LAPEL PIN

4. "I HATE JEWS" BUTTON

5. HEART MADE HARD & CRUEL BY DENYING THE HOLOCAUST MYTH AND ROOTING FOR THE ARABS

6. MUCH USED ANTI-SEMITIC HATE MANUAL

7. WALLET PACKED FULL OF FRESHLY MADE COUNTERFEIT AND BANK ROBBERY MONEY

8. RED-NECKIN', BEER-DRINKIN' SONGBOOK

9. STORMTROOPER BOOTS FREQUENTLY USED FOR WALKING ALL OVER MINORITIES AND "HELPLESS" JEWS

10. EYES BLOODSHOT FROM LOOKING FOR WOMEN AND RADAR TRAPS

11. RED NECK WITH RING AROUND THE COLLAR

12. NAZI TRAINING MANUAL

13. GRENADE FOR PLANE HIJACKING AND HARASSMENT AT THE AIRPORT METAL DETECTOR

14. ILLEGAL MARTIAL ARTS FIGHTING DEVICE

15. BOMB DETONATING DEVICE WITH WATCHBAND MADE OF HUMAN HOLOCAUST VICTIM SKIN, MATCHING LAMPSHADE AT HOME

16. MATCHES IN POCKET FOR KLU KLUX KLAN CROSSBURNING

17. HIGH-TECH ILLEGAL AUTOMATIC RIFLE

18. CHILD ABUSE INSTRUMENT

BUNCH 88
SCRIPTURES FOR AMERICA

GORDON KAHL'S ACCOUNT OF THE SLAYING
OF TWO FEDERAL MARSHALS IN NORTH DAKOTA

I, Gordon Kahl, a Christian patriot, and in consideration of the events, which have taken place within the last few hrs, and knowing to what lengths, the enemies of Christ, (who I consider my enemies) will go to separate my spirit from it's body, wish to put down on paper a record of the events which have just taken place, so that the world will know what happened.

I feel that the awesome power, which will be unleashed, to silence forever, my testimony, will, if not checked by the power of my God, who is the God of Abraham, and Isaac and Jacob, will cut short my time to leave to the world, these happenings, therefor, I'm going to make this record and leave it in the hands of those who I know will bring it to light, even though I may in the meantime be extinguished.

While urgency, or human weakness, tells me to run, my spirit says write, so this I am going to do and if my God continues to protect me, I shall write first, and flee from the hands of my enemies later.

We had just finished our meeting in Median, concerning how we could best implement the proceedings of the third Continental Congress, which was to restore the power and prestige of the U.S. Constitution up to and including the 10 articles of the Bill of Rights, and put our nation back under Christian Common Law, which is another way of saying God's Law, as laid down by the inspiration of God, through his prophets and preserved for us in the Scriptures, when word was received from someone, whose identity I am not able to give, that we were to be ambushed on our return to our homes.

I realize now that we did not take this warning as seriously as we should have. The reason for this was because it has happened so many times before, when nothing happened. I see now that the many false alarms were to cause us to lower our guard.

As we pondered what to do, someone suggested that we take two cars instead of one. Consequently, I went with Dave Brower, and my son Yorie, Scotty Faul, my wife Joan, and Vernon Wagner, went in our station wagon. At this time none of us really expected any trouble, but just to be on the safe side, my son Yorie, myself, and Scotty prepared to defend ourselves, in the event that an attack upon us should take place.

SOURCE: a photocopy of a handprinted letter received at Aryan Nations Headquarters (no return address).

As we came over one of the hills just north of Medina, I saw on the top of the next hill what looked like two cars parked on it. About this time they turned on their red lights, and I knew that the attack was under way.

We were just coming to an approach and I told Dave to pull in on it and stop. Our other car pulled in just beyond us and stopped, also.

I looked back in time to see another vehicle coming from behind with its red light on.

I picked up my mini-14, and got out and got myself and my weapon ready as the vehicle coming from behind, skidded to a stop about 20 feet away. The doors flew open on it and the two men who were in the front seat aimed their guns at us. My son Yorie had jumped out of the other car and had run over to a high-line pole. The two cars which we had seen ahead of us, pulled up and stopped behind us.

A man got out of the vehicle which had come from behind us, and ran out into the ditch on the east side of the road.

During this time there was a lot of screaming and hollering going on but nothing else so it appeared to be an impasse.

About this time a shot rang out, and the driver of the car who I believe at this time must have been supposedly in command turned around and stood up so he was looking at his man in the east ditch and toward the cars which had come from the north and yelled "Who fired, who fired?" the other man who was with him, echoed his question.

At the time the shot rang out I heard Yorie cry out "I'm hit, I'm hit."

I took my eyes off the two men who were yelling "Who fired?" and looked over at Yorie. He was still standing, but I could tell he was in pain from the way he stood.

About this time, another shot rang out, and I heard Yorie cry out again. I looked over and saw that he was hit again and laying on the ground.

I looked back toward the two men and saw the one in the passenger side aim at me and I was sure then that they felt the situation was no longer under their control, and the only thing to do was kill us all.

Before he was able to fire, I loosed a round at the door behind which he was standing, and while I don't think I hit him, it caused him to duck down behind the door.

I looked around again toward Yorie, and saw Scotty Faul running over toward him I turned my head again in time to see the driver of the vehicle which had followed us raise up from behind his door and aim his gun at Scotty. I moved my gun over and fired at him before he could shoot. I didn't hit him either, the bullet striking somewhere near the lower left-hand corner of the windshield. He ducked down behind the dash so I could only see his head. About this time the other man raised up and aimed at me again. I shot again striking the door and causing him to duck. This happened several times, with the two men alternating, and my shots causing them to duck each time before they could aim and fire. I don't know how many times I fired, until the man on the passenger side fell, and I was able to tell he was out of the fight. The driver must have seen this as he moved his gun from Scotty's direction toward me.

I fired several more shots at him, each time he raised up to shoot at me. I finally realized this could keep up 'til my 30-round clip was empty. My bullets appeared to be ricocheting off the windshield and door post. I ran around toward the side of the vehicle, firing at the door as I went to keep him down until I got around far enough to get a clear shot at him, at which time I knew he was out of the fight also.

I ran back where I could see the third man from this north-bound vehicle just in time to see him raise up to shoot at Scotty, who had run over to Yorie. Before he was able to pull the trigger I fired and he fell to the ground. At this I saw the man who was behind the front end of the green Mercury, raise up and aim at Scotty. He saw me swing my gun in his direction, and he ducked down behind his car. I could see his feet or legs beneath the car, and I fired, striking him and putting him out of the fight.

I ran over to the man in the east ditch, thinking he might still be in fighting condition. When I got nearly to him, he raised up his head and said, "Don't shoot me again, I'm all done." He had his hand on his shot-gun so I took that and his pistol which was in his holster and threw them in the back seat of the green Mercury. I didn't see the man who had been behind the Mercury, and who I thought I'd hit in the leg, so I don't know where he'd gone to.

A pick-up had pulled up behind the north-bound vehicle, but I didn't notice anyone in it or around it and I assumed it was the pick-up we saw on the top of the first hill as we came out of Medina, and which I believed belonged to the city, but as to who was driving it, I have no knowledge.

Scotty tells me he saw one and possibly two men run out into the trees and hide, but I have no way of knowing who they were.

I think from the reports I've heard on the radio which was in the Mercury, that the car which came from behind, was the one the Marshalls were in. If this is so, they weren't the ones who fired the first shots. The two men who were in the front seat were both looking in the direction of the green Mercury when they were shouting, "Who fired?"

Yorie's .45-auto, which he had in his shoulder holster had either a rifle or pistol bullet imbedded in the clip, shattering the grips on both sides. Had he not been wearing it, he would have been killed instantly.

Whether this was the first or second shot that was fired at him, I don't know. One was buckshot and the other was either a rifle or a high-powered pistol, from the way the bullet looks.

I didn't see it, but it sounded as though Yorie's gun fired after he was hit. I think probably his finger tightened on the trigger when he was hit, but I know neither he nor Scotty fired before this, and whether either of them fired afterwards, I don't know. I know that if they did, they didn't hit anyone, as I *knew* when I hit each one of them, myself.

I saw a man in the clinic, when we took Yorie in, who I think must have been the man in the pickup who pulled up behind what I think was the Marshall's vehicle. He had blood on his face, and I think he was probably hit by either a bullet or bullets which glanced off the Marshall's vehicle when I was firing at them. I didn't see him, and I know I didn't shoot at him, and I know neither Yorie nor Scotty shot at him.

Vernon Wagner was unarmed so I know he didn't shoot at anyone and Dave Brower didn't shoot at anyone either. My wife had nothing to do with it, other than the fact that she had ridden along with us so she could visit with a couple of other ladies who were coming to the meeting.

I want the world to know that I take no pleasure in the death or injury of any of these people any more than I felt when I was forced to bring to an end the fighter pilots' lives who forced the issue during WWII. When you come under attack by anyone, it becomes a matter of survival. I was forced to kill an American P-51 pilot one day over Burma, when he mistook us for Japs. I let him shoot first, but he missed and I didn't. I felt bad, but I knew I had no choice.

I would have liked nothing other than to be left alone, so I could enjoy life, liberty and the pursuit of happiness, which our forefathers willed to us.

This was not to be, after I discovered that our nation had fallen into the hands of alien people, who are referred to as a nation within the other nations. As one of our founding fathers stated, "They are vampires, and vampires cannot live on vampires, they must live on Christians." He tried to get a provision written into the U.S. Constitution that would have prevented Jews from living inside the U.S. He warned his brethren that if this was not done their children would curse them in their graves, and that within 200 years their people (the Jews) would be sitting in their counting houses rubbing their hands, while our people would be slaving in the fields to support them. This has happened exactly as was predicted.

These enemies of Christ have taken their Jewish Communist Manifesto and incorporated it into the Statutory Laws of our country and thrown our Constitution and our Christian Common Law (which is nothing other than the Laws of God as set forth in the Scriptures) into the garbage can.

We are a conquered and occupied nation, conquered and occupied by the Jews and their hundreds or maybe thousands of front organizations doing their un-Godly work.

They have two objectives in their goal of ruling the world. Destroy Christianity and the white race. Neither can be accomplished by itself. They stand or fall together.

ROBERT MATHEWS' LAST LETTER

For the past decade I have been a resident of northern Pend Oreille County. When I first arrived in Metaline Falls I had only $25 to my name, a desire to work hard and be left alone, and the dream of someday acquiring my own small farm.

During my three years at the mine and seven years at the cement plant I can safely say that I was known as a good worker. I stayed out of the bars and pretty much kept to myself. Anyone who is familiar with Boundary Dam Road knows how my late father and I carved a beautiful place out of the woods. All of the goals I had when I arrived were accomplished but one. I was not left alone.

SOURCE: published in the *Sandpoint Daily Bee*, Dec. 12, 1984.

Within months of my arrival, the FBI went to the mine office and tried to have me fired from my job. I was working in the electrical department at the time and my foreman, fortunately, had a deep and lasting dislike for the Feds. He was informed of the situation by the mine secretary. Had it been the mine manager instead of the secretary that the government goons talked to, I would have lost my job.

This campaign of harrassment and intimidation began because of my involvement in the tax-rebellion movement from the time I was 15 to 20 years old. The government was on me so much in Arizona that during one incident when I was 18, IRS agents shot at me for nothing more than a misdemeanor tax violation.

I left Arizona and the tax rebellion when I was 20. I left not out of fear of the IRS or because of submission to their tyranny, but because I was thoroughly disgusted with the American people. I maintained then, as I do now, that our people have devolved into some of the most cowardly, sheepish degenerates that have ever littered the face of this planet.

I had hoped to start a new life in the state of Washington, but the ruling powers had other plans for me. When I learned of their highly illegal attempt to have me fired, I wrote a letter to their Seattle office and told them, "I would take no more, to leave me alone, or I would respond in such a way that could be very painful to certain agents." After the letter they gradually started to let me be.

I soon settled down to marriage, clearing my land and reading. Reading became an obsession with me. I consumed volume upon volume of subjects dealing with history, politics and economics. I was especially taken with Spengler's "Decline of the West" and Simpson's "Which Way Western Man?" I also subscribed to numerous periodicals on current American problems, especially those concerned with the very increasing decline of white America.

My knowledge of ancient European history started to awaken a wrongfully supressed emotion buried deep within my soul, that of racial pride and conciousness.

The stronger my love for my people grew, the deeper became my hatred for those who would destroy my race, my heritage and darken the future of my children.

By the time my son had arrived I realized that white America, indeed my entire race, was headed for oblivion unless white men rose and turned the tide. The more I came to love my son the more I realized that unless things changed radically, by the time he was my age, he would be a stranger in his own land, a blond-haired, blue-eyed Aryan in a country populated mainly by Mexicans, mulattoes, blacks and Asians. His future was growing darker by the day.

I came to learn that this was not by accident, that there is a small, cohesive alien group within this nation working day and night to make this happen. I learned that these culture disorders have an iron grip on both major political parties, on Congress, on the media, on the publishing houses, and on most of the major Christian denominations in this nation, even though these aliens subscribe to a religion which is diametrically opposed to Christianity.

These are the same people who ex-Sen. William J. Fulbright and the late General Brown tried to warn us about. Henry Ford and Charles Lindburg tried vainly to warn us also. Had we been more vigilant, my son's future would not be so dark and dismal.

Thus I have no choice. I must stand up like a white man and do battle.

A secret war has been developing for the last year between the regime in Washington and an ever growing number of white people who are determined to regain what our forefathers discovered, explored, conquered, settled, built and died for.

The FBI has been able to keep this war secret only because up until now we have been doing nothing more than growing and preparing. The government, however, seems determined to force the issue, so we have no choice left but to stand up and fight back. Hail victory!

It is at this point that I wish to address the multitude of lies that the federals have been telling about Gary Lee Yarbrough and myself.

Gary did not "ambush" any agents. For weeks prior to this incident they had been harrassing Gary, following him everywhere, even to the hospital to visit his gravely ill daughter. The day of the mythical ambush Gary was out in his yard when he saw a forest service truck driving across his property in obvious disregard to the numerous no-trespassing signs scattered about his land. He yelled at the truck to stop but it kept coming towards his house until it crashed into and destroyed a gate. At this point Gary fired warning shots into the air and the truck drove away. That . . . was the big ambush.

The newspapers are saying now that Gary not only ambushed three agents but that he hit three of them. Gary did not even realize they were FBI at the time, which is fortunate for them because Gary is an expert marksman and had he decided to ambush the FBI he easily could have killed every fed within range of his weapon.

It was not until 8 p.m. that night that Gary realized what was actually taking place. That is when approximately 30 agents drove up to Gary's house. Gary and a young house guest went outside to investigate the commotion. When the feds started yelling at Gary he dropped to the ground and rolled into a ditch behind one of the government vehicles. The young house guest went running back into Gary's residence. After waiting for three hours the FBI used Gary's wife as a shield and a hostage and went into the house. What brave men they are.

As incredulous as it sounds Gary laid in the ditch behind the agents for five hours with his gun aimed at their backs. Had Gary really wanted to ambush these invaders then that was a wonderful opportunity to do so. Gary chose instead to give them quarter, something he would later come to regret. Gary eventually slipped out of the ditch and into the woods.

The incompetence of these gun-toting bureaucrats never ceases to amaze me. Especially after their attempted ambush and murder of myself in a Portland motel. First, let me say that the FBI was not there to arrest Gary but to ambush me. They didn't even know that Gary was in the room. The only reason they were able to find me was because a trusted friend in Room 14 was actually a traitor and an informant. The FBI has vast resources and the latest technology but the quality of their agents is going downhill with every new recruit. That's because most of the best white men in this country are starting to realize that to be an FBI agent is to be nothing more than a mercenary for the ADL and Tel Aviv.

When I stepped out of my motel room that morning, a gang of armed men came running at me. None of the men had on uniforms and the only thing they said was "Stop, you bastard." At this, I yelled to Gary who was still inside and I leaped down the stairwell and took off running into the parking lot. A woman agent shot at my back and the bullet missed and hit the motel manager. I rounded the corner of the motel and took off down the hill into a residential area. After running for two blocks I decided to quit being the hunted and become the hunter. I drew my gun and waited behind a concrete wall for the agents to draw near. When I aimed my gun at the head of the closest agent I saw the handsome face of a young white man and lowered my aim to his knee and his foot. Had I not done so I could have killed both agents and still had left the use of my hand which is now mangled beyond repair and which I might very well lose altogether. That is the last time I will ever give quarter.

As for the traitor in Room 14, we will eventually find him. If it takes 10 years and we have to travel to the far ends of the Earth we will find him. And true to our oath when we do find him, we will remove his head from his body.

I have no regrets or apologies to make for Gary or myself. In fact I am proud that we had the courage and the determination to stand up and fight for our race and our heritage at a time in our history when such a deed is called a crime and not an act of valor.

Approximately nine months ago the FBI went to my house while I was away and threatened my two-year-old son. That was a very big mistake on their part. After the Portland shootout they went to my house and threatened my 63-year-old mother. Such brave men they are.

I am not going into hiding: rather I will press the FBI and let them know what it is like to become the hunted. Doing so it is only logical to assume that my days on this planet are rapidly drawing to a close. Even so, I have no fear. For the reality of life is death, and the worst the enemy can do to me is shorten my tour of duty in this world. I will leave knowing that my family and friends love me and support me. I will leave knowing I have made the ultimate sacrifice to secure the future of my children.

> As always for blood, soil, honor,
> for faith and for race,
> Robert Jay Mathews

Appendix II

SOURCES OF DATA ON CORE CHRISTIAN PATRIOTS

	Patriots on Whom Data Were Obtained	
Sources	Number	Percent (Using Base of 493)
Exclusively secondary sources		
Commercial newspapers and magazines	75	15.2
Anti-Klan publications	19	3.9
Nonpolitical public agencies and research monographs	31	6.3
Total of secondary sources	125	25.4
Exclusively primary sources		
Face-to-face interviews	69	14.0
Telephone interviews	270	54.8
Mailed questionnaires	11	2.2
Both primary and secondary source	18	3.7
Total of primary sources	368	74.6
Nothing obtained except specific group affiliation of the patriot[a]	27	
Grand total of patriots[b]	520	

[a]These patriots were either impossible to locate, refused to cooperate, or did not receive a mailed questionnaire.

[b]In addition to the 520 core patriots in the sample, I learned the names of 140 other candidates. These were not included in the core sample for different reasons: For most, specific group affiliations could not be learned; or if they were learned, the individuals were not considered radical enough for inclusion in this study (e.g., politically or religiously unprincipled tax violators); or if they were radical enough they were not affiliated with Idaho patriot groups; or if they were so connected their inclusion in the sample would have skewed representation from certain regions of Idaho (particularly eastern Idaho). In at least one case there is evidence that the same individual was included under two names, one an alias or a misspelling in a press report. Finally, some were uncovered too late to be included in this project.

Appendix III

GEOGRAPHIC ORIGINS
OF THE PATRIOTS

Of the 458 patriots in the sample of 520 whose places of origin and final destination are known, 43.9 percent derive from Idaho itself or from its topographically and culturally similar environs, e.g., northern Utah, the border region of eastern Washington—especially the Palouse area—and the mountainous portions of western Montana. If subjects from these contiguous areas were classed as outsiders to Idaho, then the percentage of native Idaho patriots in the sample would drop to 38 percent. What this indicates, obviously, is that Idaho Christian patriotism is not entirely or even mostly homegrown.

Of the 458 patriots cited above, 342 give as their present place of domicile some place in Idaho. The remainder, while residing outside the state—several in southwest Canadian provinces—maintain contin-

Table III.1
Geographic Origins of All Idaho Christian Patriots

Place of Origin	Number	Percent
Idaho	201	43.9
California	71	15.5
Pacific Coast	88	19.2
Sun Belt[a]	121	26.4
Middle South[b]	51	11.2
Confederate South[c]	38	8.3
Industrial Northeast[d]	42	9.2
Total number of patriots whose original and final places of residence are known	458	

[a]California, Arizona, New Mexico, Texas, Louisiana, Arkansas, Oklahoma, Missouri, Alabama, Mississippi, Florida, Georgia. Note overlap with Middle South.
[b]Missouri, Arkansas, Nebraska, Texas, Kansas, Iowa, Oklahoma, Louisiana.
[c]Georgia, Virginia, Alabama, Florida, Tennessee, Carolinas, Louisiana.
[d]Massachusetts, Connecticut, New Jersey, Michigan, Illinois, New York, Ohio, Pennsylvania.

uous contact with Idaho-based patriot groups by attending conventions and workshops and by subscribing to their newsletters. It is therefore reasonable to include them as part of the Idaho movement. Using the base figure of 342 patriots now living in Idaho, 57.9 percent report themselves as being raised there. Again, this supports the contention that much "Idaho" patriotism has been imported from elsewhere. But from where? 14.6 percent of those now living in Idaho report their original place of residence as California, mostly from Los Angeles and points south. Another 3.5 percent have emigrated from western Washington and Oregon. That is, about one-fifth of all patriots now residing in Idaho were raised on the Pacific Coast, nearly half the total raised in Idaho. Another sizable contingent (8.2 percent) has moved to Idaho from the Middle South (Missouri, Arkansas, Nebraska, Texas, Kansas, Iowa, Oklahoma, and Louisiana). These figures are virtually identical for all patriots, regardless of present residence, whose places of origin are known: 15.5 percent are from California, 19.2 percent from the entire Pacific Coast, and 11.2 percent from the Middle South.

Christian Constitutionalists have a significantly different geographical biography than Identity Christians. The original and final residences of 162 Constitutionalists are known. Of these, 70.9 percent report themselves as having been brought up in Idaho. If we consider only those 110 Constitutionalists presently living in Idaho, the number soars to well over 75 percent. This tells us that Idaho's version of Christian Constitutionalism has been largely generated locally.

Contrast this with the Identity movement. Only 29 percent of the Identity Christians in the sample are native to Idaho. Even excluding those Identity adherents who now live out of state, only about 50 percent of the remainder can trace their origins to Idaho. That Idaho Identity is to a great extent a California export is indicated by 21.6 percent of movement adherents claiming to have been brought up in the Golden State. Another 11.9 percent are from the Industrial Northeast.

Recall the distinction between two major types of Identity: explicitly racist and non-racist. Although it is difficult to precisely classify individual cases, it appears that far less than one-quarter of the outspoken racist and anti-Semitic Identity Christians in the sample were raised in Idaho. The comparable percentage from California alone is close to one-third. More Idaho Identity racists issue from California than any other state in the Union, *including* Idaho itself.

To summarize, Idaho culture is over twice as likely to produce radical Constitutionalists as it is Identity racists. The racists and bigots it does have are more likely to have imported their wares from California—especially southern California—than to have learned it in Idaho. Although the numbers are far too small to place great confidence in, this is even truer for terrorists. Only four of the eighty-one terrorists are native Idahoans.

There is a second point. The two different types of Idaho Christian patriots—Constitutionalists and Identity advocates—are not evenly distributed throughout the state. Most of the Constitutionalists in the sample hail from southeast Idaho, most of the racist Identity and issue-oriented patriots from western and northern counties. As observed in the text, southeast Idaho is demographically dominated by the Church of Jesus Christ of Latter-day Saints (Mormon). In Chapter 6 I argue that Mormon doctrine has been appropriated by some Church members to color the brand of patriotism found in southeast Idaho. The attraction of racist and anti-Jewish forms of Identity elsewhere in Idaho, on the other hand, seems to be due in part to the presence in those places of Christian theologies conducive to it. In brief these are theologies of extreme fundamentalist Protestantism. This connection is thoroughly examined in Chapter 8. While some of these theologies are native to Idaho, more of them have been brought from southern California and the Middle South.

Appendix IV

THE JOHN BIRCH SOCIETY AND THE JEWISH QUESTION

The John Birch Society has explicitly and repeatedly denounced racism and anti-Semitism in its writings. In "The Neutralizers," published in 1963, Robert Welch speaks of Anglo-Israelism and the Ku Klux Klan as tools used by the "insiders" to deflect public concern from their own diabolical machinations.[1] The Society has since issued similar pronouncements on Liberty Lobby and its newsletter, *Spotlight*, on Posse Comitatus, and on the Order.[2] Nevertheless, even its own leadership admits that the Society has tended to attract Jew-baiters, among them Revilo Oliver, a University of Illinois classics professor whose work is now advertised by National Alliance, an avowed Nazi splinter group; Robert DePugh, ex-convict and founder of the Minutemen; and the original leader of the Order, Robert Mathews.[3] The Society must bear some responsibility for this embarrassing state of affairs, if for no other reason than the nature of some of its publications. Gary Allen's *None Dare Call It Conspiracy*, which has had a decided impact on countless Idaho patriots, may serve as an example.[4] While disclaiming anti-Semitism on one page, on the next Allen is marshaling evidence that Jewish banking families are indeed behind America's financial woes.

Employing the standard Birch line, Allen calls the one-world conspirators "insiders," a major division of which are the "international bankers." Although preeminent among these are the Rothschilds, he warns that "anti-Semites have played into the hands of the conspiracy by trying to portray the entire conspiracy as Jewish. Nothing could be further from the truth."[5] J. P. Morgan and John D. Rockefeller, two of the foremost conspirators, are, he says, undeniably Anglo-Saxon and Christian. (Identity Christians typically counter this by insisting that both names are merely the Anglicized Jewish surnames Morganthau and Rothschild.) "There is no denying the importance of the [Jewish] Rothschilds," Allen continues. "However, . . . it is . . . unreasonable and immoral to blame all Jews for the crimes of the Rothschilds."[6]

Let us ignore Allen's excoriation of the Anti-Defamation League of B'nai B'rith which, he says, "has never let truth or logic interfere with its highly professional smear jobs."[7] The point is that within five pages of these caveats Allen is arguing that Morgan served "as the top American agent of the English Rothschilds,"[8] playing a key role in the "fabrication" of the panics of 1893 and 1907 to sway the public to accept the concept of a national bank. For its part, he contends, the Rockefeller clan has worked "in tandem" with the Rothschilds since 1885.[9] But the character who allegedly played "the most significant part" in the conspiracy, according to Allen, was neither Morgan nor Rockefeller, but the Jewish banker Paul Warburg and his brother Felix, both of whom immigrated to the United States from Germany in 1902, leaving their brother Max at home to "finance" the Bolshevik revolution.

Allen delineates in detail an interlocking network uniting the Warburgs with the Loebs, the Kuhns, and the Schiffs, all of these with the Rothschilds of Frankfurt, Germany, and this group with Adolph Ochs, Bernard Baruch, and Henry Morgenthau. In short, despite his protests to the contrary, virtually every name mentioned in his banking history—Lehman, Lazard, Goldman, Erlanger, and Sachs are others—is a person of European Jewish heritage or a "hand dog" of these same interests in America.[10] What makes this notable and disturbing is that Congressional investigations of banking in 1912 and 1933 found that of the five banks actually controlling money and credit in this country at the time, only one—Kuhn, Loeb & Co.—can definitely be said to be "Jewish." J. P. Morgan and its affiliate, Drexel & Co., and the Rockefeller-owned First National City Bank are adjudged the most dominant institutions. All the others mentioned in the investigations are decidedly Anglo-Saxon: Lee, Higginson & Co., Kidder, Peabody & Co., and George Baker's First National City Bank of New York.[11]

Certainly the tone of Allen's (and of Cleon Skousen's) argument does not begin to approach the hostile fervency of a Jack Mohr or a Jarah Crawford, two major Identity conspiratorialists. By all appearances neither Allen nor Skousen hate a particular people merely *because* they are Jewish. Rather, their vituperation is directed to the magnates of international finance, many of whom, they claim, *happen to be* Jewish. All the same, while their dislikes do give the impression of being empirically grounded instead of being rooted in prejudgment, hostile beliefs about Jews, regardless of their source, can definitely translate into hostile feelings, and these into discriminatory actions.[12] And as just pointed out, there is a serious question about the empirical validity of associating the term "international banker" with the word "Jew." As one of the most perceptive students of the American ruling elite has said: "Alas, nothing could lead them [i.e., ultraconservatives] further from the possibility of coming to grips with the power structure they wish to understand."[13]

But the issue is not so much the personal attitudes of articulate spokesmen such as Allen and Skousen, who have undoubtedly learned to condition their statements to fend off accusations of anti-Semitism. It is the effect their pronouncements have on readers considerably less astute than themselves. The ease with which nonintellectual Constitutionalists can slip into barely veiled Judeophobia was illustrated recently in testimony before the Idaho Senate State Affairs Committee. Addressing the assembly was Archibald Roberts, a popular Constitutionalist from Fort Collins, Colorado, who has also been seen in Identity pulpits in the intermountain West. There is, he proclaimed, a "secret government" in America, the Federal Reserve System. "A criminal conspiracy," it controls American finances but is accountable to no one, not even to the president of the United States. When one of the senators asked, "who owns it?" Roberts itemized eight "proprietors"; all of them, with the exception of Chase Manhattan, a Rockefeller firm, are Jewish.[14] "The ill-gotten gains, this trillion dollar debt, a lien against all private property in the United States," Roberts concluded, "obviously is a criminal act against the people of the United States." The legislators, evidently agreeing, passed a Senate-House Joint Memorial calling for repeal of the Federal Reserve Act.

Equivocation by such celebrated spokesmen on the crucial question of who exactly is behind the conspiracy has occasioned confusion among Constitutionalists I interviewed. Described below are three accommodations I was given to the theories of Allen and Skousen. All these informants have been devoted Mormons. Hence, all have been placed in the position of having to reconcile the orthodox Mormon doctrine of "Semitic identification" with what they have read in patriot pamphlets. All three responses may be considered ways of reducing what psychologists call "cognitive dissonance." One indicator of dissonance is the emotion displayed by respondents when asked to comment on the "Jewish question."

All Jews as evil: One of the sample informants has begun contemplating a wholesale rejection of Mormon doctrine. He describes his conversion as personally painful. "When I first read [Identity preacher] Herbert W. Armstrong's *Jewish Money Trust*," he says, "I couldn't believe it." Then he evidently saw it confirmed in the *Rothschild Family* (a film) ". . . I don't like to say it, but I think it's true. It disturbs me what I've found. This may sound stupid, but it disturbs me because it is like losing Santa Claus." This informant's reading of Allen's banking history has goaded him to question his childhood teachings that Jews are the chosen people of God. He now leans in the direction of Identity, kept from full commitment only by its racist aspects and the fact that his adopted son has a dark skin.[15]

Other Constitutionalists, while decrying the Jew-baiting they find in *Spotlight* or in Identity author Sheldon Emry's pamphlets, have nonetheless been prodded by other readings to articulate their own largely unconscious prejudices. "It's still hard for me to say that all of our problems are due to Jews," one admitted. "But then I suppose that they did crucify Christ, and they have been a hiss and a byword."[16] "*Spotlight* sometimes goes too far; they overemphasize some things," another concurs. "But I shipped potatoes to Jewish brokers. The Jewish boys seemed to have control. They took no risks, but those boys got others to take risks."[17] "Let's face it," another concluded after making similar observations of *Spotlight*, "Jews have always been money people. They have always sold their souls to the company store."[18]

Abstract Jews are evil; personal Jews are nice: A psychologically more intriguing accommodation is the development of a distinction between the theoretical concept "international banker" or "Zionist," who is evil, and "the Jew that I have personally known," who is a loyal citizen. "I'm unwilling to lay it at Jewish feet. A lot of the international bankers are not Jews. . . . Many Jews are not bankers," reads a typical response. "But I have no time for [Israeli leaders] Ariel Sharon and Menachem Begin."[19] "I don't believe everything I read," another assured me. "*Spotlight* has gone too far with the Jewish thing. I'd rather leave it at international bankers. There is good and bad in everything."[20] Says still another: "Just because a few Jewish bankers are involved, doesn't mean all Jews are bad."[21]

The reaffirmation of Mormon doctrine: The overwhelming majority of Constitutionalists appear preprogrammed by their Mormon upbringing to avoid the Jewish question altogether. "It [the one-world conspiracy] has nothing to do with Judaism or the Jewish people," is a common response.[22] "I know there is a lot of anti-Jewish sentiment," another confesses. "But that is hearsay. . . . I don't believe we should put some other religion down to enhance our own."[23] At least one, a firm adherent to the notion of a banking conspiracy, even offered this warning: "The Lord knew what He was doing when He came through the Jews. Any nation that has gone against them has brought trouble on itself."[24]

Appendix V

THE ACTION ORIENTATION
OF IDENTITY CHRISTIANITY

Words are distinguishable from acts, but they are not separable from them. The word accounts for the act; the act completes the word. Far from being neutral descriptive categories, words prepare people to perform in particular ways. What is the general action orientation promoted by and implied in the words of Identity Christianity?

It should be emphasized that I speak here only of a general action orientation. This is emphatically not the same as a scientific prediction as to how specific activists will behave. Nor is it a forecast of America's political future. For the action orientation described below to be effected, other conditions would have to be met. Their simultaneous realization is so unlikely as to render the following account into something approaching fantasy. These conditions include but are not limited to governmental authorities ignoring or promoting violence by Identity adherents, or being incapable of responding effectively to revolutionary threats to the social order, widespread public indifference to and/or encouragement of rightist violence, a capacity by rightists to mobilize a very sizable treasury and armory, and, most important, a huge body of disciplined supporters, willing to sacrifice everything for the accomplishment of Identity goals. To repeat: an action orientation is simply the behavior legitimized by a specific ideology.

The action orientation implied in the most radical variants of Identity is the mass murder, enslavement, relocation, and/or deportation of American cultural and racial minorities. This is most vividly illustrated in *The Turner Diaries.* By the end of the "Great Revolution," North America has been bombed into a racially pure nuclear wasteland and "blood is flowing ankle-deep in the streets of Europe's great cities." The only remaining power center still resisting Organization control is China. Through a mixture of chemical, biological, and radiological means, its sixteen million square miles will later be "effectively sterilized," left inhabited only by roving bands of "mutants." All of this just 110 years after the birth of the "Great One," Adolf Hitler.

True, Identity Christianity can claim no monopoly over this kind of orientation, as it is characteristic of all totalistic ideologies. But the consensus of authorities is that the two most seminal psychological preconditions of mass social destructiveness are first, the dehumanization of the victim and second, the symbolic elevation of the executioner to a position of moral sanctity.[1] Rarely have these two preconditions been expressed so baldly as in racialist Identity Christianity.

There is first the verbal objectification of the Other, his rhetorical relegation to the status of object: "Not everything that walks on two legs is human." And insofar as these Others are not truly persons, then sympathetic identification with their pain and misery, the very presuppositions of moral restraint and civilized conduct toward them, is effectively minimized if not altogether eliminated. Since they are "Satan's Kids," to use the laid-back title of one of Jack Mohr's more popular pamphlets, little does it matter what is done to them. The second and more widely shared notion among Identity adherents is that whatever they do is permissible because they are God's chosen people. It is not strictly their will, but God's will working through them that motivates their politics of righteousness. They are "God's battle-axe and His weapons of war."

Given these considerations, it should come as no surprise that Jarah Crawford discovers theological support for the enslavement of pre-Adamic man,[2] and that he resurrects the admonition given Israel by Yahweh prior to its invasion of the promised land: *herem,* the commandment to exterminate every Palestinian inhabitant. "As regards the towns of those peoples which Yahweh your God gives you as your own inheritance, you must spare not the life of any living thing. . . . Thou shalt utterly destroy them" (Deut. 20:15–20). To my knowledge, in all the world's major religious creeds, there is no commandment more absolutist nor terrifying than this.[3] Believing as they do in the inerrancy of God's Word, the most rabid Anglo-Israelites have soberly taken upon themselves this same holy obligation.[4]

However, most Identity activists prefer something akin to the more "humane" recommendations of James O. Pace in his *Amendment to the Constitution,* advertised as a constitutional and nonviolent way to "avert the decline and fall of America."[5] Composed as a legal brief, the Pace amendment advocates a return to the definition of American citizenship recognized in federal courts by the Dred Scott decision in 1868 and enforced *de facto* through the 1950s by Jim Crow laws: that the only real and full citizens are descendants of European whites. The proposal involves the repeal of the Fourteenth and Fifteenth Amendments to the Constitution and the achievement of "a fair and non-burdensome adjustment" in the status of the nonwhite American population.

It is not necessary to detail all the provisions of the Pace amendment. It is enough to say that American blacks, Asians, Arabs, and Mexicans would no longer have rights as American citizens. The determination of the legal status of "nonwhite Caucasoids" from Iran, Armenia, and Asia, of Turks, Egyptians, Jews, and Pakistanis, remains to be "artfully" determined later by some combination test of blood type, ancestry, and appearance. In any case, those with any "ascertainable trace" of Negro appearance are to be classified "Negro" and considered *personae non grata*.[6]

Only bonafide, certified citizens will be permitted permanent residency in the United States. All others shall be compulsorily deported "in a manner economically beneficial to them" to their native lands.[7] Although this will involve tens of millions of American residents, and is to be accomplished in a single year, Pace assures us that deportation will be "fair" and "minimally painless." Money now "wasted" on federal welfare and public education programs can be budgeted for moving allowances and the leasing of mass transportation facilities.

Those who so wish may keep title to their property *in absentia,* at least temporarily. But failure to comply with repatriation will automatically result in its confiscation. Further enforcement procedures are not specified. On the whole, the author is optimistic that if the carrot of allowances is beguiling enough, bloodshed should be minimal. To this end, precautions will be undertaken to ensure that "the enforcers do not become over-zealous in their duties."[8]

American Indians, Aleuts, and Hawaiians, although not real citizens, will not face relocation, but will be maintained in "tribal reservations" analogous to the arrangement in South Africa. Those whose age precludes easy relocation and others who can demonstrate extraordinary hardship may apply for provisional privileges to maintain their present domicile. But since such conditions are always subject to abuse, these should be observed only in the "most extreme" cases.

The outwardly civil and calculatedly understated tone of Pace's proposal contrasts with Jarah Crawford and Andrew MacDonald's ravings. For that reason it is all the more alarming. Pace addresses a far larger audience, and his stated credentials—graduate of Columbia and Harvard, Harvard law journal editor, and partner in a New York law firm—lend an aura of intellectual respectability to his enterprise that few Identity spokesmen enjoy.

Indeed, so incredible is Pace's amendment and the apparent coolness with which he weighs his options that one may initially think it a modern version of Jonathan Swift's bitterly satirical *A Modest Proposal*. But the publishers of the Pace volume share none of the playful irony and indignation of the satirist. Instead, they are tweed-coated, morally earnest, short-haired men, far too young to have experienced the tragedies conducive to satire.[9] One identifies himself as a fifth-generation Mormon and Columbia University graduate in marketing and Japanese who now works as an international business consultant; another as a recent graduate in music from the same school who is now business manager of a major urban symphony orchestra.

Appendix VI

OTHER CONSPIRACIES

Identity historiography sees the entirety of world history as being due to a monstrous Jewish conspiracy. Chapter 4 depicted the alleged banking conspiracy, as gleaned from *The Protocols of the Learned Elders of Zion*. But insofar as the *Protocols* were issued (or, more accurately, fabricated) in the late nineteenth century, they could not have anticipated the latest tactical elaborations on the Jewish-Masonic plan to establish one-world government. This appendix will touch on recent developments in what is known in radical patriot circles as the science of conspiratology.

Protocol 11 recommends that the conspirators obtain control over the print media. According to Identity conspiratologists, media invented later—radio, television, and moving pictures—have been incorporated into the plot. The major TV and radio networks (the so-called "Jews media") and the Hollywood film colony have all become "Jewish strongholds," Hollywood a veritable "Jew town," locally known, we are told, as "Kosher Valley." This "explains" television series like "All in the Family," which portray race-conscious, loyal American patriots such as Archie Bunker as unattractive, ill-educated, blue-collar boors, and others like "The Cosby Show," which picture "so-called minorities" as articulate, sensitive professionals. It also accounts for the spate of "race" movies and TV pseudodocumentaries like "Roots," which portray blacks as being abused and persecuted by white bigots, or which continually resurrect images of the "hoax of the 20th century," the Jewish Holocaust. These art forms instill in white Christian audiences "a sense of guilt for these 'wrongs.' " "We are taught that consciousness of race is 'un-American' and a manifestation of bigotry. . . . In this respect, all Jewish propaganda squares exactly with the Hollywood line. . . . The one thing Communists fear more than anything else is a rebirth of race consciousness among the great white majority of the Christian world."[1]

Likewise, the *Protocols* could not have anticipated the metric system conspiracy, the Civil Rights conspiracy,[2] the teenage suicide, euthanasia, and abortion conspiracies, the AIDS conspiracy, or the heinous way in which "Jewish" agents have used advances in medical technology to weaken the white race by "medical allopathic slavery."

Identity documents claim that the American Medical Association was established at the behest of the Rothschild family and Lloyd's of London to protect their artificial drug and insurance companies. The AMA now works to keep the Aryan medical consumer chronically ill. This is done first by employing a regimen of "poisoning" (chemotherapy, vaccinations with infected swine and horse serums, blood transfusions from half-human homonids, and fluoridation), "burning" (radiation therapy), and "butchering" (surgical organ removal). Second, the AMA has enlisted government support to prevent competitors (otherwise known as "quacks") from practicing alternative naturopathic remedies and preventative medicines such as moderate exercise, dietary changes, and an overall healthy life style.

Among the attributes of Identity's "healthy life style" is racial segregation. But the "Jewish cabal" undermines this by promoting "The Great Immigration Conspiracy."[3] "Alien-Generated Diseases Engulf America," reads the headline of one patriot newsletter, "as swarms of invading aliens," subject to no medical screening and at tax-payer expense, "occupy America." Infected with Hepatitis B virus, liver parasites, salmonellosis, cholera, and tuberculosis, they are encouraged to seek employment as food handlers for white Christians.[4]

And there is more. In the 1920s a Dr. Koch, M.D., and his Christian Medical Research League introduced a drug called Glyoxilide. It is a peroxide-like substance which, when injected into the blood, presumably destroys toxins by oxidation. Because it works so well, killing all poisons and thus rendering hospitals, drug companies, and health insurance superfluous, "Jewish medical demagogues" sought to make its use illegal.[5] Glyoxilide is celebrated by Identity spokesmen as a spiritual "homeopathic preparation," not an "earthly substance" as are "allopathic poisons."

The most intriguing recent conspiracy involves "Soviet Electromagnetic War Actions." These are the supposed cause of well-documented weather changes throughout the northern hemisphere beginning July 4, 1976, the bicentennial of the United States Declaration of Independence. The story opens with Nikola Tesla, a Jewish Austrian electrical engineer, who in the 1930s conducted experiments on Extreme Low Frequency (ELF) waves pumped through the earth and into the ionosphere by means of magnifying transmitters.[6] At this moment the

Soviets are installing immense Tesla magnifiers in the Ust/Urst Plateau and have begun transmitting waves at 31.5 Hertz, "almost at the fourth harmonic of the earth-ionosphere Schumann Resonance." This is the earth's natural vibration frequency. "Heterodyne patterns might be expected to occur and the converging . . . waves may be able to produce magneto-sonic waves near the surface of the earth" that can alter jet stream paths and change traditional weather patterns. This "explains" the dramatic decreases in winter temperatures over North America in the 1980s. Furthermore, just as "standing columnar waves" can ionize the air, "so you can cause earthquakes with it." The rash of volcanoes and devastating earth movements along the Pacific Rim since 1976, including the Mount St. Helens eruption and the Mount Borah, Idaho, earthquake are all said to be due to Soviet electronic warfare.

The indictment grows. Animals that orient themselves with atmospheric waves are exhibiting aberrant behavior in the mid-Pacific Ocean. Fish species have disappeared, gulls avoid ancient nesting grounds, and even the reproductive cycles of coral polyps have been disturbed by Tesla wave alterations.

Worst of all, "in vitro experiments . . . demonstrate an interaction between an ELF electric field and the calcium ion equilibrium in brain tissue." One writer asks if his readers have had recent "drug-like experiences of euphoria but taken no hallucinogens?" Feeling physically run-down? he asks: the Soviets have discovered the link between ELF signals, mind control, and physical disease. "U.S.S.R. signals entrain and capture the brains of human bio-systems by placing them in forced sympathetic response." They have "broken the genetic code of the human brain" and now "almost anything can be inserted into [it] . . . words, phrases, images, sensation . . . emotions, . . . thoughts and ideas. . . . Since the start of the Soviet ELF signals, a massive and spreading mood of total surrender to Soviet goals has swept across the United States." This is the "real" reason why in 1987 the U.S.S.R. proposed to reduce by half its medium-range nuclear missiles in Europe. They are now obsolete.

Why do we know so little about this? Our ignorance is solid proof of Jewish thought-control over America. . . . Because these pro-Marxist, anti-American, degenerate Sodophiliacs control all aspects of the U.S. television industry—there should be no surprise that news of the Soviet weatherwar . . . against America has been totally covered-up and suppressed.[7]

NOTES

CHAPTER 1. INTRODUCTION

1. From Jerry Falwell's introductory comments to Richard A. Viguerie, *The New Right: We're Ready to Lead* (Falls Church, Va.: Viguerie Co., 1980).

2. Paul Weyrich, quoted without a source in *ibid.*, p. 56.

3. For anguished liberal response to this event, see *The Wall Street Journal*, July 11, 1980; *The New York Times*, Aug. 17–20, 1980; and *Newsweek*, Sept. 15, 1980.

4. For the right-wing version, see Viguerie, *The New Right*, for the liberal version, Perry Deane Young, *God's Bullies* (New York: Holt, Rinehart and Winston, 1982); and for a scholarly interpretation, see *The New Christian Right* ed. Robert Liebman and Robert Wuthnow (New York: Aldine Publishing Co., 1983).

5. Phillip Finch, *God, Guts, and Guns* (New York: Seaview/Putnam, 1983), and Patsy Sims, *The Klan* (New York: Stein and Day, 1978).

6. Quoted from the Anti-Defamation League of B'nai B'rith, "The Ku Klux Klan, 1978," from *Facts,* in Aryeh Neier, *Defending My Enemy* (New York: E. P. Dutton, 1979), p. 21.

7. Illinois, Legislative Investigating Committee, *Ku Klux Klan* (Springfield, Ill., 1976), p. vii. The report concludes: "The Ku Klux Klan in Illinois is little more than a club, whose members bestow on one another grand titles and high offices. . . . Most of their time is spent in a futile effort to recruit new members, but they fail to understand that few adults are interested in joining a boys' club. The Ku Klux Klan is like a group of noisy and mischievous adolescents whose childish ways society must tolerate, so long as they cause no harm. . . . There is nothing harmful or unlawful about parading around in robes; nor is there anything harmful or unlawful about burning crosses. Symbols are all the Klan has left, and symbols cannot hurt anyone" (p. 95).

8. House Judiciary Committee, Subcommittee on Crime, *Increasing Violence Against Minorities,* 96th Cong., 2nd sess., Dec. 9, 1980 (Washington, D.C.: Government Printing Office, 1981). This report summarizes the violent events immediately preceding the congressional investigation.

9. Membership in racist and anti-Semitic groups is said to have dropped to about 6,500 in 1984 and to 4,500–5,500 in 1987. See the Anti-Defamation League of B'nai B'rith, *The KKK and the Neo-Nazis: A Status Report* (New York, 1984), p. 1, and *The Hate Movement Today: A Chronicle of Violence and Disarray* (New York, 1987), pp. 2, 5. Such estimates are at best tentative.

Pastor Richard Butler of the Idaho-based Aryan Nations Church alone claims to have a mailing list with over 6,000 names.

10. Dept. of Justice, Idaho Advisory Committee to the United States Commission on Civil Rights, *Bigotry and Violence in Idaho* (Washington, D.C.: Government Printing Office, 1986).

11. David Chalmers, *Hooded Americanism* (New York: Franklin Watts, 1981 [1965]), p. 428.

12. Laird Wilcox, *Guide to the American Right* (Kansas City, Mo.: Editorial Research Service, 1986).

13. Cf. *Marginal Natives: Anthropologists at Work,* ed. Morris Freilich (New York: Harper and Row, 1970).

14. Seymour Martin Lipset and Earl Raab, *The Politics of Unreason* (New York: Harper and Row, 1970).

15. Robert Nisbet, *The Quest for Community* (New York: Harper and Bros., 1953).

16. Samuel A. Stouffer, *Communism, Conformity and Civil Liberties* (New York: John Wiley, 1966).

17. Pete Peters, *The Real Hate Group* (Laporte, Colo.: Scriptures for America, 1988), p. 2.

18. Pete Peters, "Authority: Resistance or Obedience?" *Scriptures for America,* June 1987, p. 16.

19. Quoted in Peters, *The Real Hate Group,* pp. 28–29.

20. Cf. *USA Today,* Sept. 27, 1985, for the story of alleged Jewish Nazi Frank Collin.

21. *"Hate Groups in America": A Critical Review,* ed. Laird Wilcox (Kansas City, Mo.: Editorial Research Service, 1987), pp. 34–40.

22. Jerry Falwell, reiterating the assertion of the president of the Southern Baptist Convention, Oct. 11, 1980, said, "I believe God does not hear the prayers of unredeemed gentiles or Jews." Falwell later recanted after public outcry from American Jewish leaders (*Facts on File* [New York: Facts on File, Inc., 1980], p. 646, column B2). For the analogous statement of the Convention president, see *ibid.,* p. 811, column B1.

23. *Facts on File* (1982), p. 194, column E2.

24. See Appendix IV for a complete statement of this position.

25. For typical rejections, see Appendix IV.

26. Informant 107, Jan. 22, 1986. Informants are numbered by the order in which they were interviewed, correspondents by the order in which their letters were received. All correspondence is quoted verbatim.

27. Informant 142, Mar. 8, 1986.

28. The Constitutional article disqualified from voting, holding office, or serving as a juror anyone "who is a bigamist or polygamist, or is living in what is known as patriarchal, plural or celestial marriage, . . . or who, in any manner, teaches, advises, counsels, aids, or encourages any person to enter into [the above] . . . or who is a member of or contributes to the support, aid or encouragement of, any order, organization, association, corporation, or society, which teaches, advises, counsels, encourages, or aids any person to enter into [the above].

29. Informant 20, Nov. 29, 1985.
30. *Churches and Church Membership in the United States 1980,* ed. Bernard Quinn et al. (Atlanta, Ga.: Glenmary Research Center, 1982), pp. 76–81.
31. Informant 89, Jan. 11, 1986.
32. Informant 148, Mar. 14, 1986.
33. Informant 178, May 5, 1986.
34. Idaho, House Joint Memorial 3, *Daily Data* (final edition), 46th–47th legislature, 1981–84. See Appendix IV of this book for excerpts from the address of Archibald Roberts on the necessity for this memorial.
35. For brief descriptions of these acts of harassment, see Dept. of Justice, Idaho Advisory Committee to the United States Commission on Civil Rights, *Bigotry and Violence in Idaho* (Washington, D.C.: Government Printing Office, 1986) pp. 2–6.
36. Scott Grant McNall, "The Freedom Center: A Case Study of a Politico-Religious Sect," Ph.D. dissertation (Eugene: University of Oregon, 1965).
37. James A. Aho, "A Community with a Heart: The Story of the Kootenai County Human Relations Task Force," mimeographed (Coeur D'Alene, Idaho: Chamber of Commerce, 1985).
38. Jack Douglas, *Investigative Social Research* (Beverly Hills, Calif.: Sage Publications, 1976).
39. Idaho, County of Kootenai, "Nehemiah Township Charter and Common Law Contract," July 12, 1982, Book 120, p. 387.
40. Rick Greenberg, "Neo-Nazism: Flash in Pan or Spark of Revolution," *Cleveland, Ohio, Plain Dealer,* July 6, 1986.
41. For the article to which the caller referred, see *Spokesman-Review,* Aug. 7, 1985.
42. J. B. Owens, "Aho Article Described As Confused, Vague, Manipulative," *Idaho State Journal,* Oct. 16, 1986. The article to which this author refers: Jim Aho, "Coeur D'Alene Violence May Teach Us: Listen to Others," *Idaho State Journal,* Oct. 7, 1986.
43. For a table itemizing my proportional reliance on these two data sources, see Appendix II.
44. *Aryan Nations Calling,* no 53.
45. Cf. *Albuquerque Journal,* July 12, 1986.
46. *Sacramento Bee,* June 21, 1987.
47. Correspondent 13, Feb. 1, 1986.

CHAPTER 2. THE GENESIS OF REVOLT

1. *Idaho Statesman,* Apr. 19, 1973. See also *ibid.,* Nov. 1, 1973.
2. Personal interview, Dec. 10, 1985. Cf. George Hansen, *To Harass Our People: The IRS and Government Abuse of Power* (Washington, D.C.: Positive Publications, 1984), pp. 131–34.
3. Hansen, *To Harass Our People,* p. 133.
4. For the memorandum with names omitted, see *ibid.,* pp. 33–34.
5. *Ibid.,* p. 42.
6. *Ibid.,* p. 33.

7. *Ibid.*, pp. 46–47. For the document authorizing the RCP, see pp. 39–40; for that giving the RCP the final go-ahead, p. 44; and for the cancellation, pp. 47–48.

8. *Ibid.*, p.144.

9. *Ibid.*, p. 134.

10. Here and elsewhere in this book all ages are calculated to 1984. The following information is based on a personal interview, Jan. 1, 1986.

11. Hansen, *To Harass Our People*, p. 156.

12. Informant 84, Jan. 10, 1986.

13. Informant 50, Dec. 20, 1985.

14. Informant 49, Dec. 20, 1985.

15. Informant 50, Dec. 20, 1985. Cf. the comments of Cliff Turner and of Andrew Melichinsky, self-proclaimed *de jure* President of the United States, *Idaho State Journal*, Mar. 3, 1983.

16. *Idaho State Journal*, Sept. 14 to 29, 1983.

17. *Ibid.*, July, 1983. For Judge Woodland's rejoinder, see *ibid.*, Sept. 14, 1983.

18. Informant 168, Mar. 27, 1986. Again: A wife whose estranged husband has willfully failed to pay income taxes has her house attached by the IRS although it was given exclusively to her by her father. During the time in question, husband and wife have had separate domiciles and she is neither informed of nor in support of his tax rebellion. She cannot understand why she should be held responsible for the actions of an independent adult, and confesses to having "long crying spells" (Informant 161, Mar. 24, 1986).

19. Hansen, *To Harass Our People*, pp. 114–20. Confirmed by personal interview, Informant 68, Dec. 31, 1985.

20. Informant 34, Dec. 7, 1985. Cf. *Idaho State Journal*, Mar. 24, 1983

21. For one such justification, see *Idaho State Journal*, Feb. 20, 1983.

22. Informant 49, Dec. 20, 1985.

23. Informant 30, Dec. 4, 1985.

24. Bing Anderton, quoted in *Idaho State Journal*, Aug. 2, 1983.

25. Red Beckman Seminar, Idaho State University, Nov. 20, 1985.

26. Herbert Howard, preface to the second edition of Walter H. Anderson, *A Treatise on the Law of Sheriffs Coroners and Constables with Forms* (1941) (Towson, Md.: Herbert D. Howard, 1982).

27. Red Beckman Seminar, Idaho State University, Nov. 20, 1985.

28. Informant 30, Dec. 4, 1985.

29. Informant 75, Jan. 6, 1986. Cf. the article concerning the founding of the Bingham County Posse Comitatus, *Idaho State Journal*, Feb. 10, 1983.

30. *Idaho Code*, article 18, section 707.

31. *Sandpoint Daily Bee*, Jan. 1, 1975; Mar. 14, 1975; June 26, 1975. For similar incidents in Stockton, California, and Pendleton, Oregon, see *Idaho Statesman*, Sept. 3, 1975 and *Oregonian*, Mar. 25, 1975.

For a foiled plot by the Multnomah, Oregon, Posse Comitatus to burn the homes of several local judges, see *Oregonian*, Apr. 10, 1985. No arrests were ever made in this affair.

32. *Sandpoint Daily Bee*, Feb. 26, 1975.

33. "Seeds of Hate," ABC News, Aug. 15, 1985.

34. Dick Cockle, "Founder of Posse Comitatus Decries Radicals, Lives Quietly," *Oregonian,* June 23, 1985.

35. Informant 75, Jan. 6, 1986.

36. Informant 20, Nov. 29, 1985.

37. Informant 75, Jan. 6, 1986.

38. Informant 30, Dec. 4, 1985.

39. *Ibid.*

40. Anonymous citation on an undated Barristers' Inn School of Common Law advertisement.

41. "The Hidden Third Party in Your Marriage," *Alert,* June 1985, and "The Trojan Horse into the Christian Marriage," *Alert,* no. 26.

42. "The Church vs. State Churches" (Boise: Barristers' Inn School of Common Law, n.d.).

43. Informant 77, Jan. 7, 1986.

44. Informant 46, Dec. 19, 1985.

45. Bob Hallstrom, public speech, Pocatello Community Center, Mar. 20, 1986.

46. Chuck Powell, untitled, undated statement, distributed by Barristers' Inn School of Common Law.

47. Frederick Haberman, *Tracing Our Ancestors* (Metairie, La.: New Christian Crusade Church, 1932). The latest edition, issued by the Lord's Covenant Church in Phoenix, adds the adjective "white" to the title "to make it more clear who is being written about." The subtitle of the edition issued by the New Christian Crusade Church asks: "Were They Descendants of Apes or of Adam?"

48. Bob Hallstrom, public speech, Pocatello Community Center, Mar. 30, 1986.

49. Thomas F. Gossett, *Race: The History of an Idea in America* (New York: Schocken Books, 1965), p. 179.

50. John Wilson, *Our Israelitish Origin* (Philadelphia: Daniels and Smith, 1850). For the most comprehensive history of the Identity movement by an outsider, see Ralph L. Roy, *Apostles of Discord* (Boston: Beacon Press, 1953), pp. 92–117. A briefer account, based on Roy, may be found in J. Gordon Melton, *The Encyclopedia of American Religions* (Wilmington, N.C.: McGrath, 1978), 1:446–52. The John Birch Society has issued an intriguing history of its own of the movement. See Robert Welch, *The Neutralizers* (Belmont, Mass.: John Birch Society, 1963). See also Gossett, *Race,* pp. 190–92.

51. For a brief analysis of the literary roots and merits of the *Protocols,* see Gustavus Myers, *Bigotry in the United States* (New York: Capricorn Books, 1960), pp. 293–98. For a thorough scholarly treatment, see Norman Cohn, *Warrant for Genocide* (New York: Oxford University Press, 1967).

52. J. H. Allen, *Judah's Sceptre and Joseph's Birthright* (Boston: A. A. Beauchamp, 1930 [1902]), p. 71. Cf. Roy, *Apostles of Discord,* p. 98.

53. Armstrong, whose TV and radio messages were seen throughout Idaho until his death in 1986, was considered "the most notable exponent of racism" in the Anglo-Israel movement by J. Gordon Melton. See his *The Encyclopedia*

of American Religions 1:448. See, for example, Herman L. Hoeh, *The Truth About the Race Question* (Pasadena, Calif.: World Wide Church of God, 1957).

54. Wesley Swift, *America: The Appointed Place* (Hollywood, Calif.: New Christian Crusade Church, n.d.).

55. Considerable debate flourishes among fundamentalists around the temporal positioning of the Rapture, the Tribulation, the Second Coming, the Millennium, the Battle of Armegeddon, and the Judgment. Premillennialists believe Jesus will appear prior to the Millennium, postmillennialists, after. The premillennial school may be further divided into those who place the Rapture at various places during the seven-year Tribulation: pretribulationists, midtribulationists, and posttribulationists. While postmillennialism predominated in the nineteenth century, premillennialism in its various guises dominates the fundamentalist scene today.

Some writers have argued that Identity espouses a postmillennial theology. This presumably explains its willingness to forcibly impose its views, i.e., God's law, on others (cf. Richard R. Holden, "Postmillennialism as a Justification for Right Wing Violence" [Central Missouri State University: Center for Criminal Justice Research, 1986]). My reading of Identity literature, however, indicates that it is impossible to fit its proponents into such a narrow theological school. The one point on which Identity preachers do dispute conventional fundamentalists, apart from the notion of who constitutes Israel, is the issue of the Rapture. Identity activists believe that the doctrine of Rapture is too often used by conventional fundamentalists as a way to escape from their responsibilities in this world.

56. All these paraphrases and quotes are from *Prepare War* (Pontiac, Mo.: CSA Bookstore, n.d.).

57. See Roy, *Apostles of Discord*, pp. 186–202, and Harry and Bonaro Overstreet, *The Strange Tactics of Extremism* (New York: W. W. Norton & Co., 1964), pp. 143–56.

58. For Smith's own tribute to Swift, see "Obituary, " *Cross and the Flag,* March 1971. For Smith's own obituary, see *New York Times,* Apr. 16, 1976.

A descendant of four generations of fundamentalist preachers, Smith served as an aid to Huey Long—indeed, cradled him in his arms at the moment of his assassination—the anti-Semitic radio hate-monger, Father Coughlin, and Henry Ford during his Judeophobic period.

An ordained minister of the Disciples of Christ Church, "Doctor" Smith was best known for his gallery of sacred art and seventy-foot Christ of the Ozarks statue on the peak of Magnetic Mountain in Louisiana. At the base of the statue a lavish Passion Play—Smith called it "a noble spectacle"—is still enacted annually. It has earned Smith the title of being America's most dangerous Jew baiter. Smith defended himself against the charge by arguing that if his shrine is anti-Semitic then "the New Testament is anti-Semitic." See Arnold Forster and Benjamin Epstein, "Gerald Smith's Road," *The New Anti-Semitism* (New York: Anti-Defamation League of B'nai B'rith, 1974), pp. 19–48; Roy, "Hitler's Ghost in American Garb," *Apostles of Discord,* pp. 59–91;

Studs Terkel, *Hard Times* (New York: Avon Books, 1970), pp. 368–76.

59. Informant 10, Mar. 15, 1985.

60. Richard Butler, quoted in Solveig Torvik, "The Earth's Most Endangered Species," *Seattle Post-Intelligencer,* Sept. 23, 1980.

61. Roy, *Apostles of Discord,* pp. 60–61.

62. *San Jose Mercury News,* Jan. 27, 1985. For a slightly different version, see Torvik, "The Earth's Most Endangered Species."

63. Richard Mauer, "Church Leader Works for Dream of Racial Purity," *Idaho Statesman,* Sept. 14, 1980.

64. *Idaho State Journal,* Aug. 25, 1985.

65. *Alert* (Barristers' Inn School of Common Law), January 1985.

66. Informant 154, Mar. 16, 1986.

67. Harry Jones, *The Minutemen* (Garden City, N.Y.: Doubleday & Co., 1968).

68. *Ibid.,* p. 129. At one time a trusting follower of Butler, Gilbert claims that Butler sent Mower as a go-between to try to talk him into going through with King's murder. He believes that when he balked, Butler and Mower told the FBI where he was hiding. The Royal Canadian Mounted Police then arrested him in Vancouver, British Columbia, and had him extradited to California to stand trial for possession of explosives (personal correspondence, June 19, 1985).

Gilbert has since established his own Socialist Nationalist Aryan Peoples Party as a competitor to Butler's Aryan Nations Church. In 1982 he sued Butler for $6,666,666.66, "the number of the beast," for defamation of character (*Spokesman Review,* July 24, 1982).

69. *Facts on File* (New York: Facts on File, Inc., 1976), p. 952, column D3.

70. A number of in-depth series on the Aryan Nations Church have appeared in Pacific Northwest newspapers and magazines since 1980. I used the following in preparing this section:

Richard Mauer, "Aryan Nations," *Idaho Statesman,* Sept. 14–17, 1980.

"The New Nazis: Rifles, Religion, and Racism," *The Spokesman Review,* Apr. 14 and 21, 1985.

Joshua Hammer, "Trouble," *People Weekly,* Aug. 29, 1983, pp. 44–48.

Torvik, "The Earth's Most Endangered Species."

Elly Everitt, "A Light for the White Race," *Twin Falls News-Times,* Jan. 3, 1983.

"Violence on the Right," *Time,* Mar. 4, 1985.

Paul Henderson, "We're Not Saluting Hitler—We're Saluting God," *Seattle Times,* Apr. 17, 1983.

"Heavenly Reich," *Lewiston Morning Tribune,* July 17, 1983.

Mike Martin and Anne Russell, articles in the *Gonzaga Bulletin,* Oct. 7 and 14, 1983.

John Harris, "Hitler's Legacy," *Seattle Post-Intelligencer,* Jan. 5, 1985.

Peter Lake, "An Exegesis of the Radical Right," *California Magazine,* Apr. 1985.

71. Anti-Defamation League of B'nai B'rith, *Extremism on the Right: A Handbook* (New York, 1983), p. 9. Because they are undocumented, there is always some question of the validity of ADL biographical claims.

72. *Ibid.*, pp. 5–6. See also Phillip Finch, *God, Guts and Guns* (New York: Seaview/Putnam, 1983), pp. 130–31, 188–91, 203–22.

73. For excellent analyses of the CSA and Ellison, see Ahmed Safir, "Zealot Liked to Tote Bible in His Youth," *St. Louis Post-Dispatch,* Apr. 24, 1985, and Bill Terry, "Up Against the Wall, Sinners," *Arkansas Times,* August 1983.

74. Idaho, County of Kootenai, "Nehemiah Township Charter and Common Law Contract," July 12, 1982, Book 120, p. 387.

75. Mauer, "Church Leader Works for Dream of Racial Purity."

76. Founded in 1959 by Ed White, a prosperous New Orleans real estate magnate, the Tuscumbia Klan attracted a following of one-time affiliates of the National Socialist White Peoples Party, one of several Nazi splinter groups formed after the assassination of George Lincoln Rockwell in 1967. Headed after White's death by David Duke and Don Black, both college graduates, the Tuscumbia Knights employ a tactical rhetoric palatable to the suburban, educated, white middle class. See Harry Crews, "The Buttondown Terror of David Duke," *Playboy,* Feb. 1980, and Patsy Sims, *The Klan* (New York: Stein and Day, 1978), pp. 173–223. Duke has since left the group to form his own National Association for the Advancement of White People, and in 1987 was spoken of as a possible presidential candidate on the Populist Party ticket, along with Idaho's ex-Congressman George Hansen. In 1988 Duke was elected to the Louisiana state legislature as a Republican.

I have identified seven persons at one time associated with the Tuscumbia Klan who have played at least minor roles in the Aryan Nations Church: William Fowler, the Rev. Thom Robb, James Warner, Thomas Metzger, Don Black, Karl Hand, and Louis Beam. Biographies of some of these individuals may be found in Anti-Defamation League, *Extremism on the Right.*

For a thorough analysis of the Canadian right wing, including its ties to American groups, see Stanley R. Barrett, *Is God a Racist?* (Toronto, Canada: University of Toronto Press, 1987).

77. "Wanted: Christians and/or Patriots, especially veterans, who are unprepared for the coming economic, political, social, and military crises. Write: Christian-Patriots Defense League or Citizens Emergency Defense System . . . Flora, Ill." (advertising prototype from the *National Educator*).

78. Peter Arnett, "Armed and Angry," *Salt Lake City Tribune,* Mar. 2–5, 1981. The third article in this four-part series, "The Mobile Home Militia," describes a Posse Comitatus compound in Tigerton Dells, Wisconsin, headquarters of James Wickstrom.

79. Quoted from a Jan. 1978 interview in John Irwin, *Prisons in Turmoil* (Boston: Little, Brown and Co., 1980), p. 180.

80. *Idaho State Journal,* Dec. 11, 1985.

81. David Ledford, "Cassell: Neo-Nazi Life Wasn't for Him," *Spokesman Review,* Apr. 21, 1985.

82. For daily coverage of the trial, see both the *Seattle Post-Intelligencer* and the *Oregonian,* Sept. 13–Dec. 31, 1985.

83. Pierce had also moved on from the Birch Society. A Ph.D. in physics from the University of Colorado and a former physics instructor at Oregon State University, he quit his $29,000-a-year job at Pratt-Whitney to become an unpaid secretary to American Nazi Party chief George Lincoln Rockwell. He formed the National Alliance following Rockwell's assassination (*Oregonian*, Dec. 30, 1984).

84. Andrew MacDonald, *The Turner Diaries* (Arlington, Va.: National Vanguard Books, 1978), pp. 51–52.

85. Michael D. Wiggins, "The Turner Diaries: Blueprint for Right-Wing Extremist Violence," (Central Missouri State University: Center for Criminal Justice Research, 1986).

Laird Wilcox, one of the foremost authorities on extremist violence, has expressed doubt about links between *The Turner Diaries* and the Order. He believes the Order may have modeled itself after the leftist Weather Underground of the 1960s (personal correspondence, Jan. 18, 1987).

86. Lake, "An Exegesis of the Radical Right," p. 99.

87. "Mathews Last Letter," *Sandpoint Daily Bee*, Dec. 12, 1984. For this last letter in full, see Appendix I.

88. Informant 170, Apr. 1, 1986. Cf. the comments of Debbie Mathews in *Sandpoint Daily Bee*, Dec. 12, 1984, and the *Spokesman Review*, Dec. 23, 1984.

By way of clarification, it should be pointed out that if Mathews did not strictly "hate" his fellow citizens, he did assert in his last epistle that they had "devolved into some of the most cowardly, sheepish degenerates that have ever littered the face of this planet" (see Appendix I). Mathews fathered the child of the daughter of Order member Jean Craig.

89. Several witnesses testified to Robert Mathews's apologetic and civil manner during armed robberies, in one case even wishing his victims a merry Christmas.

90. MacDonald, *The Turner Diaries*, p. 42.

91. *Ibid.*, pp. 101 and 120.

92. *Ibid.*, pp. 63 and 94.

93. *Ibid.*, p. 73.

94. *Ibid.*, p. 204.

95. *Ibid.*, p. 203.

96. *Oregonian*, Oct. 30, 1985.

97. Correspondent 7, July 12, 1985.

98. A number of articles have appeared on Order members:

(Jean Craig) *Idaho Statesman*, Apr. 17, 1985.

(Suzanne Tornatsky) *Idaho Statesman*, July 25, 1985.

(Eugene Kinerk) *Idaho Statesman*, Mar. 31, 1985.

(Randall Duey and Denver Parmenter) *Spokesman Review*, Dec. 16, 1984 and Apr. 14, 1985.

(David Tate) *Idaho State Journal*, Apr. 19, 1984.

(Gary Yarbrough) *Denver Post*, Jan. 6, 1985 and *Seattle P-I*, Dec. 31, 1985.

(Thomas Martinez) *Oregonian*, Apr. 18, 1985.

(William Soderquist) *Seattle P-I*, Sept. 25, 1985.

(Robert Merki) *Seattle P-I,* Sept. 28, 1985.

(James Dye) *Seattle P-I,* Oct. 16, 1985.

(Kenneth Loff) *Seattle P-I,* Nov. 11 1985.

(Charles Ostrout and Ronald King) *Seattle P-I,* Oct. 25, 1985.

(Randall Rader) *Seattle P-I,* Nov. 2, 1985.

(Dennis Schlueter) *Idaho Statesman,* Nov. 13, 1985.

(Robert Mathews), L. J. Davis, "Ballad of an American Terrorist," *Harper's,* July 1986, pp. 53–62.

(Bruce Carroll Pierce) *Oregonian,* Aug. 13, 1986.

99. *Spokesman Review,* Apr. 4, 1985. Cf. *Coeur d'Alene Press,* Mar. 25, 1985.

100. Informant 169, Mar. 28, 1986.

CHAPTER 3. MADNESS, MONEY, MESSIAHS

1. Correspondent 3, July 3, 1985.

2. Frank Silva, "Letter to the Editor," *Tacoma News Tribune,* quoted in *Idaho Statesman,* June 24, 1985.

3. Randall Duey, "An Open Letter to the Movement," *Aryan Nations Calling,* no. 50, pp. 6–7.

4. Correspondent 4, July 27, 1985.

5. Thom Robb, Keynote Address, Aryan World Congress, Hayden Lake, Idaho, July 12, 1986.

6. Correspondent 11, Aug. 6, 1986.

7. Correspondent 16, Oct. 27, 1987.

8. Correspondent 11, Aug. 8, 1987.

9. For a clear characterization of this distinction, see C. Wright Mills, "Situated Actions and Vocabularies of Motive," *American Sociological Review* 5 (Dec. 1940), 904–13. Mills's analysis is based in part on the now classic work of rhetorician Kenneth Burke.

10. For an excellent introduction to this research style together with a critique of conventional sociological research, see Hugh Mehan and Huston Wood, *The Reality of Ethnomethodology* (New York: John Wiley & Sons, 1976).

11. The classic discussion of these ideal-types may be found in Max Weber, *The Theory of Social and Economic Organization,* trans. and ed. by Talcott Parsons (New York: Free Press, 1964 [1947]), pp. 15–16. A simpler and more readable account may be found in Randall Collins, *Sociological Insight: An Introduction to Nonobvious Sociology* (New York: Oxford University Press, 1982), pp. 3–29.

12. Field research in mental hospitals demonstrates that the label "insane" is routinely bestowed on conduct when said authorities are confronted with behaviors whose stimuli are unknown or remote, or when the behavior itself is immutable. "Crazy" or "insane" are often less conclusions of objective scientific diagnoses or medical intelligence than they are admissions of professional ignorance passing as science (cf. Thomas J. Scheff, *Being Mentally Ill: A Sociological Theory,* 2d ed. (New York: Aldine, 1984).

13. Joshua Hammer, "Trouble," *People Weekly,* Aug. 29, 1983, pp. 44–48.

14. Quoted in *Gonzaga Bulletin,* Oct. 14, 1983.

15. Personal correspondence, July 9, 1985.

16. For this tragic story in detail, see James A. Aho, "Reification and Sacrifice: The Goldmark Case," *California Sociologist* 10 (Summer 1987), 79–95.

17. David L. Rice, Psychological Evaluation, Prosecuting Attorney, King County, Washington, Jan. 2, 4, 6, 7, 9, 13, 1986.

18. Talcott Parsons, the translator of Weber's discussion of this distinction, says: "[In substantive rationality] there is no question either of rational weighing of this end to others, nor is there a question of 'counting the cost' in the sense of taking account of the possible results other than the attainment of the absolute end. [But functional] rationality involves . . . the weighing of the relative importance of their realization . . . and consideration of whether undesirable consequences would outweigh the benefits to be derived from the course of action. . . . 'Expediency' is often an adequate rendering of [the term]" (Weber, *The Theory of Social and Economic Organization,* p. 115, n. 38).

19. See Max Weber's classic study, *The Protestant Ethic and the Spirit of Capitalism,* trans. Talcott Parsons (New York: Charles Scribner's Sons, 1958), pp. 117–19.

20. Quoted in Anti-Defamation League of B'nai B'rith, *The Hate Movement Today,* p. 10.

21. Thom Robb, keynote address, Aryan World Congress, Hayden Lake, Idaho, July 12, 1986.

22. Kitty Carpella, " 'Days Numbered' for FBI's Neo-Nazi Insider," *Oregonian,* Apr. 18, 1985. Cf. the recruitment stories of Charles Ostrout and Dennis Schlueter in the *Seattle Post-Intelligencer,* Oct. 25, 1985, and the *Idaho Statesman,* Nov. 13, 1985, respectively.

23. *Philadelphia Daily News,* Feb. 18, 1988.

24. M. Williams, letter to the editor, *Sandpoint Daily Bee,* Jan. 1985.

One of the most notable cases of movement profiteering involves Harold W. "Hal" Hunt, Butler's cohort who moved with him from California to Idaho in the early 1970s. In a sworn affadavit Helene P. Pierre, Hunt's fourth wife (or seventh, depending on which account one reads), claims that Hunt, who is now over ninety, has supported himself by marrying wealthy widows endeared to him by his outspoken political demeanor. Once he gains title to their assets, to use her word, he "destroys" them. Pierre, who has identified herself as one of the victims, goes on to say that the entire million-dollar estate of an earlier, now deceased wife of Hunt's, Suzanne Caum, heiress to a huge Pennsylvania dairy fortune, was embezzled and plundered in just this way with the legal aid of several of Richard Butler's Hayden Lake associates. (For tax purposes, Hunt himself reported the value of the estate at $70,715; the Internal Revenue Service put it at about $200,000.) Several thousand dollars of the estate, Pierre claims, were given in the form of an automobile and an airplane to Butler, another portion to underwrite the construction of his house. Other amounts allegedly went to the printing press mentioned in the text. The fine Hayden Lake home Hunt allegedly secured through these shenanigans was recently seized from Hunt by these same lawyers. Caum's exposé of the so-called cancer conspiracy, *Cancer Cures Crucified,* published just prior to her own death from the disease, is still sold at the Aryan Nations compound. For her part Pierre, now divorced from Hunt, lives on welfare (Richard Mauer, " 'Cult Victim' Accuses Aryans of Money Fraud," *Idaho Statesman,* Sept. 15, 1980).

25. Personal interview, Aug. 20, 1985.

26. Carpella, " 'Days Numbered' for FBI's Neo-Nazi Insider."

27. Jarah Crawford, *Last Battle Cry* (Middlebury, Vt.: Jann Publishing, 1984), pp. 395–98.

28. *Ibid.,* p. 396.

29. See Appendix I.

30. *Ibid.*

31. J.T., "American Hero," *National Vanguard* (Mar./Apr. 1985), p. 3. See also the well-written if disturbing editorial, "What Will It Take," *Ibid.* (Jan./Feb. 1985), pp. 2–4.

32. Ernest Becker, *Escape from Evil* (New York: Free Press, 1975). This is one of the most intellectually challenging volumes on the subject of heroism ever written.

33. *Ibid.,* p. 148.

34. Quoted from a letter by an anonymous Hayden Lake, Idaho, Identity Christian, June 28, 1986, to Christopher Bryan in response to a letter to the editor of the *Coeur d'Alene Press* in which Bryan closes by urging that the readers all "begin to live as brothers." Father Bill Wassmuth was at that time chairman of the Kootenai County Human Relations Task Force. His home was bombed on September 15, 1986, but he escaped injury.

CHAPTER 4. "SATAN'S KIDS" AND JACOB'S SEED

1. Correspondent 3, July 3, 1985.

2. For the classic statement of this proposition, see Peter Berger and Thomas Luckmann, *The Social Construction of Reality* (Garden City, N.Y.: Doubleday-Anchor, 1967).

3. Of course, strictly speaking, apart from signifying rain, clouds can also serve a symbolic function. In principle, anything can be symbolically charged.

4. This is the basis of my *Religious Mythology and the Art of War* (Westport, Conn.: Greenwood Press, 1981).

5. Informant 85, Jan. 10, 1986.

6. I Enoch 1–36, *The Old Testament Pseudepigrapha,* vol. 1, ed. James H. Charlesworth (Garden City, N.Y.: Doubleday, 1983). Cf. Genesis 6:1–4.

7. Wesley Swift, *The Mystery of Iniquity* (Hayden Lake, Idaho: Church of Jesus Christ Christian, n.d.).

8. *Ibid.,* pp. 23–24.

9. David Lane, "Race, Reason, Religion" (unpublished manuscript, 1984).

10. Although not strictly an Identity message, *The Turner Diaries* uses images seen frequently in Identity literature. Liberalism is spoken of as a "salient symptom" of a "disease" that permeates American civilization. It is a "cancer" so "deeply rooted in our flesh" that it can be eradicated only by "surgery."

11. Tony Lapan, "Truth," *National Chronicle,* May 6, 1976. Though Lapan

is not an Identity Christian, his letter was published by editor Hal Hunt apparently because it reflected his own views.

12. The following account is based on Swift, *The Mystery of Iniquity.*

13. There exists a sizable right-wing literature connecting Bolshevism to Jewry. There have been just enough Jewish Marxists to give this claim some plausibility. Two such pamphlets I consulted are the anonymous *Communism Is Jewish: Quotes by the Jews* (Dandridge, Tenn.: The Battle Axe N.E.W.S., 1976) and Frank Britton, *Behind Communism* (n.p., n.d.).

14. Correspondent 8, Oct. 27, 1985.

15. *Protocols of the Learned Elders of Zion,* trans. from the Russian of Nilus by Victor E. Marsden (n.p., n.d.).

16. *Ibid.,* p. 60.

17. MacDonald, *The Turner Diaries,* pp. 23–24.

18. Sheldon Emry, *Billion$ for Banker$* (Phoenix, Ariz.: Lord's Covenant Church, 1984), p. 17.

19. Sheldon Emry, *Bible Law on Money* (Phoenix, Ariz.: Lord's Covenant Church, 1981), pp. 40–42.

20. *Ibid.,* pp. 43, 57–59.

21. Emry, *Billion$ for Banker$,* p. 19.

22. *Ibid.,* p. 24. See Appendix VI for more elaborate conspiracies.

23. Allen, *Judah's Sceptre and Jacob's Birthright,* pp. 62–78.

24. *Ibid.,* pp. 46–62.

25. See especially, *Articles of Faith and Doctrine* for Dan Gayman's Church of Israel, p. 5.

26. Informant 175, May 6, 1986.

27. Allen, *Judah's Sceptre and Jacob's Birthright,* pp. 23–35. The import of Allen's discussion may be seen in Gayman's attempt to reconcile Christ's evident promise of universal salvation with Identity exclusivity. "The living Church" must, he begins, "move forward with a plan of racial purity." And this necessitates the development of criteria "to discern those who are white and yet border-line when it comes to outward appearance." But to devolve into ascertaining "correct" eye color, cranial structure, "or degrees of whiteness of skin," says Gayman, is simply self-defeating. Instead, we must "become fruit inspectors" and employ "scriptural criteria for racial purity," which means discerning "by the fruits they bear." What follows is a list of allegorical "racial standards" with which most orthodox Protestants would be comfortable: one's character, his "endurance and perseverence in the truth," his "testimony," "the witness of [his] Christian living," and whether or not he has certain faith in his election to salvation. True, these criteria apply only to "white" people, but Gayman is explicitly disconnecting himself from literal renderings of the word white used by some churches and assuming a more orthodox position (Dan Gayman, "Racial Purity and the Living Church," *The Watchman,* Spring 1986, pp. 9–10).

28. Gordon "Jack" Mohr, *Know Your Enemies* (Merrimac, Mass.: Destiny, 1982).

29. *Ibid.,* p. 12.

30. *Ibid.,* p. 19.

31. *Ibid.,* p. 26.
32. *Ibid.,* pp. 37–38.
33. *Ibid.,* p. 37. Mohr cites a letter from a "born-again" Jew to prove this point on pp. 27–29.
34. *Ibid.,* p. 62.
35. Including, presumably, ritual murder of Christian children. A popular book among racist Identity affiliates is Arnold Leese, *Jewish Ritual Murder,* first published in London in 1938 by the International Fascist League.
36. Mohr, *Know Your Enemies,* p. 62.
37. *Ibid.,* p. 64.
38. Justin Bonaventura Pranaitis (d. 1917) was a Russian Roman Catholic priest. *The Talmud Unmasked* was translated from Latin into English in 1939. A compilation of quotations from the classic anti-Semitic text (2,120 pp.) of the same title by the German-professor Johann Eisenmenger in 1700, it is also based in part on *Der Talmudjude* (1839–41), by anti-Jewish Catholic priest Augustus Rohling. The Pranaitis Talmud was introduced to America by Colonel E. L. Sanctuary, a cohort of fundamentalist minister Gerald Winrod, the "Jayhawk Nazi" as his detractors called him. Now standard fare in rightist circles, including the Aryan Nations Church, it is the main source of Dilling's *The Plot Against Christianity.* See Roy, *Apostles of Discord,* pp. 37–39. For a scholarly treatment of Eisenmenger's text together with an assessment of its historical influence, see Jacob Katz, *From Prejudice to Destruction: Anti-Semitism 1700–1933* (Cambridge, Mass.: Harvard University Press, 1980).
39. Mohr, *Know Your Enemies,* pp. 51 and 68 from John 8:44.
40. *Ibid.,* p. 50.
41. *Ibid.,* p. 51.
42. *Ibid.,* p. 68.
43. Crawford, *Last Battle Cry,* p. 325.
44. Biblical contextualists maintain there was only one creation, but two separate renditions of the event written at widely disparate times to different audiences. The first story is said to have issued from "priestly" sources given the sparsity of the narrative and its emphasis on law; the second from "Yahwistic" sources, given its use of God's name as revealed to Moses—"Yahweh."
45. Crawford, *Last Battle Cry,* pp. 333–34.
46. *Ibid.,* p. 337.
47. *Ibid.,* pp. 338–41.
48. *Ibid.,* p. 32.
49. Cf. Pete Peters, *The Greatest Discovery of Our Age* (Laporte, Colo.: Scriptures for America, 1985), p. 9. Pastor Peters's church has a number of southern Idaho adherents, and at least three members of the Order are alleged to have attended services with his congregation.
50. Crawford, *Last Battle Cry,* p. 34.
51. *Ibid.,* pp. 36–37. Cf. Peters, *The Greatest Discovery of Our Age,* pp. 27–28.
52. Crawford, *Last Battle Cry,* p. 37.
53. *Ibid.,* p. 67.
54. *Ibid.,* p. 91.

55. *Ibid.*, pp. 87–88.
56. *Ibid.*, pp. 98–99.
57. Bertrand Comparet, *Your Heritage: An Identification of the True Israel Through Biblical and Historic Sources* (Hayden Lake, Idaho: Aryan Nations, n.d.), p. 2.
58. Allen (*Judah's Sceptre and Jacob's Birthright*, pp. 259–69) claims that a thesaurus of European place names can be attributed to Dan. In Ireland: *Dans*-lough, *Don*-sower, *Dun*-dalke, *Dun*-drum, Lon-*don*-derry, *Din*-gle, and *Duns*-garven. In England and Scotland: *Dun*-kirk, *Dun*-bar, *Dun*-dee *Dun*-raven, Ed-*din*-burg, and of course, Lon-*don*.
59. *Ibid.*, pp. 143–44, 247–48. One of the most impressive analyses of this sort is E. Raymond Capt., *Missing Links Discovered in Assyrian Tablets* (Thousand Oaks, Calif.: Artisan Sales, 1985).
60. Frederick Haberman, *Tracing Our Ancestors*, pp. 44–58. See also Allen, *Judah's Sceptre and Jacob's Birthright*, pp. 207–15, 228–29, 248–58.
61. For a fanciful genealogy from Adam (4000 B.C.) through Judah (b. 1752 B.C.) down to England's King George VI (d. A.D. 1952), see Allen, *Judah's Sceptre and Jacob's Birthright*, pp. 369–77.

CHAPTER 5. CHRISTIAN IDENTITY PROVEN

1. For the classic study of prophetic failure actually solidifying religious belief, see Leon Festinger, *When Prophecy Fails* (Minneapolis: University of Minnesota Press, 1956).
2. Allen, *Judah's Sceptre and Jacob's Birthright*, pp. 279–99.
3. Haberman, *Tracing Our Ancestors*, p. 38, and Allen, *Judah's Sceptre and Jacob's Birthright*, pp. 274–75. For an extensive list of Hebrew words and their presumed English derivatives, see Capt, *Missing Links Discovered in Assyrian Tablets*, pp. 187–98.
4. Haberman, *Tracing Our Ancestors*, p. 4.
5. *Ibid.*, p. 77.
6. *Ibid.*, p. 7.
7. *Ibid.*, pp. 34–38.
8. *Ibid.*, pp. 46–48.
9. Allen, *Judah's Sceptre and Jacob's Birthright*, pp. 320–24, 341–43. For the most thorough attempt to correlate prophecy, heraldic signs, and national destinies, see Capt, *Missing Links Discovered in Assyrian Tablets*, pp. 203–16.
10. Wesley Swift, *Standards of the Kingdom* (Hayden Lake, Idaho: Aryan Nations, n.d.), p. 24. See also pp. 21–22.
11. Franklin Snook, *America: 13th or All 13?* (Phoenix, Ariz.: Lord's Covenant Church, n.d.), especially p. 3.
12. Swift, *Standards of the Kingdom*, p. 25.
13. *Ibid.*, pp. 28–29.
14. *Ibid.*, p. 22.
15. *Ibid.*, p. 26.
16. *Ibid.*
17. *Ibid.*, p. 23.

18. *Ibid.*, p. 28.
19. *Ibid.*, p. 25.
20. *Ibid.*
21. Allen, *Judah's Sceptre and Jacob's Birthright,* pp. 324–27. Cf. Snook, *America,* pp. 21–22.
22. Haberman, *Tracing Our Ancestors,* p. 172. For other, more inventive numerological interpretations regarding the unification of the British Empire, see pp. 145 and 173, as well as Allen, *Judah's Sceptre and Jacob's Birthright,* pp. 315–17.
23. Comparet, *Your Heritage,* p. 9.
24. *Ibid.*, pp. 15–16.

CHAPTER 6. CHRISTIAN CONSTITUTIONALISM AND MORMONISM

1. Brigham Young, "The Priesthood and Satan," *Journal of Discourses* 2:182. See also *ibid.* 6:152–53 and 7:15.
2. Robert Welch, *The Blue Book* (Belmont, Mass.: John Birch Society, 1960).
3. Of the many books treating this subject, one of the best is Benjamin Epstein and Arnold Forster, *The Radical Right: Report on the John Birch Society and Its Allies* (New York: Vintage Books, 1967).
4. For one exposé, see T. George Harris, "The Rampant Right Invades the GOP," *Look,* July 16, 1963, pp. 19–25.
5. Epstein and Forster, *The Radical Right,* p. 201. Quoted without a source.
6. A photocopy of this advertisement is found in Mike W. Hatch, "Extremism in Idaho Politics," M.S. thesis (Salt Lake City: University of Utah, 1966), p. 210. A similar letter inviting church members to an upcoming JBS meeting quotes Joseph Smith and Presidents John Taylor and McKay. It closes with the words: "Your help is needed to preserve freedom under the God-inspired Constitution of the United States."
7. *Salt Lake City Tribune,* Mar. 21, 1963.
8. *Idaho State Journal,* Nov. 21, 1963. Cf. Hatch, "Extremism in Idaho Politics," pp. 126–27.
9. *Idaho State Journal,* Mar. 26, 1985.
10. Informant 125, Feb. 4, 1986.
11. *Congressional Record,* Ralph A. Harding, "The John Birch Society," 88th Cong. 1st sess. January 1963, House rept. 1010–11.
12. Letter signed by the First Presidency of the LDS Church, Aug. 1, 1963, cited in *Congressional Record,* Wallace Bennett, "The Attitude of Latter-day Saints Toward John Birch Society," 88th Cong., 1st sess., August 1963, Senate rept. 14171–2.
13. Hatch, "Extremism in Idaho Politics," pp. 138–41, 147, 149–50.
14. For the flavor of Benson's remarks, see his *The Red Carpet,* an exposé of the "royal road" to Communism (Salt Lake City, Utah: Bookcraft, 1962) and *A Nation Asleep* (Salt Lake City, Utah: Bookcraft, 1963).
15. Joseph Fielding Smith, letters to Ralph Harding dated Oct. 30 and Dec. 23, 1963, in *Idaho State Journal,* Feb. 20, 1964.

16. For expressions of remorse by Smith and David O. McKay's son, Robert, see *Idaho State Journal,* Feb. 21, 1964.

17. *Ibid.* For analysis of these and other comments and their bearing on the 1964 congressional election, see Hatch, "Extremism in Idaho Politics," pp. 132–36 and 151.

18. Book of Mormon, Alma 51:5–6. For a brief but well-documented history of the Freemen Institute, see John Heinerman and Anson Shupe, *The Mormon Corporate Empire* (Boston: Beacon Press, 1985), pp. 152–56.

19. Robert Gottlieb and Peter Wiley, *America's Saints: The Mormons* (New York: G. P. Putnam's Sons, 1984), pp. 91–92.

20. *Ibid.,* p. 93. Quoted without a source.

21. Cf. Ed Decker and Dave Hunt, *The Godmakers* (Eugene, Ore.: Harvest Books, 1984), pp. 253–54.

22. For the argument supporting the claim of a coalition between the fundamentalist Right and the Mormon Church, see John Heinerman and Anson Shupe, "Mormonism and the New Christian Right: An Emerging Coalition?" *Review of Religious Research* 27 (Dec. 1985), 146–57. For the counterargument, see Merlin B. Brinkerhoff, Jeffrey C. Jacob, and Marlene M. Mackie, "Mormonism and the Moral Majority Make Strange Bedfellows?: An Exploratory Critique," *Review of Religious Research* 28 (March 1987) 236–51.

23. For detailed analyses of CAUSA's connections to "soft-core fascists" in Asia, see Scott Anderson and John Lee Anderson, *Inside the League* (New York: Dodd, Mead, 1986), pp. 66–70, 129–30, 232–34.

24. *Idaho State Journal,* June 14, 1985.

25. Informant 238, Sept. 29, 1986.

26. In fairness to the Rev. Moon, it should be mentioned that as friends of the court forty national political, civil rights, and religious groups joined in the Supreme Court appeal to have his conviction overturned.

27. *Idaho State Journal,* Aug. 22, 1985.

28. Ezra Taft Benson, *This Nation Shall Endure* (Salt Lake City, Utah: Deseret Book Co., 1977), p. 23.

29. Revelation to Joseph Smith, Dec. 16, 1833, Kirtland, Ohio, *Doctrine and Covenants* 101:80. Cf. the revelation dated Aug. 6, 1833, *ibid.* 98:5–7.

30. Brigham Young, "The Constitution and Government of the United States," *Journal of Discourses* 2:175.

31. Benson, *This Nation Shall Endure,* pp. 18–19.

32. Brigham Young, "The Priesthood and Satan," *Journal of Discourses,* 2:184–88.

33. Revelation to an assembly of elders, Aug. 17, 1835, Kirtland, Ohio, *Doctrine and Covenants* 134:11.

34. These phrases taken from W. Cleon Skousen, *The Making of America* (Washington, D.C.: National Institute for Constitutional Studies, 1985).

35. *Doctrine and Covenants,* 98:6–7.

36. Joseph Fielding Smith, *Journal of Discourses* 23:71.

37. John Taylor, *Journal of Discourses* 23:66–67. For other selections used by patriots to justify insurgency, see *ibid.* 12:119–20; 24:64–71; 2:309–13;

14:31; and 23:110–11. All the quotations in this and the previous paragraph are taken from this source.

38. Book of Mormon, Alma 51:5–6.

39. Book of Mormon, Helaman 3:23.

40. *Pearl of Great Price*, Moses 5:29.

41. *Ibid.* 5:31.

42. *Ibid.* 5:40. Cf. Alma 3:7.

43. Book of Mormon, II Nephi 26.

44. Whitney R. Cross, *The Burned Over District* (New York: Harper and Row, 1965).

45. Fawn Brodie, *No Man Knows My History* (New York: Alfred A. Knopf, 1966 [1945]), p. 64.

46. Helaman, 2:4.

47. For "secret combination," see II Nephi 9:9, 26:22, Alma 37:30–31; Helaman 3:23; III Nephi 4:29; Mormon 8:27; Ether 8:19, 22; 9:1; 13:18; and 14:8. For "secret society," III Nephi 3:9; Ether 9:6; 11:22. For "secret band," Helaman 11:10.

48. III Nephi 4:7.

49. Helaman 6:21–22.

50. For typical fundamentalist Protestant accusations of Mormon borrowing from Masonic ritual and myth, see Decker and Hunt, *The Godmakers*, pp. 116–31, and Jerald and Sandra Tanner, *Mormonism: Shadow or Reality*, enlarged edition (Salt Lake City: Utah Lighthouse Ministry, n.d.), pp. 69–72, 484–92. For scholarly support of this contention, see David John Buerger, "The Development of the Mormon Temple Endowment Ceremony," *Dialogue: A Journal of Mormon Thought* 20 (Winter 1987), 33–76.

51. Informant 135, Feb. 15, 1986.

52. Informant 142, Mar. 8, 1986.

53. Speech at John Birch Society meeting by LDS member, Pocatello, Idaho, Mar. 18, 1986.

54. W. Cleon Skousen, *The Naked Capitalist* (Salt Lake City, Utah: W. Cleon Skousen, 1974 [1968]).

55. Gary Allen, *None Dare Call It Conspiracy* (Seal Beach, Calif.: Concord Press, 1971).

56. Carroll Quigley, *Tragedy and Hope* (New York: Macmillan Co., 1966).

57. Allen, *None Dare Call It Conspiracy*, p. 75. For a more detailed presentation of Allen's and Skousen's conspiracy theories, see Appendix IV.

58. Skousen, *The Naked Capitalist*, p. 24.

59. Quigley, *Tragedy and Hope*, pp. 938, 945. Quigley praises their work in promoting peace, helping advance backward countries, and spreading democracy (p. 954).

60. Allen, *None Dare Call It Conspiracy*, p. 29.

61. Skousen, *The Naked Capitalist*, pp. 26–28.

62. Allen, *None Dare Call It Conspiracy*, p. 80.

63. Unless otherwise indicated, all of these phrases are taken from Benson, *The Red Carpet*.

64. Bruce McConkie, *Mormon Doctrine* (Salt Lake City, Utah: Bookcraft,

1979 [1966]), pp. 389–90. McConkie takes this quote from Joseph Smith, *History of the Church of Jesus Christ of Latter-day Saints* (Salt Lake City, Utah: Deseret Book Co., 1967), 3:380. Brigham Young concurs: "Joseph said that the gentile blood was actually cleansed out of their veins, and the blood of Jacob made to circulate in them." (*Journal of Discourses* 2:269).

65. McConkie, *Mormon Doctrine*, pp. 455–48.

66. Charles A. L. Totten, "The Romance within the Romance, or the Philosophy of History': Tea Tephi David's Daughter, Jeremiah's Ward," *Our Race Quarterly* 3, 1st series (March 1891), n.p.

67. Howard H. Barron, *Judah, Past and Future* (Bountiful, Utah: Horizon Pub., 1979), pp. 47–48.

68. Helaman 6:10 and 8:21.

69. I Nephi 10:11; 19:13–14.

70. I Nephi 20.

71. I Nephi 11:35.

72. I Nephi 1:19–20; 2:13; 3:17; 4:36; 7:14; II Nephi 6:9–11; 10:3, 5–6.

73. I Nephi 13:31. For typical unofficial usage of these passages to interpret Jewish sufferings over time, see Barron, *Judah, Past and Future*, pp. 45–60. Barron says that seen in light of Jewish transgressions against God, "Hitler [may be viewed] as an instrument in the hand of God" (pp. 56–57).

74. Informant 13, Nov. 17, 1985.

75. Armand Mauss, "Mormonism and Minorities," Ph.D. dissertation (Berkeley: University of California, 1970), p. 60.

76. Personal correspondence, Mar. 21, 1988.

77. For a detailed statement to this effect, see Ezra Taft Benson, "A Message to Judah from Joseph," an address to Mormons, non-Mormons, and Jews at the Jubilee Auditorium, Calgary, Alberta, Canada, May 2, 1976. This is reprinted in Benson, *This Nation Shall Endure*.

78. Quoted in Mauss, "Mormonism and Minorities," pp. 62–63.

79. I Nephi 22:6, 7; II Nephi 10:7–22.

80. I Nephi 15:12–17.

81. I Nephi 15:19–20.

82. Benson, "A Message to Judah from Joseph," pp. 5–6. For Hyde's official message, see Barron, *Judah, Past and Future*, p. 76. See also pp. 76–87. For other official church missions to the Holy Land, see pp. 87–95.

83. For excerpts from the Pace amendment, see Appendix V.

CHAPTER 7. SKETCHING THE MOVEMENT CAUSES

1. For an excellent introduction to this view, see Thomas R. Dye and L. Harmon Zeigler, *The Irony of Democracy* (Belmont, Calif.: Wadsworth, 1970), especially pp. 137–40.

2. William Kornhauser, *The Politics of Mass Society* (New York: Free Press 1959), p. 188.

3. Robert Nisbet, *The Quest for Community* (New York: Harper and Bros., 1953), p. 34.

4. Seymour Martin Lipset, "Working Class Authoritarianism," in *Political Man* (Garden City, N.Y.: Doubleday, 1960), pp. 97–126.

5. Samuel Stouffer, *Communism, Conformity and Civil Liberties* (New York: John Wiley, 1966).

6. Herbert McCloskey, "Personality and Attitude Correlates of Foreign Policy Orientation," *Domestic Sources of Foreign Policy* (New York: Free Press, 1967), pp. 51–110.

7. Monica Blumenthal, Robert Kahn, Frank Andrews, and Kendra Head, *Justifying Violence* (Ann Arbor: University of Michigan Press, 1972).

8. Seymour Martin Lipset and Earl Raab, *The Politics of Unreason* (New York: Harper and Row, 1970), pp. 328, 330–31.

9. *Ibid.*, pp. 320–24.

10. *Ibid.*, pp. 429–33.

11. Harold Quinley and Charles Glock, *Anti-Semitism in America* (New York: Free Press, 1979), pp. 33–49.

12.   Student Performance on Graduate Record Examinations:
           Percentages Above or Below the 1981–82 National Average[a]

	GRE, % above or below 1981–82 average	
Undergraduate Major	Verbal	Quantitative
Fine arts	+1.7	−8.4
English	+14.5	−5.7
Foreign languages	+7.9	−4.2
History	+10.8	−5.5
Philosophy	+17.6	+4.6
Political science	+3.5	−5.0
Psychology	+3.1	−4.0
Sociology	−5.0	−15.0
Other social science	−0.4	−7.2
Chemistry	+2.1	+18.3
Mathematics	+2.7	+26.3
Physics	+6.6	+29.5
Business administration	−9.1	−2.3
Education	−10.4	−15.8
Engineering	−7.3	+25.1

[a]Adapted from Clifford Adelman, National Institute of Education.

13. For an unmatched history and critique of this theory, see Anthony Oberschall, *Social Conflict and Social Movements* (Englewood Cliffs, N.J.: Prentice-Hall, 1973), pp. 102–45. For early statements of the theory, see Ortega y Gassett, *The Revolt of the Masses* (New York: W. W. Norton, 1932), and Erich Fromm, *Escape from Freedom* (New York: Avon Books, 1965 [1941]).

14. For example, see Elton Mayo, *The Social Problems of an Industrial Civilization* (Boston: Harvard School of Business Administration, 1945); Norman Cohn, *The Pursuit of the Millennium* (New York: Oxford University Press, 1970); Seymour Martin Lipset and Philip Altbach, "The Quest for Community on Campus," in *The Quest for Community in Modern America*, ed. E. Digby Baltzell (New York: Harper & Row, 1968), pp. 123–47; James Coleman, *Community Conflict* (Glencoe, Ill.: Free Press, 1957); Mancur Olson, Jr., "Socioeconomic Change and Third World Instability," in *When Men Revolt and Why*, ed. James Davies (New York: Free Press, 1971), pp. 215–27; Talcott Parsons, "Some Sociological Aspects of the Fascist Movement," *Social Forces* 21 (1942), 138–47; Mark Colvin, "The New Mexico Prison Riot," *Social Problems* 29 (June 1982), 449–63.

15. Robert Crain et al., *The Politics of Community Change* (New York: Bobbs-Merrill, 1969).

16. Raymond Wolfinger et al., "America's Radical Right," in *Ideology and Discontent* ed. David Apter (New York: Free Press, 1964), pp. 262–93.

17. Richard Hamilton, *Who Voted For Hitler?* (Princeton, N.J.: Princeton University Press, 1982), p. 41.

18. *Ibid.*, p. 40.

19. Aida K. Tomeh, "Formal Voluntary Organizations: Participation, Correlates, and Interrelationships," in *The Community*, ed. Marcia P. Effrat (New York: Free Press, 1974).

20. For data regarding geographic mobility at the national, regional, and state levels, see U.S. Dept. of Commerce, *County and City Data Book* (Washington, D.C.: Government Printing Office, 1983), Table A, items 13–16.

21. *Ibid.*, Idaho, Table B, items 13–16.

22. For a provocative argument to this effect, see Evelyn Reed, *Woman's Evolution: From Matriarchal Clan to Patriarchal Family* (New York: Pathfinder Press, 1975).

23. Hugh Carter and Paul C. Glick, *Marriage and Divorce: A Social and Economic Study* (Cambridge, Mass.: Harvard University Press, 1970), p. 83.

24. *Ibid.*, pp. 23–25.

25. *Ibid.*, pp. 20–23.

26. Sidney Verba and Norman Nie, *Participation in America* (New York: Harper & Row, 1972), p. 31.

27. Kornhauser, *The Politics of Mass Society*, pp. 51–61.

28. For the classic statment of the theory of rising expectations, see Alexis de Tocqueville in *When Men Revolt and Why*, ed. James C. Davies (New York: Free Press, 1971), pp. 92–98.

29. Clark Kerr and Abraham Siegel, "The Inter-Industry Propensity to Strike: An International Comparison," in *Industrial Conflict*, ed. Arthur Kornhauser, Robert Dubin, and Arthur Ross (New York: McGraw-Hill, 1954), pp. 189–212.

30. Kornhauser, *The Politics of Mass Society*, pp. 183–93.

31. *Ibid.*, pp. 207–11.

32. *Ibid.*, pp. 212–22.

33. *Ibid.*, pp. 197–201.

34. *Ibid.*, pp. 201–7.

35. *Ibid.*, pp. 76–90.

36. J. Gordon Melton, *Encyclopedia of American Religions*, 2 vols. (Wilmington, N.C.: McGrath, 1978).

37. Cited in David A. Roozen, "What Hath the 1970s Wrought: Religion in America," in *Yearbook of American and Canadian Churches: 1984*, ed. Constant H. Jacquet, Jr. (Nashville, Tenn.: Abingdon Press, 1984), pp. 273–81.

38. *Yearbook of American and Canadian Churches: 1984*, p. 238.

39. *Churches and Church Membership in the United States*, ed. Bernard Quinn et al. (Atlanta, Ga.: Glenmary Research Center, 1982), pp. 13–14.

40. Rodney Stark and William Sims Bainbridge, *The Future of Religion* (Berkeley: University of California Press, 1985), pp. 74–78.

41. I did not inquire into occupations of the sample before they got involved in the movement because most could not tell specifically when they became patriots. As shall be seen in Chapter 9, for most the process of patriot commitment involved a series of small steps and not a single, one-time conversion. One problem with the mass theory of extremism is that it fails to depict accurately what actually occurs in radicalization, presenting it instead as a relatively simple mechanical cause and effect. The reason for this is that few if any mass theorists to my knowledge have ever interviewed activists directly or participated with them in the field. Rather, they rely on secondary data.

CHAPTER 8. THE RELIGIOUS ROOTS OF PATRIOTISM

1. Testifying to the popularity of this theory is an entire handbook dedicated to research on it: *Handbook of Political Socialization*, ed. Stanley A. Renshon (New York: Free Press, 1977).

2. James C. Davies, "The Family's Role in Political Socialization," *Annals of the American Academy of Political and Social Science* 361 (Sept. 1965), 11.

3. M. K. Jennings and R. G. Niemi, "The Transmission of Political Values from Parent to Child," *American Political Science Review*, 62 (1968), 169–84.

4. Renshon, ed., *Handbook of Political Socialization*, pp. 115–328.

5. *Ibid.*, pp. 428–29.

6. Gordon Allport, "The Composition of Political Attitudes," *American Journal of Sociology* 35 (1929), 220–38.

7. For the Jewish-leftist association, see Seymour M. Lipset, "University Student Politics," in *The Berkeley Student Revolt*, ed. Lipset and Sheldon Wolin (Garden City, N.Y.: Doubleday-Anchor, 1965). For the non-religious connection to the left wing, see R. E. Peterson, "The Student Left in American Higher Education," *Daedalus* 97 (1968), 293–317.

8. For example, see W. Morris, "Houston's Superpatriots," *Harper's*, Oct. 1961, pp. 248–56, or M. Chesler and R. Schmuck, "Participant Observation in a Superpatriot Discussion Group," *Journal of Social Issues* 19 (1963), 18–30.

9. See the pieces by A. D. Elms, F. W. Grupp, Jr., and I. S. Rohter in *The*

American Right Wing, ed. R. Schoenberger (New York: Holt, Rinehart and Winston, 1969).

10. Anson Shupe and William Stacy, "The Moral Majority Constituency," in *The New Christian Right,* ed. Robert Liebman and Robert Wuthnow (New York: Aldine, 1983), pp. 104–17.

11. See Seymour Martin Lipset, "Working Class Authoritarianism," in *Political Man* (Garden City, NY: Doubleday, 1960), pp. 97–126.

12. For information on religious affiliation in the United States, see *Yearbook of American and Canadian Churches: 1984,* ed. Constant H. Jacquet, Jr., (Nashville, Tenn.: Abingdon Press, 1984), p. 244. For Idaho, *Churches and Church Membership in the United States,* ed. Bernard Quinn et al., (Atlanta, Ga.: Glenmary Research Center, 1982), pp. 13–14. See the comments at Table 8.2, note a.

13. George Gallup, Jr., and David Poling, *The Search for America's Faith* (Nashville, Tenn.: Abingdon Press, 1980), pp. 106–8 and the last page (unnumbered).

14. Research on apostasy rates indicates that Jews, Protestants, and Catholics are inclined to leave their faiths in this order (David Caplovitz and R. Sherrow, *The Religious Dropouts* [Beverly Hills, Calif.: Sage, 1977]). Since there are no Jews in the sample, they are ignored here.

I use the 1980 religious census compiled by Quinn et al. to retrospectively estimate the proportions of different church affiliations in Idaho for the period during which most of those in the sample were youngsters (ca. 1935–45). If it is true that Methodism, Congregationalism, Presbyterianism and other denominations considered liberal have been losing members at higher rates than fundamentalist sects since the fifties, then this means that I have probably overestimated the proportion of Idahoans who actually were raised fundamentalists and underestimated the proportion raised in "liberal" churches. These probable errors in estimation of religious upbringing skew the ration comparisons in Table 8.2 in such a way as to work against the argument presented in this chapter. If I were to statistically control for different rates of apostasy among liberal and fundamentalist church-goers, the data in this chapter would demonstrate an even stronger association between fundamentalism and patriotism than reported in the text.

15. James A. Aho, "Suffering, Redemption and Violence: Albert Camus and the Sociology of Violence," *Rendezvous* 9 (Spring 1974/Winter 1974–75), 51–62; "The Protestant Ethic and the Spirit of Violence," *Journal of Political and Military Sociology* 7 (Spring 1979), 103–19; and *Religious Mythology and the Art of War* (Westport, Conn.: Greenwood Press, 1981), pp. 147–53.

16. Ed Decker and Dave Hunt, *The God Makers* (Eugene, Ore.: Harvest House Books, 1984), pp. 20–33, 60–61, 65–68, and 116–31.

17. John Calvin, *On God and Man,* ed. F. W. Strothmann (New York: Frederick Ungar, 1956), p. 26.

18. Quoted without a source in Phillip Finch, *God, Guts and Guns* (New York: Seaview/Putnam, 1983), p. 53.

19. For one example of a growing literature on this subject, see Wolfgang Lederer, *The Fear of Women* (New York: Harcourt, Brace, Jovanovich, 1968), pp. 153–68.

20. Richard G. Butler, *The Aryan Warrior* (Hayden Lake, Idaho: Aryan Nations Church, n.d.), p. 11.

21. Max Weber, *The Sociology of Religion*, trans. Ephraim Fischoff (Boston: Beacon Press, 1964), pp. 166–83.

22. J. B. Stoner, letter to the editor, *Calling Our Nation* 52:26–27.

23. McConkie, *Mormon Doctrine*, pp. 715–34.

24. David Mauer, "Couple Finds Answers in Butler's Teachings," *Idaho Statesman*, Sept. 14, 1980.

25. Rosemary Ruether, *Faith and Fratricide: The Theological Roots of Anti-Semitism* (New York: Seabury Press, 1979). Ruether is Catholic.

For one of the first recent Jewish assertions to this effect, see Jules Isaac, *The Teaching of Contempt: The Christian Roots of Anti-Semitism* (New York: McGraw-Hill, 1964). See also Samuel Sandmel, *Anti-Semitism in the New Testament?* (Philadelphia: Fortress Press, 1978). For a readable if less scholarly history of Christian-inspired anti-Semitism, see Malcolm Hay, *The Roots of Christian Anti-Semitism* (New York: Anti-Defamation League of B'nai B'rith, 1981 [1950]). Hay's anti-Catholic bias is evident in this volume. His book may be likened to the more emotional Dagobert Runes, *Let My People Live!* (New York: Philosophical Library, 1975). For detailed bibliographies on this subject, see Ruether and Isaac.

26. Sandmel, *Anti-Semitism in the New Testament?*, pp. 1–5.

27. See Ruether, *Faith and Fratricide*, for the history of this myth.

28. Hay, *The Roots of Christian Anti-Semitism*, p. 88.

29. Cf. James Brown, "Christian Teaching and Anti-Semitism: Scrutinizing Religious Texts," *Commentary* (Dec. 1957), pp. 494–501.

30. Charles Glock and Rodney Stark, *Christian Beliefs and Anti-Semitism* (New York: Harper and Row, 1966). For the index, see pp. 94–98. By orthodoxy, the authors mean assent to specific doctrinal assertions concerning a personal God, Jesus Christ as savior, and the universalism of Christianity. By particularism, they are referring to belief that Christianity has an exclusive monopoly on salvation. Images of ancient Jewry include the Jews as killers of Christ; modern Jews are pictured as having shady business dealings, etc.

31. *Ibid.*, pp. 136, 175. For the quotation, see Harold Quinley and Charles Glock, *Anti-Semitism in America* (New York: Free Press, 1979), p. 176. See also pp. 94–109.

32. Armand Mauss, "Mormonism and Minorities," Ph.D. dissertation (Berkeley: University of California, 1970).

33. *Ibid.*, pp. 63–64. See also Armand Mauss, "Mormon Semitism and Anti-Semitism," *Sociological Analysis* 29 (Spring 1968), 11–27.

34. For the critique of the Glock-Stark research program, see Robin Williams, Andrew Greeley, and Daniel Levinson, "Review Symposium," *American Sociological Review* 32 (Dec. 1967), 1004–13. For the Glock-Stark rebuttal, see *Wayward Shepherds* (New York: Harper and Row, 1971), pp. 63, 81, 83.

35. The image of a passive subject being "brainwashed" by authority figures has come under considerable criticism by sociologists conducting field research on cults. For one critique, see James T. Richardson and Brock Kilbourne, "Classical and Contemporary Applications of Brainwashing Models: A Comparison and Critique," in *The Brainwashing/Deprogramming Controversy*, ed. David Bromley and Richardson (Toronto: Edwin Mellen Press, 1983), pp. 23–45.

36. Informant 250, Sept. 15, 1987.

CHAPTER 9. SOCIAL NETWORKS AND PATRIOT RECRUITMENT

1. Malcolm Hay, *The Roots of Christian Anti-Semitism*, p. 3.

2. One of the first large-scale research projects to discover and analyze the dynamics of the multi-step process of mobilization is Paul F. Lazardsfeld, Bernard Berelson, and Hazel Gaudet, *The People's Choice* (New York: Columbia University Press, 1948). Quality studies elucidating and elaborating on this theory include; Tamotsu Shibutani, *Improvised News: A Sociological Study of Rumor* (Indianapolis, Ind.: Bobbs-Merrill, 1966); Clark McPhail and Ronald T. Wohstein, "Individual and Collective Behaviors within Gatherings, Demonstrations, and Riots," *American Review of Sociology* 9 (1983), 579–600; for fads and fashions, David L. Miller, *Introduction to Collective Behavior* (Belmont, Calif.: Wadsworth, 1985), pp. 152–53; James H. Copp, Maurice L. Sill, and Emory J. Brown, "The Function of Information Sources in the Farm Practice Adoption Process," *Rural Sociology* 23 (1958), 146–57; Eliot Friedson, "Client Control and Medical Practice," *American Journal of Sociology* 65 (1960), 374–82; Philip Selznick, *TVA and the Grassroots* (Berkeley: University of California Press, 1949); Aldon Morris, "Black Southern Sit-In Movement: An Analysis of Internal Organization," *American Sociological Review* 46 (1981), 744–67; Frederic J. Flerion, Jr., "The Malevolent Leader: Political Socialization in American Subculture," *American Political Science Review* 62 (June 1968), 564–75.

3. Anthony Oberschall, *Social Conflict and Social Movements* (Englewood Cliffs, N.J.: Prentice-Hall, 1973), p. 135.

4. The classic statement of the conversion process as gleaned from participant observation of the Unification Church is John Lofland and Rodney Stark's "Becoming a World-Saver: A Theory of Conversion to a Deviant Perspective," *American Sociological Review* 30 (Dec. 1965), 862–75. For an update of this theory in light of recent studies of recruitment into the Mormon Church, among other groups, see Rodney Stark and William S. Bainbridge, "Networks of Faith: Interpersonal Bonds and Recruitment to Cults and Sects," *American Journal of Sociology* 85 (May 1980), 1376–95. For Lofland's own development away from this theory, see his " 'Becoming A World-Saver' Revisited," *American Behavioral Scientist* 20 (July/August 1977), 805–18.

5. James T. Richardson and Mary Stewart, "Conversion Process Models and the Jesus Movement," in *Conversion Careers*, ed. Richardson (Beverly Hills, Calif.: Sage, 1978), pp. 24–42.

6. Luther Gerlach and Virginia Hine, *People, Power, Change* (New York: Bobbs-Merrill, 1970).

7. Roger Straus, "Changing Oneself: Seekers and the Creative Transformation of Life Experience," in *Doing Social Life*, ed. John Lofland (New York: Wiley and Sons, 1976).

8. Robert Balch, "Looking Behind the Scenes in a Religious Cult: Implications for the Study of Conversion," *Sociological Analysis* 41 (1980), 137–43.

9. Cf. Stark and Bainbridge, "Networks of Faith."

10. James T. Richardson and Rex Davis, "Experiential Fundamentalism: Revisions of Orthodoxy in the Jesus Movement," *Journal of the American Academy of Religion* 51(1983), 397–425.

11. For five such cases, see *Seattle P-I*, Sept. 25 and Oct. 16, 1985, and *Idaho Statesman*, Nov. 13, 1985.

12. Cf. Lofland and Stark, "Becoming a World-Saver." These authors call this stage the "turning point."

13. A number of articles deal with this fact, confirmed in my own interviews: Roy Wallis, "Network and Clockwork," *Sociology* 15 (Feb. 1982), 102–7; James T. Richardson, "The Active vs. Passive Convert: Paradigm Conflict in Conversion/Recruitment Research," *Journal for the Scientific Study of Religion* 24 (1985), 163–79; and also the Balch and Straus articles cited in notes 7 and 8 above. The word "seeker" is borrowed from Straus.

14. I profited from correspondence with Armand Mauss concerning this issue. For one of the earliest statements of the theory, see Oberschall, *Social Conflict and Social Movements*, pp. 157–72. For a later version of the theory, which loosens the requirement of complete rationality, see Bert Klandermans, "Mobilization and Participation: Social Psychological Expansions of Resource Mobilization Theory," *American Sociological Review* 49 (Oct. 1985), 583–600.

15. Rodney Stark and William Sims Bainbridge, *The Future of Religion: Secularization, Revival and Cult Formation* (Berkeley: University of California Press, 1985), esp. pp. 5–8 and 172–73.

16. I thank James T. Richardson for gently reminding me of this rather obvious fact which, nonetheless, I had overlooked until reading the article by Richardson, Jan van der Lans, and Frans Derks, "Leaving and Labeling: Voluntary and Coerced Disaffiliation from Religious Social Movements," *Research in Social Movements, Conflicts and Change* 9 (1986), 97–126.

17. See James A. Aho, "Out of Hate: A Sociology of Defection from Neo-Nazism," *Current Research on Peace and Violence* 11 (1988), 159–68.

18. Oberschall, *Social Conflict and Social Movements*, p. 107.

19. Some respondents went into great detail describing their political conversions. Many more others were relatively tight-lipped. Had I not arbitrarily limited all of them to revealing the single most important factor influencing their politics, the responses of the verbal subjects would have been given undue weight in Table 9.3.

20. Informant 48, Dec. 19, 1985.

21. Informant 55, Dec. 23, 1985.

22. Informant 56, Dec. 23, 1985.

23. Informant 61, Dec. 24, 1985.
24. Informant 63, Dec. 27, 1985.
25. Informants 59 and 60, Dec. 24, 1985.
26. For a scholarly introduction to Upper Snake River history, see Samuel M. Beal, *The Snake River Fork County* (Rexburg, Idaho: Rexburg Journal, 1935). A treasure trove of information on Mormon families can be found in the various histories compiled by local church wards kept at the David O. McKay Library on the Ricks College Campus in Rexburg. There too may be found detailed genealogies kept by prominent Mormon families from the surrounding area. My account is based on interviews conducted Dec. 20 and 23, 1985, and Jan. 17, 1986, with informants 51, 57, 58, and 98. It could not have been completed without the aid of Professor Jack Reinwand of Ricks College, who conducted his own interviews with members of the Foreman* and Peters* families during the fall of 1986.
27. Jerreld Newquist, *Prophets, Principles, and National Survival* (Salt Lake City, Utah: Publishers Press, 1964).
28. One of the best books written on the social sources of the New Left: Richard Flacks, *Youth and Social Change* (Chicago: Markham, 1973). Using data collected via interviews, Flacks repudiates the conventionally popular theory of generational conflict, showing instead that most leftists in the 1960s came from liberal, agnostic families. See also the articles on political mobilization cited in note 2 above.
29. My own experience confirms this. An Ayn Rand aficionado at the time, I was invited to an organizational meeting for the Students for a Democratic Society (SDS) by my graduate-school office mate. He was a devoted, well-read Marxist with a working-class background. Although skeptical of a speech given that night by a national SDS leader, within days I was sitting at an information table disseminating left-wing literature, running the local chapter's mimeograph machine, and printing posters announcing demonstrations. In the end, I helped compose the SDS charter for my campus.

A major moment in my transformation occurred during the course of a vigorous debate with an older, charismatic fellow graduate student concerning unemployment. He gave me C. Wright Mills's "The Promise," an excerpt from his classic *Sociological Imagination.* Mills's distinction between "private troubles" and "public issues" had a profound effect on my viewpoint: Unemployment, I learned, is not necessarily due to private vice, but to the institutional structure of corporate capitalism.

A third moment in my political conversion occurred when I came under the influence of a popular philosophy professor who had been a conscientious objector in World War II. Through him I discovered my own pacifism and got a job with the American Friends Service Committee organizing draft counseling services. Contacts formed on this job eventually led to my affiliation with West Coast draft resistance and participation in the underground railroad running draft evaders to the Canadian border.

It is clear that while I was throughout this time an intellectually active seeker, had I not had access to this leftist opportunity structure, I might very well have ended up a different kind of political animal than I am today.

CHAPTER 10. THE BIG PICTURE

1. Seymour Martin Lipset and Earl Raab, *The Politics of Unreason* (New York: Harper and Row, 1970).

2. For the classic case study of status politics, see Joseph Gusfield, *Symbolic Crusade: Status Politics and the American Temperance Movement* (Westport, Conn.: Greenwood Press, 1980 [1963]).

3. Lipset and Raab, *The Politics of Unreason*, p. 484.

4. *Ibid.*, p. 90.

5. *Ibid.*, pp. 117, 118.

6. *Ibid.*, pp. 391–92.

7. *Ibid.*, p. 488.

8. *Ibid.*, pp. 460–61.

9. *Ibid.*, pp. 38–39. Cf. the equally plausible account of the Know Nothing Party of the middle 1850s (pp. 55–58).

10. *Ibid.*, pp. 83–87.

11. *Ibid.*, p. 89.

12. *Ibid.*, pp. 153–54, 165–66.

13. *Ibid.*, pp. 210–11.

14. Seymour Martin Lipset and Earl Raab, "The Election and the Evangelicals," *Commentary* 71 (Mar. 1981), 25–32.

15. John H. Simpson, "Moral Issues and Status Politics," in *The New Christian Right*, ed. Robert C. Liebman and Robert Wuthnow (New York: Aldine, 1983), pp. 187–205.

16. Lipset and Raab, *The Politics of Unreason*, p. 152.

17. Richard Hofstadter, "The Pseudo-Conservative Revolt (1955)," in *The Radical Right*, ed. Daniel Bell (Garden City, N.Y.: Anchor Books, 1963), pp. 75–96.

18. Richard Hoftstadter, "Pseudo-Conservatism Revisited: A Postscript (1962)," in *The Radical Right*, ed. Bell, p. 103.

19. *Ibid.*, p. 100.

20. Lipset and Raab, *The Politics of Unreason*, pp. 62, 63.

21. *Ibid.*, p. 64. My italics.

22. The reader may wish to compare this itinerary with Max Weber's in his description of the sins and felonies of Reformation England, circa 1600, or to assertions concerning womanhood and the world by early Church fathers Tertullian and Jerome. See Max Weber, *The Protestant Ethic and the Spirit of Capitalism*, trans. Talcott Parsons (New York: Charles Scribner's Sons, 1958), pp. 155–83.

23. There are serious questions of whether Coughlin's National Union for Social Justice or Huey Long's contemporaneous "Share the Wealth" clubs were bonafide right-wing movements. For an excellent discussion of this question, see Lipset and Raab, *The Politics of Unreason*, pp. 194–97. To be sure, Coughlin espoused anti-Zionism, but this is not unique to right-wing groups. In any case, there is little evidence that his radio audience shared his anti-Semitism. On the contrary, the most anti-Semitic Americans of that time were also anti-Catholic and possibly anti-Coughlinite (pp. 184–89).

24. Arthur M. Schlesinger, Jr., *The Cycles of American History* (Boston: Houghton Mifflin, 1986), p. 97.

25. Arthur M. Schlesinger, Sr., "Extremism in American Politics," *Saturday Review* (Nov. 17, 1965), pp. 21–25.

26. Schlesinger, Jr., *The Cycles of American History,* p. 30. For an earlier statement to this same effect, see Arthur M. Schlesinger, Jr., *Paths to the Present* (Boston: Houghton Mifflin, 1964), pp. 92–93. For a restatement of the theory offering further support, see Samuel P. Huntington, "Generations, Cycles, and Their Role in American Development," in *Political Generations and Political Development* (Lexington, Mass.: Lexington Books, 1977), pp. 9–28.

27. Two exceptions are: Joseph Gusfield, "The Problem of Generations in an Organizational Structure," *Social Forces* 35 (May 1957), 323–30, and Bennett M. Berger, "How Long Is a Generation?" *British Journal of Sociology* (March 1960), pp. 10–23.

28. Karl Mannheim, "The Problem of Generations," in *Essays in the Sociology of Knowledge* (London: Routledge & Kegan Paul, 1952), p. 297.

APPENDIX IV. THE JOHN BIRCH SOCIETY AND THE JEWISH QUESTION

1. Robert Welch, *The Neutralizers* (Belmont, Mass.: John Birch Society, 1963).

2. "Memorandum on *The Spotlight*" (Belmont, Mass.: John Birch Society, Apr. 2, 1980); "A Critical Look at Sheriff's Posse Comitatus" (Belmont, Mass.: John Birch Society, 1974); Don Fotheringham, "Wolves in Jackals' Clothing," *The New American* (Jan. 27, 1986).

3. For other prominent anti-Semites whose names have since been removed from Birch membership rolls, see Benjamin Epstein and Arnold Forster, *The Radical Right: Report on the John Birch Society and Its Allies* (New York: Vintage Books, 1967), pp. 110–14, 129–34.

4. Gary Allen, *None Dare Call It Conspiracy* (Seal Beach, Calif.: Concord Press, 1971). The copy before me from the third printing is advertised as a "runaway bestseller! Over 5 million in print."

5. *Ibid.,* p. 39. Was this a Jewish conspiracy? asks W. Cleon Skousen: "No student of the global conspiracy should fall for the Hitlerian doctrine that the root of all evil is a super 'Jewish conspiracy' " (*The Naked Capitalist* [Salt Lake City, Utah: W. Cleon Skousen, 1974]).

6. Allen, *None Dare Call It Conspiracy,* p. 39.

7. *Ibid.,* p. 40. Cf. Skousen's equally critical remarks concerning the ADL, *The Naked Capitalist,* p. 8.

8. Allen, *None Dare Call It Conspiracy,* p. 44.

9. *Ibid.,* p. 98.

10. Besides these names, Skousen adds the Jewish bankers Shroder, Seligman, Speyer, Mirabaud, Mallet, and Fould.

11. Of the nearly seventy names listed in the 1913 "Pujo" investigation report as directors of America's dominant banking houses, only five can be

said to be "Jewish." See House Committee on Banking and Currency, *Concentration of Money and Credit,* 62nd Cong. 3d sess., Feb. 28, 1913 (Washington, D.C.: Government Printing Office, 1913).

According to neo-Marxist historian Gabriel Kolko, "there was no conspiracy during the Progressive Era" (*The Triumph of Conservatism* [New York: Free Press, 1963]), p. 282. See also pp. 139–58.

12. For an excellent discussion of this process, see Charles Glock and Rodney Stark, *Christian Belief and Anti-Semitism* (New York: Harper and Row, 1966).

13. G. William Domhoff, *The Higher Circles* (New York: Vintage Books, 1970), pp. 296–97. Cf. the conclusions of Martin Mayer, *The Bankers* (New York: Ballantine Books, 1976), p. 11.

14. Archibald E. Roberts, "A Nation in Hock," *Bulletin* (Fort Collins, Colo.: Committee to Restore the Constitution, 1983): "Owner number one, Rothschild Banks of London and Berlin; Owner number two, Lazard Brothers banks of Paris; Owner number three, Israel Moses Seif banks of Italy; Owner number four, Warburg Bank of Hamburg and Amsterdam; Owner number five, Lehman Brothers Bank of New York; Owner number six, Kuhn, Loeb Bank of New York, . . . ; Owner number eight, Goldman, Sachs Bank of New York."

15. Informant 14, Nov. 18, 1985. A former school teacher from Seattle, Washington, whom I met at the Aryan World Congress in the summer of 1986 related a similar story. "I picked up Identity by accident," he said, after reading *None Dare Call It Conspiracy.* The book served as a "triggering mechanism," and he went back to consult the sources cited in the Allen volume. One of these, he says, was Henry Ford's *The International Jew,* which he found stored in the pornography section of the Seattle Public Library. "I was thunderstruck by the book-burning phenomenon" and "now began my research in earnest." He was subsequently introduced to full-fledge Identity doctrine through the writings of Sheldon Emry (Informant 226, July 12, 1986). I am unable to find any reference to *The International Jew* in *None Dare Call It Conspiracy.*

16. Informant 17, Nov. 25, 1985.
17. Informant 115, Jan. 28, 1986.
18. Informant 45, Dec. 15, 1985.
19. Informant 25, Dec. 15, 1985.
20. Informant 130, Feb. 11, 1986.
21. Informant 128, Feb. 10, 1986.
22. Informant 78, Jan. 7, 1986.
23. Informant 21, Nov. 30, 1985.
24. Informant 101, Jan. 18, 1986.

APPENDIX V. THE ACTION ORIENTATION OF IDENTITY CHRISTIANITY

1. See especially chapters 3, 8, and 9 in *Sanctions for Evil,* ed. Nevitt Sanford and Craig Comstock (Boston: Beacon Press, 1971).

2. Jarah Crawford, *Last Battle Cry,* (Middlebury, Vt.: Jann, 1984), pp. 384–85.

3. Aho, *Religious Mythology and the Art of War,* pp. 175–79.

4. Crawford, *Last Battle Cry,* pp. 398, 404–5.

5. James O. Pace, *Amendment to the Constitution* (Los Angeles: Johnson, Pace, Simmons & Fennell, 1985).

6. *Ibid.,* pp. 106–9.

7. *Ibid.,* p. 109.

8. *Ibid.,* p. 118.

9. I interviewed one of the publishers of the Pace volume at the 1986 Aryan World Congress, at which he gave a workshop on implementing its proposals.

APPENDIX VI. OTHER CONSPIRACIES

1. Frank Britton, *Behind Communism* (n.p., n.d.), pp. 92–96.

2. Kent H. Steffgen, *The Bondage of the Free* (Berkeley, Calif.: Vanguard Books, 1966), and Joseph P. Kamp, *Lawless Tyranny: An American Conspiracy Against We, the People* (Fairfield, Conn.: Headlines, n.d.).

3. C. B. Baker, "The Great Immigration Conspiracy," *Youth Action News,* Apr. 1984.

4. C. B. Baker, "Alien Terror over America," *Youth Action News,* Sept. 1985.

5. Cf. "The Persecution of H. Ray Evers, M.D.," *National Chronicle,* May 6, 1976, for the comparable story of Chelation, and *ibid.,* Nov. 6, 1975, for the stories on Krebiozzen and Mucorhicin.

6. C. B. Baker, "Soviet Electromagnetic War Actions," *Youth Action News,* Nov. 1983.

7. C. B. Baker, "Soviet Weather Mayhem," *Youth Action News,* Nov. 1985.

BIBLIOGRAPHY

This bibliography of references consulted is arranged into three parts: government documents; secondary works; and publications by Christian patriots. With the exception of newspaper series on radical patriot groups, individual articles cited in the text are omitted here. Newspapers consulted in this research are listed.

GOVERNMENT DOCUMENTS
Idaho Code
Idaho. County of Kootenai. "Nehemiah Township Charter and Common Law Contract." July 12, 1982. Book 120, p. 387.
Idaho. Legislature. House Joint Memorial 3. *Daily Data* (final edition). 46th–47th Legislature, 1981–84.
Illinois. Legislative Investigating Committee. *Ku Klux Klan*. Springfield, Ill., 1976.
U.S. Congress. House. "The John Birch Society." Report prepared by Ralph A. Harding. 88th Cong., 1st sess., Jan. 1963. *Congressional Record*, 1010–11.
U.S. Congress. House. Committee on Banking and Currency. *Concentration of Money and Credit*. 62d Cong., 3d sess. Washington, D.C.: Government Printing Office, 1913.
U.S. Congress. House. Subcommittee on Crime of the Committee of the Judiciary. *Increasing Violence Against Minorities*. 96th Cong., 2d sess., Dec. 9, 1980. Washington, D.C.: Government Printing Office, 1981.
U.S. Congress. Senate. "The Attitude of Latter-Day Saints Toward John Birch Society." Report prepared by Wallace Bennett. 88th Cong., 1st sess., Aug. 1963. *Congressional Record*, 14171–72.
U.S. Dept. of Commerce. *County and City Data Book*. Washington, D.C.: Government Printing Office, 1983.
U.S. Dept. of Commerce. *1980 Census of Population, Detailed Population Characteristics, Idaho*. Washington, D.C.: Government Printing Office, 1981.
U.S. Dept. of Commerce. *1980 Census of Population, General Social and Economic Characteristics*. Washington, D.C.: Government Printing Office, 1981.
U.S. Dept. of Commerce. *Statistical Abstract of the United States 1986*. Washington, D.C.: Government Printing Office, 1986.
U.S. Dept. of Justice. Idaho Advisory Committee to the United States Com-

mission on Civil Rights. *Bigotry and Violence in Idaho.* Washington, D.C.:
Government Printing Office, 1986.

U.S. Dept. of Treasury. Criminal Investigation. Office of Intelligence. "Illegal
Tax Protester Information Book." Washington, D.C.: Government Printing
Office, n.d.

SECONDARY SOURCES

Aho, James A. "Coeur d'Alene Violence May Teach Us: Listen to Others."
Idaho State Journal, Oct. 7, 1986.

———. "A Community with a Heart: The Story of the Kootenai County
Human Relations Task Force." Mimeographed. Coeur d'Alene, Idaho:
Chamber of Commerce, 1985.

———. "Out of Hate: A Sociology of Defection from Neo-Nazism." *Current
Research on Peace and Violence* 11 (1988), 159–68.

———. "The Protestant Ethic and the Spirit of Violence." *Journal of Political
and Military Sociology* 7 (Spring 1979), 103–19.

———. "Reification and Sacrifice: The Goldmark Case." *California Sociologist*
10 (Summer 1987), 79–95.

———. *Religious Mythology and the Art of War.* Westport, Conn.: Greenwood
Press, 1981.

———. "Suffering, Redemption and Violence: Albert Camus and the Sociology of Violence." *Rendezvous* 9 (Spring 1974/Winter 1974–75), 51–62.

Allport, Gordon. "The Composition of Political Attitudes." *American Journal
of Sociology* 35 (1929), 220–38.

Anderson, Scott, and John Lee Anderson. *Inside the League.* New York: Dodd,
Mead, 1982.

Anti-Defamation League of B'nai B'rith. *Extremism on the Right: A Handbook.*
New York, 1983.

———. *The Hate Movement Today: A Chronicle of Violence and Disarray.* New
York, 1987.

———. *The KKK and the Neo-Nazis: A Status Report.* New York, 1984.

Arnett, Peter. "Armed and Angry." 4-part series. *Salt Lake City Tribune,* Mar.
2–5, 1985.

Balch, Robert. "Looking Behind the Scenes in a Religious Cult: Implications
for the Study of Conversion." *Sociological Analysis* 41 (1980), 137–43.

Barker, William E. "The Aryan Nations: A Linkage Profile." Coeur d'Alene,
Idaho: William E. Barker, 1986.

Barrett, Stanley R. *Is God a Racist?* Toronto: University of Toronto Press,
1987.

Beal, Samuel M. *The Snake River Fork Country.* Rexburg, Idaho: Rexburg
Journal, 1935.

Becker, Ernest. *Escape from Evil.* New York: Free Press, 1975.

Berger, Bennett M. "How Long Is a Generation?" *British Journal of Sociology,*
Mar. 1960, pp. 10–23.

Berger, Peter. *Invitation to Sociology.* Garden City, N.Y.: Anchor Books, 1963.

————, and Thomas Luckmann. *The Social Construction of Reality.* Garden City, N.Y.: Doubleday-Anchor, 1967.

Blank, Robert. *Regional Diversity of Political Values: Idaho Political Culture.* Washington, D.C.: University Press of America, 1978.

Blumenthal, Monica, Robert Kahn, Frank Andrews, and Kendra Head. *Justifying Violence.* Ann Arbor: University of Michigan Press, 1972.

Book of Mormon. *See* Church of Jesus Christ of Latter-day Saints.

Brinkerhoff, Merlin B., Jeffrey C. Jacob, and Marlene M. Mackie. "Mormonism and the Moral Majority Make Strange Bedfellows?: An Exploratory Critique." *Review of Religious Research* 28 (Mar. 1987), 236–51.

Brodie, Fawn. *No Man Knows My History.* New York: Alfred A. Knopf, 1966 (1945).

Brown, James. "Christian Teaching and Anti-Semitism: Scrutinizing Religious Texts." *Commentary* (Dec. 1957), pp. 494–501.

Buerger, David John. "The Development of the Mormon Temple Endowment Ceremony." *Dialogue: A Journal of Mormon Thought* 20 (Winter 1987), 33–76.

Calvin, John. *On God and Man.* Edited by F. W. Strothmann. New York: Frederick Ungar, 1965.

Caplovitz, David, and R. Sherrow. *The Religious Dropouts.* Beverly Hills, Calif.: Sage, 1977.

Carpella, Kitty. " 'Days Numbered' for FBI's Neo-Nazi Insider." *Oregonian,* Apr. 18, 1985.

Carter, Hugh, and Paul C. Glick. *Marriage and Divorce: A Social and Economic Study.* Cambridge, Mass.: Harvard University Press, 1970.

Chalmers, David. *Hooded Americanism.* New York: Franklin Watts, 1981 (1965).

Chesler, M., and R. Shmuck. "Participant Observation in a Superpatriot Discussion Group." *Journal of Social Issues* 19 (1963), 18–30.

Church of Jesus Christ of Latter-day Saints. Book of Mormon. Translated by Joseph Smith. Salt Lake City, Utah, 1961.

————. *Doctrine and Covenants.* Salt Lake City, Utah, 1985.

————. *Pearl of Great Price.* Translated by Joseph Smith. Salt Lake City, Utah, 1921.

Cohn, Norman. *Warrant for Genocide.* New York: Oxford University Press, 1967.

Collins, Randall. *Sociological Insight: An Introduction to Nonobvious Sociology.* New York: Oxford University Press, 1982.

Copp, James H., Maurice L. Sill, and Emory J. Brown. "The Function of Information Sources in the Farm Practice Adoption Process." *Rural Sociology* 23 (1958), 146–57.

Crews, Harry. "The Buttondown Terror of David Duke." *Playboy,* Feb. 1980.

Cross, Whitney R. *The Burned Over District: The Social and Intellectual History of Enthusiastic Religion in Western New York.* New York, Harper and Row, 1965.

Davies, James C. "The Family's Role in Political Socialization." *Annals of the American Academy of Political and Social Science* 361 (Sept. 1965).

————, ed. *When Men Revolt and Why.* New York: Free Press, 1971.

Davis, L. J. "Ballad of an American Terrorist." *Harper's,* July 1986, pp. 53–62.

Doctrine and Covenants. See Church of Jesus Christ of Latter-day Saints.

Domhoff, G. William. *The Higher Circles.* New York: Vintage Books, 1970.

Douglas, Jack. *Investigative Social Research.* Beverly Hills, Calif.: Sage, 1976.

Dye, Thomas R., and L. Harmon Zeigler. *The Irony of Democracy.* Belmont, Calif.: Wadsworth, 1970.

E740.J6 Epstein, Benjamin, and Arnold Forster. *The Radical Right: Report on the John*
E59   *Birch Society and Its Allies.* New York: Vintage Books, 1967.

Everitt, Elly. "A Light for the White Race." *Twin Falls News-Times,* Jan. 3, 1983.

Festinger, Leon. *When Prophecy Fails.* Minneapolis: University of Minnesota Press, 1956.

Finch, Phillip. *God, Guts and Guns.* New York: Seaview/Putnam, 1983.

Flacks, Richard. *Youth and Social Change.* Chicago: Markham, 1973.

Flerion, Frederic J., Jr. "The Malevolent Leader: Political Socialization in American Subculture." *American Political Science Review* 62 (June 1968), 564–75.

Forster, Arnold, and Benjamin Epstein. *The New Anti-Semitism.* New York: Anti-Defamation League of B'nai-B'rith, 1974.

———. *The Radical Right: Report on the John Birch Society and Its Allies.* New York: Vintage Books, 1967.

Freilich, Morris, ed. *Marginal Natives: Anthropologists at Work.* New York: Harper and Row, 1970.

Gallup, George, Jr., and David Poling. *The Search For America's Faith.* Nashville, Tenn.: Abingdon Press, 1980.

Gerlach, Larry. *Blazing Crosses in Zion.* Logan: Utah State University Press, 1982.

Gerlach, Luther, and Virginia Hine. *People, Power, Change.* New York: Bobbs-Merrill, 1970.

Glock, Charles, and Rodney Stark. *Christian Beliefs and Anti-Semitism.* New York: Harper and Row, 1966.

———. *Wayward Shepherds.* New York: Harper and Row, 1971.

Gossett, Thomas F. *Race: The History of an Idea in America.* New York: Schocken Books, 1965.

Gottlieb, Robert, and Peter Wiley. *America's Saints: The Mormons.* New York: G. P. Putnam's Sons, 1984.

Greenberg, Rick. "Neo-Nazism: Flash in Pan or Spark of Revolution." *Cleveland Plain Dealer,* July 6, 1986.

Gusfield, Joseph. "The Problem of Generations in an Organizational Structure." *Social Forces* 35 (May 1957), 323–30.

———. *Symbolic Crusade: Status Politics and the American Temperance Movement.* Westport, Conn.: Greenwood Press, 1980 (1963).

Hamilton, Richard. *Who Voted for Hitler?* Princeton, N.J.: Princeton University Press, 1982.

Hammer, Joshua. "Trouble." *People Weekly,* Aug. 29, 1983, pp. 44–48.

Harris, John. "Hitler's Legacy." *Seattle Post-Intelligencer,* Jan. 5, 1985.

Harris, T. George. "The Rampant Right Invades the GOP." *Look,* July 16, 1963, pp. 19–25.

Hay, Malcolm. *The Roots of Christian Anti-Semitism.* New York: Anti-Defamation League of B'nai B'rith, 1981 (1950).

"Heavenly Reich." *Lewiston Morning Tribune,* July 17, 1983.

Heinerman, John, and Anson Shupe. "Mormonism and the New Christian Right: An Emerging Coalition?" *Review of Religious Research* 27 (Dec. 1985), 146–57.

———. *The Mormon Corporate Empire.* Boston: Beacon Press, 1985.

Henderson, Paul. "We're Not Saluting Hitler—We're Saluting God." *Seattle Times,* Pacific Magazine, Apr. 17, 1983.

Hofstadter, Richard. "Pseudo-Conservatism Revisited: A Postscript (1962)." In *The Radical Right,* edited by Daniel Bell. Garden City, N.Y.: Anchor Books, 1963.

———. "The Pseudo-Conservative Revolt (1955)." In *The Radical Right,* edited by Daniel Bell. Garden City, N.Y.: Anchor Books, 1963.

Holden, Richard R. "Postmillenialism as a Justification for Right Wing Violence." Central Missouri State University: Center for Criminal Justice Research, 1986.

Huntington, Samuel P. "Generations, Cycles and Their Role in American Development." In *Political Generations and Political Development.* Lexington, Mass.: Lexington Books, 1977.

Irwin, John. *Prisons in Turmoil.* Boston: Little, Brown and Co., 1980.

Isaac, Jules. *The Teaching of Contempt: The Christian Roots of Anti-Semitism.* New York: McGraw-Hill, 1964.

Jacquet, Constant H., Jr., ed. *Yearbook of American and Canadian Churches: 1984.* Nashville, Tenn.: Abingdon Press, 1984.

Jennings, M. K., and R. G. Niemi. "The Transmission of Political Values from Parent to Child." *American Political Science Review* 62 (1968), 169–84.

Jones, Harry. *The Minutemen.* Garden City, N.Y.: Doubleday, 1968.

Katz, Jacob. *From Prejudice to Destruction: Anti-Semitism 1700–1933.* Cambridge, Mass.: Harvard University Press, 1980.

Kerr, Clark, and Abraham Siegel. "The Inter-Industry Propensity to Strike: An International Comparison." In *Industrial Conflict,* edited by Arthur Kornhauser, Robert Dubin, and Arthur Ross. New York: McGraw-Hill, 1954.

Klandermans, Bert. "Mobilization and Participation: Social Psychological Expansions of Resource Mobilization Theory." *American Sociological Review* 49 (Oct. 1985), 583–600.

Kolko, Gabriel. *The Triumph of Conservatism.* New York: Free Press, 1963.

Kornhauser, William. *The Politics of Mass Society.* New York: Free Press, 1959.

Lake, Peter. "An Exegesis of the Radical Right." *California Magazine,* Apr. 1985.

Lazardsfeld, Paul F., Bernard Berelson, and Hazel Gaudet. *The People's Choice.* New York: Columbia University Press, 1948.

Lederer, Wolfgang. *The Fear of Women*. New York: Harcourt Brace Jovanovich, 1968.

Ledford, David. "Cassell: Neo-Nazi Life Wasn't for Him." *The Spokesman-
Review,* Apr. 21, 1985.

Liebman, Robert, and Robert Wuthnow, eds. *The New Christian Right*. New
York: Aldine, 1983.

Lipset, Seymour Martin. "University Student Politics." In *Berkeley Student Revolt,* edited by S. M. Lipset and Sheldon Wolin. Garden City, N.Y.: Doubleday-Anchor, 1965.

———. "Working Class Authoritarianism." In *Political Man,* edited by S. M.
Lipset. Garden City, N.Y.: Doubleday, 1960.

———, and Earl Raab. "The Election and the Evangelicals." *Commentary* 71
(Mar. 1981), 25–32.

———. *The Politics of Unreason*. New York: Harper and Row, 1970.

Lofland, John. " 'Becoming a World-Saver' Revisited." *American Behavioral
Scientist* 20 (July/Aug. 1977), 805–18.

Lofland, John, and Rodney Stark. "Becoming a World-Saver: A Theory of
Conversion to a Deviant Perspective." *American Sociological Review* 30 (Dec.
1965), 862–75.

Mannheim, Karl. "The Problem of Generations." In *Essays in the Sociology of
Knowledge*. London: Routledge & Kegan Paul, 1952.

Martin, Mike, and Ann Russell. Two-part series. *Gonzaga Bulletin,* Oct. 7 and
14, 1983.

Mauer, Richard. "Aryan Nations." *Idaho Statesman,* Sept. 14–17, 1980.

Mauss, Armand. "Mormonism and Minorities." Ph.D dissertation. Berkeley:
University of California, 1970.

———. "Mormon Semitism and Anti-Semitism." *Sociological Analysis* 29 (Spring
1968), 11–27.

Mayer, Martin. *The Bankers*. New York: Ballantine Books, 1976.

McCloskey, Herbert. "Personality and Attitude Correlates of Foreign Policy
Orientation." In *Domestic Sources of Foreign Policy*. New York: Free Press,
1967.

McNall, Scott Grant. "The Freedom Center: A Case Study of a Politico-Religious Sect." Ph.D. dissertation. Eugene: University of Oregon, 1965.

McPhail, Clark, and Ronald T. Wohstein. "Individual and Collective Behaviors within Gatherings, Demonstrations, and Riots." *American Review of
Sociology* 9 (1983): 579–600.

Mehan, Hugh, and Huston Wood. *The Reality of Ethnomethodology*. New York:
John Wiley & Sons, 1976.

Melton, Gordon. *The Encyclopedia of American Religions*. 2 vols. Wilmington,
N.C.: McGrath, 1978.

Miller, David. *Introduction to Collective Behavior*. Belmont, Calif.: Wadsworth,
1985.

Mills, C. Wright. "Situated Actions and Vocabularies of Motive." *American
Sociological Review* 5 (Dec. 1940), 904–13.

Morris, Aldon. "Black Southern Sit-In Movement: An Analysis of Internal
Organization." *American Sociological Review* 46 (1981), 744–67.

Morris, W. "Houston's Superpatriots." *Harper's,* Oct. 1961, pp. 248–56.
Myers, Gustavus. *Bigotry in the United States.* New York: Capricorn Books, 1960.
Neier, Aryeh. *Defending My Enemy.* New York: E. P. Dutton, 1979.
"The New Nazis: Rifles, Religion, and Racism." Two-part series. *Spokesman-Review,* April 14 and 21, 1985.
Nisbet, Robert. *The Quest for Community.* New York: Harper and Bros., 1953.
Oberschall, Anthony. *Social Conflict and Social Movements.* Englewood Cliffs, N.J.: Prentice-Hall, 1973.
Overstreet, Harry, and Bonaro Overstreet. *The Strange Tactics of Extremism.* New York: W. W. Norton, 1964.
Owens, J. B. "Aho Article Described As Confused, Vague, Manipulative." *Idaho State Journal,* Oct. 16, 1986.
Pearl of Great Price. See Church of Jesus Christ of Latter-day Saints.
Peterson, R. E. "The Student Left in Higher Education." *Daedalus* 97 (1968), 293–317.
Quigley, Carroll. *Tragedy and Hope.* New York: Macmillan, 1966.
Quinley, Harold, and Charles Glock. *Anti-Semitism in America.* New York: Free Press, 1979.
Quinn, Bernard, et al. *Churches and Church Membership in the United States.* Atlanta, Ga.: Glenmary Research Center, 1982.
Reed, Evelyn. *Woman's Evolution: From Matriarchal Clan to Patriarchal Family.* New York: Pathfinder Press, 1975.
Renshon, Stanley A., ed. *Handbook of Political Socialization.* New York: Free Press, 1977.
Richardson, James T. "The Active vs. Passive Convert: Paradigm Conflict in Conversion/Recruitment Research." *Journal for the Scientific Study of Religion* 24 (1985), 163–79.
———, and Brock Kilbourne. "Classical and Contemporary Applications of Brainwashing Models: A Comparison and Critique." In *The Brainwashing/Deprogramming Controversy,* edited by David Bromley and James Richardson. Toronto: Edwin Mellen Press, 1983.
Richardson, James T., Jan van der Lans, and Frans Derks. "Leaving and Labeling: Voluntary and Coerced Disaffiliation from Religious Movements." *Research in Social Movements, Conflicts and Change* 9 (1986), 97–126.
Richardson, James T., and Mary Stewart. "Conversion Process Models and the Jesus Movement." In *Conversion Careers,* edited by James Richardson. Beverly Hills, Calif.: Sage Publications, 1978.
Richardson, James T., and Rex Davis. "Experimental Fundamentalism: Revisions of Orthodoxy in the Jesus Movement." *Journal of the American Academy of Religion* 51 (1983), 397–425.
Roozen, David A. "What Hath the 1970s Wrought: Religion in America." In *Yearbook of American and Canadian Churches: 1984,* edited by Constant H. Jacquet, Jr. Nashville, Tenn.: Abingdon Press, 1984.
Roy, Ralph L. *Apostles of Discord.* Boston: Beacon Press, 1953.
Ruether, Rosemary. *Faith and Fratricide: The Theological Roots of Anti-Semitism.* New York: Seabury Press, 1979.

Runes, Dagobert. *Let My People Live!* New York: Philosophical Library, 1975.

Safir, Ahmed. "Zealot Liked to Tote Bible in His Youth." *St. Louis Post-Dispatch,* Apr. 24, 1985.

Sandmel, Samuel. *Anti-Semitism in the New Testament?* Philadelphia: Fortress Press, 1978.

Sanford, Nevitt, and Craig Comstock, eds. *Sanctions for Evil.* Boston: Beacon Press, 1971.

Scheff, Thomas J. *Being Mentally Ill: A Sociological Theory,* 2d ed. New York: Aldine, 1984.

Schlesinger, Arthur M., Jr. *The Cycles of American History.* Boston: Houghton Mifflin, 1986.

———. *Paths to the Present.* Boston: Houghton Mifflin, 1964.

Schlesinger, Arthur M., Sr. "Extremism in American Politics." *Saturday Review,* Nov. 17, 1965, pp. 21–25.

Schoenberger, R., ed. *The American Right Wing.* New York: Holt, Rinehart and Winston, 1969.

Selznick, Philip. *TVA and the Grassroots.* Berkeley: University of California Press, 1949.

Shibutani, Tamotsu. *Improvised News: A Sociological Study of Rumor.* Indianapolis, Ind.: Bobbs-Merrill, 1966.

Shupe, Anson, and William Stacey. "The Moral Majority Constituency." In *The New Christian Right,* edited by Robert Liebman and Robert Wuthnow. New York: Aldine, 1983.

Simpson, John H. "Moral Issues and Status Politics." In *The New Christian Right,* edited by Robert Liebman and Robert Wuthnow. New York: Aldine, 1983.

Sims, Patsy. *The Klan.* New York: Stein and Day, 1978.

Smith, Joseph. *History of the Church of Jesus Christ of Latter-day Saints.* 3 vols. Salt Lake City, Utah: Deseret Book Co., 1967.

Stark, Rodney, and William Sims Bainbridge. *The Future of Religion: Secularization, Revival and Cult Formation.* Berkeley: University of California Press, 1985.

———. "Networks of Faith: Interpersonal Bonds and Recruitment to Cults and Sects." *American Journal of Sociology* 85 (May 1980), 1376–95.

Stouffer, Samuel A. *Communism, Conformity and Civil Liberties.* New York: John Wiley, 1966.

Straus, Roger. "Changing Oneself: Seekers and the Creative Transformation of Life Experience." In *Doing Social Life,* edited by John Lofland. New York: Wiley and Sons, 1976.

Terkel, Studs. *Hard Times.* New York: Avon Books, 1970.

Terry, Bill. "Up Against the Wall, Sinners." *Arkansas Times,* Aug. 1983.

Tomeh, Aida K. "Formal Voluntary Organization: Participation, Correlates and Interrelationships." In *The Community,* edited by Marcia P. Effrat. New York: Free Press, 1974.

Torvik, Solveig. "The Earth's Most Endangered Species." *Seattle Post-Intelligencer,* Sept. 23, 1980.

Verba, Sidney, and Norman Nie. *Participation in America.* New York: Harper and Row, 1972.

"Violence on the Right." *Time,* Mar. 4, 1985.

Wallis, Roy. "Network and Clockwork." *Sociology* 15 (Feb. 1982), 102–7.

Walls, Dwayne. *The Klan: Collapsed and Dormant.* Nashville, Tenn.: Race Relations Information Center, 1970.

Weber, Max. *The Protestant Ethic and the Spirit of Capitalism.* Translated by Talcott Parsons. New York: Charles Scribner's Sons, 1958.

———. *The Sociology of Religion.* Translated by Ephraim Fischoff. Boston: Beacon Press, 1964.

———. *The Theory of Social and Economic Organization.* Translation and edited by Talcott Parsons. New York: Free Press, 1964 (1947).

Wiggins, Michael D. "The Turner Diaries: Blueprint for Right-Wing Extremist Violence." Central Missouri State University: Center for Criminal Justice Research, 1986.

Wilcox, Laird. *Guide to the American Right.* Kansas City, Mo.: Editorial Research Service, 1986.

———. *"Hate Groups in America": A Critical Review.* Rev. ed. Kansas City, Mo.: Editorial Research Service, July 1987.

Williams, Robin, Andrew Greeley, and Daniel Levinson. "Review Symposium." *American Sociological Review* 32 (Dec. 1967), 1004–13.

Young, Perry Deane. *God's Bullies.* New York: Holt, Rinehart and Winston, 1982.

Newspapers carrying in-depth articles on Northwest radical patriot groups and individuals during the 1980s:
Idaho Statesman. Boise, Idaho.
Oregonian. Portland, Oregon.
Seattle Post-Intelligencer. Seattle, Washington.
Seattle Times. Seattle, Washington.
Spokesman Review. Spokane, Washington.

PUBLICATIONS BY CHRISTIAN PATRIOTS

Allen, Gary. *None Dare Call It Conspiracy.* Seal Beach, Calif.: Concord Press, 1971.

Allen, J. H. *Judah's Sceptre and Joseph's Birthright.* Boston: A. A. Beauchamp, 1930 (1902).

Barron, Howard H. *Judah, Past and Future.* Bountiful, Utah: Horizon, 1979.

Beam, Louis R., Jr. *Essays of a Klansman.* Hayden Lake, Idaho: AKIA Pub., 1983.

Benson, Ezra Taft. *A Nation Asleep.* Salt Lake City, Utah: Bookcraft, 1963.

———. *The Red Carpet.* Salt Lake City, Utah: Bookcraft, 1962.

———. *This Nation Shall Endure.* Salt Lake City, Utah: Deseret Book Co., 1977.

Britton, Frank. *Behind Communism.* N.p., n.d.

Butler, Richard G. *The Aryan Warrior*. Hayden Lake, Idaho: Aryan Nations, n.d.

———. *To Lose Our Sovereignty: On the Dismantling of a Christian Nation*. Hayden Lake, Idaho: Aryan Nations, n.d.

Calvin, John. *On God and Man*. Edited by F. W. Strothmann. New York: Frederick Ungar, 1965.

Capt, E. Raymond. *Missing Links Discovered in Assyrian Tablets*. Thousand Oaks, Calif.: Artisan Sales, 1985.

Communism Is Jewish: Quotes by the Jews. Dandridge, Tenn.: The Battle Axe N.E.W.S., 1976.

Comparet, Bertrand. *Your Heritage: An Identification of the True Israel Through Biblical and Historic Sources*. Hayden Lake, Idaho: Aryan Nations Church, n.d.

Crawford, Jarah. *Last Battle Cry*. Middlebury, Vt.: Jann, 1984.

Decker, Ed, and Dave Hunt. *The Godmakers*. Eugene, Ore.: Harvest Books, 1984.

Edwards, Lee, and Anne Edwards. *Rebels with a Cause*. New Rochelle, N.Y.: Arlington House, 1968.

Elmer, Slaisier A., and Evelyn Elmer. *Sociobiology and Immigration: The Grim Forecast for America*. Monterey, Va.: American Immigration Control Foundation, 1984.

Emry, Sheldon. *Bible Law on Money*. Phoenix, Ariz.: Lord's Covenant Church, 1981.

———. *Billion$ for Banker$*. Phoenix, Ariz.: Lord's Covenant Church, 1984.

Fotheringham, Don. "Wolves in Jackels' Clothing." *The New American,* Jan. 27, 1986.

Gayman, Dan. *Articles of Faith and Doctrine for the Churches of Israel*. Schell City, Mo.: Church of Israel, 1982.

———. *Heirs of the Promise*. Schell City, Mo.: Church of Israel, 1983.

———. *The Last Will and Testament of Jesus Christ*. Schell City, Mo.: Church of Israel, n.d.

———. *Tracing Our Ancestors*. Schell City, Mo.: Church of Israel, n.d.

George, Wesley Critz. *The Biology of the Race Problem*. New York: National Putnam Letters Committee, 1962.

Haberman, Frederick. *Tracing Our Ancestors*. Metairie, La.: New Christian Crusade Church, 1932.

Hansen, George. *To Harass Our People: The IRS and the Abuse of Power*. Washington, D.C.: Positive Publications, 1984.

John Birch Society. "A Critical Look at Sheriff's Posse Comitatus." Belmont, Mass., 1974.

———. "Memorandum on *The Spotlight*." Belmont, Mass., Apr. 20, 1980.

Kahl, Gordon. "Victim of Federal Ambush Attempt and Massive Manhunt Tells His Side in North Dakota Slaying of Two Federal Marshalls." Mimeographed. N.p., n.d.

Kamp, Joseph P. *Lawless Tyranny: An American Conspiracy Against We the People*. Fairfield, Conn.: Headlines, n.d.

Lane, David. "Race, Reason, Religion." Mimeographed. N.p., 1984.

————. "Under This Sign You Shall Conquer: Identity." Mimeographed. N.p., n.d.

Leese, Arnold, *Jewish Ritual Murder*. London: International Fascist League, 1938.

MacDonald, Andrew (William L. Pierce). *The Turner Diaries*. Arlington, Va.: National Vanguard Books, 1978.

Mathews, Robert. "Mathews Last Letter." *Sandpoint Daily Bee*, Dec. 12, 1984.

McConkie, Bruce. *Mormon Doctrine*. Salt Lake City, Utah: Bookcraft, 1979 (1966).

McManus, John F. *The Insiders*. Belmont, Miss.: John Birch Society, 1983.

Mohr, Gordon. *Exploding the "Chosen People" Myth*. Bay St. Louis, Miss., n.d.

————. *Know Your Enemies*. Merrimac, Mass.: Destiny, 1982.

————. *Woe Unto Ye Fundamentalists!* Bay St. Louis, Miss., n.d.

Newquist, Jerreld. *Prophets, Principles and National Survival*. Salt Lake City, Utah: Publishers Press, 1964.

Pace, James O. *Amendment to the Constitution*. Los Angeles: Johnson, Pace, Simmons & Fennell, 1985.

Peters, Pete. *The Greatest Discovery of Our Age*. Laporte, Colo: Scriptures for America, 1985.

————. *None Ever Call It Conspiracy*. Laporte, Colo.: Scriptures for America, 1988.

————. *The Real Hate Group*. Laporte, Colo.: Scriptures for America, 1988.

————. *The Real Meaning of the Rich Man and Lazarus*. Laporte, Colo.: Scriptures for America, n.d.

Pranaitis, Justin Bonaventura. *The Talmud Unmasked*. Schell City, Mo.: Church of Israel, 1917.

Prepare War. Pontiac, Mo.: Covenant, Sword and the Arm of the Lord Bookstore, n.d.

Protocols of the Learned Elders of Zion. Translated by Victor E. Marsden. N.p., n.d.

Republic vs. Democracy Redress. "America Where Are You? You're Too Young to Die." Oregon City, 1986.

————. "Communism in America: Do You Live Under Communist Rule in the U.S.S.A. (U.S.A.)?" Oregon City, 1986.

————. "Preamble to the United States Constitution: Who Are the Posterity?" Oregon City, 1986.

Roberts, Archibald E. "A Nation in Hock." *Bulletin*. Fort Collins, Colo.: Committee to Restore the Constitution, 1983.

Skousen, Cleon. *The Making of America*. Washington, D.C.: National Institute for Constitutional Studies, 1985.

————. *The Naked Capitalist*. Salt Lake City, Utah: W. Cleon Skousen, 1974 (1968).

————. *What Is Behind the Frantic Drive for a New Constitution?* Provo, Utah: Freemen Institute, n.d.

Snook, Franklin. *America: 13th or All 13?* Phoenix Ariz.: Lord's Covenant Church, n.d.

————. *The Rebirth of America*. Phoenix, Ariz.: Lord's Covenant Church, n.d.

Steffgen, Kent H. *The Bondage of the Free*. Berkeley, Calif: Vanguard Books, 1966.

Swift, Wesley. *America: The Appointed Place*. Hollywood, Calif.: New Christian Crusade Church, n.d.

———. *The Mystery of Iniquity*. Hayden Lake, Idaho: Church of Jesus Christ Christian, n.d.

———. *Standards of the Kingdom*. Hayden Lake, Idaho: Aryan Nations, n.d.

Tanner, Jerald, and Sandra Tanner. *Mormonism: Shadow or Reality*. Enlarged edition. Salt Lake City: Utah Lighthouse Ministry, n.d.

Totten, Charles A. L. " 'The Romance within the Romance, or the Philosophy of History': Tea Tephi David's Daughter, Jeremiah's Ward." *Our Race Quarterly* 3 (1st series), March 1891, n.p.

Viguerie, Richard. *The New Right: We're Ready to Lead*. Falls Church, Va.: Viguerie Co., 1980.

Welch, Robert. *The Blue Book*. Belmont, Mass.: John Birch Society, 1960.

———. *The Neutralizers*. Belmont, Mass.: John Birch Society, 1963.

Wilson, John. *Our Israelitish Origin*. Philadelphia: Daniels and Smith, 1850.

Patriot periodicals consulted:

Alert. Boise, Idaho: Barristers' Inn School of Common Law.

America's Promise Newsletter. Phoenix, Arizona: Lord's Covenant Church.

Aryan Nations Calling (Calling Our Nation). Hayden Lake, Idaho: Aryan Nations Church.

The Classical Liberal. Caldwell, Idaho: Center for the Study of Market Alternatives.

The Cross and the Flag. Los Angeles, Calif.: Christian Nationalist Crusade.

Flying Eagle. Malta, Idaho.

Journal of Discourses. Salt Lake City, Utah: The Church of Jesus Christ of Latter-day Saints.

National Chronicle. Hayden Lake, Idaho.

National Educator. Fullerton, California.

National Vanguard. Arlington, Virginia: The National Alliance.

The New American. Belmont, Mass.: The John Birch Society.

The Pathfinder. Spokane, Wash.: Christ's Gospel Fellowship, Inc.

Posse Noose Report. Evansville, Wisconsin: Posse Comitatus.

Scriptures for America. Laporte, Colorado: Laporte Church of Christ.

The Spotlight on the News. Washington, D.C.: Liberty Lobby.

Youth Action News. Alexandria, Virginia.

SUBJECT INDEX

Abel and Cain, 97; in Mormonism, 124, 125
Abolitionist movement, 219
Abortion, 4, 5, 15, 17, 59, 75, 76, 87, 202, 221, 265; as evil fetish, 81–82, 173
Adam and Eve, 97
ADL. *See* Anti-Defamation League of B'nai B'rith
Ages of patriots. *See* Demographics of patriots
AIDS, 85; as conspiracy, 266; as God's vengeance, 174
Alienation of patriots. *See* Mass theory
Amendment to the Constitution (Pace), 132, 261–63
America: as Manasseh, 53, 110, 111–12; as New Jerusalem, 53, 121
American Israelism. *See* Identity Christianity
American Protection Association, 214, 215
An Enemy Has Done This to Us (Benson), 125
Anglo-Israelism. *See* British Israelism
Anglo-Saxon Federation of America, 52
Anne Frank's Diary: A Hoax (Felder), 96
Anti-Catholicism, 24, 88, 173, 203
Anti-Defamation League of B'nai B'rith, 16, 29, 56, 57, 82; on American Nazi movement, 6, 267n9; as "defamatory," 256
Anti-Judaism. *See* Anti-Semitism
Anti-Mormonism, 22, 24, 173, 268n28
Anti-Semitism, 25; fundamentalism and, 179, 180, 181; as left hand of Christianity, 178–79; Mormon rates of, 179, 180–81; Mormon rules against, 130; Posse Comitatus and, 46–47. *See also* Jews; Judaism
Apostasy rates, 289n14
Are We of Israel? (Reynold), 128

Arizona Patriots, 7
Armageddon, War of, 53, 54, 174
Aryan Brotherhood, 60, 61
Aryan Nations Calling, 30, 187
Aryan Nations Church, 9, 10, 12, 17, 28, 32, 51, 55, 78, 166, 187, 279n9, 274n76; as tax write-off, 77; and Boise Valley American Israelites, 196; and connection to CSA, 58; Jews for, 93; and Ku Klux Klan, 59; move to Idaho of, 56–57; Order and, 24, 65; recruitment to, 59–61, 187, 188. *See also* Aryan World Congress; Butler, Richard G.; Cutler, Gary and Cindy; Identity Christianity; Minor, Ed and Lisa
Aryan Warrior (Butler), 172
Aryan World Congress, 7, 9, 10, 32, 33, 58, 76; announcements for, 229–30; as recruitment tool, 59
Asher, Tribe of, 108; as Sweden, 111

Banking conspiracy. *See* International banking conspiracy
Baptist Church, 175, 200; and patriots, 169, 170
Barristers' Inn School of Common Law, 193; Boise Valley American Israelites and, 196, 201; constitutional roots of, 48; courtroom tactics of, 49–50; financial success of, 49, 77; founding of, 48–49; Identity Christianity and, 51; nonviolence of, 50
"Becoming a World-Saver" (Stark and Lofland), 196
Behind Communism (Britton), 96
Benjamin, Tribe of, 95, 100, 108; as Vikings, 110–11
Bible Presbyterian Church, 54
Bigotry. *See* Anti-Catholicism; Anti-Mormonism; Anti-Semitism
Bilderbergers, 18, 173
Black Legion, 7

Black Muslims, 60

Blue Book (Welch), 114–15

B'nai B'rith. *See* Anti-Defamation League of B'nai B'rith

Boise Valley American Israelites, 204; attitude of toward Order, 197; and connection to other groups, 196, 201; leadership of, 197; member profiles of, 198–99; recruitment to, 197–203

Bolsheviks, 115, 137, 256, 279n13. *See also* Communist conspiracy

Brainwashing: critique of, 291n35. *See also* Political socialization

British Israelism, 57; and British as covenant people, 107; and British as Phoenicians, 107–8; disintegration of, 53; influence of, on Identity Christianity, 51–53; world authority in, 53, 93, 101, 104, 110, 128

Bruders Schweigen. See Order

Busing, 5. *See also* Race-mixing

Cain and Abel, 97, 124, 125

Cancer Cures Crucified (Caum), 277n24

Catcher in the Rye (Salinger), 17

Catholic Church, 136, 160; and Jews, 179, 181; and National Union for Social Justice, 215; and patriots, 167–70, 177

CAUSA, 21, 119–20, 131, 136; Freemen Institute and, 120; Idaho membership in, 120

Causes of patriotism, 222–24; sociological view of, 12–13, 35; types of, 12, 136–38; vs. motives for, 70. *See also* Cyclical theory; Formal education; Mass theory; Multi-step theory; Political socialization; Projective politics; Resource mobilization theory; Rising expectations; Status displacement

Center for Market Alternatives, 21

Children of God: recruitment into, 188

Christ, Followers of, 24, 136

Christian American Advocates, 10

Christian Anti-Communist Crusade, 55, 147

Christian Constitutionalism: CAUSA and, 119; defined, 18; enemy in, 79; Mormonism and, 22, 120–23; racism in, 132; and representative groups, 19;

violence in, 132. *See also* Christian Constitutionalists

Christian Constitutionalists: average age of, 148; equivocation toward Jews by, 257–59; formal education of, 140–41; geographic mobility of, 49–50; geographic origins of, 253; gender of, 148; in Idaho, 22, 254; and marital stability, 152; numbers of, 20; and occupational isolation, 158; political participation of, 154; religious background of, 175–77; religious isolation of, 160. *See also* Upper Snake River Constitutionalists

Christian economics, 21

Christian fundamentalism. *See* Fundamentalism

Christian Identity. *See* Identity Christianity

Christian Patriot Defense League, 58, 94; advertisement for, 274n77. *See also* Mohr, Gordon "Jack"

Christian patriotism, 13–17; authority vs. power in, 14–15; as deviant career, 210–11; and Devil's consortium, 173; ends and means in, 15; geography of, in Idaho, 21–24. *See also* Causes of patriotism; Christian Constitutionalism; Identity Christianity; Issue-oriented patriotism; Motives of patriotism

Christian patriots: average age of, 148; geographic origins of, 253–54; gender, 148; numbers of, 18, 20; representative groups of, 19; sources of data on, 251; typical career of, 223–26. *See also* Christian Constitutionalists; Identity Christians; Issue-oriented patriots

Christ's Gospel Fellowship, 93. *See also* Schott, Karl

Church of Christ, 52; Laporte branch of, 190–91, 202. *See also* Peters, Pete; Scriptures for America

Church of Christ Scientist, 115

Church of I Am, 160

Church of Israel, 58, 59, 93, 96

Church of Jesus Christ Christian. *See* Aryan Nations Church

Church of Jesus Christ of Latter-day Saints. *See* Mormon Church

Citizen's Emergency Defense System, 58

Citizen's Tax Council, 41, 42

Civil Rights conspiracy, 264
Committee for Better Government, 44, 45
Committee of the States, 7
Communist conspiracy, 17, 194, 208; as bankers' plot, 126; Eisenhower and, 116; as evil fetish, 81; as Jewish plot, 88, 279n13; John Birch Society and, 114–15
Communist Worker Party U.S.A., 6
Congregational church, 167, 170; and Jews, 181
Conspiracy Against God and Man (Kelly), 125
Conspiratology, Institute for, 132
Conspiratorialism, 15, 18; as cultural baggage, 213; in fundamentalism, 173, 220; in Identity Christianity, 88–92, 264–66; in Mormonism, 124–25. *See also specific conspiracies*
Constitution, organic, 14, 71, 75, 79, 119; as sacred to Mormonism, 22, 39, 44, 122, 204
Constitutionalism. *See* Christian Constitutionalism
Council on Foreign Relations, 127
Covenant, Sword, and the Arm of the Lord, 9, 59; Aryan Nations Church and, 58; fundamentalism in, 54; national convocation and, 231; Order and, 24, 65
Creation, dual, 97
Credit card conspiracy, 91
CSA. *See* Covenant, Sword, and the Arm of the Lord
Cult Awareness Center, 27
Cyclical theory of politics: and business cycles, 222; and extremism, 217–18, 221; and patriots, 222–23

Dan, Tribe of, 101; European place names and, 108
Dearborn (Michigan) *Independent,* 52
Decline of the West (Spengler), 62
Demobilization, 193. *See also* Resource mobilization theory
Demographics of patriots: average age, 148; geographic mobility, 149–50; geographic origins, 252–54; gender, 148
Denmark. *See* Dan, Tribe of

Devil's consortium, 173
Dispossessed Majority (Robertson), 62
Divorce. *See* Marriage stability
Doctrine and Covenants, 121–22, 176
Dualism (Manicheism), 213; in fundamentalism, 171–72, 220; in Identity Christianity, 85–88, 105; in Mormonism, 123
Duck Club, 74

Eagle Forum: Freemen Institute and, 119
Eclipse of community. *See* Mass theory
Education. *See* Formal education; Home schooling
ELF waves. *See* Weather war conspiracy
Elijah, Voice of, 24
Encyclopedia of American Religions (Melton), 159
England. *See* Ephraim, Tribe of
English: as Hebraic word, 107
Ephraim, Tribe of, 53, 100, 108; as England, 110; in Mormonism, 128
Episcopal Church, 167–70, 177
Euro-American Alliance, 57
Evil. *See* Sin

Federal Reserve System, 25, 46, 91, 257. *See also* International banking conspiracy
Females: attitude toward, 32, 87, 153, 172; demography of, 148; and home schooling, 183, 200–3
Fifth Amendment tax return, 39, 41
Finland. *See* Issachar
Flirty fishing, 188
Followers of Christ, 24, 136
Force X, 18
Formal education, right-wing: and colleges attended, 145–46; and college majors, 143–45; during McCarthy era, 139; and levels attained, 139–43; and reliability of survey, 141–42; summary of, 142–46, 159; theory of, 136–37, 138
Four Square Gospel Church, 52, 200
Freedom: Center, 26; Festival, 59
Freemasonry: as archenemy, 173, 221; as conspiracy, 53, 89–90, 127; in Identity Christianity, 89, 90; in Mormonism, 124–25

Freemen, 118, 123
Freemen Institute, 21, 131, 207;
    CAUSA and, 120; founding of, 118;
    Mormon symbolism in, 118–19. *See
    also* Skousen, Cleon
Fundamentalism: anti-Mormonism in,
    119; asceticism in, 172–73; as cause
    of extremism, 218–19, 223; conspir-
    acy in, 173, 220; as "cultural baggage,"
    213–14; defined, 53–54; Identity
    Christianity and, 53–54, 254; and last
    dispensation, 54, 173–74, 220; and
    millennialism, 272n55; and misogyny,
    172; and sin, 171–72, 220. *See also*
    Abel and Cain; Adam and Eve
Fundamentalists: and Jews, 179–81;
    Klan leaders as, 214; location of, in
    Idaho, 22, 24; preachers of, as Levites,
    111; as recruits, 174; representation
    of, among all patriots, 169, 170; rep-
    resentation of, among Identity Chris-
    tians, 175–77; status of, in America,
    216

Gad, Tribe of, 101, 110; as Goths and
    Lombards, 111; as Scots, 108
Gadianton robber conspiracy, 124–27,
    176
Gender. *See* Demographics of patriots
Generations, 222–23; conflict between,
    293n28
Geographic mobility. *See* Demographics
    of patriots
Geographic origins of patriots, 252–54
Germany. *See* Judah
Glenmary Research Center, 159
Glyoxilide, 265
Golden Mean Society, 16, 41, 42, 193
Gospel of Christ Kingdom Church, 24,
    93, 132, 160
Government of God (Taylor), 208
Guide to the American Right (Wilcox), 10

Handbook of Political Socialization (Ren-
    shon), 165
Hate, 68–69. *See also* Anti-Catholicism;
    Anti-Mormonism; Anti-Semitism; Ho-
    mosexuality; Misogyny; Racism
Herem (holocaust), 105, 261
Heritage Library, 201. *See also* Hum-
    phries, Larry

Heroism, 70; and Christian patriotism,
    78–81, 172; dangers of, 81–82; di-
    alectic of, 78–79
Hidden Hand, 18
Hoax of the Twentieth Century (Butz), 96
Home schooling, 21, 200, 210. *See also*
    Montgomery Institute
Homosexuality, 4, 15, 25, 76, 220; as
    evil fetish, 81–82, 173; death sentence
    for, 54, 86, 105; NEA "support" of,
    120
Hooking, 188

Iceland. *See* Benjamin, Tribe of
Identity Christianity, 18, 19, 21, 93–94;
    action orientation of, 260–63; Adamic
    man in, 55, 98; anti-Catholicism in,
    24, 88–89; anti-Judaism in, 18, 24,
    79, 93–94, 95, 96; as pro-"Semitic,"
    100; Caucasians as Chosen People in,
    52, 98–100; conspiracy in, 18, 88–
    92; dual creation in, 97; and evil, 85–
    87; fundamentalism in, 53–54, 254;
    Israel in, 100–4; Manicheism in, 85–
    88, 105; Mormonism and, 127–29;
    origins of, 51–57; and postmillennial-
    ism, 272n55; and racism, 53, 97–100;
    and scepter of world authority, 110.
    See also Christian patriots; Proofs of
    Identity Christianity
Identity Christians: average age of, 148;
    formal education of, 140–41; gender
    of, 148; geographic mobility of, 149;
    geographic origins of, 253; location
    of, in Idaho, 23–24, 254; marital sta-
    bility of, 152, 153; numbers of, 20;
    occupational isolation of, 158; political
    participation of, 154; religious back-
    ground of, 175–77; religious isolation
    of, 160. *See also* Boise Valley American
    Israelites; Cutler, Gary and Cindy; Mi-
    nor, Ed and Lisa
Illuminati, Order of the, 127, 173, 214
Immigration conspiracy, 265
Imperium (Yockey), 96
Insanity: defined, 276n12. *See also* Moti-
    vation for patriotism
Insiders, 18, 79, 207; as evil fetish, 81;
    as international bankers, 2–8, 255
Institute for Conspiratology, 132
Internal Revenue Service, 10, 15, 32, 39,

206; abuses by, 42–43, 270n18; as corrupt, 123; Returns Compliance Project, 38–39

International banking conspiracy, 25, 87, 90, 91–92; and Jews, 255–57. *See also* Pujo investigation; Rothschild family

International Jew (Ford), 96

IRS. *See* Internal Revenue Service

Israel: astrological banners of, 108, 109, 110; camping array of, 109; evidence of, in Europe, 101; identity Christian history of, 95, 100–5; scepter of world authority in, 101, 104. *See also specific tribes;* British Israelism

Israel, Church of, 58, 59, 93, 96

Issachar, Tribe of, 108; as Finns, 111

Issue-oriented patriotism, 19, 20, 177

Jacob, 104; descendants of, 102–3. *See also* Israel

Jesuit Order (Society of Jesus), 127

Jesus Movement, 188

Jewish Money Trust (Armstrong), 258

Jews, 18, 92–93; as archenemy, 76, 79, 81, 95–96, 129, 136, 173, 220; as Canaanites, 98, 100; as Christ killers, 47, 96, 129, 179, 201, 258; as conspirators, 88–90; and constitutionalists, 257–59; John Birch Society and, 255–57; as leftists, 165; Mormonism and, 129–31, 258–59; New Testament and, 178; as Satan's children, 54, 55, 96–98, 178; as urban symbol, 87. *See also* Judaism

John Birch Society, 16, 17, 18, 131, 136, 192, 193, 207; denunciation of racism by, 255; Idaho membership in, 116; Jews and, 255–57; Kootenai County chapter of, 22, 116; Mormon Church and, 115–18, 174; on international banking conspiracy, 255–57; Order and, 65; Pocatello chapter of, 116–17; Robert Mathews and, 62

Joseph, Tribe of, 53, 100, 110

Judah, Tribe of, 94, 100, 105, 108, 131; as Germans, 110; as Jutes, 93, 95, 101

Judah's Sceptre and Joseph's Birthright (Allen), 202

Judaism, 18; as Satan worship, 93–94, 95, 96, 197; origins of, 95; ritual murder in, 96, 280n35; vs. Israel, 94–95, 100. *See also* Israel; Jews

Justice Times, 41, 59

King James Bible, 71, 86, 105

Kingdom Message, 52

Kingdom of Yahweh, 160

Kingmen, 123, 124, 126

"Know Your Enemies" (Mohr), 94–96

Kootenai County Human Relations Task Force, 28, 149, 278n34

Ku Klux Klan, 7, 9, 16, 29, 33, 54, 62, 194, 214, 218; Aryan Nations Church and, 59, 274n76; as "tool" of Insiders, 255; in Illinois, 6; Wesley Swift and, 55

Lamanites, 52, 122, 129

Last Battle. *See* Armageddon, War of

Last Battle Cry (Crawford), 97–100

Latter-day Saints. *See* Mormon Church; Mormonism

Law (Bastiat), 208

Learning theory. *See* Multi-step theory; Political socialization

Lehi, 129

Levi, Tribe of, 95, 100; and fundamentalist preachers, 111

Liberty Lobby, 16, 18, 59, 207, 256

Liberty Ranch, 201

Life Science Church, 77, 160

Lombardy. *See* Gad

Lord's Covenant Church, 77, 201. *See also* Emry, Sheldon

Love bombing, 188

Lutheran Church, 167, 200; and patriots, 170; and Jews, 181

McCarthy era, 139, 215, 218

Manasseh, Tribe of, 100, 108; America as, 53, 110, 111–12

Marriage stability and patriots, 150–53

Market Alternatives, Center for, 21

Mass theory, 204, 215; description of, 137, 146–47; summary of findings on, 161–63; weaknesses of, 288n41. *See also* Demographics of patriots; Marriage stability; Occupational isolation; Political participation; Religious isolation

Master Mahan, 124–27

Media conspiracy, 264
Medical conspiracy, 18, 265
Mein Kampf (Hitler), 66, 73
Methodist church, 54, 167; and patriots, 170
Metric system conspiracy, 18
Militia, Oregon, 10
Ministry of Christ Church, 9, 24, 56, 62, 160
Minutemen, 54, 57, 59, 62, 132, 194, 255
Miscegenation. *See* Race-mixing
Misogyny, 87, 172
Mobility. *See* Demographics of patriots
Mobilization. *See* Multi-step theory; Resource mobilization theory
Montgomery Institute, 201
Moonies. *See* Unification Church
Moral Majority, Inc., 4, 27, 221; Freemen Institute and, 119; fundamentalists in, 165–66
Mormon, Book of, 123, 132; Jew in, 129–30, 176; origin of name of, 124. *See also* Abel and Cain; Gadianton robber conspiracy
Mormon Church, 160, 166, 168, 174, 257, 263; anti-radicalism of, 47; and John Birch Society, 115; and Jews, 180, 181; in Idaho, 22; political neutrality of, 116, 117, 120–21; and Constitutionalists, 175–77; and patriots, 167; ritual adoption in, 128; temple recommends in, 206–7; tithing in, 206
Mormonism: conspiracy in, 123–24, 127, 176; and Constitution, 22, 39, 40, 47, 121–23, 176, 254; discrimination against, 22; dispensationalism in, 121, 174; dualism in, 123; fundamentalists against, 119, 171; Identity Christianity and, 110, 127–29; Masonic symbolism in, 124–25; pro-Judaism in, 22, 130–31, 176, 257, 258–59
Motivation for patriotism, 70, 75, 78; and functional vs. substantive rationality, 75–77, 277n18; irrational, 72–74; nonrational, 71–72. *See also* Heroism
Mulek, 129
Multi-step theory: applied to left-wingers, 210, 293n29; applied to patriots, 187–90, 193–94; described, 186–87,

193–94, 212; qualitative evidence for, 196–203; quantitative evidence for, 194–96
Mystery of Iniquity (Swift), 88–89
Mythos Makers, 76, 238–39

Naked Capitalist (Skousen), 18, 126–27
Naphtali, Tribe of, 108; as Norwegians, 111
National Alliance, 62, 65, 255. *See also* Pierce, William
National Association for the Advancement of White People, 274n76
National Center for Constitutional Studies, 118. *See also* Freemen Institute
National Council of Churches, 210, 220
National Educator, 41
National Socialism. *See* Nazism
National Suicide (Sutton), 125
National Union for Social Justice, 215. *See also* Coughlin, Father
Nazarene, Church of the, 51, 54, 200
Nazism, 5–6, 16, 24, 32–33, 54, 56, 60, 72, 73, 159, 274n76; alienation and, 137, 147; as heroic, 81; as rhetorical term, 68; as totalistic, 126. *See also* Hitler, Adolf; National Alliance; Socialist Nationalist Aryan Peoples Party
Nehemiah Township Charter, 28, 58
Nephites, 118, 123, 124, 125, 129
Network, The, 18
New Covenant Theocracy, 160
New Guard, 4
New Nation U.S.A., 131
New Right: demise of, 221; origin of, 4–5; representative groups of, 19
None Dare Call It Conspiracy (Allen), 18, 91, 126, 207, 255–57
Norway. *See* Naphtali

Occupational isolation, 154–57
Occupational Safety and Health Administration (OSHA), 45, 49, 123
"On the Jews and Their Lives" (Luther), 178
Opportunity structure: for patriots, 210; and rising expectations, 216
Order, the *(Bruders Schweigen)*, 21, 40, 197, 255, 275n85; anti-Catholicism of, 88; and educational profiles of members, 66; founding of, 65; and non-racism of one member, 65; prose-

cution of, 24, 61, 77; and race-mixing, 83, 86; recruitment to, 188; and sources of members, 65; structure of, 63; violence of, 7, 8–9, 27, 63, 64. *See also* Duey, Randall; Mathews, Robert; Silva, Frank; Yarbrough, Gary

Order of Servant's Church, 24

Order Strike Force II, 10

Organic Constitution. *See* Constitution, organic

OSHA. *See* Occupational Safety and Health Administration

Our Israelitish Origin (Wilson), 52

Pace amendment, 132, 261–63

Pathfinder Radio Ministry, 52

Patriotism, right-wing. *See* Causes of patriotism; Christian patriotism; Demographics of patriots; Geographic origins of patriots; Motivation for patriotism; Political participation of patriots

Pearl of Great Price, 176

Pentateuch, 79, 113; defined, 14

Pentecostalism, 188, 200

Plot Against Christianity (Dilling), 96

Political activism, 153–55

Political socialization, 164, 166–71, 175–77; family and, 165; limits of evidence for, 181–82; neglect of religion in, 165–66; theory of, 137–38, 164–65

Politician (Welch), 116, 125

Politics of righteousness, 15, 17, 173, 211, 212, 216; defined, 13–14

Politics of Unreason (Lipset and Raab), 212, 213–15

Populist Party, 16, 21, 192, 193, 274n76; Boise Valley American Israelites and, 196

Posse Comitatus, 9, 10, 16, 17, 18, 22, 55, 58, 59, 136, 192, 194, 255; anti-Semitism and, 46–47; in Idaho Code, 45; Madison County chapter of, 44–47; Mormon Church and, 47; violence of, 25, 46; tax avoidance by, 77

Posse Noose, 46

Presbyterian Church, 21, 54, 160, 167; divine transcendence in, 171–72; and patriots, 169, 170

Projective politics: described, 219–20; weakness of, 221

Proofs of Identity Christianity: architec-

tural, 107; astrological, 108–10; and God's promises fulfilled, 112–13; and Hebraism in English language, 106–7; and Jacob's blessings, 110–11; numerological, 111–12; totemic, 108, 109

Prophetic Herald Ministry, 52

Prophets, Principles, and National Survival (Newquist), 208

Pro se litigation, 18, 19, 47–48, 136, 192. *See also* Barrister's Inn School of Common Law

Prosperity: and right-wing extremism, 218

Protestantism: and Jews, 181; conservatism and, 165, 214; and patriots, 166–68. *See also specific denominations;* Fundamentalism

Protocols of the Learned Elders of Zion, 96, 264; as fantasy, 89–90; enumerated, 90; sources of, 52–53

Quondam Complex, 214, 215

Race-mixing: as sin, 83, 173, 220; as source of evil, 85; punishment for, 86

Race Relations Information Center, 6

Racism, 24, 26, 54. See also *Amendment to the Constitution* (Pace); Anti-Semitism; Jews; Race-mixing

Recruitment: prison and, 60–61; summarized, 222–24. *See also* Multi-step theory; Resource mobilization theory

Red Carpet (Benson), 125

Reformed Church of Christ–Society of Saints. *See* Socialist Nationalist Aryan Peoples Party

Religious backgrounds, 166–71; of Christian Constitutionalists, 175–77; of Identity Christians, 175–77; of issue-oriented patriots, 177

Religious isolation, 159–60; of Christian Constitutionalists, 160; of Identity Christians, 160

Religious Round Table, 27

Reorganized Church of Jesus Christ of Latter-day Saints, 128, 132

Resource mobilization theory, 190–93. *See also* Demobilization

Restoration Church of Jesus Christ, 160

Reuben, Tribe of, 110

Right-to-Life, 20, 21. *See also* Abortion

Right-to-Work, 25

Right-wing extremism. *See* Christian patriotism
Rising expectations, theory of, 155, 216
Rocky Mountain Family Bible Retreat, 191; advertisement for, 232–33
Rothschild Family (film), 258

Sample: size of, 18, 20; sources of data for, 251; strategies in developing, 28–29; weaknesses of, 135–36, 142
Satan's Kids (Mohr), 96
Schooling. *See* Formal education; Home schooling
School of Prophets, 160
Scientology, 188
Scotland. *See* Gad, Tribe of
Scriptures for America, 77. *See also* Peters, Pete
Secret Brotherhood. *See* Order
Secular humanism, 87, 123, 183, 220
Semitic-identification, 180, 257. *See also* Mormonism: pro-Judaism in
700 Club, 27, 33, 221
Shotgun News, 59
Silver Shirt Legion, 55, 194
Simeon, Tribe of, 110; as Spanish, 111
Sin, 173, 219, 220. *See also* Abortion; Busing; Homosexuality; Misogyny; Race-mixing; Secular humanism; Usury
Slavic peoples. *See* Zebulum, Tribe of
SNAPP. *See* Socialist Nationalist Aryan Peoples Party
Socialist Nationalist Aryan Peoples Party (SNAPP), 9, 24, 28, 29, 61, 273n68; brochure for, 234–35. *See also* Gilbert, Keith; Spisak, Frank
Socialization. *See* Political socialization
Society for Educated Citizens, 7
Sociology, 5, 11–13; of knowledge, 83–84, 105; right-wing extremism and, 26. *See also* Causes of patriotism; Sample
Soldier of Fortune, 59
Sons of Liberty, 62
Spain. *See* Simeon, Tribe of
Spotlight, 18, 59, 188, 207, 255, 258
Status displacement, theory of: and patriots, 215–16; described, 213–14; loose definitions in, 214–15; test of, 216–18
Stockholm Syndrome, 29
Superimposed segmentalism, 193
Survivalism, 59, 60, 131

Sweden. *See* Asher, Tribe of
Sympathetic understanding, 11

Talmud Unmasked (Bonaventura), 96, 280n38
Talmudjude, Der (Rohling), 280n38
Tamar Tephi, 101, 129
Tax-resistance, 18, 59, 131, 136, 192, 193; non-violence of, 40, 41–42; origins of, in Idaho, 39–40; Upper Snake River Constitutionalists and, 206, 207, 208. *See also* Golden Mean Society
Terrorists: defined, 18; number of, 20, 62. *See also* Violence, right-wing
To Harass Our People (Hansen), 40
Tracing Our Heritage (Haberman), 203
Tragedy and Hope (Quigley), 126–27
Trilateralists, 18, 173
Turner Diaries (MacDonald), 62, 63, 64–65, 260; Robert Mathews and, 63–64
Two Babylons (Hislop), 203

UFO Crusade, 188
Unemployment in America, 216–18
Unification Church (Moonies), 119; recruitment to, 188. *See also* CAUSA
Upper Snake River Constitutionalists: and disconfirming mass theory, 203–4; genealogy of, 205; member profile of, 204; recruitment to, 204, 206, 207, 208
Usury, 15, 220; death sentence for, 86, 92, 105. *See also* International banking conspiracy

Verstehen (sympathetic understanding), 11
Vigilant Committee (of 10,000), 37
Violence, right-wing, 261; Christian Constitutionalism and, 132; Christian patriotism and, 62, 72; in Idaho, 7; Identity Christianity and, 260–61; Ministry of Christ and, 56; in 1980s, 6, 8–10; Order and, 7, 8–9, 27, 63, 64; Posse Comitatus and, 25, 46. *See also* Kahl, Gordon; Mathews, Robert; Rice, David L.; Spisak, Frank
Voice of Elijah, 24

Weather war conspiracy, 18, 265–66
West Bank incident, 41, 42–43

Western Guard, 32, 59
White American Bastion. *See* Order
White American Resistance, 194
White Student Union, 33
Women: attitudes toward, 32, 87, 153, 172; demographics of, 148; and home schooling, 183, 200–3
World Wide Church of God, 51. *See also* Armstrong, Herbert W.

Yahweh Believers, 24; "Jew" for, 85
Yearbook of American and Canadian Churches, 159
Young Americans for Freedom, 4, 192

Zebulum, Tribe of, 108; as Slavic peoples, 111
Zionist Occupation Government (ZOG), 15, 210

NAME INDEX

Allen, Gary, 18, 91, 126, 207, 257; and anti-Semitism, 255–56
Allen, J. H., 52, 53, 132, 202; and "race versus grace," 94
Allenby, Field Marshal Edmund, 53
Andrus, Cecil, 37
Armstrong, Herbert W., 51, 53, 203

Bainbridge, William, 159, 190
Beach, Henry L. "Mike," 45, 46, 55
Becker, Ernest, 81
Beckman, Red, 42–45
Bennett, W. H., 51
Bennett, Wallace, 117
Benson, Ezra Taft, 125, 204, 207; on America as Chosen Land, 121; on Communist subversion, 116, 117; on Freemen Institute, 119; on John Birch Society, 115
Benson, Mark, 119
Benson, Reed, 115, 117
Berg, Alan, 63, 66, 77
Berlin, Isaiah, 17
Boeing, William, 120
Brabham, Leonard, 45
Broadbent, Larry, 28
Bryan, William Jennings, 216
Butler, Jefferson, 58
Butler, Norwin, 58
Butler, Richard G., 46, 59, 132, 182; disparagement of, 77, 94; establishment of Aryan Nations by, 58; Keith Gilbert and, 273n68; racism of, 56; Wesley Swift and, 55; on women, 172. See also Aryan Nations Church

Calvin, John, 171
Cameron, William J., 52
Camus, Albert, 69
Carter, Hugh, 152
Carter, Steve, 43
Caum, Suzanne, 277n24
Chalmers, David, 7

Christ, Jesus, 16; as "racist," 98–100
Christopher, Joseph, 9, 62
Church, Frank, 25, 37
Clerkin, Donald, 57
Cohn, Norman, 52
Comparet, Bertrand, 100, 112, 202
Cooley, Marvin, 39, 40, 41; Robert Mathews and, 62
Coolidge, Calvin, 221
Coors, Joseph, 120
Coughlin, Father, 16, 215, 221. See also National Union for Social Justice
Cowan, Frederick, 72
Crain, Robert, 147
Crawford, Jarah, 96, 256, 262; on heroic violence, 79–80, 261; racism of, 97–100
Cutler, Gary and Cindy, 174–75, 179

Darby, John Nelson, 53
Davis, Roger, 45
DePugh, Robert, 132, 255. See also Minutemen
De Tocqueville, Alexis, 155
Douglas, Jack, 28, 31
Duey, Randall, 63; as Christian, 68–69
Duke, David, 274n76

Edwards, Lee, 4
Eisenhower, Dwight D., 116, 204
Ellison, Jim, 58
Emerson, Sandy, 27
Emry, Sheldon, 91–92, 201, 202, 203, 258. See also Lord's Covenant Church
Eshelman, M. M., 52

Falwell, Jerry, 4, 94, 119. See also Moral Majority, Inc.
Finch, Phillip, 5
Ford, Gerald, 5
Ford, Henry, 52, 296n15
Fowler, William, 46

Franklin, Joseph P., 9, 62
Fulbright, William, 137

Gale, William P., 45, 46; Richard Butler and, 55, 56. *See also* Ministry of Christ Church
Gandhi, Mahatma, 40, 42
Gayman, Dan, 58–59, 96; as equivocal racist, 93, 94
Genghis Khan, 89
Gilbert, Keith, 57, 60, 73; Richard Butler and, 273n68. *See also* Socialist Nationalist Aryan Peoples Party
Glick, Paul C., 152
Glock, Charles, 179, 212
Goldmark family, 73
Goldwater, Barry, 221–22
Gordon, George, 48–49
Gurr, Ted, 6

Haberman, Frederick, 51, 107, 108, 203
Hallstrom, Bob, 50, 51. *See also* Barristers' Inn School of Common Law
Hammer, Armand, 63
Hansen, George, 38, 39, 40, 118, 120; John Birch Society and, 117
Harding, Ralph, 117, 118
Harrell, John, 58
Harrelson, Thomas, 61
Hayek, F. A., 208
Hays, Henry, 9
Hegel, G. W. F., 79
Herzl, Theodor, 89
Hitler, Adolf, 45, 56, 59, 65, 66, 260; as "great" Christian, 73; as Elijah, 234–35
Hofstadter, Richard, 218–19, 223
Holm, DelRay "Rebel," 37
Hoover, J. Edgar, 208
Hounsell, Janet, 61
Huberty, James, 10
Humphries, Larry, 33. *See also* Heritage Library
Hunt, Hal, 46, 106; as profiteer, 277n24
Hunt, Nelson Bunker, 120
Hyde, Orson, 115, 131

Irwin, John, 60

Javits, Jacob, 63
Jeffers, Joe, 53
Jesus Christ. *See* Christ, Jesus

Kahl, Gordon, 9, 132; as hero, 80; last testament of, 242–46
Kerr, Clark, 155
Kinerk, Eugene, 9
King, Martin Luther, Jr., 57
Kirk, Arthur, 9
Knowles, James, 9
Koch, Dr., 265
Kornhauser, William, 155, 215; on freelance intellectuals and alienation, 137, 155–56

LaRouche, Lyndon, 21, 94, 136
Lear, Norman, 63
Lilienthal, Alfred, 94
Lincoln, Abraham, 92
Lipset, Seymour Martin, 212, 220; on extremism and prosperity, 218; on projective politics, 219; on theory of formal education, 138, 143, 166; on theory of status displacement, 12, 213–16
Lofland, John, 196
Long, Huey, 16
Lovell, James, 53
Luther, Martin, 178
Lutz, Joe, 201
Lyman, Asael, 37

McBrearty, Ardie, 40, 41, 63
McCloskey, Herbert, 139
McConkie, Bruce, 128, 174
McGovern, George, 44
McGrath, Don, 9
McIntire, Carl, 53. *See also* Christian Anti-Communist Crusade
McKay, David O., 115, 116
McMillan, John, 9
McNall, Scott, 26
Mannheim, Karl, 222
Manson, Charles, 72, 182
Martinez, Thomas, 77
Mason, Gary, 40, 41, 42
Mathews, Robert, 9, 25, 40, 61, 62, 63, 80, 188, 255, 275nn88, 89; last testament of, 246–50. *See also* Order
Matson, Gary, 40–42
Mauss, Armand, 129, 180
Mencken, H. L., 216
Merkie, Robert, 63
Miles, Robert, 10
Miller, Glenn, 9

Minor, Ed and Lisa, 182–84, 193
Mohr, Gordon "Jack," 58, 257, 262; on
  Jews, 94–96
Moon, Myung, 119, 120. *See also*
  CAUSA
Morgan, J. P., 255, 256. *See also* International banking conspiracy
Mower, Dennis, 57

Nielson, Shreve "Duke" and Joan, 56
Nisbet, Robert, 137
Nixon, Richard, 5

Oberschall, Anthony, 186–87
Oliver, Revilo, 255
Ostrout, Charles, 65

Pace, James O., 261
Pak, Bo Hi, 120
Parmenter, Denver, 63
Paul, Saint, 89
Pelley, William Dudley, 55
Peters, Pete, 14, 202. *See also* Church of
  Christ; Scriptures for America
Peyson, Walter, 57
Pierce, William, 62; background of,
  275n83. *See also* National Alliance
Pierre, Helene P., 277n24
Pires, Robert, 10
Pranaitis, Justin Bonaventura, 96,
  280n38

Raab, Earl, 212–16, 218, 220
Rader, Randall, 63
Rand, Howard D., 52
Reagan, Ronald, 25, 215, 221
Record, Robert, 203
Rhodes, Cecil, 126–27
Rice, David, 9, 62, 73, 74
Richardson, James, 192
Rigby, Larry, 40
Robb, Thom, 69, 76
Roberts, Archibald, 257
Robertson, Pat, 33. *See also* 700 Club
Rockefeller, John D., 255, 256. *See also*
  International banking conspiracy
Rockefeller, Nelson, 5
Rockwell, George Lincoln, 73, 274n76,
  275n83
Rollins, Tommy, 33, 193
Rothschild, Baron Elie de, 63
Rothschild family, 91, 255, 256, 265.

  See also International banking conspiracy
Rousselot, John, 117
Ruether, Rosemary, 178
Ruskin, John, 127

Schiffner, Alexander, 52, 132
Schlafly, Phyllis, 119
Schlesinger, Arthur, Jr., 222
Schlesinger, Arthur, Sr., 221–22
Schmitz, John, 44
Schott, Karl, 52, 93. *See also* Christ's
  Gospel Fellowship
Schwarz, Fred, 118, 208
Siegel, Abraham, 155
Silevin, Everett, 201
Silva, Frank, 68
Simplot, Jack, 120
Simpson, John H., 215–16
Sims, Patsy, 5
Singer, John, 10, 132
Singer, Vickie, 10
Skousen, Cleon, 18, 118, 120, 126, 127,
  207, 256–57. *See also* Freemen Institute; *Naked Capitalist*
Smith, Gerald L. K., 53, 55, 272n58
Smith, Joseph, 52, 119, 121, 123, 124;
  as Freemason, 125; and ritual adoption, 128
Smith, Joseph Fielding, 118, 123, 204
Snell, Ralph, 9
Snook, Franklin, 110
Soderquist, William, 63
Spencer, Herbert, 208
Spisak, Frank, 9, 72–73
Stark, Rodney: and American church
  membership, 159; and anti-Semitism
  study, 179–80, 212; "Becoming a
  World-Saver," 196; and resource mobilization theory, 190
Stoner, J. B., 174
Stouffer, Samuel, 139
Strakal, Barbara, 27
Swapp, Addam, 10, 132
Swift, Wesley, 53, 55, 56, 57, 202; on
  evil, 86; on tribes of Israel and modern
  nations, 110–11

Tate, David, 9, 63
Taylor, Zachary, 122
Tesla, Nikola, 265
Thornton, Robert, 52

Totten, Charles A. L., 128
Tucker, Richard, 43
Turner, Cliff, 40, 41

Viguerie, Richard, 4
Von Mises, Ludwig, 208

Wallace, George, 44, 214
Wallington, James, 58
Walls, Dwayne, 6
Warburg, Paul and Felix, 256. *See also*
   International banking conspiracy
Warthan, Perry "Red," 9, 72
Wassmuth, Bill, 82, 278n34
Weber, Max, 172
Weishaupt, Adam, 127

Welch, Robert, 114–17, 125, 255. *See
   also* John Birch Society
West, Walter, 63
White, Ed, 274n76
Wickstrom, James, 46, 47
Wiggins, Donald, 57
Wilcox, Laird, 10, 275n85
Wilson, John, 52
Wilson, Kenneth, 72
Withrow, Greg, 33, 193
Woodruff, Wilford, 122
Woods, John, 93, 132. *See also* Gospel of
   Christ Kingdom Church

Yarbrough, Gary, 61, 63, 66, 248–49
Young, Brigham, 114, 122
Young, David and Doris, 10